HUMAN RESOURCE
Management

Issues and Strategies

HUMAN RESOURCE
Management

Issues and Strategies

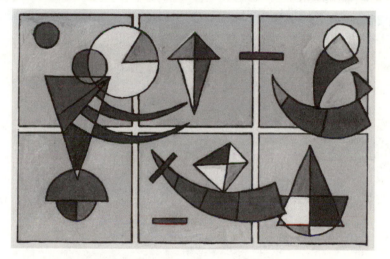

Rosemary Harrison

University of Durham Business School

Addison-Wesley Publishing Company

Wokingham, England • Reading, Massachusetts • Menlo Park, California • New York
Don Mills, Ontario • Amsterdam • Bonn • Sydney • Singapore
Tokyo • Madrid • San Juan • Milan • Paris • Mexico City • Seoul • Taipei

© 1993 Addison-Wesley Publishers Ltd.
© 1993 Addison-Wesley Publishing Company, Inc.

Many of the designation used by manufacturers and sellers to distinguish their products are claimed as trademarks. Addison-Wesley has made every attempt to supply trademark information about manufacturers and their products mentioned in this book. A list of trademark designations and their owners appears below.

Cover designed and illustrated by Arthur op den Brouw, Reading
and printed by The Riverside Printing Co. (Reading) Ltd.
Typeset by Colset Private Limited, Singapore
Printed and bound in Great Britain at the University Press, Cambridge

First printed 1993.
ISBN 0-201-62440-0

British Library Cataloguing in Publication Data
A catalogue record for this book is available from the British Library.

Library of Congress Cataloging in Publication Data
Applied for.

Contents

Preface   vii

List of contributors   xi

Acknowledgements   xiii

**Part 1 Concepts and Issues in Human Resource
Strategy**   1

1. **The nature of strategic management**   3
    Susan Miller

2. **Concept and issues in strategic human resource
    management**   35
    Rosemary Harrison

3. **Roles, relationships and skills in developing a
    strategic approach to human resource
    management**   67
    Rosemary Harrison

4. Strategies for human resource management:
    issues in larger and international firms   85
    Adrian Wilkinson, Mick Marchington and Peter Ackers

5. Strategies for human resource management:
    challenges in smaller and entrepreneurial
    organizations   111
    John Ritchie

6. Industrial relations, employment relations and
    strategic human resource management   137
    David Bright

Part 2 Human Resource Strategies in the Workplace   161

7. Communicating organizational vision, goals
    and human resource strategy   163
    Stephen Pain

8. Achieving equality of treatment and
    opportunity in the workplace   189
    Monica Shaw

9. The strategic management of recruitment and
    selection   219
    Robin Evenden

10. Performance management: its role and
    methods in human resource strategy   247
    Gordon Anderson and Robin Evenden

11. Choosing and using relevant financial reward   275
    systems
    David Bright and Frank Needham

12. Developing people – for whose bottom line?   299
    Rosemary Harrison

Part 3 Applying the Concepts: Practical Assignments and Case Studies 331

1. Assignments: Strategic management 333
   Susan Miller

2. Case study: Strategic human resource management at HMH Sheetmetal Fabrications Ltd, 1993 335
   Rosemary Harrison

3. Case study: Putting TQM into practice – the role of the personnel function 341
   Adrian Wilkinson and Mick Marchington

4. Case study: Analysing the links between employee involvement, strategic human resource management and organizational change 347
   Peter Ackers, Mick Marchington and Adrian Wilkinson

5. Case study: In search of enterprise – a consultancy assignment 351
   John Ritchie

6. Assignment: Moving to local bargaining arrangements 355
   David Bright

7. Assignment: How well do you know your employees? 357
   Stephen Pain

8. Assignments: Equality in the workplace 359
   Mhnica Shaw

9. Assignments: Strategic aspects of selection in human resource management 361
   Robin Evenden

10. Case study: The Fair Value case study 363
    Robin Evenden

11. **Case study: Wharfedale Water**   369
     David Bright

12. **Case study: Thorn Lighting Ltd, UK – a
     learning organization**   375
     Rosemary Harrison

Appendix A: Industrial disputes   381

References and useful reading   385

Index   411

Preface

The purpose of the book is to help practitioners, and students on MBA and similar courses, to understand important concepts, issues and strategies related to Human Resource Management (HRM) in organizations. Although the book has been produced by a team of writers, it is intended to be a cohesive, integrated text with clear, practical guidelines about how to relate human resource strategies to business needs and goals, and about some of the most vital issues to consider when trying to implement HRM strategy in the workplace. It therefore aims to complement, not compete with, compilations of readings produced in the last few years (see, for example, Sisson, 1989a; Storey, 1989; Salaman, 1992; Blyton and Turnbull, 1992; Towers, 1992).

The book's focus on strategy is an acknowledgement of the crucial role that a coherent, business-led approach to HRM has in today's organizations, and of the need for the function to be concerned with long-term as well as immediate business goals. It illustrates ways in which the function should make a proactive as well as reactive contribution to business strategy, and it emphasizes that: corporate strategy should take human resource considerations fully into account; business units should have detailed human resource plans; and in the workplace there should be a consistent and well-managed approach to the acquisition, performance, reward, retention and development of teams and of individuals.

The book's purpose can be further clarified by explaining what it will *not* do: it will not encompass the theory of personnel management, nor will it enter significantly into the debate about whether 'personnel management' and 'human resource management' are the same or different functions. These issues have already been comprehensively examined in a wide range of texts and articles (for example Mackay and Torrington, 1986; Guest, 1989, 1990;

Sisson, 1989b; Storey and Sisson, 1989; Legge, 1989; Storey, 1992).

Finally, the book is not a research study of HRM practice (for that, see for example Storey, 1992). While valuable research findings are presented in Chapter 4, in the study of Multichem, the other practical examples that appear in each chapter and the assignments at the end of the book have been chosen simply to bring HRM to life for readers, helping them in their attempts to apply HRM concepts to the complex reality of their organizations.

Readership

The book's student market is primarily that of MBA and other masters' courses where human resource management is a key component. There is no doubt that for postgraduate students of management the subject is assuming a high profile: it is evidenced in the United Kingdom by the number of MBA foundation and elective courses in HRM and related areas and the steadily growing number of MA courses focusing on the management or development of human resources.

The book's practitioner market is envisaged as being those line managers and human resource specialists who have significant HRM responsibilities in their organizations, and who recognize in the book's list of contents issues relevant to their work. The primary orientation of the book is British practice, although especially in Part 1 there are references to a wider international stage and to some of its key human resource implications for organizations.

Main themes covered in the book

The book revolves around two overall themes: concepts and issues related to the development of a strategic approach to HRM in organizations (Part 1); and issues and strategies related to the functional components of HRM, focusing especially on practice in the workplace (Part 2).

In Chapter 1 Susan Miller introduces key concepts and issues in strategic management, examining the nature of the strategy process and identifying factors critical for strategic success. She concludes her chapter by looking at implications for HRM. The chapter assumes little if any previous knowledge of the area on the reader's part, and covers a wide range of business strategy concepts and models because these are so crucial to an understanding of the part that strategic HRM can play in a business.

In Chapter 2 Rosemary Harrison links themes raised in Chapter 1 to an analysis of whether HRM is, should, or can be, a truly strategic function, examining the tensions inherent in attempts to fit HRM strategies to business needs and the human processes that affect HRM strategy's implementation in the workplace. In Chapter 3, she looks at data on the kinds and levels of HRM roles in organizations in the United Kingdom and further afield; at the impact they appear to be having on corporate strategy and down through the organization; and at the skills that are needed if HRM is to be a truly strategic activity. The chapter ends by highlighting critical tasks facing HRM in organizations operating in an international context.

That last theme reappears in Chapter 4, the first of two chapters exploring strategies for HRM in specific contexts. In the Multichem study, Adrian Wilkinson and his co-writers present a major original case concerning changing patterns of HRM and employment relations in a chemical company. They use it to identify issues and challenges for HRM strategy in large organizations, including those either entering the international market or directly affected by international issues. Critical issues of direction, control and social interactions that were signalled in Chapters 1 and 2 come to the fore in this important chapter.

In Chapter 5 John Ritchie moves to the other end of the spectrum and enters the world of small, medium-sized and/or entrepreneurial organizations where the real question is how far HRM can in fact be a discrete function, let alone a strategic one. The chapter presents a typology of such organizations, and thus offers to researchers, students and practitioners a valuable tool for the collection and analysis of further data in these major sectors of employment.

In Chapter 6 David Bright traces the historical development of changing patterns of employment relationships, mainly in the United Kingdom, but with some reference to practice in other countries. He returns to a number of concepts and issues raised in previous chapters in his analysis of the implications of those patterns for strategic HRM today.

Part 2 covers some key functions of HRM in the workplace. The first two, despite their importance, have so far attracted little detailed attention in British textbooks on HRM: Chapter 7 (Stephen Pain) analyses the role to be played by communications in organizational change and the implementation of business and related human resource strategies in the workplace. It is written from a communication practitioner's viewpoint, and focuses on three BET case studies. It contains important practical insights into the relationship between HRM strategy on the one hand and the organization's culture and structure on the other. Chapter 8 (Monica Shaw) takes the theme of 'equality' and uses data relating to British and wider European practice to argue the case for bringing issues of equality in the workplace to the forefront of human resource strategy in all organizations.

Turning to the attraction, retention and development of people, in Chapter 9 Robin Evenden identifies key trends in human resource planning and in the recruitment and selection of employees, relating these to wider human resource strategy on the one hand, and to the achievement of business goals in the workplace on the other. In Chapter 10 he and Gordon Anderson then focus on the management of performance – a topic which is now of particular concern as more organizations decentralize and managers of business units have direct budgetary and personnel control, and are answerable for the achievement of defined performance (and, to an increasing extent, behavioural) targets of their people. Tensions are examined between the use of performance management systems on the one hand to control individuals and teams and on the other to develop their potential.

The place of financial rewards in the management of performance is obvious but also controversial. In Chapter 11 David Bright and his colleagues look at some current trends and problems, and make recommendations about the components of an effective financial incentive and reward system. Finally, in Chapter 12, Rosemary Harrison examines the vital role to be played in strategic management by the consciously planned learning and development of everyone in the organization, and the benefits such activity offers to the business as well as to the individual.

Part 3 contains a range of practical assignments that test and extend the learning built up throughout the book. Most of these require readers to apply their learning to their own organizations, and are thus of particular value as aids to understanding and action.

Each chapter in the book starts with a list of learning objectives indicating purpose and scope, and practical examples are interwoven throughout the text in order to aid reflection, analysis and problem-solving.

Acknowledgements

I would like to thank, in particular, the team of writers who worked so hard and collaboratively with me to produce an integrated, up to date book in such a complex and dynamic field; Maggie Pickering, Jane Hogg, Davina Arkell, and Susan Keany at Addison Wesley Publishers who were always so helpful and enthusiastic; and my family – Malcolm, Piers and Dominic – without whose generous support this book certainly could not have been written.

Rosemary Harrison
August 1993

List of contributors

Peter Ackers
Lecturer in Industrial Relations, University of Loughborough Business School

Gordon Anderson
Director of MBA Programmes, University of Strathclyde Business School

David Bright
Lecturer in Employment Relations and Co-director of Human Resource Development Unit, University of Durham, Department of Adult and Continuing Education

Robin Evenden
Management Development Consultant and External Human Research Tutor, University of Strathclyde Business School

Rosemary Harrison
Lecturer in Human Resource Management and Co-director of Human Resource Development Unit, University of Durham Business School

Mick Marchington
Senior Lecturer in Industrial Relations, Manchester School of Management, University of Manchester Institute of Science and Technology

Susan Miller
Lecturer in Organizational Behaviour and Business Strategy, University of Durham Business School

Frank Needham
General Secretary, National and Provincial Building Society Staff Association

Stephen Pain
Head of Corporate Communications, BET plc

John Ritchie
Lecturer in Organizational Behaviour and Director of Undergraduate Programmes, University of Durham Business School

Monica Shaw
Dean of the Faculty of Social Sciences, University of Northumbria at Newcastle upon Tyne

Adrian Wilkinson
Lecturer in Human Resource Management, Manchester School of Management, University of Manchester Institute of Science and Technology

Acknowledgements

Grateful acknowledgement is made to the following sources for permission to reproduce material in this book.

Thomson, K. *The Employee Revolution*, and Brewster, C. and Tyson, S. *International Comparisons in Human Resource Management* reproduced by permission of Pitman Publishing. Drucker, P. *The New Realities*, reproduced by permission of Butterworth Heinemann. Majaro, S. *The Creative Gap: Managing Ideas for Profit*, reproduced by permission of Longman Law, Tax and Finance and McGraw-Hill Book Company Europe. Hart, N.A. *Effective Corporate Relations*, © McGraw-Hill Book Company Europe. Toffler, A. *The Adaptive Corporation*, © McGraw-Hill Inc. Extracts from The Telegraph 18 September 1991 and 6 November 1991, reproduced by permission of © The Telegraph plc, 1991. Thompson, A.A. Jr and Strickland, A.J. *Strategic Management: Concepts and Cases*, 6th Ed, © 1992 Richard D. Irwin, Inc. Paper delivered to the Institute of Personnel Management Annual Conference (1989) Sue Lewis, Personnel Development Manager, reporting on these developments in 1989 concluded: reproduced by permission of British Telecommunications plc. Extract from Assessing E.O. Policies, *Personnel Review*, **18**(1), 1989, and extract from Refashioning Industrial Relations? The Experience of a Chemical Company Over the Last Decade, *Personnel Review*, **22**(2), 1993 reproduced by permission of MCB University Press Ltd. Straw J. *Equal Opportunities* reproduced by permission of © 1990 IPM. Extract from *When Line Managers Welcome Equal Opportunities*, reproduced by kind permission of Personnel Management, monthly magazine of the Institute of Personnel Management. Foster, J. (1989) Sex Discrimination – the Enemy of Effective Resourcing, Harrogate, *Institute of Personnel Management Conference*. Armstrong, M. and Murlis, A.D. *Reward Management*; and Brewster, C. *Managing Industrial Relations* in Towses, B. (editor) *Handbook of Industrial Relations Practice*, reproduced by permission of © Kogan Page. Wickens, P. *The Road to Nissan* © 1987: Macmillan Ltd. Fox, A. *Managements Frame of Reference* reproduced from Industrial Relations Review and Report with kind permission of Industrial Relations Services, Eclipse Group Ltd, 18–20 Highbury Place, London N5 12P. Reports reproduced by permission of ACAS, Rover Group, Keith Reynolds Allen and Basil Blackwell Publisher Ltd. Silverman, D. © 1970 Sage Publications Ltd. Hayes, F.C. (The Prospect Centre) *Training: the Problem for Employers* reproduced by permission of the Employment Policy Institute. De Vries, M. and Miller, D. *The Neurotic Organization* reproduced by permission of Addison-Wesley Publishing Company. HM Customs and Excise; A. Fowler; BET plc; Institute of Personnel Management; Thorn Lighting Ltd UK; Coca-Cola & Schweppes Beverages; K. Riley and M. Sloman (Natwest Markets); L. McKee (Woolworths plc.); C. Coulson-Thomas (Adaptation Ltd); B. Webster; S. Marlow and D.A. Patton; C.J. Brewster and C. Smith; J.E. Burgoyne; and P. Miller.

PART 1

Concepts and Issues in Human Resource Strategy

1 The nature of strategic management

2 Concepts and issues in strategic human resource management

3 Roles, relationships and skills in developing a strategic approach to human resource management

4 Strategies for human resource management: issues in larger and international firms

5 Strategies for human resource management: challenges in smaller and entrepreneurial organizations

6 Industrial relations, employment relations and strategic human resource management

1

The nature of strategic management

Susan Miller

By the end of this chapter the reader will:

1. understand the concept of strategic management and its historical development;

2. understand the nature of the strategy process and have an overview of some of the critical issues and debates in this area;

3. appreciate the significance of the human resource element in strategy formulation/implementation;

4. be able to analyse, by reference to theory and practice, their own organization's strategy process.

Introduction

Like human resource management, strategic management is a relatively new subject area and is still evolving. In addition, the body of knowledge which makes it up is informed by a multiplicity of specialist disciplines. The evolutionary and multidisciplinary nature of the subject means that there are many different views about what strategic management is and how it is carried out in organizations.

This chapter aims to provide the reader with an overview of some of the main issues and debates in the area, since a sound understanding of concepts and issues related to business strategy is an essential prerequisite to any analysis of issues in human resource management strategy. It begins with a brief chronology of the development of the subject before discussing some of the more widely known techniques for strategic analysis. The issue of how strategy is actually made in practice in different types of organizations is explored. This is followed by an examination of some of the factors which are deemed to contribute to strategic success. Finally, the implications for human resource management are addressed. Throughout, one of the main themes of the chapter is the distinction between studies which prescribe solutions for managerial *problems* (the aim being to identify appropriate strategies for managers to take), and studies which attempt to understand managerial *processes* (the aim being to understand those processes which lead to strategic action).

The intention is to help the reader gain a better insight into this complex and multilayered topic, in order both to be in a better position to shape strategic action in his/her own organization, and to move into the discussion of human resource management as a strategic function that follows in Chapter 2. Figure 1.1 shows the seven themes covered in this first chapter.

What is meant by 'strategy'

Historical development

The broad area which is encompassed by strategic management is also known by different names, for example, business policy, corporate strategy and business strategy. It can be argued that each of these refers to a specific subset of issues, but they are often used interchangeably.

It is of interest briefly to trace the historical development of the area, since this provides clues as to the changes in emphases which have been

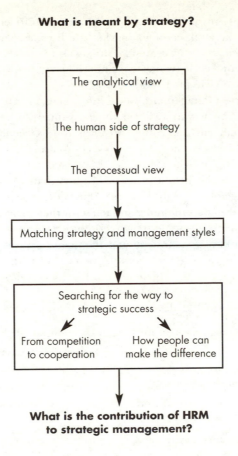

What is meant by strategy?

The analytical view

The human side of strategy

The processual view

Matching strategy and management styles

Searching for the way to strategic success

From competition to cooperation

How people can make the difference

What is the contribution of HRM to strategic management?

Figure 1.1 *The seven themes of Chapter 1.*

attributed to the concept. During the early part of this century the emphasis in business firms was firmly centred on **budgeting and control**. The main thrust of strategic direction was based on the assumption that past conditions would prevail in the future. The overriding need for managers was therefore to oversee resource allocation and ensure that budgetary targets were met.

In the 1950s **long-range planning** became the focus of managerial activity. The notion here was that past trends could be examined to predict future events and activities. A longer perspective was being taken, but obviously for historical trends to be useful predictors, the future needed to be relatively similar to the past. This worked reasonably well until the 1960s when it was becoming clear that environments and markets were increasingly unstable, rendering past events less accurate in forecasting future trends. So

corporate planning came into being, a comparatively sophisticated attempt to focus on the total, complex market and business environment in which the firm operated. But corporate planning was still based around the old concept of the 'planning cycle' which was undertaken at regular intervals – the annual plan, the five-year plan, and so on.

Strategic management came into currency from about the mid-1970s onwards, when it was realized that any analysis of the firm's position in relation to current and future business trends needed to be carried out on a continual basis, rather than being compulsorily fitted to a predetermined review cycle. The whole process broadened out at this point to take in a wider view of the firm's business, rather than merely concentrating on a narrow range of economic factors. Alongside this, it was clear that management needed to become more proactive in their strategic aims and activities.

In passing, it should be noted that nowadays all kinds of organizations talk of having a strategy and the need to adopt a strategic view – both manufacturing and service organizations, and both profit and not-for-profit sectors. Strategic management is of critical relevance to every type of organization.

So this historical development has centred on a number of areas:

- a move towards a more long-term view of the organization,
- the analysis of a wider range of factors (both environmental and internal to the firm) which are deemed to affect a firm's present position and future development,
- a more sophisticated understanding of the complexities of managing the strategy process, and
- an acceptance of the need for continual monitoring and evaluation of the firm's strategic position.

The tendency is to attempt to adopt a more holistic approach towards understanding the firm in its environment, and paralleling this, there is a greater recognition of the need to ensure congruence within the organization as a whole. Thus all functions, departments, divisions, strategic business units or whatever, must be aware of the strategy and understand the part which they play in it. It is argued that strategy can only be achieved if all the component parts of the organization, though having different responsibilities, are working together in some coordinated way towards an identifiable, coherent and agreed set of strategic objectives.

The multidisciplinary nature of strategic management

As with other functional areas (such as HRM), strategic management attracts interest from writers and researchers from a variety of disciplines. Hence the body of knowledge which makes up the subject borrows from such areas as economics, organizational behaviour, sociology and psychology. The topics considered under the umbrella title of strategic management are equally diverse – from industry economics to product life cycles, from team building to organizational change.

This makes for lively reading and debate; but it also leads to writers giving different emphases to different aspects, and inevitably there is dispute over which factors play the most crucial part in determining the way in which strategy is formulated and put into effect. Is the key to business success the precision with which the firm's strategy is matched to a thoroughly analysed industry and market? Or is it more to do with the way in which people in the organization are motivated to innovate, integrate and share a common strategic vision? Such a stark dichotomy is somewhat simplistic, and most writers would agree that both perspectives are relevant. Nevertheless, there are discernible differences in emphasis between authors, as will be seen later.

There are also differences in the way writers approach the subject. On the one hand, there are those (both academics and consultants) whose work involves prescriptions – finding solutions to managerial problems – who are therefore preoccupied with the applied nature of their findings. On the other hand, there are those whose aim is simply to understand strategy and the nature of strategic management, and who therefore carry out 'basic' or 'fundamental' research with this intention. Their results are usually of interest and significance for practising managers, but their prime aim is not to solve managerial problems, but to provide insight into the issues.

It is therefore important to recognize that all the work cited in this chapter is embedded in particular frames of reference and ways of seeing the world. These stem in part from the prescripts and frameworks legitimized by individual academic disciplines. So there is bound to be variation, argument and dissent. All disciplines display such internal heterogeneity; a multidisciplinary subject like strategic management inevitably does so more than most.

Towards a definition of strategic management

There are probably as many definitions of strategic management as there are writers on the subject. To attempt a summary in a single sentence or paragraph is perhaps unwise (especially bearing in mind the foregoing comments about the variety of perspectives), so the following are some key elements which a study of strategic management would encompass.

Strategic management is about the present and future direction of the organization. This includes:

- assessing the organization's internal competences and capabilities,
- assessing environmental threats and opportunities,
- deciding the scope of the organization's activities,
- creating and communicating a strategic vision,
- managing the process of change in an organization.

Importantly, strategic management is not just about finding a congruence between organizational strengths and weaknesses and environmental opportunities and threats (the so-called SWOT analysis), though this is part of the strategic process. There is far more scope for proactive behaviour – shaping the environment and redefining strengths and weaknesses – than this infers. Similarly, strategy is not just about communicating the chief executive's vision down the line. It is also about harnessing the abilities, innovative capacity and drive of everyone in the organization. It involves the values, expectations and goals of those in a position to influence strategy (Johnson and Scholes, 1989), and this means everyone concerned with the formulation and implementation process. The implications of all of this for human resource management and development are thus already beginning to emerge; these will be analysed in detail in Chapter 2.

If strategic management is seen as an organizational process, touching everyone in the organization, then this adds to its complexity. There are then a huge number of factors which need to interrelate for strategy to be successful. This will become apparent later in the chapter.

Levels of strategy

One view of strategy is that it is something of a 'free-flowing' process, happening everywhere at all times in organizations. Another view is that different parts of the organization are responsible for separate parts of the strategy. Table 1.1 gives an indication of how, in theory, different levels can take on responsibilities for different strategic objectives. This usually only applies in a large, diversified company.

The table gives an indication of the way corporate strategic objectives are allocated throughout the organization, and how the overarching, corporate vision is apportioned to each subunit in a 'trickle-down' pattern, though in practice such clear-cut distinctions may become blurred. The model does attempt to illustrate how the activities of lower level units can shape the strategies of those above. Obviously, information and intelligence about customers, markets, products and competitors gained from those operating at the 'grass roots' level should feed upwards in the organization, influencing corporate strategy. This continuous feedback loop is critical for strategic success. This raises questions about the extent to which strategic decision-

Table 1.1 *Levels of strategy (after Thompson and Stickland, 1992).*

Strategy level	Primary responsibility	Areas of focus
Corporate	The chief executive and other senior executives	Building and managing a high-performing portfolio of business units (making acquisitions, strengthening existing business positions, divesting businesses that no longer fit into the company's plans). Capturing the synergy among related business units and turning it into competitive advantage. Establishing investment priorities and steering corporate resources into businesses with the most attractive opportunities. Reviewing/revising/unifying the major strategic approaches and moves proposed by business-unit managers.
Business	General manager/head of business unit	Devising approaches to compete successfully and secure competitive advantage. Forming responses to changing external conditions. Uniting the strategic initiatives of key functional departments. Taking action to address company-specific issues and operating problems.
Functional	Functional managers	Crafting approaches to support business strategy and to achieve functional/departmental performance objectives. Reviewing/revising/unifying strategy-related moves and approaches proposed by lower level managers.

making can be neatly divided into 'upstream' and 'downstream' functions, with, for example, HRM pigeonholed in the downstream category. This important issue will be discussed at more length in Chapter 2.

Having given an overview of the concept of strategic management, and having looked briefly at some of the elements which make it up, the next section looks in detail at some tools and techniques for strategic analysis. It concentrates particularly on the work of Porter (1980, 1985), whose seminal contributions have made him one of the most widely known and discussed writers in this area. In many ways Porter's work epitomizes an approach to strategic management which places great emphasis on detailed analytical models, often based on rational economic assumptions. This approach to strategy occupies a central position within the field and it is therefore crucial to have a fairly detailed understanding of its main themes and findings. The implications of this work are critical for both strategic management and HRM.

The analytical view of strategic management

This section discusses work which, it is argued, takes an overtly analytical view of strategy. Such work appears to have two central concerns:

- the necessity of finding accurate ways of analysing a firm's competitive position in its industry or market, in order to facilitate the above;
- the definition and delimitation of a range of appropriate strategies at the corporate and business unit level.

Firms are usually perceived as profit-maximizing; corporate goals are assumed to be generally explicit, agreed and stable over time. The prime job of managers is therefore to understand their industry and competitors in order to find ways of gaining and maintaining competitive advantage over rivals.

Work in this area is generally normative in nature and is based on the view that strategy is (or ought to be) a relatively logical, sequential process of analysis and choice. The behavioural aspects of choice and implementation are largely ignored.

For our purposes it is important to note that the implications for functional managers (such as HRM specialists), resulting from different strategic choices, are not addressed, nor is much consideration given to the effects of such strategies on employees.

Porter, a Harvard university professor, has been responsible for introducing a number of analytical techniques which have been widely reproduced in textbooks and frequently debated in the literature. His inspiration has been primarily drawn from industrial economics and his focus has been on what he sees as the crucial strategic question for any organization: how firms gain and maintain competitive advantage over rivals. This section will discuss three of his most prominent concepts: the five force framework; generic strategies; and the value chain.

The five force framework

Porter argues that the intensity of competition within an industry is governed by five forces. Competition is not just determined by a firm's immediate

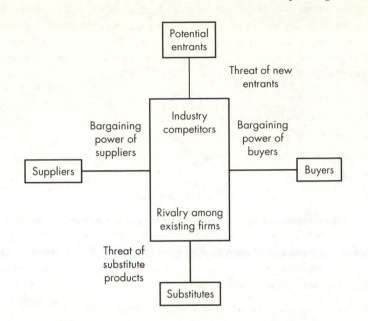

Figure 1.2 Porter's five force framework (from Porter, 1980).

competitors – this is only one of the forces – but also by the threat of new entrants, the threat of substitutes, and the bargaining power of suppliers and buyers (see Figure 1.2). Together these competitive forces determine the strength and nature of competition within the industry. Hence the intensity of competition, and thus the level of profitability, will vary from industry to industry.

Taking the central box first, Porter considers that the intensity of rivalry among existing firms depends mainly on the following:

- *The size of competitors* Where they are more or less equal, competition is likely to be strong as each jostles for dominance; industries with dominant organizations in them tend to be more stable.

- *The rate of market growth* Slow market growth leads to increased competition to retain market share, or to outlast competition.

- *The level of fixed costs* High fixed (or storage) costs may lead to firms cutting prices to maintain turnover.

- *The degree of differentiation* Low product differentiation or low switching costs allow customers to move between competitors, or to play one off against another.

- *High exit barriers* May lead to industry overcapacity.

- *Extra capacity only available in large increments* May lead to overcapacity, even if only in the short term.

Moving on to the next box, Porter believes the threat of new entrants, as well as actual entrants, will stimulate competition. Whether potential newcomers will enter the industry depends on the degree to which there are barriers to entry. The main barriers to entry are:

- economies of scale
- product differentiation
- capital requirements
- access to distribution channels
- government policies
- cost disadvantages independent of size

The degree to which substitute products are a threat depends on how well they can serve the same function as the industry product. Their existence can constrain prices and therefore profits.

Threats from buyers will depend upon how powerful the buyer group is. Buyers tend to be powerful when:

- they are concentrated, or purchase large volumes
- switching costs are low
- they are buying undifferentiated products
- the product represents a significant proportion of the buyer's total cost
- buyers can threaten backward integration

Finally, suppliers will be similarly powerful when:

- they are a concentrated group
- the costs of switching from one supplier to another are high, perhaps because of high differentiation
- the supplier's customers are not considered important to the supplier
- the supplier produces a product which is important to the buyer's business
- suppliers can threaten forward integration

The five force framework is a useful heuristic device for analysing where competition comes from within a particular industry. The main area of debate centres on the question of defining the industry in the first place. For example, is a brewer who owns a number of inns with restaurants and perhaps accommodation, really in the brewing industry, the restaurant/hotel business, or the wider leisure industry? Who are its main competitors – other brewers, or holiday firms offering substitute leisure products?

For Porter, this is a key issue. Drawing a boundary round the central 'existing competitors' box is not necessarily a straightforward, objective activity. Any boundary is drawn as a result of the perspectives and beliefs of organizational members – the firm decides with whom it wishes (or is best able) to compete, and this then defines the industry.

Similarly with the other forces. Not everyone in the organization may share a common definition of potential entrants, or see the firm's buyers or suppliers in quite the same terms. The framework is a useful aid in organizing thinking about competition, and in helping to break the mould of past beliefs. What it cannot do is explain the social processes whereby particular threats and opportunities are identified and agreed upon. Yet it is this process of identification and agreement which legitimizes these threats and opportunities, thus prompting action.

The second concept to be dealt with here is Porter's notion of **generic strategies**, which is somewhat more controversial.

Generic strategies

In Porter's view there are only three main strategies by which a firm can cope with the forces of competition at business unit level – by achieving overall cost leadership, by differentiating, and by focusing.

Overall cost leadership is achieved by having the lowest cost structure in the industry. This increases margins, helps ward off price increases from suppliers, provides a bulwark against substitutes, increases barriers to entry and helps to prevent buyers pushing prices down too far.

Differentiation is achieved by being able to offer a product which is in some way unique in the industry. Uniqueness may be acquired in a number of ways, by having specific features, by offering special services to customers, by having a distinct design, and so on. Whatever the source of differentiation, a product must be unique in a way which is valued by the customer. Differentiation creates a brand image, which in turn creates customer loyalty, allows higher margins and erects entry barriers.

Focus is the third generic strategy which relates specifically to the scope of the market being targeted. The first two strategies are assumed to be adopted for the market as a whole, but it is clear that either may be directed at particular segments only. It is possible to aim to be the lowest cost producer in one (or a few) market segments only (a **cost focus** strategy), or to direct a differentiated product at a similarly narrow target market (**differentiation focus**).

Porter's diagram in Figure 1.3 illustrates these strategies.

So these three strategies (or should it be four?) represent the ways of combating competitive forces and gaining competitive advantage. To do anything other than choose one of these is to be 'stuck in the middle' (Porter, 1985, p. 17), and therefore to be disadvantaged. Strategies can be pursued simultaneously, but this is rare and to be discouraged:

> . . . achieving cost leadership and differentiation are usually inconsistent, because differentiation is usually costly.
>
> (Porter, 1985, p. 18)

But several writers have queried this view of the three strategies being, for all practical purposes, mutually exclusive. Murray (1988) offers his 'contingency view' of Porter's concept, arguing that since a viable cost leadership strategy largely emanates from an industry's structural characteristics (for example, economies of scale, preferential access to inputs or distribution channels, and the 'experience curve' effect), and a viable differentiation strategy emanates primarily from consumer tastes (for example, perceived quality, reliability or service), the two strategies could be pursued together:

> Because these two sets of exogenous factors are independent, the possibility of a firm pursuing cost leadership and product differentiation simultaneously is not precluded.
>
> (Murray, 1988, p. 395)

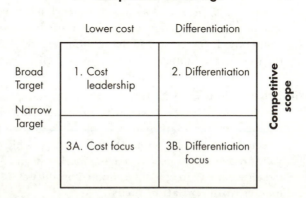

Figure 1.3 *Three generic strategies (from Porter, 1985).*

Murray also points out that empirical findings based on the concept of generic strategy have been contradictory, and that some authors (Phillips *et al.*, 1983; Fine, 1983) have demonstrated positive links between elements of differentiation and costs, suggesting that there are associations between these dimensions.

Some of these thoughts are echoed by Hill (1988), who suggests that 'differentiation can be a means for firms to achieve an overall low-cost position' (p. 401). Furthermore, many industries, especially mature ones, do not have a unique low cost position (since many firms have similar minimum-cost structures) so there is a need to pursue both low cost and differentiation strategies in order to try and obtain competitive advantage.

It can be seen that the concept of generic strategies is not without problems. It is important because the debate about what is an appropriate (and therefore successful) business level strategy is a central theme of strategic management. However, confusion over the exact nature of each strategy and the doubts raised by empirical work about how they operate in practice has muddied the waters.

Murray's contingency view is a useful step forward, but he does recognize that the contingency approach can be overdeterministic, assuming managerial choice is overconstrained by environmental factors. In reality managers may enjoy considerable freedom to follow their own preferred strategic choices (Child, 1972). Furthermore, supposedly exogenous factors such as consumer perceptions and preferences can be manipulated by a firm (for example, by using advertising) to the firm's own advantage.

The generic strategy concept tends to assume that firms have accurate knowledge about competitor and customer behaviour. Additionally, and perhaps more importantly, it does not dwell on how the choice about which strategy to follow is arrived at. The tendency is to assume that the choice of strategy is based on a logical and rational evaluation of the strategic options for an organization. This neglects the fact that decisions in organizations are often made within a political setting (Pettigrew, 1973) and that individuals operate within a bounded rationality (Simon, 1957). Decision-making is therefore hampered by a lack of complete and accurate information and is also constrained by having to accommodate numerous interest groups.

The third of Porter's major contributions is that of the **value chain**, and it is here that some attention is given to the way in which intra-organizational activities can contribute to the achievement of strategy.

The value chain

The value chain breaks down an organization into its constituent parts in order to illustrate the **activities** which add value (value as perceived by the

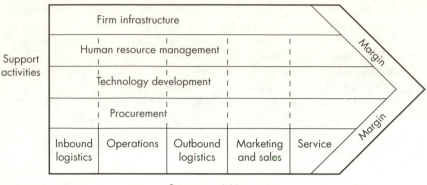

Primary activities

Figure 1.4 *The value chain (from Porter, 1985).*

customer) to the product. The value chain (Figure 1.4) is an analytical tool which can be used to identify strategic resources and sources of competitive advantage. It cuts across traditional departmental boundaries such as marketing, finance and production to focus on the process by which a product (or service) is produced and delivered. Porter suggests it is the **linkages** between these activities which may be crucial in distinguishing sources of competitive advantage. Because many activities are carried out outside an individual firm, any analysis also needs to take account of the value chains of other suppliers, distributers and buyers.

The nature of the primary activities is fairly self-explanatory. They are concerned with bringing in the product or service inputs, transforming them into the final product, distributing them to buyers, and marketing, selling and servicing them. The four support activities are linked to the primary activities and cover the following areas:

Firm infrastructure: Includes functions which support the whole chain, such as finance, planning, quality management.

Human resource management: Includes the recruitment, selection, training, development and rewarding of all personnel.

Technology development: Includes the 'know-how' associated with all value activities, not just production technology.

Procurement: Includes all processes associated with purchasing inputs needed for the primary activities.

One of the uses of the value chain is that it shows how the total value of the product is made up. Since customers will only pay a certain value for a product, 'the goal of any generic strategy is to create value which is greater than the costs of its creation; the difference between the two being margin' (Moore, 1992, p. 54).

So the value chain can help to show how resources are being used to create a product; it can be used to isolate those activities which are of strategic importance; and it can show which activities and linkages between activities (in the firm's own value chain, or between this and those of its suppliers, buyers and so on) are sources of competitive advantage. An example of this last point is when a company insists that its suppliers achieve certain quality standards, which then reduces its own costs of inspection and quality assurance, and reduces the need for skilled staff involved in the procurement support activity within inbound logistics.

The value chain begins to look inside the organization to understand how competitive advantage is achieved. However, the mere act of grouping and labelling activities can seem somewhat mechanistic, perhaps static, and at worst arbitrary. With reference to HRM, Porter is not particularly explicit about how human resource activities support the primary activities. However, he does point out that human resource management has a role to play in helping to secure competitive advantage for a firm by: 'determining the skills and motivation of employees and the cost of hiring and training' (1985, p. 43). Indeed, in some firms HRM is the crucial key to competitive advantage. Additionally, Porter draws attention to the way in which linkages in the value chain can influence organizational structure. The appropriate grouping of activities can help HRM and other 'support' managers to see how they relate to the firm's overall competitive position (1985, p. 61). This is useful because they often do not have a clear view of how they link to the overall competitive strategy of the organization.

The value chain is a framework for organizing thinking and facilitating insight. At this level it can be said to be a tool to aid analysis. It suggests areas in which it may be fruitful to search for competitive advantage, but not how to change the value chain so that the firm can actually achieve one of the generic strategies.

But there is a lack of attention to what actually happens in practice inside the firm, in terms of strategic processes. Porter is not alone in his comparative neglect of this area (and his later work does recognize some of the inertial characteristics of strategic models, as will be seen later in this chapter).

There are a number of other techniques for analysing a firm's competitive position and the portfolio of products it chooses to produce, and many take a similarly rational approach. Many of these have been developed and popularized by consultants as an aid to practising managers, for example, Boston Consulting Group's well-known BCG matrix and General Electric's Business Screen.

This is not the place to provide a comprehensive view of such models (but for an interesting analysis of how portfolio planning strategies may affect HRM policies, see Purcell, 1992); it is sufficient to note that there are a number of such tools which can aid analysis of the firm's present position and evaluate alternative competitive opportunities and strategic ways forward for the company. But it is a mistake for managers to assume that familiar-izing themselves with these analytical tools is enough to ensure that the most profitable strategy is chosen and will be implemented smoothly. Over-emphasis on the analytical skills of managers may neglect the political and behavioural skills required for a more complete understanding of the strategic management process.

Many models seem to be predicated on the unspoken assumption that strategy is a linear process which happens in a set series of stages: first the current position of the firm is analysed in terms of its strengths and weak-nesses; these are then compared to opportunities and threats in the environ-ment; an appropriate strategy is selected; it is then put into effect. The *implementation* of strategy is neglected because it tends to be assumed that what has been decided will inevitably happen. Because rather too little attention is given to the *process* of strategy formulation, that is, the social and political processes which lead to strategic decisions, the potential difficulties of imple-mentation are not addressed. Furthermore, it is not recognized that the process of strategy may be a nonlinear iterative one, in which formulation and implementation are often fused.

This point will be returned to later in this chapter. Meanwhile, the next section looks at work which has begun to refocus attention on the 'people' side of strategic management, and this includes an examination of imple-mentation issues.

Refocusing the issues – the human side of strategy

In many ways it was Peters and Waterman (1982) who repopularized the idea that it is people in organizations who 'make the difference' and contribute towards 'excellent' (that is, successful) companies. At first glance this begins to suggest a role for the HRM practitioner, for example in helping to select and train personnel so that they can operate in the appropriate way to achieve organizational excellence. However, as will be shown, such key relationships are given a relatively superficial and simplistic treatment.

Although their research received criticism for lack of methodological rigour and their results were hampered by many of their excellent companies becoming less successful after their book *In Search of Excellence* was published, their ideas about the importance of the 'people side' hit a chord. Even though many of their ideas were by no means new, their resurrection occurred at a receptive period, and because of the impact those ideas made, and have continued to make on the world of management, it is important to examine them briefly here.

Companies across the world, and American ones in particular, had become shaken by the ability of the Japanese consistently to beat them in world markets. A new theory of doing business appeared to be what was called for. Peters and Waterman, and subsequently Peters again in 1989, drew attention to the need for new templates for action. Particularly, they criticized business school approaches to strategy with their emphasis on analytical techniques and their overreliance on 'hard', quantitative data:

> The numerative, rationalist approach to management dominates the business schools. It teaches us that well-trained professional managers can manage anything. It seeks detached, analytical justification for all decisions. It is right enough to be dangerously wrong, and it has arguably led us seriously astray.
>
> (Peters and Waterman, 1982, p. 29)

> The word 'strategy', which used to mean a damn good idea for knocking the socks off the competition, has often come to be synonymous with the quantitative breakthrough, the analytic coup, market share numbers, learning curve theory, positioning business on a 4-, 9- or 24-box matrix (the matrix idea, straight from mathematics) and putting all of it on a computer.
>
> (Peters and Waterman, 1982, p. 30)

They argue that the business paradigm promotes conservatism and stops experimentation. This encourages an organization where mistakes are punished, rather than innovation being rewarded. What is really required is a new approach whereby organizational members are encouraged to try out new ideas, where *action* is valued, even if things go wrong. This certainly draws attention to the implementation side of strategic management. The message is clear – do not get hung up on analysis, but concentrate on getting things done.

Peters and Waterman have a number of prescriptions for the way in which companies ought to be operating, but the nub of their approach is that what excellent companies share is the '. . . ability to achieve extraordinary results through ordinary people' (1982, p. 239). Productivity can only be achieved through the workforce, so everyone needs to get involved, to contribute. Senior management need to be leaders, role models and heroes, and their job is to shape the culture and values of the organization.

One of the major criticisms of this kind of approach (apart from worries about the reliability of the data) was that this was a static analysis. The research did not look at the way these companies had become excellent, so it was difficult for other, non-excellent companies to know what to do to improve. Furthermore, the prescripts looked very much like a blueprint for action, a kind of 'one best way' approach which had been discredited with Taylorism back in the 1930s (for a more detailed critique see Guest, 1992).

Some of these criticisms were recognized by the authors, and Peters responded in his next book *Thriving on Chaos* in 1989. Once again, one clear message which came through was the need to have highly trained, flexible personnel and use them as a principal means of adding value. Strategy should be very much a 'bottom-up' exercise, rather than being the sole province of top management. Organizational leaders have to provide the strategic vision and culture whereby people are induced to love change as much as they hated it before.

The use of the concept of culture in this way has attracted much debate. The concept itself is often poorly defined and researchers are not agreed that corporate culture is a tangible, identifiable aspect of organizations which can be manipulated in quite so cavalier a manner. The problem is that in fact organizations may have a number of different cultures (or subcultures). This means that people may have different understandings about what the symbols, myths, legends and heroes mean – and these may change over time. The imposition of an overarching, corporate culture may not be possible, or even morally defensible.

Issues of culture will be explored in more detail in Chapter 2 (see also Pettigrew's article in Wilson and Rosenfeld, 1990). Suffice it to say here that the oft-cited view that organizational culture is a panacea for a number of organizational ills and that it is management's job to manage cultural change is not without difficulties – as is any process of change (Wilson, 1992).

Peters and Waterman's contribution is to place *people* firmly back on the agenda. Although the relationship between individual and organizational performance is treated somewhat simplistically, and the prescriptions for HRM are implicit rather than explicit, there still appears to be a role for the human resource specialist in making sure that the workforce is equipped to play a more proactive part (but this concern must be shared by all managers). There is now an acknowledgement that people in organizations should be selected to be innovative; and that employees will require training and continual development to contribute fully to the strategic objectives of the firm. The management of strategy requires that personnel are trained to manage it for themselves.

However, it is still very much a formula-based approach (Storey, 1992) and provides little in the way of clear direction to functional specialisms. Although the emphasis is on implementation – getting things done in an organizational setting – it is not really clear how this happens in practice. We need to know what goes on inside the firm really to understand what managers have to do to bring about strategic change.

Peters and Waterman begin to take the lid off the 'black box', but they leave many questions only partially answered (see Guest, 1992). The next section discusses further work which begins to look in more detail at the process by which strategy is enacted.

The processual view of strategic management

Much of what has been discussed up to now has been prescriptive and normative. Writers have been concerned to offer ways of analysing and thinking about strategy in order to provide guidelines for managerial action.

As discussed, one overriding assumption promulgated particularly by Porter and colleagues at Harvard appears to be that strategy is an outcome of a rational, planned process, whereby the current situation is analysed, choices are made about future strategic options, and implementation realizes them. Peters and Waterman (1982) and Peters (1989) have been much more at pains to investigate the nonrational and chaotic aspects of strategy, but they too have offered prescriptive, 'how to' formulae. However, other empirical research looking at how the strategic process occurs in organizations has thrown up a rather different picture, encompassing such notions of incremental and emergent change.

Lindblom's work (1959; Braybrooke and Lindblom, 1963) depicts the process as one of 'muddling through' or 'disjointed incrementalism'. The argument is that strategic decisions are problematic because managers are dealing with a complex, dynamic world, and are having to make choices about a future which is inherently unpredictable. Hence the period of implementation may throw up new information, or may present a set of changed circumstances for which the original strategy may not be appropriate.

The incrementalist approach is therefore aimed at simplifying things by focusing on a limited number of choices which are only marginally different from the *status quo*. Implementation does not follow from formulation in one fell swoop. Instead, it occurs in small steps so that unsuccessful actions can be 'undone' before too much damage is wreaked. So analysis, choice and implementation are not linear. Further decision-making is often required after initial implementation, which may require re-analysis of the policy, attention to different choices, and so on. Because each step on its own does not present too great a change, any unforeseen consequences should not be too severe, and resistance to change minimized.

Dror (1964) suggested that this could be a recipe for inertia, but Lindblom (1969) countered that radical change can be effected '. . . as rapidly through a sequence of incremental steps as through drastic – hence less frequent – alterations' (p. 172). This is a model of action which is both descriptive and prescriptive. According to Lindblom, this is not only what managers appear to do, it is also what they ought to do to manage in a complex environment.

Lindblom's work in this area has been primarily concentrated in the public sector, however Quinn's research (1978, 1980) extended to the private sector and tended to confirm the view that incrementalist approaches were helpful and were used in firms. He had this to say about what he called 'logical incrementalism':

> The most effective strategies of major enterprises tend to emerge step by step from an iterative process in which the organization probes the future, experiments, and learns from a series of partial (incremental) commitments rather than through global formulations of total strategies. Good managers are aware of this process, and they consciously intervene in it.
>
> (Quinn, 1980, p. 58)

This notion of emergent strategies and organizational learning has been taken up and expanded by Mintzberg and colleagues (Mintzberg and Waters, 1985; Mintzberg, 1987). The argument is that the view which sees strategy as an analytic process for establishing long-range goals and action plans, where formulation precedes, and is separate from, implementation, is 'seriously limited' (Mintzberg and Waters, 1985, p. 257) since it rarely accords with what happens in practice.

Strategy is conceptualized as 'a pattern in a stream of decisions' and the researchers suggest that strategies may vary in their degree of 'deliberateness'. That is, some strategies appear to be more **deliberate** in that the strategy is realized as intended by the strategist, while others appear to be more **emergent**, that is, they happen despite, or in the absence of, intentions. Deliberate and emergent strategies are in fact two ends of a continuum and, in real life, most strategies lie somewhere along this, rather than being placed at either extreme.

A perfectly deliberate strategy must have precisely articulated and communicated intentions which are actioned without interference from exogenous factors. A perfectly emergent strategy is one where there is a consistency about the organization's actions over time, even though there are no explicit intentions. Both pure forms of strategy are rare, but Mintzberg and Waters maintain that some patterns they have observed do come close to them. They then distinguish a number of strategic processes which they place along the continuum.

This notion that strategies do not come about in identical ways is novel and challenges the analytical view of strategy formation. The concern in not so much about the content of strategy, or which strategies are the most successful, but more about the process by which strategy occurs. This broadens the area of debate and interest. As the authors say:

> . . . the fundamental difference between deliberate and emergent strategy is that whereas the former focuses on direction and control – getting desired things done – the latter opens up this notion of 'strategic learning'. Defining strategy as intended and conceiving it as deliberate, as has traditionally been done, effectively precludes the notion of strategic learning.
>
> (Mintzberg and Waters, 1985, p. 270)

Mintzberg has continued his critique of various traditional schools of thought in further work (1990a, 1990b, 1991). His views on what he calls the 'design', 'planning' and 'positioning' schools (he places Porter's work in the 'positioning' school) are that they are overly narrow, being based on assumptions of rationality, with an overemphasis on economic and quantifiable data and the exclusion of any analysis of social or political phenomena. They are also almost totally concerned with big business, ignoring the way in which other organizations formulate strategy (see Chapter 5).

The emphasis on the processual nature of strategic management does not define a formal role for different managers in the organization – that is not its intent, so human resource management is not considered *per se*. Nevertheless, if strategic action results not only from planned deliberation by the chief executive but also by a process in which participation is widened out in the organization, then the scope for others to become involved is greater – a point taken up in Chapter 12 when the concept of 'the learning organization' is discussed.

The next section broadens out this question by looking at the kinds of strategic styles which firms actually use and examines which are the most appropriate.

Matching strategies and management styles

There is work which suggests that the strategies which firms adopt are influenced by managers' perceptions of the appropriate business 'recipe'. The recipe is a set of assumptions and beliefs about how to succeed in a particular business. Such recipes have evolved over time, and are not always explicit, but can nevertheless influence the formulation of strategy (Johnson and Scholes, 1989). Whether such recipes are successful or not is a moot point, since they may only serve to limit strategic vision as managers hesitate to alter the formula.

Other work, such as that carried out by Goold and Campbell (1991) has explicitly looked at what managers do to arrive at a strategy and has compared managerial styles with their firm's competitive success. Goold and Campbell base their conclusions on the results of research into 16 British firms, carrying out interviews with a number of senior managers. All the companies involved are large, diversified organizations (including such names as BP, Hanson Trust, Cadbury Schweppes and Plessey), and this must be taken into account when assessing the generalizability of their findings.

The researchers were anxious to find out what role the company headquarters played in diversified organizations and how it added value to them. Their studies appeared to show two extremes. In companies like BTR, GEC, Hanson Trust and Tarmac, the centre's role was limited to a few essentials such as approving proposals and appointing managers, and decision-making was devolved to the Strategic Business Unit (SBU) level. However, tough profit targets were set and failure to meet them could mean dismissal.

At the other extreme were companies like BOC, Lex and STC, where the way of operation was very different. In these companies the centre had a leadership role, giving direction to SBUs and helping them to develop strategies. The centre was much more involved in decision-making and coordination, while targets were mainly concerned with progress against competition and a shared commitment towards goals was sought (Goold and Campbell, 1991, p. 8).

Essentially, Goold and Campbell found that the centre's influence over SBUs varied along two dimensions. The first of these was the degree to which the centre influenced *planning* in the SBUs, that is, how far strategy was formulated in a 'top-down' manner. The second dimension related to how far the centre actually exercised *control* over the SBU, in terms of setting targets and monitoring results.

Using these two dimensions, eight different styles of strategic management were distinguished, the three most popular being:

Strategic planning style   This combines a high planning influence by the centre with flexible forms of control. The aim is to build up a number of 'core' businesses, often with coordinated, global strategies (p. 10). Ambitious, longer term goals are pursued, but decisions are slower and reaction to poor performance is less decisive. There appears to be less ownership of the strategy at the SBU level. In passing, Goold and Campbell note that companies using this style make little formal use of portfolio planning techniques to allocate corporate resources (p. 64).

Financial control style   This is where the centre has a low planning influence in terms of setting competitive strategy, but exerts tight financial controls over the SBUs. The portfolio is expanded through acquisition, and although success criteria are clear the style can promote risk aversion and 'short-termism'.

Strategic control style   This again is where the centre has a low planning influence but combines this with tight strategic controls. This means that both competitive and financial ambitions are targeted. Longer term thinking is more prevalent but there is a danger that planning processes can become superficial and bureaucratic (p. 10). The researchers found that four of the five companies in this category made use of portfolio planning techniques (p. 95).

Each style can be successful, but, as is briefly indicated, each has its own drawbacks. Goold and Campbell's major conclusion is that: '. . . different styles achieve different sorts of results, and that no one style is conclusively superior to all others' (p. 294). They go on to remark that: 'Each style therefore emphasizes different objectives, and achieves success in different dimensions' (p. 296).

In searching for the reasons why different styles should exist, the authors conclude that managers have different underlying assumptions about how to build a successful organization (p. 297). Thus strategic planning companies stress collaboration and cooperation, while strategic control and financial control companies place more emphasis on personal responsibility and accountability, with financial control companies insisting on tough performance criteria.

Although the writers do not provide any details about how this affects individual functions within organizations, it might appear that the human resource function would be given differing scope within different styles. For example, it may be thought that the strategic planning style might give more emphasis to training and development as a way of achieving long-term strategic goals, although SBUs might well need to match the centre's own HRM policies. Both strategic control and financial control styles allow greater freedom for the SBU in decision-making, but the emphasis on profitability might suggest that HRM policies are either restricted, or need to be carefully costed to show a distinct return. This point will be returned to in the next chapter.

Goold and Campbell's work provides an insightful account of the assumptions on which strategy-making is based, and consequently the way in which strategies vary in diversified companies. Their study demonstrates the poverty of one best way prescriptions and also the multifaceted nature of 'success', which can be measured along several dimensions.

But what other factors account for strategic success – and not just in diversified organizations? The next section analyses various views about what is necessary for a firm to compete in today's complex and turbulent environments, and thus what action has to be undertaken to improve a company's chances in the marketplace. This is a crucial area, for if there is little certainty about what factors lead to success, then it is that much harder for all functions in the organization, including HRM, to understand and fulfil their strategic roles.

Searching for the way to strategic success

It has been seen that authors have different opinions about how to achieve strategic success and this chapter has already explored the views expressed by Porter, Peters and Waterman and others. This is an important issue, since if the factors which lead to success can be clearly specified, then the role of internal organizational functions in helping to achieve strategic objectives becomes easier to define.

From competition to cooperation?

It has been suggested that for companies to be successful they need to find a sustainable source of competitive advantage over rival firms. Porter has continued his arguments for this point of view in recent work (1990). Because he recognizes that competition and markets are becoming ever more global, he aims to set the issue of competitive advantage in a national context. This is an important development as it begins to recognize the wider context in which strategy is carried out, and the limits on strategic vision which a national 'business recipe' can foster (for example, the issue of short-termism and expectations on return on capital in the UK and USA, as compared to the longer time frame and more modest returns expected by Japanese companies).

Porter makes a number of points about the way that governments can help national companies to be successful internationally:

- by focusing on specialist 'factor creacion' initiatives, such as specialized apprenticeship schemes, university research programmes, and trade association activities;
- by avoiding intervention in factor and currency markets;
- by enforcing strict product, safety and environmental standards;
- by sharply limiting direct cooperation among industry rivals;
- by promoting goals which lead to sustained investment;
- by deregulating competition;
- by enforcing strong domestic anti-trust policies; and
- by rejecting managed trade.

In contrast, companies themselves have a different agenda, which should include:

- creating pressures for innovation;
- seeking out the most capable competitors as motivators;
- establishing 'early warning' systems to help take opportunities early;
- improving domestic rivalry;
- using alliance with foreign companies very selectively; and
- choosing the best home base to support competitive advantage for each business.

Porter stresses that companies should not seek out alliances with foreign companies, believing that these have 'become another managerial fad and cure-all' (p. 92). In his view such alliances exact significant costs and involve coordinating two separate operations, creating a competitor and giving up profits. However, writers such as Clarke and Brennan (1988) see the strategic alliance as a powerful tool which can aid competitive strategy, despite the pitfalls, while Ring and Van de Ven (1992) note the increasing interest which cooperative relationships are receiving in the strategic management literature.

However, many forms of cooperative venture do have unforeseen drawbacks. Although acquisitions and mergers can bring in new expertise, products and profit potential, alliances between different organizations also bring issues of harmonization and integration. In the author's own research (Miller, 1990) looking at the factors which contributed towards the successful implementation of strategic decisions, it was found that the difficulties of combining two ways of operating after a merger could lead to significant problems. Of particular difficulty were the human resource problems of managing two workforces with different value systems, expectations and norms. It is then that the human resource function can ease integration by devising integrative training, development and reward systems that cut across traditional boundaries. These human resource issues will be explored in more detail towards the end of Chapter 12.

Cooperative strategies may therefore help some firms to gain competitive advantage, but their inherent problems should not be underplayed and the human issues, especially, should be thought through. In this area, the HRM function might well need to be more proactive.

How people can 'make the difference'

Forms of interorganizational cooperation and global competition may be attracting more attention at present, but what are the intrafirm processes which give birth to strategic success?

While macro-economic variables need consideration, macro-economists tend to neglect the possibility of discretionary behaviour at the level of individual firms (Nelson, 1992). But if people really can 'make the difference', then we need to know more about how this can be made a reality.

As Hamel and Prahalad (1989) point out, the notions of 'strategic fit' and 'generic strategies' may in fact have helped the process of competitive decline (p. 63) by encouraging imitative behaviour, rather than by fostering innovative strategies. They remark that:

> It is not very comforting to think that the essence of Western strategic thought can be reduced to eight rules for excellence, seven S's, five competitive strategies, and innumerable two-by-two matrices.
>
> (Hamel and Prahalad, 1989, p. 71)

All this leads to 'predictable strategies that rivals easily decode' (p. 72).

They argue that since competitor analysis focuses on the existing resources (human, technical and financial) of competitors, the question of **resourcefulness** (the pace at which new competitive advantages are being built) is rarely considered (p. 64). Their concept of **strategic intent** tries to overcome these limitations by centring on what management can do to build on their resourcefulness and so further their competitive ambitions. They suggest a number of active management processes directed towards the internal operation of the firm, including leaving room for individual and team contributions and motivating people by communicating the value of what is to be achieved.

Hamel and Pralahad maintain that strategic intent is more valuable in planning, in that it motivates personnel and allows more ambitious targets to be achieved. As such, it is very clear about what the objectives are, but it is more flexible as to the means by which such objectives are achieved.

In a sense this perspective can be compared to the idea of 'strategic vision' but the authors go further to indicate how intent may be realized in practice. In particular, they emphasize that every employee should be able to 'benchmark' his or her efforts against the best competition, 'so that the challenge becomes personal' (p. 67). Additionally, there is a great need for employees to be provided with the skills they need to work effectively, for example, training in problem-solving, team-building and so on. They also stress 'reciprocal responsibility' for all levels of personnel so that all employees share in the 'gain and pain' of success.

In a second paper Prahalad and Hamel (1990) continue this theme, drawing attention to the **core competences** of an organization which the managers of the firm need to create and consolidate. What might these be? Prahalad and Hamel do not provide a succinct, operationalized definition, but instead give a number of examples. Core competences are referred to as 'the collective learning in the organization', and the 'communication, involvement, and . . . deep commitment to working across organizational boundaries' (p. 82). Such competences should enable the firm to access a wide variety of markets (p. 83), should make a significant contribution to perceived customer benefits, and should be difficult for a rival to imitate (p. 83).

This is still somewhat vague and it is not clear how the organization is to identify and build on its competences. Nevertheless, the authors emphasize that business-level managers need to isolate the human skills that 'embody' core competences, and must be prepared to justify their holding on to people who carry the company's competences.

What appears to be the message here is that the organization has a corporate responsibility to audit its human resource and promote what it sees to be its central areas of expertise. It must then ensure that such competences are used to best advantage and assigned to wherever in the organization they can be best put to use. Human resources should be considered on an organization-wide basis, not allocated to particular business units for all time, but mobilized to whenever competitive advantage can be consolidated. To this end, reward systems which focus on career paths that seldom cross business unit boundaries may engender competition between unit managers, to the detriment of the firm as a whole. The message is: 'the people critical to core competences are corporate assets to be deployed by corporate management' (p. 90). Strategy is thus based on an understanding of abilities, rather than generated by a toolkit of analytical techniques.

This begins to delimit a key function for the HRM specialist, alongside other managers. It is one of auditing the human resource, applying organization-wide personnel systems which do not generate harmful interbusiness-unit rivalry, developing people to consolidate core competences and facilitating the mobilization of the human element across the organization.

Stalk *et al.* (1992) pick up some of these threads. Indeed it could be said that they go further. They put forward what they believe to be a new concept in corporate strategy, that of 'capabilities-based competition'. The central plank of this belief is that the question of how to compete is as important, if not more so, than the question of where to compete. That is, it is the dynamic, behavioural processes of the firm which are a source of advantage: 'The building blocks of corporate strategy are not products and markets but business processes.' (p. 62). Such capabilities are collective and cross-functional, in other words: 'a small part of many people's jobs, not a large part of a few' (p. 62). And the way towards becoming a capabilities-based company is to change managerial roles and responsibilities to encourage the new behaviour required and make sure employees have the necessary skills and resources to achieve the chosen capability.

This emphasis on harnessing the skills and knowledge of the workforce to build organizational capabilities for business advantage is shared by others. Hall (1992) includes employee know-how, personal relationships and organizational culture in his analysis of intangible resources which a company possesses. His survey of 847 chief executives found that they believed employee know-how to be one of the three most important contributors to overall success (the other two were company and product reputation). Additionally, Giles (1991) maintains that the technical side of strategy generation is overemphasized, to the neglect of the human aspect of strategy. He suggests that wider ownership of the strategy among the organizational members is the key to successful implementation.

So it would appear that the most recent writings in this area have once again discovered people as a 'new' source of competitive advantage, while the traditional emphasis on analytical tools and techniques has come under increasing scrutiny. The main criticisms are that such analysis is over-simplistic; it results in strategies which are obvious to the competitor and easy to imitate; and it pays too little attention to the way in which strategy is activated and translated by human action.

This would seem to be welcome news to the HRM specialist. On the surface at least such evidence would appear to underline the importance of the human side of strategic management and to legitimize the HRM function. But just how much practical direction do such studies give in terms of what needs to be done? From one perspective, the answer is, in fact, very little. In the final section the relationship between the strategic management literature and human resource management is examined and the issue of what all this means for HRM as a function is explored in more detail.

What is the contribution of HRM to strategic management?

Strategic management – where we are now

This chapter has covered much ground in the strategic management literature. It has been shown that the area of strategy is complex and fragmented. Although one of the major themes is how firms seek and maintain competitive advantage, there is a multitude of factors which different authors stress as being the most significant.

Of course, on the one hand, it could be asserted that there is no great difference of views. It is merely that some writers take a macro-economic view and suggest appropriate competitive strategies based on a 'global' understanding of the way firms compete, while others take a more micro-economic perspective, focusing on intrafirm competences or capabilities.

But this will not suffice. Both views can be shown to be equally limited. On the one hand, macro-economic analyses appear to suggest strategies which are oversimplistic and easy to imitate. They do not address how particular strategies are translated and activated by human action, and they understate the importance of political behaviour in strategic choice. By failing to attend to the process of strategic management they neglect the dynamic processes which shape strategy at the firm level.

On the other hand, writers who do take a closer look at the internal workings of the organization give prominence to the human side of strategy. Unfortunately, they use concepts which are insufficiently operationalized, so it is unclear what capabilities or competences are being advocated, or how the 'culture' is to be 'managed'. The result too often is a series of 'motherhood' statements about the significance of employees, but with little in the way of guidelines about how personnel are to be motivated, communicated with, or can learn to take 'ownership' of strategy.

Additionally, and perhaps more worryingly, the empirical evidence to substantiate such claims is impoverished. Where is the carefully analysed data to support the view that competences, capabilities or whatever, are associated with (let alone lead to) improved performance? What is offered in the way of evidence is often little more than self-selected single or comparative examples, with minimal description of methodological detail or analytical rigour. If the 'sample' is larger, then it is often restricted to the opinion of the chief executive, or senior managers. In many cases, too, results are only applicable to large-scale organizations.

When research does stop to look at what actually happens in firms then the insights gained are more detailed, and richer in content. So-called process research does provide a more comprehensive understanding of what goes on inside the firm. It suggests that what happens in practice is often a more iterative, incremental or emergent process, tempered by learning, rather than a preplanned, linear sequence of decision–choice–implementation. But this picture of strategy-making, even if more recognizable to the practising manager, provides less in the way of prescriptive guidelines for action. This research does not distinguish the components of 'best practice', in fact it begins to look as though any attempt to look for them is misplaced.

Chakravarthy and Doz (1992) agree with many of the misgivings outlined above. They distinguish between **strategy content** research and **strategy process** research, the former being centred on 'what strategic positions of the firm lead to optimal performance under varying environmental contexts'. The latter is more concerned with '. . . how a firm's administrative systems and decision processes influence its strategic positions' (p. 5). While pointing out the shortcomings of the former, they believe that to be of relevance for practising managers, strategy process research should be more normative, focusing on the performance implications for the firm.

The call for research to be more normative may not be accepted by those whose main consideration is better understanding. The offering of superficial 'solutions' to managerial problems may not be considered a priority when our understanding is still relatively unsophisticated. Nevertheless, it is the case that even the supposedly prescriptive research sheds little light on what managers actually have to do to reap advantage. As has been suggested, this makes the task of those who are directly responsible for the overarching human resource strategy that much more difficult.

Writing the agenda for strategic HRM

As can be seen from the foregoing, the way in which human resource management needs to address itself to the issues of strategic management are not spelled out. While there appears to be consensus that HRM, in common with other organizational functions, needs to support corporate strategy, the specific actions that HRM specialists need to take in this matter are not made explicit. Indeed, to extrapolate from the view of some writers, there would appear to be little of an additional, strategic nature for HRM experts to undertake. If the choice of corporate strategy is an inevitable outcome of rational, calculative analyses carried out by the chief executive alone or in conjuction with senior managers, then the personnel function remains reactive, occupied with the traditional demands of personnel management. However, if the whole thrust of a firm's competitive strategy is crucially dependent on the particular strategic capabilities of its workforce, then this offers a much more proactive role for the HRM function in auditing and developing human potential to meet strategic objectives. It also implies that the line manager's role in the planning and implementation of human resource management strategy is a crucial one – and there is considerable evidence now to show that such a shift of role is taking place (see Chapters 2 and 3). Thus not only is the move towards strategic HRM predicated on this new way of looking at the HRM role, but the role itself also appears to be undergoing a significant shift away from personnel specialists into the hands of line managers.

Hendry and Pettigrew (1992) have argued than human resource management should be consistently linked to the strategy of the organization. They remark that:

> [HRM] . . . should be judged against criteria of coherence and appropriateness – that is, whether aspects of the employment system are internally consistent with one another and are aligned with business strategy.'
>   (Hendry and Pettigrew, 1992, p. 137)

Their study utilizes the concept of organizational life-cycles to investigate the process of strategic change and the evolution of HRM. In the course of their paper they note that companies need to create the conditions whereby employees can relate their activities to one another, and their requires the adoption of HRM as a holistic approach to the management of people (p. 137). This requires HRM to be a much more proactive function than personnel management. Whereas personnel management is about the maintenance of personnel and administrative systems, HRM is about the forecasting of organizational needs, the continual monitoring and adjustment of personnel systems to meet current and future requirements, and the management of change. Of course all this begs the question of whether the HRM function itself has enough influence in the organization to transcend its traditional 'operational' status – an issue that will be explored in Chapter 3.

Since the strategic management writers are apparently so reluctant to spell out the agenda for functional specialisms, human resource practitioners must be proactive in this too. They must take the initiative in deciding what their role must be, and how they can best add to the strategic capability of the firm. They need to take part in the discussion about strategic intentions, and use their expertise to put forward policies to recruit, train, reward and develop personnel in order to meet strategic objectives. Even if the relationship between action and outcomes is not so clear-cut, the HRM manager needs to be represented at the strategic level to influence thinking about the implications of policy for the HRM function.

To become truly strategic, HRM must initiate its own agenda. The next chapter tackles the matter of how this can be done.

Conclusion

This chapter has attempted to provide an overview of some of the main writers and key themes in the broad area of strategic management. The intention has been to offer a critical evaluation of the literature, in terms of its methodological soundness and rigour, and its utility to the practising manager.

Some well-known analytical techniques have been introduced and discussed, the 'excellence' literature addressed, and some processual models of strategy described. Some of the factors believed to be associated with successful strategies have been highlighted and evaluated.

The conclusion has been that, in general, work in this area does not offer a detailed description of what different functional areas need to do to contribute to the strategic direction of a firm. It is therefore up to functional specialists to take the initiative, and to spell this out for themselves.

In HRM it can be argued that the crucial need is for specialists (where they exist) to work closely with line management to develop a truly strategic direction for the function so that it can play its full part in strategy formulation and implementation. However, whether this means that HRM really needs to be a more proactive, 'upstream, first order' function, rather than a 'downstream, third order' function (Purcell, 1992) is a fundamental issue which remains open to debate. This debate is addressed in the next chapter.

2

Concepts and issues in strategic human resource management

Rosemary Harrison

By the end of this chapter the reader will:

1. understand the meaning of 'strategic human resource management', and the practical ways in which a coherent, integrated, business-led function can contribute to the achievement of an organization's mission and corporate goals;

2. understand some of the key processes, ambiguities and tensions involved in taking a strategic approach to HRM in an organization;

3. understand the contingency-based view of HRM strategy, and its practical implications for an organization, division or strategic business unit;

4. be able to identify some of the key triggers to a more strategic approach to HRM in organizations.

Strategic human resource management

As we have seen in Chapter 1, the essence of strategic management is a focus on coherent long-term vision, goals, planning and direction, and the effective fusion of strategic activities and processes. This chapter is concerned primarily with two issues; first, the relationship between human resource strategy and wider business strategy, and secondly, the processes whereby consistency in decision-making and actions can emerge from the choice and formulation of HRM strategies, their implementation, and the feeding back of their outcomes into the strategic decision-making process – the continuous feedback loop referred to on p. 8. Figure 2.1 shows the sequence of themes for the chapter.

But first, what is Human Resource Management (HRM)? There is much debate about this question in academic literature. The concerns range from whether the HRM function, as such, exists at all, to whether it is or should be quite distinct from traditional personnel management. These concerns are outlined in Chapter 3, and are discussed comprehensively in Blyton and Turnbull (1992), Salaman *et al.* (1992) and in Storey's account of employment practices in a sample of around 40 UK organizations (1992).

At this point let us offer a definition of HRM as a strategic function. The majority of managers in the field would probably agree with the following description:

> Strategic HRM can be defined as the overall and coherent long-term planning and shorter term management, control and monitoring of an organization's human resources so as to gain from them the maximum added value and to best position them to achieve the organization's corporate goals and mission.

Such a definition of strategic human resource management may well be:

> . . . directed mainly towards management needs for human resources to be provided and deployed, with a greater emphasis on planning, control and monitoring rather than on problem solving and mediation. It is totally identified with management interests and is relatively distant from the work-force as a whole.
>
> (Mackay and Torrington 1986, p. 178)

However, it is with management's needs that, at this point in the text, we are concerned.

Principles related to strategic HRM

There are a number of factors directly associated with the development of a strategic approach to HRM. They are outlined here, and will be discussed in more detail during the course of this chapter:

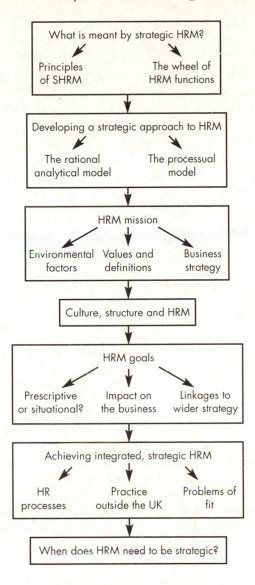

Figure 2.1 *The seven themes of Chapter 2.*

- *The extent to which human resource management is a strategic activity in an organization is mainly dependent upon the philosophy, values and commitment of top management.*

    In the small to medium-sized business, this is self-evident: without such support, the function will barely exist, let alone be seen as a key contributor to success. In larger concerns the support of top management is equally essential to ensure not only that human resources management is a strategic activity, but also that strategy is then implemented and sustained throughout the organization.

- *The effective implementation of human resource strategy is significantly dependent upon those who exercise key influence in the workplace.*

In smaller firms the founder/MD is both the most powerful member of the top management team and the key influence in the workplace. It could be argued that many small and medium-sized organizations are therefore more, not less, likely than larger organizations to approach HRM in a cohesive and consistent way. Whether this would amount to a deliberate strategic approach is open to question, but Marlow and Patton (1992) concluded from their study of employment relations and HRM strategies in the smaller firm that:

> Small firms do have a profile which is accessible to an HRM approach to the employment relationship. The lack of formal or professional policy towards employee management enables an individualized approach to the employment relationship, where the role of employee management is largely undertaken by the owner him/herself . . . (and) by the lack of collective employee representation which owners and managers consider unnecessary.
> (Marlow and Patton, 1992, p. 18)

Others would disagree, as is made clear in Chapter 5. Be that as it may, it is indisputable that those who exercise real (as distinct, often, from formal managerial) leadership at different levels of an organization, not only at the top, have a crucial influence over the direction and outcomes of human resource strategy. It is they who dominate the workplace culture – the set of values, beliefs and attitudes that underpin and explain typical ways of behaving and performing at work – and it is they who either give or withhold the support needed to ensure that HRM strategy is implemented in different parts of the organization according to the formal plans established at corporate and at business-unit level. This, of course, takes HRM into the political arena, and later in this chapter we shall return to this theme.

- *Human resource management strategy must be aligned with corporate strategy in order to serve business needs.*

This requires information to be available to corporate decision-makers regarding the acquisition, performance, development, retention and rewarding of people. There must be analysis of the type, size, performance levels and potential of the required and available labour force once business strategy has been determined. Ideally, such analysis should take place at a point where it can influence choice, not just implementation, of strategy, but in practice HRM strategy (at least in UK organizations) seems generally to be viewed as a 'third order' function, coming well downstream of the processes by which long-term business goals and business strategy are determined (Purcell, 1989, p. 72). Of course, if we view strategy as an emergent process, incrementally changed by organizational learning (as described on p. 22), then HRM takes on a different and more proactive complexion. These are all issues to which more attention will be paid later in the chapter.

■ *For human resource management to produce value for the firm, it must be sustained by and, in turn, sustain an appropriate organizational culture.*

Schein (1992) defines organizational culture as the pattern of basic assumptions that a given group has invented, discovered, or developed in learning to cope with its problems of adapting to its external environment and of internal integration. He explains that when these basic assumptions have worked well enough to be considered valid by the group they will be taught to new members as the ways in which they too should perceive, think and feel in relation to the problems of adaptation and integration. The need for strong linkages between HRM and culture are obvious in the sense that the key HRM processes – such as recruitment, training, development and rewards – clearly have an obvious impact on values, attitudes and behaviour in an organization, but the linkages are also complex, nebulous, and differ from one situation to the next (for a current assessment of 'cultural strategies' see Salaman, *et al.*, 1992, Part 3). In a subsequent section of this chapter there will be a more searching analysis of these linkages.

■ *There are tensions and contradictions within human resource management: they cannot be eliminated but must be recognized and managed.*

Figure 2.2 shows a rational approach to what has been called the 'human resource cycle' (Fombrun *et al.*, 1984). The concept is one of a smooth interaction between the various HRM functions relating to performance, and then integration of the entire human resource cycle with business goals. While the need for coherence and integration in strategic management is obvious (p. 6), Storey's research (1992) shows that there appear to be very few organizations where the ideal is to be found. The points of tension involved in achieving both external and internal consistency are too great and the expertise required, as well as the levels of collaboration and commitment needed between the key parties, are too high.

One major source of tension, to which reference has already been made, lies in the culture of the organization. The tension comes not only from the fact that where people do not 'fit' they will probably be marginalized, excluded or actually forced to leave, it also arises when the prevailing culture of an organization no longer 'fits' the external environment. Tensions also arise when organizational structure and systems change – particularly in the cases of mergers, acquisitions and decentralization.

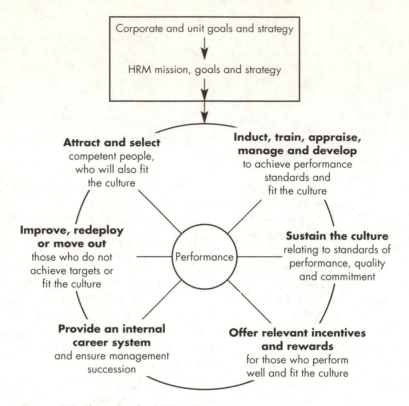

Figure 2.2 *The wheel of HRM functions.*

We shall examine these and other tensions involved in a strategic approach to HRM in more depth shortly.

Developing a strategic approach to human resource issues

The conclusion thus far is that it is easy enough to prescribe a set of principles related to strategic HRM, but, as observed in Chapter 1, it is much less easy to identify ways in which, in practice, human resource and business planning issues and processes should interact.

Let us look first at a practical example involving human resource planning. In this example there is a summary of some general views on that topic, followed by examination of the difference that can be made in a specific situation by developing a coherent, long-term response to human resource problems instead of simply applying reactive short-term remedies.

CASE STUDY: *Human resource strategies – supply of manpower*

Warwick University research identified skill supply as one of the key issues that typically triggered movement into a more strategic approach to human resource management in the organizations studied (Hendry *et al.*, 1988). David Bell (1989) too found that demographic issues were beginning to prompt a return to the longer term planning of the human resource.

Allen elaborated

> The key problem which personnel professionals will have to help solve in the 1990s is that manpower numbers are not going to add up if present policies continue. . . . One aspect of the human resources role is to stop last-minute 'seat of the pants' responses to these problems, . . . by urging and offering strategic and practical solutions. . . . This implies . . . radical changes of policy on the age at which people are recruited, on internal training and retraining, on whether work is done in-house or outside and on the hours in which the work is done.
>
> (Allen, 1991, p. 42)

Research done on behalf of 17 major city organizations in the UK by the Institute of Manpower Studies (Bell, 1989) concluded that a strategic approach to manpower acquisition was needed, and that it should cover in-house human resource planning and development, the re-examination of recruitment and deployment practices, matching technology and workers more effectively, and the creation of flexible working structures. The survey included an example of the kind of organization that had hitherto relied heavily on school leavers as a source of labour supply, and now confronted an environment characterized by a projected steady decline in the school leaver population. Bell pointed out that for such an organization it would be essential to generate alternative objectives that did not rely on a continuous supply of school leavers. Such objectives might be:

- to adjust the age pattern of recruits, or
- to adjust the structure of the jobs, or
- to adjust the expenditure on automation, or
- to adjust all of these.

Each of these objectives should be considered in relation to the kinds of rewards, training, career development, industrial relations climate, other human resource policies and systems that the organization could offer. By analysing and comparing alternative courses of action and their wider implications in relation to HRM in the organization, a manpower strategy could be chosen that would produce an optimum balance of advantage for the organization in relation to achieving its business goals.

In this illustration we can see how a carefully chosen strategy on supply offers the organization the possibility of greater control over a key area in HRM, thus placing it in a better position to solve specific recruitment problems as they arise. The example also points to the need for an overall human resource strategy whose policies of attracting, retaining, rewarding and developing people are consistent one with the other; a principle illustrated in the case study about HMH Sheetmetal Fabrications in Part 3, and in Figure 2.2 (p. 40).

Table 1.1 demonstrated the levels of strategic management in an organization. From that table it is clear that developing a strategic approach to HRM requires not only a human resource strategy at corporate level, but that a strategic perspective must also characterize HRM at the level of business units, where shorter term strategies and plans need to be made and systems put in place to ensure they can be implemented and monitored. This in turn requires that HRM practitioners and line managers work together in the kind of collaborative relationship that will ensure every business-unit plan contains a detailed HRM policy and plans.

Finally, effective HRM needs to be part of managers' daily operations and dealings with people, so that it is built into their management strategy at the operational level. Here, HRM needs to be concerned with achieving for every individual effective and efficient recruitment, training, target setting, appraisal and development, incentives and rewards, and so on. Actions in one area must be supported by consistency of actions in all the rest if, throughout all operations, there is to be a clear, integrated approach to HRM that will ensure the right people are in the right place at the right time with the right skills and motivation to achieve performance targets and develop their potential to aid future organizational growth. In this way a strategic approach to the management of people has a real chance of becoming part of the culture of the workplace rather than a peripheral activity which has no support from the key influencing parties.

It is vital that the processual aspects of HRM strategy are grasped. The confused, often chaotic nature of business strategy, explained in Chapter 1, characterizes human resource strategy also: we should not envisage it as a fixed state, arrived at after a rational process of decision-making, choice and agreement on business goals and a route to reach them, leading to the generation of goals to take the workforce along that route. That may be an ideal to aim for, and at different times activities may be taking place that seem to conform to that ideal; written plans, reports and other documentation may support the perception of some that life is proceeding in an orderly fashion, dominated by rational economic considerations. However, time and again the ways in which people – the key actors in the situation – behave and interact will reshape, change the course of, and sometimes destroy what the formal plans and processes intend.

Thus the 'rational economic model of human behaviour' is quite inadequate as a way of explaining or predicting organizational life. People in organizations have their own views and aims related to formal strategies and plans, and will act accordingly, whatever economic rationality may dictate. Entrenched interests will often block the paths of change, resisting forces of innovation either overtly or with various forms of what has been termed 'organizational inertia' (McKinlay and Starkey, 1992, p. 121). Somehow, human resource strategy must find ways of turning that inertia into commitment to its formal goals.

At British Airways in the early 1980s, the inertia produced by an entrenched bureaucracy was only overcome by: getting rid of top managers who represented and reinforced that culture; putting in across the whole organization a major culture-change training programme that focused on changing every individual's self-image as well as their image of the company and of its customers; installing appraisal and reward systems to support the new focus on high quality, customer service, and commitment to the company; and carrying out radical structural change. To maintain those changes and ensure that there is no return to the old culture, the company has subsequently subscribed to a continuing pattern of 'change events' as well as to a stringent auditing of its human resource function (which, in the early 1990s, led to that function's delayering, downsizing and decentralization, to use the jargon words of the time).

To cope with the political and dynamic nature of strategic HRM processes, there is a major need for sensitivity, creativity and political skill: sensitivity to what is going on between key parties and to the main areas of tension and tolerance; creativity in thinking up responses which will keep strategy on track while also making necessary adjustments through time; and political skill in knowing how to recognize and deal with the 'nonrational aspects of organizational behaviour' and how to 'mobilize those intangible social forces which perpetuate organizational inertia' (McKinlay and Starkey, 1992, p. 121).

In Chapter 3 we shall look at some of the ways in which such skills can be applied to the management of human resource strategy in the organization. At this point, here is a brief illustration of creativity in progressing the achievement of HRM goals.

CASE STUDY: *Developing strategic decision-making skills at Digital Equipment, UK in the late 1980s*

With acknowledgements to Bell D. (1989).

At Digital Equipment Corporation in the late 1980s Tony Attew, human resource strategist, identified a gap of language, culture, knowledge and organizational perspective between HRM specialists and the rest of the management group that impeded the development of a meaningful manpower plan and associated recruitment policy for the firm. He therefore held a series of workshops for line managers and manpower planners which helped the former to understand manpower constraints involved in business and technological goals and the latter to understand those goals.

The outcome of the workshops was the achievement of a scenario approach to the skills needs of future markets, technology and economic situations. This allowed joint exploration of the skills capabilities of the company, so that a 'statement of capability' (key issues which help or hinder business goals) could be drawn up, followed by computer analysis of current capabilities and future competencies within functions.

This example, brief though it is, is a useful illustration of creativity being exercised at a point when formal human resource goals were being threatened by negative interactions between two parties – the specialists on the one hand, the line managers on the other. The creative device chosen – a series of workshops – tackled the ostensible tasks to be done through processes that were also designed to draw the parties together and break down those barriers of knowledge, attitudes and culture that had been separating them.

The device was apt and successful. However, because it brought about a new pattern of human interactions, it would have created expectations in the parties that the new style of relationship would continue. The task for Attew and his colleagues thereafter would be twofold: to continue to work towards achieving the formal human resource tasks, but to do so in new ways that would build on and sustain the new kind of interactions between the specialists and the line managers. There is no general prescription to apply to such a dynamic situation. Sensitivity, creativity and political skill are needed to continue what has been begun. If such skills are not applied, then the old culture will take over, and once again the barriers between the parties will obstruct the achievement of formal tasks – only this time there will be added barriers created by frustration, cynicism and disappointed expectations: 'We always knew they wouldn't really change', will typify the feelings likely to develop on both sides.

Planned interactive processes take time to show benefits since they are to do with changing people's values, attitudes and customary ways of behaving and interacting; the concept of interaction and the need for creativity in fostering it must therefore be built into HRM strategy.

In the previous sections we have looked at a definition of strategic HRM, explored key issues, and concluded that, to be truly 'strategic', HRM must be built into corporate planning, into strategy at business-unit level, and into the everyday culture, policies and practices at the operational level of the business (Fombrun *et al.*, 1984, p. 42). It has also been stressed that human resource strategy must be a dynamic, creative and political process. This realization gives a particular edge to Gluck's statement that:

> Management is measured by the skill and sensitivity with which it manages and develops people, for it is only through the quality of their people that organizations can change effectively.
>
> (Gluck, 1985)

HRM mission

Now let us look at the concept of the HRM mission. It is customary in textbooks to assert that the first essential for human resource strategy is to have a clear, relevant and agreed human resource mission or overall policy, derived from a philosophy that sees people as the key to an organization's success and growth and from a vision which can inspire and direct the behaviour and performance of the workforce. Such prescriptions, of course, make eminent sense; but in practice they are hard and often impossible to follow.

Examples of corporate mission statements abound. Like HRM mission statements, they are relatively easy to produce. A familiar convention is for the top management team, plus other key parties (however defined) to go off on a weekend of contemplation, often 'facilitated' by an external consultant, and to return like Moses from the mountain with organizational truths embedded in minds, hearts, transparencies and flip charts. However, to ensure that a mission reflects the primary values within the organization is very hard, and the consequences for many employees can be dramatic. In 1981, with British Airways in a state of virtual bankruptcy, the advent of Lord King and Colin Marshall, as chairman and chief executive respectively, heralded a period of sustained and radical change. The new corporate mission of aiming to make BA 'the Harrods of the airways of the world' led to: getting rid of those top managers whose culture was antipathetic to that mission; restructuring BA to turn it from a rigid, introverted bureaucracy to a customer-orientated, high-quality and world-class airline; and radically changing its financial, technological and human resource systems (Thomas, 1985). The corporate mission statement had looked innocuous, if ambitious – the reality behind it proved harsh for many.

Achieving commitment

A mission needs to capture the 'hearts and minds' of all employees. However, such commitment can have its downside: 1993 saw the battle between British Airways and a small but dangerous competitor, Virgin, reach an unexpected culmination – Richard Branson, of Virgin, won a half-million pound court award in recognition of the validity of his accusations that BA had conducted a sustained campaign of 'dirty tricks' against his airline. The campaign itself was a wide-ranging, illuminating example of the kind of commitment that a 'successful' corporate mission and a powerful and charismatic leadership can produce in certain members of its workforce. A former BA employee said at the time in an affidavit that the behaviour of staff towards Virgin could be explained by an environment created at the very top of the organization, and that most individuals had been reacting in a way that reflected their concern that if they too did not take a very aggressive line then they might be regarded as weak or lacking (Blackhurst, 1993). The danger of this kind of commitment is clear, and the backfire was obvious too: if a world-class airline could go to such lengths against a small competitor, what might it not do, or be doing, against other competitors?

In theory, the HRM mission must serve the corporate mission, and should reflect the organization's philosophy about its workforce and the kind of contribution they are expected to make to the business, as well as the reciprocal treatment they can expect from the organization. Therein, too, can lie complexities, not least when the HRM mission statement is all too clearly belied by the reality: the way human resource management is actually carried out at different levels of the workforce.

We shall explore such tensions later in the chapter, but here, let us look at a different issue, that of whose interests, exactly, are to be served by HRM and corporate missions.

Values and definitions of key parties

Malloch (1992) cites the case of a labour-dominated metropolitan borough council in a deprived urban area of the North East of England. In its formulation of a human resource mission and strategy the council's top management were concerned to reflect their determination to maintain job security for council employees as part of a wider mission of commitment to the local community.

The council's corporate mission was summarized by the phrase 'to build the community'. At Hutton (the pseudonym given to the council in the case study) new top managers had arrived in the early 1980s who saw the council's environment as a community to be served:

> They did not see their environment as a set of product and labour markets
> to be exploited. They saw the poor economic and social conditions in Hutton
> as an environment to be improved. The main point is that organizations can
> and do have the power to define the environment in which they operate.
>
> (Malloch, 1992, p. 134)

The council's HRM mission and policies were driven by the same values that
had produced the corporate mission. There was a tactical approach to tendering, aimed at ensuring that few if any outside contractors won council
tenders, and there was a policy of redeployment which had a clear economic
rationale – it increased the utilization of human resource capacity; it transferred employees' learning and skills between locations; and it permitted a
greater range of work to be done with the existing workforce. However, for
the policy-makers its most powerful rationale was that it honoured the
council's commitment to internal employment security.

Thus moral values shaped HRM strategy and policies at Hutton, just
as they shaped corporate mission and goals. But Hutton is not unique.
Malloch also undertook research in, *inter alia*, a National Health Service
hospital, a brewery, and two large multinational chemical producers (1990),
and in every case he found that management values drove the manpower
system both directly and indirectly. He found that they worked directly by
defining certain manpower policies as being appropriate on grounds of
morality, personal interest or tradition; they worked indirectly by shaping
decisions on technology, work organization, how costs were to be reduced and
changing definitions of market domains.

As Malloch observed in his commentary on the local council, there are
a number of private sector organizations too who partly define their environment as a community and are to a degree driven by social as well as purely
economic values in strategic decision-making. However, the council acted in
a very different way from many other local authorities placed in a similar
situation. Again we can see the impact on strategy of the values and social
interactions of those who make the key decisions:

> What actually occurs in such a situation will, therefore, be the outcome of
> the relative capacity of different actors to impose their definition of the
> situation upon others, rather than of a mechanistic relationship between an
> organization's needs and the problems with which the system is faced
>
> (Silverman, 1970, p. 165)

So although it is inarguable that the human resource mission must derive
from the corporate mission, the processes involved are complex:

> Analyses of human resource management which purport to be driven solely
> by economics and the environment . . . need to be treated with considerable
> reserve and scepticism
>
> (Malloch, 1992, p. 134)

As was pointed out in Chapter 1 (pp. 15, 18), managers may enjoy considerable freedom to follow their preferred strategic choices, and social and
political processes do indeed have a significant effect on strategic decisions.

To summarize:

- The corporate mission derives from top management's definition of the environment in which the organization must operate.

- That mission will, to a greater or lesser extent, be influenced by social as well as economic values, and those values will be a key differentiating factor in the choice of strategy, goals and policies for the organization. Organizations cannot be typified as driven purely by economic ends.

- The definitions and values that shape corporate strategy will also shape human resource strategy, adding further complexity to the many processes by which that strategy is determined and implemented in the workplace.

Culture, structure and human resource management

Organizational culture

It is conventional wisdom that the mission and strategy of an organization need to be underpinned by an appropriate primary organizational culture and that human resource strategy and the culture are and must be tightly interrelated. To quote Fowler (1987):

> First . . . every aspect of employee management must be wholly integrated with general business management and reinforce the desired company culture. Second . . . a dominant emphasis on the common interest of employer and employed in the success of the business will release a massive potential of initiative and commitment within the workforce.

The importance of culture in relation to corporate success has been emphasized in the 'excellence' literature and in considering innovation (Kanter, 1983). Peters and Waterman (1982) stressed that the culture of the organization is shaped from the top, and that a number of simple, positive values permeate the most successful corporations. The point has been debated, particularly on the grounds that such values, generalized as they are, can never in themselves be enough to explain or ensure organizational 'success' – a term in any case capable of many different interpretations. However, despite the criticisms of such literature to which Chapter 1 has already referred (pp. 19, 20) and about which David Guest has written a telling account in Salaman *et al.* (1992), values do matter, because they help to guide and explain behaviour. To the extent that people have shared values about certain key aspects of behaviour and performance in an organization, the task of tackling goals collaboratively becomes easier, and their achievement more likely. Thus in his examination of Hutton Borough Council Malloch (1992, p. 133) found that there was strong evidence of a culture and working practices that were consistent with corporate mission and strategy, and that both culture and external environmental factors had a clear impact on the council's HRM policies.

However, the real point at issue here is that getting sufficient shared values to secure the kind of commitment that Fowler describes is far harder than populist literature admits. Fowler (1987) makes this clear in his observation that strategic human resource management, in its drive to secure commitment, may really be 'a covert form of employee manipulation dressed up as mutuality'.

Certainly, fundamental changes in business strategy and consequent organizational restructuring have been identified (Hendry *et al.*, 1988) as among the key triggers to attempts to take a coherent, strategic approach to HRM; and as noted in Chapter 1, such changes are frequently accompanied by attempts to develop across the organization the kind of culture that will encourage and reward the attitudes and behaviour that the drive for change demands. This, in turn, leads to a major focus on communications, so that it is not surprising that a survey by Collinson Grant Consultants (PM Plus, 1993) of directors and personnel managers in 52 UK firms in manufacturing, retailing, distribution, professional services and construction should show over 90% of respondents having communications as their major concern (even though nearly half did not have a formal policy on the subject). We shall see in Chapter 7 how BET used communication strategy to underpin and extend its radical programme of strategic, structural and cultural change.

Most typically, 'culture' manifests itself in the workplace in:

- the ways in which people interact with their environment, and the working practices that exist;

- the ways in which people interact with each other, for example within teams and across different hierarchical and horizontal levels of the organization;

- the kind of performance and behavioural goals that are set;

- the levels of performance and behavioural goals that are achieved;

- the kinds of managerial style that characterize and are rewarded by the organization (an increasing number of organizations are now using peer group and even subordinate assessment to identify the extent to which managers behave in ways that contradict rather than reinforce the primary culture desired by top management);

- the ways in which communications and motivation are tackled by management, and typical responses by the rest of the workforce.

From this, one important realization should emerge: culture in the workplace is *not* necessarily either a unifying force or one always dominated by management and operating in its interests:

> It would be difficult to explain the 1984 strike of the British coal miners either in terms of the collective will of the corporation or in terms of the internalization of dominant norms and values. . . . Norms and values have as much potential for creating conflict within organizations as they do for creating social cohesion.
>
> (Meek, 1992, p. 197)

It is not unusual to find organizations where a 'primary culture' has been systematically imposed and reinforced by management and where compliance rather than internalization of values has been achieved. The tensions inherent in such systems demonstrate that having a clear mission, and a managerial culture and business policies and systems to support it, may not be enough to ensure sustained high performance of the workforce. Attempts to create a 'unifying' culture, if they ignore the inevitable plurality of interests in organizations, can lead to a high potential for damaging conflicts, as Gouldner's classic study of a gypsum plant showed (1965).

> Integration, in the sense of getting the members of the organization working together with a sense of common purpose, is an important aim of HRM, but this must take account of the fact that all organizations are pluralist societies in which people have differing interests and concerns which they may well feel need to be defended collectively.
>
> (Armstrong, 1987, p. 32)

So we should dismiss the ideas that developing or changing 'organizational culture' is easy, can be achieved by quick fixes, and can in the relatively short term build up a workforce unified in its fundamental values, beliefs and commitment to corporate goals. There may be examples of such workforces – but where they exist the explanation for them is complicated and is likely to lie not in management action alone but in the interaction of many forces over a long period of time. Even where the appearance of a 'unifying culture' does exist, the true state is more likely to be either of compliance because of the complete domination of one party over all the rest, or of the achievement of a balance of advantage between different interest groups – a state of equilibrium that will need constant exercise of political skill if it is to be maintained.

This is not to deny the contribution that HRM can make to changing behaviour, because of course people's perceptions, motivation, interactions and performance in an organization are influenced by HRM processes such as recruitment, training and development, and rewards; but they are also fundamentally affected by the manifest beliefs and behaviour of those in key positions of power and influence (Silverman, 1970; Gouldner, 1965). As Meek concludes: 'Culture *as a whole* cannot be manipulated – although it needs to be recognized that some are in a better position than others to attempt to intentionally influence aspects of it.' (Meek, 1992, p. 209).

All of these points have a particularly strong applicability to large and multinational organizations, and are strikingly illustrated in the Multichem case study presented in Chapter 4. Interestingly, it is in the smaller not larger enterprises where, because of the domination of a strong central influence, a unifying primary culture can probably be most easily developed – as can be seen from the example of Albert Moss at HMH Sheetmetal in Part 3.

Organizational structure

Another truism is that the structure of an organization, its key processes and operating and decision-making mechanisms must be consistent with its culture and facilitate the achievement of its mission and the implementation of its business strategy. The aim is for the culture and structure of the organization, together with the corporate plan, to form the context within which human resource strategy must operate, and with which it must interact. However, this interaction is complex, dependent on a range of internal as well as organizational imperatives specific to the particular situation.

Structural change, like attempts to change culture, is therefore far harder to achieve than may on the surface seem to be the case. Systems theory has done a service to managers in enabling them to map the organization in terms of its interlocking components. The value of that analytical framework is the attention it draws to the need for certainty about the mission of the organization, and about the elements key in achieving its goals, and to the repercussions that will take place within it whenever change is introduced in any of the elements. But the weakness of many areas of systems theory is that they lead to a reification of 'the organization'; and a tendency to present organizations as static entities rather than as the product of the continuing social interactions of their members, and of those members with forces in the external environment. They also present people as a predictable, manipulable component – indeed the term 'human resource management', which carries just such an implication, was common in American systems theory literature in the 1960s, twenty years or more before it was widely encountered in UK texts.

The deterministic view of human nature is misleading. Organizational structures, after all, come into being because people decide that they should, for reasons associated with the particular values, perceptions and ideas of those people, in that situation, at that time. Structures then continuously evolve as the result not only of a variety of external pressures, but also of continuous human interactions at every organizational level. Some of those interactions will support a prescribed structure, others will challenge or seek to change it, the outcome being decided at the point where the real power to influence events resides. This was brought out in Gouldner's famous study (1965) of a wildcat strike at an American gypsum mine and, again, is very clearly illustrated in the Multichem study in Chapter 4.

As a conclusion to this section we can expand our original definition of strategic HRM to take in an awareness of the reality of organizational life:

> Strategic HRM can be defined as the overall and coherent long-term planning and direction, and the shorter term management, monitoring and control of an organization's human resources so as to gain from them the maximum added value, and to best position them to achieve the organization's corporate goals and mission.
>
> To the extent that people have shared values about certain key aspects of behaviour and performance in an organization, the task of tackling goals collaboratively will become easier, and their achievement more likely. However, because organizations are pluralist, not unitary systems, there is a major need for sensitivity, creativity and political skill, treating strategy as a continuous and uncertain process, not a fixed state.

HRM goals and their contribution to 'the business'

In discussing the HRM mission and the linkages between HRM strategy and culture and structure, we have perhaps missed a step: the nature of HRM goals. Goals derive from the mission, and represent the specific outcomes that strategy seeks to achieve. Without goals, strategy is meaningless: the dangers of taking a route to nowhere in particular should be obvious.

In their detail, the goals of HRM will vary from one organization to another, dependent on specific internal factors and on external pressures and challenges. In essence, however, they are to do with 'utilizing labour to its full capacity or potential' (Storey, 1989, p. 9). This, as we shall shortly see, may follow a 'soft' or 'hard' approach, contingent upon the pressures of the situation.

At this point, we look at three research studies that give important insights into the goals of HRM, the impact of their achievement on business performance, and the extent, if any, to which HRM is in fact becoming a 'strategic' function in the United Kingdom.

Guest's model of HRM goals

Guest (1989a, b) proposes certain overall policy goals for strategic HRM. He emphasizes that these are relevant only for organizations seeking to obtain a leading edge in their field, needing high-quality products or services produced by a skilled, flexible workforce that is fully committed to the business goals of management. He emphasizes, too, that to achieve these HRM goals there must be a commitment to HRM among organizational leaders, and a related willingness to make a high level of investment (of time, money and expertise) in human resource over a long rather than short time span. To be successful, strategic HRM also requires (he suggests) either no union presence or a management–union relationship where management is the dominating party, and that it will be greatly facilitated by a greenfield site situation.

The goals he proposes are to do with achieving:

- strategic integration of HRM issues and plans at every level of the organization;

- a high level of commitment of the workforce to the goals and culture of the organization;

- high-quality recruitment, management and development of employees;

- flexibility of function and of structure to enhance the ability to innovate.

Guest (1989b, pp. 42–3) quotes certain companies that are successful by reference to their financial status, their innovative and turnaround capacity, and their ability to remain nonunion, and observes that they are also companies who have adopted HRM policies in pursuit of the above aims. However, he admits (Guest, 1990) that there is as yet no large-scale evidence either in the United Kingdom or in the United States of America (where, it is usually thought, HRM is at a sophisticated stage in many organizations) of any causal links between strategic HRM and business performance. He concludes that so-called leading-edge HRM companies should at present be viewed simply as illustrating what can be achieved when a strategic, business-led HRM approach is used, rather than as providing any convincing proof that the model he proposes will invariably lead to such results. The Multi-chem study in Chapter 4 demonstrates the practical complexities involved in trying to impose overarching HRM goals of the kind Guest suggests in a multinational corporation.

Impact of HRM strategy on business performance

There are some promising signs, none the less. Fox *et al.* (1992) quote from a recent research project covering 60 companies in the United Kingdom of which 49 were comparable financially and statistically and whose structures were diverse – holding companies, multidivisional companies, and smaller, undivisionalized firms without subsidiaries and operating in one product line. The project examined the companies' financial performance over a

10-year period (1978–88), interviewing executives responsible for HRM in each company, and 'in many cases' (p. 2) a number of other managers. They examined key HRM practices as they affected the firm's management populations, and in each company they looked at four measures of HRM as practised:

1. *Systematization*   How   systematically   were   these   HRM   practices conducted?

2. *HRM integration*   How far was there integration between different components of human resource strategy, such as recruitment and selection, appraisal, reward systems, human resource development?

3. *Integration with corporate strategy*   How far did HRM practices influence, for example, choice of decision-makers at corporate level, and the processes as well as the plans related to strategic decision-making and implementation?

4. *Meritocracy of HRM*   'For example, did they give each manager at a certain level the same chance to have his or her work recognized?' (p. 3).

They produced, from their research, statistics which showed broad patterns of linkages between HRM, corporate strategy and financial performance. Their main conclusions were that:

> High scores on all of our four measures of HRM are associated with higher degrees of financial performance, although the measure which is most robust is the degree of integration between HRM practices and corporate strategy. High degrees of integration between HRM strategy and corporate strategy were most strongly associated with high financial performance, and low degrees of integration between HRM strategy and corporate strategy were strongly associated with low financial performance.
>
> (Fox *et al.*, 1992, pp. 11–12)

Of course financial performance *per se* may not be the only, or even primary, goal of every organization, and other measures of HRM's impact on the organization also need to be devised. However, it is a goal that undeniably has universal business significance and so is one with which HRM strategy must always be concerned.

Integration of HRM and corporate strategy

Storey's research (1992) concludes that such internal consistency and external integration is rare in British organizations. His project covered 40 organizations in the United Kingdom, 15 of them in detail. It focused on large, complex, mainstream employing organizations, and involved 350 in-depth interviews with managers at all levels, approximately 80% of whom were line and general managers as distinct from personnel specialists. Some interviews were also held with shopfloor and union employees.

Storey's aim was different from that of Guest or of Fox *et al.*: it was to explore the nature and extent of change in the management of labour in Britain (Storey, 1992, p. 263). He found a significant degree of change in managerial approaches to handling human resources, in part propelled by a greater general movement towards hard measures such as site closures, delayering, demanning, and a greater focus on target-setting and control of individuals; in part driven by the fact that senior managers 'had a view' about desired people-management approaches 'and tended to share a broad sense of the direction in which their organization should be heading in employment matters' (p. 266). Common trigger words were: corporate culture, flexibility, quality of service, core beliefs, vision, and the communication process. However, managers were focusing their HRM practices and initiatives – of which there were a striking variety and number – on the individual employee, leaving industrial relations managers to deal with collective issues.

Thus Storey concluded that: 'Human resource management type initiatives had been "bolted on" to the embedded system' (p. 269). The management of change emerged as a slow, uncertain process, not one of transformation but rather of evolution, and HRM emerged less as a cohesive alternative strategy to traditional personnel/IR than as a 'set of movements' quite separate from it. Everywhere there seemed to be a lack of integration between employment practices, both individual and collective, and wider business strategy.

The general conclusion seems to be that while there is, in the United Kingdom, a marked growth in the variety of HRM initiatives being pursued as organizations search for competitive advantage, growth and achievement of corporate goals, there is little sign yet of a coherent, long-term, internally consistent approach to HRM, nor of confirmed links between specific kinds of HRM goals on the one hand, and business performance on the other.

We therefore end where we began: first, clear HRM goals must be set, but their nature must depend on the specifics of the situation; secondly (in default of evidence to the contrary), if HRM strategy is to contribute to the 'bottom line', especially in the longer term, then there must be an internally consistent set of HRM policies, with HRM strategy itself tightly aligned to corporate strategy. This latter point does, however, beg an important question: what other types of impact for HRM strategy can replace, or add, the strictly financial as measured by the research of Fox *et al.*? In Chapter 12 of this book an attempt will be made to at least partly answer that question, when the concept of 'the learning organization' is explored.

Achieving integrated and strategic HRM processes

Light can be shed on the ambiguity that, in the literature at least, relates to discussions of the goals and outcomes of strategic HRM by looking again at the key HRM functions (p. 40) – what Fombrun *et al.* (1984, p. 41) call 'the HRM cycle' – that influence human performance:

■ selection

■ appraisal

■ rewards

■ development

These represent pivotal HRM processes. It is quite logical to argue (as in Chapter 1) that, having recruited expensive human beings into an organization, they should then be trained, rewarded and developed according to some overall human resource strategy which aims to improve their performance and ensure their effectiveness, motivation and efficiency. Japanese employment practices seem to confirm this view: in most Japanese organizations except the very small (that is, employing fewer than 25 people (Koike, 1988)) the preferred strategy is to recruit well-educated workers, offering them relatively long-term security and an internal career system, together with continuous development and improvement of their skills, knowledge and experience. This human resource strategy is often thought to explain much of the success of Japanese organizations and it therefore merits some attention here.

Japanese employment practices: what is the lesson?

As we have just seen, integration and consistency seem to be rarely achieved in HRM in the United Kingdom (Storey, 1992). However, Japanese practice must be viewed with caution. Koike (1988), who carried out primary comparative research across a number of countries including the United States, observed that internalized career systems were not unique to Japanese companies: for example, they could be found on quite a wide scale in US organizations. He also pointed out that in those Japanese organizations where long-term security of employment appeared to exist, it only lasted until around 50 years of age, and between the ages of about 27 and 50 employees underwent very stringent assessment at every stage of their, usually slow, progression up the hierarachy of promotion. The average length of time taken to move into a managerial position was 10 years, and thereafter the pace became ever more competitive and rigorous. Rewards in terms of money and promotion were accumulated slowly through time, and only in return for the sustained achievement of very demanding standards of job performance.

Dore (1987, pp. 20–47) pointed out that a strategic approach to human resource management and development is facilitated in Japan by the structure of industry and patterns of ownership and control which encourage long-termism generally. Ackroyd *et al.* (1988) also noted the importance of the interrelationships in Japan between economic structures, economic systems, organizational units and employment practices in explaining the success of Japanese businesses. Finally, the Bank of Japan has questioned the view that Japanese industrial competitiveness is, in any case, due mainly to the flexibility and efficiency of Japanese factories; it sees the availability of cheap finance in the 1980s as a more likely cause (Leadbetter, 1993b).

Such underlying structures and systems, like cheap finance itself, are now, however, being subjected to increasing strains as the economy moves into a more recessionary period, and Leadbetter (1993a) forecasts that the severity of Japan's current economic downturn is likely to lead to the lifetime employment system being reformed, with companies demanding more in return for the security they offer, and a particular threat to job security after the age of 50 if high performance standards in that age group are not maintained. Indeed in 1991 Briggs (1991, p. 36) was already reporting that only about 30% of Japanese workers were being offered lifetime employment with the major companies, a figure that was decreasing steadily. She also explained that the alternatives in Japan to staying with a single employer are not attractive (Briggs, 1991, p. 41), and that because Japanese workers are brought up in a culture which clearly separates personal emotions from work behaviour, they accept and endure work conditions and levels of effort that would be unacceptable to, for example, many British workers (see also Chapter 5). For both these reasons Japanese workers do tend to try to remain with one employer for the long term, despite quite widespread lack of job satisfaction and lack of pride in the firm (Briggs, 1991, pp. 41–2).

Finally, looking at Japanese overseas subsidiaries, researchers like Gleave and Oliver (1990, p. 68) and Sawers (1986) found important keys to Japanese business success in the successful 'fit' or 'compromise between local ideas and corporate preferences', not simply in the strategic nature of HRM in those companies.

Employment practices in other countries

This is not the place for a detailed survey of HRM outside the United Kingdom (see, for example, Brewster and Tyson, 1991; Towers, 1992). However, some brief comments are relevant here. In the United States the general entrepreneurial culture and the higher academic and practical status of the personnel/human resource profession and function go far to explain the widespread acceptance of HRM as a key strategic function for the business – although the poor American secondary educational system and the long period of recession have meant a decline in the general level of investment in employees' development over the long term. Then again, in most European countries except the United Kingdom, state, employers and unions tend to work collaboratively in key aspects of HRM, notably in ensuring high standards of vocational education and training for the young, and in adult training and development (see Harrison, 1992, Chapter 4). In all of these countries there is, compared to the United Kingdom, a significantly higher level of commitment to strategic HRM, particularly evidenced by a greater HRM boardroom presence (see Chapter 3).

In the United Kingdom, by contrast, there has been a markedly *laissez-faire* approach to the development of people, be it through vocational education in schools, or through patterns of education and training in and out of work thereafter (Harrison, 1992b, Chapter 3). This failure to make long-term, continuous and high-level investment in the people who will become or who already constitute the country's available workforce reflects a view of human beings as costs, not as assets needing careful management to become a productive resource for country or individual organization. It is a failure that goes some way to explain the lack of influence of personnel professionals at various levels of organizations, and of the generally low level of proactivity of human resource practitioners – specialists or line managers – in the crucial area of corporate strategy and planning (see Chapter 3).

The point being made by this digression into non-UK employment practices is that we should avoid making generalizations about the links between HRM and the bottom line; about appropriate policy goals for strategic HRM; or about the reasons why organizations invest in a strategic approach to the function and the kind of outcomes that can result from it. Even very generalized comparisons between competitor countries demonstrate that HRM can only be fully understood, and its goals and organization should only be determined, against a wider backcloth of the external environment as well as in the context of the opportunities and constraints facing it within an organization – exactly the point made by Legge (1977) in her exposition of a contingency-based approach to personnel management, and by Malloch (1992) in his analysis of strategic HRM in a local authority in the United Kingdom.

Problems of 'fit'

We have already concluded that to make an effective contribution to achieving business goals, HRM strategy must achieve both internal and external 'fit'. However, in the United Kingdom at least, such fit is virtually never found (Storey, 1992). Many of the problems involved have been comprehensively described by Legge (1989, pp. 29–39), but to understand why achieving fit in HRM is so difficult, some of them will also be analysed here.

Hard or soft HRM?

The 'hard' approach is quantitative, calculative and concerned with managing an organization's headcount 'rationally'. It is typified by the organization which is either demanning, or preoccupied for other reasons with cost-cutting, increased productivity and efficiency.

The 'soft' approach seeks to achieve people's 'commitment' to the organization by focusing on communication, motivation and leadership. It is typical of the American school of organizational psychology of the 1950s and rests on values that see no essential conflict between the interests and needs of the organization on the one hand (as represented in its corporate goals) and those of individuals on the other.

We have already discussed this unitary concept and its shortcomings earlier in the chapter. The tensions involved in trying to reconcile hard and soft approaches under a single banner of strategic HRM become evident when both states are desired simultaneously – when the employer demands both an efficient, pared-down workforce and one that is highly motivated and committed. 'Tough love' is the jargon phrase for the balance that then has to be achieved, and it well describes IBM's dilemma in the early 1990s; committed to its philosophy of long-term employment and internal career development, yet unable to maintain that philosophy in practice when a viciously competitive market gave rise to the need for demanning as part of a changed business strategy. It also becomes evident in Marks & Spencer's notable move away from paternalism in the early 1990s, when redundancies took place in the interests of a leaner, more efficient, more competitive company, and a tougher management style showed signs of developing at the top.

When an organization is driven by short-term financial considerations and cost minimization, and/or is facing severe reduction in market share, tough love in fact becomes indistinguishable from the hard HRM approach, and it is at that point that many begin to question whether 'personnel management' with its traditional 'concern for the interests of individuals and working groups' (Institute of Personnel Management, 1980) is indeed a different function altogether from HRM. To illustrate these tensions let us look at an example of a company apparently moving from soft to hard HRM in an attempt to fit human resource strategy to the needs of the business.

CASE STUDY: *Rover moves to a tough love strategy*

The overall purpose of strategic HRM is to get best value from an organization's human resources. This may be done by a 'soft' strategy, focusing on effective recruitment, deployment and development, or it may be attempted by a 'hard' strategy, reducing the headcount and then pushing for greater efficiency in the leaner and tougher workforce that remains. In some organizations, the approaches are combined – a 'tough love' strategy.

Such a strategy was perhaps illustrated in the case of Rover, the British Aerospace subsidiary, which announced in November, 1991, that it was aiming to cut costs by 30% over the next four years, and planning a further reduction in the number of jobs, in response to the threat from the growing competition and efficiency of Toyota and Nissan. In previous years Rover had expressed its belief in its workforce as one of its greatest potential assets by investing heavily in wide-ranging programmes of training and development, and in September, 1991, 'it effectively offered its employees jobs for life in return for the adoption of Japanese-style working practices' (Maguire, 1991):

> The firm told its 35 000 workers that it wanted to end the distinction between blue- and white-collar employees, sweep away demarcation lines and introduce a new procedure to deal with disputes. . . . The firm, while conceding that existing manning would be reduced, says it has no target and wants to provide secure employment. . . .
>
> Rover . . . already has some of the most modern working practices after securing a deal last year that introduced 24-hour production at Longbridge in return for a $31\frac{1}{2}$-hour week for some shift workers. Under the latest proposals, remaining demarcation lines will go. Workers will be taught a range of skills and anyone capable of doing a task could be asked to do it. Team working, as in Japan, would be introduced.
>
> Mr George Simpson, Rover chief executive, said under its programme, called the New Deal, it intended to guarantee job security as far as possible, with compulsory redundancies virtually ruled out and lay-offs a thing of the past.

In November, 1991, the company said that the workforce was being cut to 34 000 in 1991. George Simpson said:

> 'I don't see the workforce dropping by a huge amount. It will be a slow, steady decline. But everything depends on our ability to increase productivity.'
>
> A Japanese newspaper yesterday quoted Mr Simpson as saying that Rover would have to shed a third of its workforce over the next four years unless sales grew.
>
> (Gribben, 1991)

What is happening in such cases appears to be less a new HRM strategy of tough love than a reactive tactic in response to intense competitive pressures and the adverse impact of continuing economic recession. Of course it can be claimed that the long-term human resource strategy will remain, with only temporary adaptations in the light of critical business needs – and certainly in Rover's case, given the major investment they continue to make in developing their employees (as we shall see in Chapter 12), this is the reality. However, the case does underline the difficulties inherent in trying to maintain a consistent strategy for HRM – by definition a long-term activity – while also trying to contend with short-term imperatives that argue for 'rationalization' of the workforce.

It would therefore seem from such considerations as these that HRM must always be a downstream strategic function, dominated in a crisis by the demands of business strategy as defined by those stakeholders, internally and externally, who 'control' the business – a point to which we shall return in our discussion of 'tight–loose' tensions.

Commitment to what?

We have already analysed some of the tensions involved in trying to get the commitment of the workforce. From the sort of examples we are looking at now, it is clear that a sustained strategy to produce a committed workforce may backfire when decisions to reduce that workforce are made. This was particularly evident in the case of the decision to shut down the highly productive Ravenscraig steelworks in Scotland, in 1992. From the time the mine was opened, the workforce had been fully committed to the company, achieving very high levels of productivity. Yet business strategy – heavily influenced, no doubt, by national political strategy – dictated closure of the mine, despite the job losses this entailed for workers who were the more vulnerable because they formed so great a proportion of the local community from which they had been drawn. Commitment, in that case, brought few rewards for the workforce. In Chapter 4, we shall see in the Multichem case study a practical illustration of the problems of gaining and retaining commitment in the face of such pressures.

Tight or loose HRM?

In principle, HRM policies should mesh with business strategy and fit the stage of development at which the organization has arrived – in terms of product or geographical diversity, and of associated organizational form. The work of Sparrow and Pettigrew (1988), for example, showed the variety of ways in which human resource strategy was being adapted to the particular business needs and situation of the firm. Firms like DEC and ICL had a general strategy of linking personnel programmes to the needs of business plans and forecasts; on the other hand companies like ICL, Honeywell Bull, Hewlett-Packard and Wang followed a general strategy of identifying the firm's human resource strengths and then gearing business strategies around them to achieve a competitive advantage. An organization like (at that time) IBM pursued a general strategy of using coherent employment policies which formed part of the organizational culture.

A more difficult question facing many organizations is how far it is possible to integrate HRM policy with strategy at business-unit/divisional level *and* achieve an integrated company-wide HRM policy (Legge, 1989, p. 29). The issue is critical, given the increasing tendency of multidivisional organizations to decentralize and to push HRM down to the business units. At British Airways in 1989 (Personnel Management, 1989) after its new personnel director had concluded an audit of the impact and value of its HRM function for the organization, that function was reorganized along two main dimensions to better serve the business:

- grouping 'field' teams and central services staff under a single manager to eradicate the conflict and competition that existed in the past and to improve links between the various units; and

- decentralizing many of the tasks previously managed by the human resource department to line management.

Similar restructuring of HRM functions took place in the late 1980s and early 1990s in UK organizations such as BP, National Power and the London Underground, always as part of a general drive for increased efficiency and improved performance or service. In 1989 a British Institute of Management/ Aston University survey noted in Britain a twin movement towards increasing decentralization of personnel responsibilities to field levels and increasing centralization of the crucial policy, strategy and control function.

The problems of striking the right balance between tight and loose in HRM clearly have no easy solution. As we shall see shortly, too tight a 'fit' with corporate strategy and culture, and there are dangers both of rigidity in relation to the outside world (for example, IBM), and of a failure to be sensitive to the needs of divisions and units. Too tight a fit with the decentralized parts of the organization, and the dangers are of insularity between parts, and between parts and the corporate whole, together with the loss of any meaningful overall HRM strategy and coordination. Yet, as explained in Chapter 1, business strategy often has to be differentiated within an organization. Thus, especially in many large, multidivisional companies, each division may have to pursue a different kind of business strategy: for example, one aiming for cost leadership, another for differentiation; or one pursuing high growth and high market share, another following a strategy of cost-paring, perhaps leading to closure, because it has low growth potential and low market share. Consequent diversification of HRM policies and practices seems inevitable in such cases, to meet the needs of business strategy – even if it then becomes virtually impossible to retain identification with any overarching corporate HRM strategy (Ahlstrand and Purcell, 1988).

It follows, then, that HRM initiatives must be:

> . . . consistent with those initiatives taken in other functional areas of the business, and consistent with an analysis of the product market situation. They key is to make operational the concept of 'fit' – the fit of human resource management with the strategic thrust of the organisation.
>
> (Ahlstrand and Purcell, 1988)

If we recall at this stage the discussion in Chapter 1 (pp. 24–5) of the different styles of strategic management, the problems of fit for HRM strategy become even more complex. The financial control style will tend to lead to a hard approach to HRM in the SBUs, even if there is a soft HRM strategy advocated across the business as a whole; the strategic control style may produce HRM planning processes that are superficial and bureaucratic across the organization as a whole, and therefore lead to a reduced ability of HRM at unit level to relate closely to the needs of that unit. The strategic planning style (combining high planning influence by the centre with flexible forms of control) is perhaps the style most likely to offer freedom to HRM managers and practitioners to tailor the function to the needs of business strategy at the SBU level, and Storey's research does offer some interesting support to that view (Storey, 1992, p. 270) – but the danger then is that of few, if any, meaningful linkages to corporate strategy. (For a full discussion of this issue, see Miller (1987) and Purcell (1989).)

Strong corporate culture?

Earlier in this chapter it was noted that many organizations are increasingly trying to recruit those who, besides having the appropriate skills to offer, also bring 'attitudes' appropriate to the primary culture of the orgadization (see, for example, Herriot and Fletcher, 1990). The use of assessment centres as an aid to recruitment, development and promotion features, usually, a strong emphasis on cultural factors, and it is becoming more common to find that behavioural as well as performance targets are being set, especially at managerial level, and measured not only by superiors but also by reference to peer, or even subordinate, ratings (Mumford and Buley, 1988).

However, there are dangers in attempts to impose a strong corporate culture. It can breed organizational rigidity – and indeed many view the problems facing IBM in the early 1990s as stemming in large part from the very tight and all-pervasive corporate culture that was 'arrogant and intro-verted' (Faith, 1992) and dominated the company and its relationship with its customers for far too long. At the level of individuals, too close an iden-tification with a strong culture can reduce the ability to respond flexibly to change, so that strength of culture becomes the enemy, not the guarantor, of flexibility (Legge, 1989, pp. 35–6).

When does HRM need to become a more strategic activity in an organization?

In our discussion of HRM goals (p. 52) we noted Guest's point about a strategic approach to HRM being appropriate for organizations seeking to obtain a leading edge in their field, needing high-quality products or services produced by a skilled, flexible workforce. Research at Warwick University (Hendry *et al.*, 1988) confirms this view, indicating that a strategic approach to HRM is likely to be triggered by a more competitive external environment pushing an organization into carrying out a complex set of internal changes, which in turn have widespread human resource implications. These changes tend to be a mix of the following:

- competitive restructuring to meet new patterns of competition (as at the TSB and Pilkingtons);
- decentralization of key areas of decision-making to get closer to clients and improve response and service levels;
- internationalization of operations (for example, GKN, Pilkingtons);
- acquisition and merger, which often encourage new HRM initiatives such as assessment centres, career planning and development;
- quality improvement in products and/or services;
- technological change in product, process or management tools, which in turn trigger a broad range of HRM development requirements; and
- new concepts of service provision and distribution (for example, a move to provide edge-of-town superstores).

Many of these triggers are discussed in the Multichem study in Chapter 4, where it will be seen that such changes require, in turn, new operating structures and systems and new cultures (Harrison, 1992, Chapter 6). Such changes are unlikely to transform employment practices and relationships in an organization – the process of change is slow, uncertain and subjected to a variety of human pressures. They will, however, bring a need for new skills, knowledge, competency levels and attitudes from line managers and personnel/HRM practitioners, and this is a focal point in Chapter 3.

Conclusion

In this chapter strategic HRM has been discussed in ways that explain the managerial goals it can serve. It has also been analysed in terms of the human issues and interactions that make it a dynamic and unpredictable process. Finally, there has been an examination of areas of tension involved in developing a more strategic approach to HRM while also acknowledging the need for pragmatism in managing the function.

3

Roles, relationships and skills in developing a strategic approach to human resource management

Rosemary Harrison

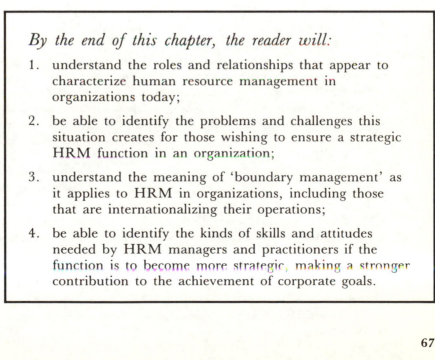

By the end of this chapter, the reader will:

1. understand the roles and relationships that appear to characterize human resource management in organizations today;

2. be able to identify the problems and challenges this situation creates for those wishing to ensure a strategic HRM function in an organization;

3. understand the meaning of 'boundary management' as it applies to HRM in organizations, including those that are internationalizing their operations;

4. be able to identify the kinds of skills and attitudes needed by HRM managers and practitioners if the function is to become more strategic, making a stronger contribution to the achievement of corporate goals.

If HRM is to become a strategic function, those in key HRM roles must be able to exercise a direct influence at board level, in divisions/strategic business units, and at the operational levels of the organization. We shall therefore look first of all at what appears to be happening to HRM roles in organizations today, both inside and outside the United Kingdom.

Human resource management as a board-level function in organizations

HRM in the boardroom

> Having a personnel director as a member of the main board demonstrates that manpower is one of the elements which need to be developed if the enterprise is to be successful. Finance, sales, production and technical directors are all essential, but each function depends on the performance of employees if it is to make its proper contribution to the success of the business . . . (I am not) arguing that the people element should be dominant (but that) it should be there; and, if it is not, it will to an extent be neglected.
> (Sir Richard O'Brien who served on the board of Delta Metal, and became chairman of the Manpower Services Commission, UK (Coulson-Thomas, 1991).)

Given the need for HRM to be represented at board level if it is to become a truly strategic function for the organization, what is the evidence about its actual position currently? There is data to indicate that in the United Kingdom, if to a lesser extent than in major competitor countries, HRM is a board-level function in about two-thirds of organizations employing over 200 people; on the other hand, again in the United Kingdom more than elsewhere, it does not appear to be a widely proactive function at that level; and it is increasingly a general management function, with even the board-level role occupied in many organizations by nonpersonnel practitioners (Brewster and Smith, 1990).

The fact that in the United Kingdom the role of 'director of human resources' is often held by a nonpersonnel specialist is partly to do with the poor track record as 'business managers' that some feel personnel practitioners hold (Thurley, 1981; Allen, 1991); partly it is because in a number of organizations, and especially in those that are decentralized, the management of human resources (as was noted on p. 32) is seen to be primarily the responsibility of line managers (Storey, 1992, p. 266); and partly it is because in a number, more especially the medium-sized to small, there is still no specialist personnel department yet none the less there is a concern with developing a consistent, even if not a truly strategic, approach to the management and development of employees.

At the international level, a 1989 report from Korn Ferry and Columbia Business School indicated that HRM could be emerging as the second most important area of expertise for the chief executive of the future, overtaking marketing and sales, and second only to strategy formulation. The survey looked at the views of 1500 top executives from 20 countries and drew 5 main conclusions from their findings:

- human resource planning must be an intrinsic part of corporate strategy,
- the human resource executive should belong to the top management team,
- the human resource function must be transformed so that it becomes a key activator in sourcing and deployment,
- management training and development is essential to organizational success, especially for chief executives,
- it is essential to choose as leaders and managers those who have internalized the corporate culture, values and goals of the organization.

Research carried out by Cranfield and Price Waterhouse into HRM in France, Sweden, the United Kingdom, West Germany and Spain gives some support to these conclusions. Data relating to the United Kingdom in 1990 (Brewster and Smith, 1990) showed that about two-thirds (63%) of organizations above 200 people had the head of personnel or human resources function on the main board or equivalent. The percentages were higher in Spain (76%), France (84%) and Sweden (87%). The situation in West Germany is not comparable, because in all major German companies the executive board must by law include a labour director, and most aspects of personnel management are defined by laws or quasi-laws, so that the human resources/personnel manager occupies primarily a 'contract manager' role (see later in this chapter). In Japan there is a personnel director on the board of major companies and he/she is usually the most senior director after the chief executive, 'sitting in the position of influence more usually occupied here by the finance director' (Parry Rogers, in Coulson-Thomas, 1991).

HRM as a proactive corporate function

If HRM is increasingly reaching the boardroom, the crucial question then is: how far do HRM views influence the determination of strategy? In the Cranfield surveys, 51% of UK respondents said, both in 1990 and again in 1991, that the personnel function took part in developing their organization's corporate strategy from the outset. This was a significantly lower figure than for France, Spain, Sweden or Germany (the latter two having the highest figure, 62%) (Arkin, 1991). Survey data further indicates that in the United

Kingdom 32% of personnel/HRM directors are consulted about corporate strategy, 9% are involved in planning its implementation, and 9% have no impact on strategy at all.

What these figures do not tell us is how far those with a responsibility for strategic HRM, *regardless of whether or not they are personnel specialists*, do make an impact on corporate strategy. Here, Storey (1992 p. 266) is enlightening. His research revealed that:

> General managers, manufacturing directors, quality directors and others, have not been content to respect specialist boundaries when matters relating to the utilization of the human resource are involved. . . .
>
> Senior executives were found to be having a far more extensive exposure to, and involvement in, issues pertaining to labour matters than has so far been reflected in the literature.

Storey found, encouragingly, that concerns about aspects of corporate culture, change management, employee commitment, quality of service, flexibility, core beliefs, vision and communications were on 'the agenda of chairman's groups and senior management workshops' and concluded:

> To what extent the diagnoses and action plans actually filtrated into business strategy as it unfolded was more difficult to determine. But at the very least, senior executives were found to 'have a view' about desired people-management approaches and tended to share a broad sense of the direction in which their organization should be heading in employment matters.

So what seems to be happening is that HRM *is* getting significant representation in the board room, if in a somewhat bitty, nonintegrated way, but its spokespersons are tending to be the senior executives of the organization, not specialist directors – a trend that may not sound hopeful for the personnel profession, but may be encouraging for the future of HRM as a strategic, top-level function in the business, provided that senior managers are committed to and well informed about HRM issues.

Strategic HRM as a business-led function

The role of HRM in the UK boardroom – whoever carries responsibility for the function – does seem to be dominated by bottom-line concerns in the broad sense:

> 'Strategic human resource management' encompasses those decisions and actions which concern the management of employees at all levels in the business and which are directed towards creating and sustaining competitive advantage.
>
> (Miller, 1987)

So is it inevitable that HRM strategy is led not only by business strategy but also by the top management values that underpin that strategy? Views such as the following indicate that it is:

> To be accepted as potential board material a person must make it entirely
> clear that his first and overriding priority is a successful, tough and cost-
> conscious company.
> (Henry Fairweather, Group Services Director, Scottish and Newcastle
> Breweries, in Coulson-Thomas, 1991, p. 39)

The same point is made by Reitsperger (1986) in his analysis of the
difference between personnel management as a mediating or as a merely
operational function, and HRM as a true strategic force. He points out, in
his study of Japanese management, that in the Japanese companies he
surveyed in Britain the tight and pragmatic integration of industrial relations
strategy with marketing and especially manufacturing strategies, and the sub-
ordination of all these functional strategies to a single overriding strategic goal
(in those cases, perfection in production), explained both what strategic
human resource management really meant and the values that should lie
behind it.

The debate about how far the personnel specialist should identify with
the concerns of line management is not new. Total commitment to the values
and goals of top management in an organization is something many personnel
practitioners have found to be the most sensible and feasible strategy given
their particular situation at the time, and seen in this way, human resource
management could be rationalized now as simply the chosen, most appropriate role for most personnel practitioners to occupy today. Perhaps all that
has really changed is that for an increasing number it is not in fact a matter
of choice at all, but of necessity:

> The role of the personnel practitioner as the 'in-between' person seems to
> have gone. Personnel managers appear to be managers first and personnel
> people second.
> (Mackay and Torrington, 1986, pp. 161–2, commenting on data from their
> survey of personnel practice in the United Kingdom)

Miller's explanation of the change in role is simple:

> The key issue (to fit human resource management with the strategic thrust
> of the organization) is made difficult because it seeks to bring together two
> traditionally disparate functions and disciplines – strategy development and
> personnel management.
> (Miller, 1987)

The difference was appreciated by the American Society of Personnel
Administration in 1989, when it underwent a change of name to The Society
for Human Resource Management. Its chairman, Thomas Kelly, explained
at its annual conference:

> The use of the word 'personnel' is waning among organizations as we take
> on increasingly strategic roles within our organization . . .
> (Personnel Management, 1989)

The attempt to bring together those two functions will, as Keenoy observes, cause a painful dilemma for many personnel professionals:

> In embracing the very real power offered by involvement in strategic human resource management, personnel managers may have to relinquish any claim to be the guardians of *humane* HRM.
>
> (Keenoy, 1990, p. 9)

But, again, is there any choice in the matter?

> It is now a totally out of date concept to think of the personnel professional either as an intermediary between workers and management or having any representational role in either direction.
> (Parry Rogers, who served on boards of companies that include IMB UK, Plessey, and ICL, in Coulson-Thomas, 1991, p. 39)

To be quite clear about the origins of the tensions we have just been exploring, compare Miller's definition of strategic HRM with the Institute of Personnel Management's official definition (1980) of personnel management:

> Personnel management is that part of management concerned with people at work and with their relationships within an enterprise . . . its aim is to bring together and develop into an effective organization those men and women working in an enterprise and, having regard to the well-being of the individual and of working groups, to enable them to make their best contribution to its success.

The difference between the two definitions lies less in content than in emphasis. What is missing from the IPM definition is an unambiguous focus on the direct linkage between people management and the achievement of business goals and strategy; what is present is the implication that personnel management is in some sense the conscience of the business. Those differences in focus summarize the essence of the case that there *is* a difference between HRM as a strategic, business-led function and personnel management as defined by its UK professional body. It might therefore be argued that 'humane HRM' is no longer a significant issue – although this point is strongly disputed, as we shall see, by Robin Evenden in Chapter 9.

Formalized HRM strategy at corporate level

Organizations like IBM and Cummins Engines have a written human resource strategy as part of the corporate business plan. That is untypical of UK practice according to Brewster and Smith (1990), where it appears from the Cranfield survey that: . . . only four out of every 10 UK organizations have a written HR strategy compared to the six out of 10 which have a written corporate strategy, and only seven out of 10 claim to have any kind of personnel strategy, written or unwritten.

Of course, another interpretation can be attached to such figures: if only 60% of organizations have a corporate strategy, then to have in the same sample as many as 40% of organizations with a written human resource strategy could be viewed as an encouraging sign of the perceived importance of HRM planning. Storey (1992) found that there were clear signs of a major take-up of HRM initiatives in organizations in the United Kingdom but that, as yet, the focus was on the individual rather than on the collective, and was not yet resulting in an internally integrated, coherent set of activities with a long-term vision. He found very few significant signs of a *strategic* HRM function (which could explain the dearth of written human resource strategy), but HRM none the less seemed to be a valued area of activity, attracting much more interest from managers than hitherto.

The role of personnel specialists in relation to HRM strategy

Let us now examine in more detail the role and impact – if any – of personnel specialists on the HRM scene. It is essential, first of all, to differentiate between the specialist personnel management function and the function of HRM which is taken in this book to mean the whole spread of activities that relate to the planning, management and performance of people as a key resource in an organization.

In 1981 Thurley wrote:

> Personnel specialists are caught in a mismatch between a pretentious abstract model of human resource management and the reality of a fragmented set of activities carried out with little recognition of their value by other managers.

This negative view of the influence of personnel specialists at board level reappears at middle management level in the work of Allen (1991) who found managers sceptical about the contribution such specialists were making to the business, and who criticized them for being out of touch with managers' needs and problems.

It is relevant here to recall one of the best-known typologies of personnel roles, that of Tyson and Fell (1986):

Clerk of works The role that involves dealing with routine personnel matters. Mainly carried out, either full- or part time, by unqualified staff, reporting to a line manager or a personnel manager. However, in some organizations, particularly highly bureaucratized and in the public sector, even very senior personnel practitioners are often, in essence, occupying no more than this role.

Contracts manager   A more senior position, heavily involved in making and interpreting procedures and agreements, especially on the industrial relations front. In Germany, as we have already seen, personnel directors tend to be mainly carrying out this kind of role because of the legalistic and proceduralized nature of much of HRM in Germany.

Architect   A member of the senior management team with a seat on the Board and a broad portfolio, with the emphasis on being a proactive business manager first, personnel manager very much second.

In the 15 case organizations Storey (1992) surveyed in depth, only the architect role was found to be particularly consonant with the HRM model; only two had personnel specialist teams of the architect type; and most of the major change programmes in those 15 cases originated outside the personnel function.

Storey (1992, p. 187) makes the important point that:

> In most of the mainstream companies personnel had found it 'safer' and more attractive to remain attached to the proceduralist symbolic realm.

In other words, most personnel practitioners were engaged in contract or clerk of works activities. He adds that where the specialists were in an architect role, this was usually in smaller companies, varied in terms of ownership and sector – a point to which we will return in Chapter 5. He continues:

> It was in these large, unionized and proceduralized organizations that . . . personnel had remained more attached to the traditional mode. (*ibid.*)

This is assumed to be because the 'traditional' is by definition the role in which most expertise and power are likely to be vested, and because of the pressure from unions and others in the larger, more proceduralized organizations.

Finally, about half of the personnel managers and directors in Storey's survey did aspire to more of an architect or change agent role, and many could point to the introduction of initiatives in the company which were recognizably to do with HRM 'albeit lacking in consistency and strategic integration'. The specialist personnel function, then, emerged in this important study as standing in the wings of anything approaching 'strategic human resource management', yet moving gradually and in a pragmatic fashion towards a more centre-stage position.

This impression of an essentially pragmatic function, moving only with caution from the familiar and secure to the more speculative and ill defined, does conform with the way in which personnel management has developed in the United Kingdom, where there has never been a single role for the personnel practitioner, nor a single set of objectives (Mackay and Torrington, 1986; Legge, 1988, 1989; Sisson, 1989). Personnel managers have come from a diversity of backgrounds into a diversity of organizations and contexts. Backgrounds, organizations, contexts, needs and expectations – their own and those of the role sets they have joined – have shaped the particular role in the particular situation. The 'personnel profession' itself has always been an open one, uneasily balanced, sometimes torn, between a concern for people and their needs and rights and a preoccupation with managerial goals; between some universal view of the values and 'mission' of personnel management and a localized preoccupation with its day-to-day survival and practice in the specific organization where the personnel manager worked. This conflict of concerns was well explained by Karen Legge as long ago as 1977, when she suggested a typology of roles for personnel managers that was less to do with their level of operations as with the stance they took towards the organization's core values and goals.

Legge formulated a contingency-based approach to the practice of personnel management and to the organization of the function in specific cases, with dominating variables being the type of culture and structure in which the personnel practitioner has to operate, the level they are at in the organization, and the stage they have reached in their career.

Fuller discussion about what exactly is happening to 'personnel management' and its practitioners in the United Kingdom can be found in a number of texts and articles, notably Legge (1988), Sisson (1989) and Storey (1989), although the most comprehensive and up-to-date treatment are probably those by Guest (1991) and by Storey (1992).

Line managers and HRM

In many organizations line managers do hold the main responsibility for HRM. However, the explanation is not in all cases that the personnel practitioners have proved inadequate and so have lost their credibility and positions. In some, perhaps many, instances it is true that they are little valued by their managerial colleagues (as shown in Allen, 1991). In many others, however, the reason for line management 'taking over' HRM direction is to do with business strategy – because HRM has long-term implications and is integral to the core performance of the organization, it is judged to be necessarily a major concern of line managers (Storey and Fenwick, 1990; Storey, 1992). Other reasons are probably to do with the organization structure and culture, the size and stage of the organization's development, and ownership of the business – a range of factors dealt with in detail by Sisson (1989, pp. 35–8).

Overall, what evidence there is in the United Kingdom indicates that middle managers are expanding their spheres of influence, and 'readily embracing the general "business manager" role alongside their acceptance of the prime responsibility for people management. . . . Meanwhile, at junior line-management level, compatible developments (are) discernible.' (Storey,

1992, p. 267). One of the major reasons for this change is the decentralization of organizations and the consequent increased importance of business units (a pattern very clear in the public as well as the private sector in the United Kingdom) which gives to managers of those units extensive budgetary control, business planning responsibility, and responsibility for the individual performance levels of their workforce:

> Line and general managers have been central to the people-management changes in two senses – both as drivers/devisers of new patterns, and as implementers/deliverers of the preferred approaches.
>
> (Storey, 1992, p. 266)

Skills of HRM professionals and managers

It will by now be clear that the human resource role requires expertise of many kinds, a close collaboration between managers and specialists, and the ability to convince of its real value to the organization. Furthermore, unless the specialist practitioners are to lose out altogether in playing an influencing role in the direction and implementation of HRM strategy, it is essential for them to develop both the specialist expertise related to making the key processes and activities of HRM serve business needs, and the collaborative and political skills related to forging and sustaining productive working relationships with key parties in their organizations.

Here is a case study illustrating an attempt to develop such skills in the HRM team, as well as ensuring the effective implementation of business-led human resource strategy.

CASE STUDY: HRM strategy in a British investment bank
(From Riley and Sloman, 1991)

■ The task for the personnel department at County NatWest

County NatWest, a leading investment bank, in 1991 asked all its business units, including its personnel department, to establish strategic milestones for a five-year period against which, by specified target dates, their performance would be measured. Thus the personnel department was forced to consider its contribution to the organization at the strategic level, in the context of the bank's overall five-year business plan.

■ The business environment

The department's overall objective was 'to add value and increase productivity within a limited resource allocation'. It had to be achieved in a dynamic, exceptionally competitive environment in which huge contractions had just taken place after the October, 1987, stock market crash and economic recession. County NatWest had in fact jumped from employing 650 in 1985 to 2350 worldwide in 1991, but there was fierce competition for scarce skilled individuals in some product areas, while labour was being shed in others. The bank had acquired and integrated three separate businesses in that time, and so there was a variety of business subcultures. 'The quest for flexibility had to be balanced by a professional approach where pragmatic short-term solutions would not undermine long-term strategic decisions.' There had to be slimming down and a tight control on costs, with productivity being improved while costs were held level or reduced.

The requirement to produce strategic milestones as an input to the business plan 'marked an important watershed in defining the contribution of personnel to the business at a strategic level. It forced the department to reflect on the nature of that contribution.' The department had three teams – the personnel management, the administration, and the staff development teams, with an executive director at their head who herself was a member of the bank's management committee. Each personnel manager had a link with a designated number of business departments, while administration and staff development had more specialist functional responsibilities.

□ *Developing a human resource strategy*

At first, each of the three teams produced its own 'milestones'. These made sense in relation to the overall function of the teams concerned, and had clearly defined methods of measuring achievement. However, 'they did not . . . add up to a coherent whole. There was no evidence of a common philosophy, synergy or a shared vision which would be needed to underpin the milestones' success and achievement. What we had was a compartmentalized approach.'

The issue was focused on at a personnel training weekend that took place shortly afterwards. The theme of the weekend happened to be 'teamworking', and offered to these three teams the opportunity to put together all the milestones they had produced, and to examine them as a whole, in the light of the overriding needs of the five-year business plan for County NatWest.

Back at work, they decided to begin again, and new milestones were created through a process of continuing meetings of small cross-team groups. Out of this exercise, 18 separate strategic milestones were produced, and were duly authorized by the senior management of the bank. The milestones were consistent one with the other and, overall, addressed issues which consultation within business units and across the three personnel teams had shown to be critical to business success.

Each milestone was then assigned to a designated individual within the department for completion, helped by a small group from a different part of the department.

> The obligations of ownership were identified as a separate performance objective for the individual concerned as part of the annual performance review. Quarterly reviews on progress, involving the whole department, are held to ensure that the milestones are on target.

The milestone on career development was an important integrative milestone and one of the most difficult to achieve. There was a willingness on the part of the business areas to allow staff to move at junior level; there was also support for movement within the graduate training scheme. It was anticipated that at senior management level there would be a reluctance to lose valued staff; however, absence of cross-career movements was a major barrier to integration and had to be addressed.

Table 3.1 *Example of a strategic milestone: cross-career movements*

Milestone	Date	Measure of success	Reaction/behaviour by business area
Cross-career movements	4th quarter 1992	One in 10 of staff will have worked in more than one business area	Cultural acceptance. Acceptance of milestones on remuneration.

Success in achieving this milestone (see Table 3.1) depended on positive support from the business units: expressing strategic objectives in this way underlined the need for a collaboration between line and specialist managers in order to achieve business targets at unit level.

To the authors of the article 'it would . . . be a great disappointment if the milestone exercise proved other than to have been a major turning point in defining the role of a proactive professional personnel department'. To the reader, the case study shows how, at the level of business units, HRM can only begin to become a strategic, integrated function if there is a continuing process of close collaboration between human resource/personnel practitioners and line management to define the needs that the function should serve, to set targets to be achieved, and to agree on how plans can be measured in order to monitor their progress and evaluate their effectiveness.

The importance of setting targets and measuring outcomes in HRM is emphasized in this case study. The situation that exists more widely in this respect, as revealed in Brewster and Smith's 1990 survey, is instructive: only

46% of UK personnel departments surveyed had their work systematically evaluated. Admittedly, this figure was the highest among the five countries surveyed, but there is ambiguity here: does a greater preoccupation in the United Kingdom with measuring the value of the work of personnel departments represent a greater professionalization of the function than elsewhere? Or does it perhaps spring from a greater scepticism by management about the value of personnel activities, or – relatedly – from anxious attempts by personnel specialists to justify their existence? Weight is given to the latter interpretation by the statement:

> Our data must raise questions about the role of personnel specialists at board level. Many of them seem not to be significantly involved in the development of corporate strategy and not to have created human resource strategies for their organizations; nor have they developed work programmes or targets against which the personnel department can be measured.
>
> (Brewster and Smith, 1990)

The County NatWest study shows the benefits to the personnel function of a rigorous process of target-setting: not only does it facilitate the achievement of key business goals, but it also provides criteria whereby the work of the department can, in part at least, be measured, and the process itself helps to raise the credibility of the function.

Skills related to planning, target-setting, monitoring and evaluation are essential to the success of HRM, whoever holds the responsibility for that function in an organization. Now let us look at other crucial skills, especially those relating to what can simplistically be called **boundary management**.

National and international HRM: crossing the boundaries

Boundaries mark the frontiers between people, cultures, organizations and countries. To bind the parts into a whole, and to position the whole so that it can interact effectively with the wider world beyond, means bringing down boundaries, or managing them in such a way that productive interactions are still possible. When the American Society of Personnel Administration in 1989 changed its name to The Society for Human Resource Management, its chairman explained that a change of title was needed to overcome boundaries of focus, of role and of function. Particular emphasis was placed on the need of human resource managers to take an increasingly international vision (Personnel Management, 1989).

In the 1960s a seminal work on organization structures was published (Burns and Stalker, 1966). The authors identified the need for organizations in a world of shifting boundaries – an 'unstable' environment – to debureaucratize their structures, to adopt matrix forms, flexible jobs and attitudes, and to recruit cosmopolitans rather than localites: people with knowledge of the outside world, who could speak its languages, operate in its cultures, import its innovations and meet its challenges head on. The essence of the book was boundary management.

In 1989 Armstrong (1989a) put a similar focus on boundary management, on the need for flexible structures and cultures in a continuously changing world, but this time in the context of personnel/human resource management. Armstrong advocated an entrepreneurial role for personnel practitioners, observing that the business context within which they had now to operate was aggressive, competitive and increasingly global (1989b). He pointed out in a speech to the Institute of Personnel Management Conference (Armstrong, 1989c) that these features were linked to developments such as acquisitions and mergers, privatization, deregulation, the rise of the multinationals and consumerism.

Storey and Sisson (1989) have questioned the universality in British organizations of the trends outlined by Armstrong, and their analysis deserves careful reading. However, we have already seen in this chapter that there is a clear need for human resource strategists to break down a variety of barriers and to play a leading role in developing more cosmopolitan cultures and flexible structures, and to establish innovative approaches to HRM at corporate, business-unit and operational levels. Likewise, within any organization where there is a need to develop a business-led HRM function it will be essential to develop the skills, relationships and processes needed to produce and implement human resource strategies that meet cross-functional and cross-sector needs. The case study about County NatWest has shown some of the ways in which such boundaries can be managed in an organization, and Allen (1991) gives many examples of the alienation between line managers and personnel/HRM practitioners that occurs in too many organizations where those practitioners have protected their traditional territory, and failed signally to make a real place for an HRM function even when managers themselves recognize the need for it.

Crossing the international boundaries: the role of HRM strategy

In a conference organized by the Economist Unit in 1989 in Belgium, '1992 and beyond: Practical approaches to the human resource and management development issues' was the theme of the two days, and a variety of speakers from different countries narrated their practical HRM strategies. Repeatedly they focused on the need to react positively to:

- the impact of the European Commission directives;

- demographic changes and the consequent recruitment crisis;

- the need for training and development strategies which would produce culture change and skilled, flexible and productive workforces; and

- issues of succession planning, mobility and executive remuneration.

Research done by Scullion (1992) indicates that in the United Kingdom at least there is a long way to go: British owned multinationals are still not recruiting and developing the international managers they will need to take advantage of the single European market, and the French appear to have a head start over the United Kingdom in graduate recruitment strategies aimed at the post-1992 era (Keenan, 1991). On the other hand, work done by BP when setting up a new European finance centre in Brussels, with staff drawn from 13 nations, shows the kind of innovative training that can be delivered to develop a shared vision and culture across boundaries of national identity (Neale and Mindel, 1992).

In the attempts to pull down one set of boundaries, however, it is essential to avoid setting up others, more powerful and ultimately more rigid. Thus membership of the single European market must avoid a protectionism that will reduce the benefits offered by that union; insularity will mean inability to understand, let alone cope with, the chaotic changes that occur, as in the wake of the breaking down of East–West barriers, and the increasing industrial and economic domination of countries in the Far East.

The expertise needed to produce and implement effective human resource strategies to help overcome boundary problems, at whatever level and for whatever reason, in and between organizations, is wide ranging. At the Economist Conference already mentioned, Roy Williams, director of the Development Associates Group, stressed the importance of human resource practitioners and managers finding 'new and more powerful ways of operating, influencing and contributing', especially in organizations moving towards or into an international arena. He identified the following as the areas where a high level of knowledge, skill and competence is essential:

- the planning and management of organizational and cultural change,

- the proactive and business-orientated design of human resource strategy,

- the planning of reward, recruitment and career management of employees, especially those in key jobs,

- developing and funding more powerful and faster ways of developing and training people, and

- taking an active and influential leadership role in the business.

This list suggests that, while boundary management is a key issue in international HRM, it is by no means the only one. Indeed in one sense, HRM issues are the same across the world:

> . . . employment organisations in all countries have to address the same human resource management issues: how to obtain and keep people to perform relevant tasks; how to develop them to be able to fulfil such tasks; how to resolve the dilemma of control and commitment.
>
> (Brewster and Tyson, 1991, p. 5)

The authors concede that cultural differences play a part in differentiating human resource strategies at the international level. However, they also observe that:

> . . . the notion . . . must be modified to consider the interaction between cultural norms and legal institutions and underlying economic factors.
>
> (p. 257)

What really differentiates human resource strategies and policies, they believe, are internal variables, such as:

> . . . management style, the personalities involved as well as the history of the organisation, its industrial relations traditions and the markets in which it trades.
>
> (p. 257)

Prokopenko (1992) underlines the importance of the leadership factor when he comments that studies of economic and social progress in the developed and developing world reveal that: 'even the best macro-economic models (strategies and policies) fail without enlightened and competent leadership'. He stresses, however, that East European and other developing countries share many more managerial and HRM practices and problems than may at first appear to be the case, 'because the commonalities of centralised socio-economic structures have a more powerful impact than cultural and technical differences'.

Conclusion

Thus in the realm of international HRM some of the most important skills are those that we have already seen to be relevant to the practice of HRM in any organization: the ability to identify the problems, challenges and opportunities that the internal and external environments of the organization present in order to make the most appropriate strategic choices and implement them effectively; to formulate differentiated human resource strategies and policies to fit particular contingencies and systems; and to recognize and build on the many areas of commonality between diverse systems and cultures.

Such skills, and the tasks to which they relate, are not the natural prerogative of personnel/human resource specialists. The shift that is making HRM a managerial function at all levels is probably inevitable; it requires a new and positive response from specialist practitioners and the forging of proactive, collaborative relationships if HRM is to become a coherent, long-term strategic process in organizations.

As was concluded in Chapter 1 (p. 29), there is a key function for the HRM specialist, alongside other managers, to perform:

> It is one of auditing the human resource, applying organization-wide personnel systems which do not generate harmful interbusiness-unit rivalry, developing people to consolidate core competences, and facilitating the mobilization of the human element across the organization.

4

Strategies for human resource management: issues in larger and international firms

Adrian Wilkinson, Mick Marchington and Peter Ackers

By the end of this chapter the reader will:

1. understand the key issues and concepts relating to the development of strategies for HRM in larger organizations, including those whose operations are moving into some kind of international context;

2. be able to identify, through examining the major case described in this chapter, the typical ways in which changes in organizational structure, culture and strategy are reflected in the changing patterns of human resource strategy and management in such organizations;

3. be able to identify the particular barriers likely to face the implementation of HRM strategy in such organizations;

4. appreciate the kinds of processes that are most important in securing commitment to the HRM mission and goals in such organizations.

Strategic HRM in large and international organizations

Introduction

It is in large and international corporations that we expect to find the most sophisticated human resource strategies. More than a decade ago, Alan Fox (1974) characterized such large manufacturing organizations as 'sophisticated moderns' who recogized trade unions, not for purely defensive reasons, but as part and parcel of a proactive and farsighted policy of winning consent from employees. To some today, that was the strategy of yesteryear, and certainly the limelight has shifted to those 'sophisticated paternalists' who seek such employee commitment without the mediating influence of trade unions. Nevertheless, large international companies – albeit different ones – remain the 'mainstream' (Storey, 1992) benchmarks for strategic HRM.

As with human beings, organizational influence is related to size and age. The paradigms of HRM tend, in the main, to be older organizations with deeply entrenched cultures. In some cases, as with the giant Japanese corporations, these tried and tested cultural legacies may be regarded as essential mystery ingredients in a successful business recipe. By contrast, in British industry, they are more like to be regarded as rigidities and obstacles to change. Hence managing and changing culture – be it 'adversarial' us-and-them or 'paternalist' (Ackers and Black, 1991) – is usually at the heart of strategic change in large international firms.

With size comes complexity, so that giant corporations are almost inevitably pluralist in the broadest sense of that term (Smith *et al.*, 1991; Dawson, 1992). Hence any idea of a unified management strategy, designed by the chief executive and simply passed down the organization, is questionable. Instead, the development of strategy is more of an ongoing dialogue between different stakeholders and management functions. As we saw in Chapter 2, the danger of pluralism is inertia – the inability to move as rapidly as external circumstances demand. Pluralism also implies potential resistance to new human strategies from groups of employees and sections of management. For this reason, industrial relations has assumed a more prominent place in large complex organizations.

Consequently, winning the support of managers and employees alike is central to HRM in the large corporation. This may involve negotiating the terms of consent, from the traditional 'arm's length' control and cooperation philosophy of British manufacturing to an emphasis on more active employee commitment and engagement. The trade unions may feel threatened by any such new approach, particularly where it affects their position as a conduit between management and the shopfloor. Certainly, innovation in the sphere of employee involvement (Marchington *et al.*, 1992) is central to communicating the management mission and involving employees in its realization.

The Multichem case study as a learning vehicle

We are going to use a major case study of 'Multichem' as the vehicle for identifying and analysing strategies and issues in HRM in large organizations. At this point, therefore, it is relevant to outline the nature of the study and the analytical approaches we shall use.

Multichem is a pseudonym for a chemical company which has been analysed previously by Marchington and Parker (1988, 1990) based on research undertaken in the mid-1980s; this focused on the changes in employee relations following a turnaround project of the early 1980s. Here we focus on a different site of the same company where the changes had the same trigger of the business turnaround programme and had virtually identical objectives and development plans. Thus in our analysis, we can draw on sustained observation and interaction over several years to examine managerial attempts to transform the employment relationship.

Multichem illustrates all four themes listed as learning objectives at the start of the chapter and briefly developed in previous paragraphs. First, it is a human resources strategy trendsetter, *par excellence*. In the past a model sophisticated modern (see p. 86), it is now in the process of redefining its management style. Second, it is a large multinational with deeply rooted traditions and philosophies for managing labour, many of which it is trying to modify in an HRM direction. Third, it is truly a complex, pluralist organization in which 'strategy' emerges through the interplay between various management and employee stakeholders, any of whom can threaten its implementation (see p. 43). In particular, strong trade unions pose a formidable obstacle to any radical change in management style. Fourth, the change process described below utilized new direct methods of communicating with and involving employees.

The chemical industry has been characterized by the large size of companies, rapid growth (especially in the 1950s and 1960s with product and process discoveries in plastics and fibres), capital intensity and large scale of production, and a high emphasis on research and development. The industry is international by orientation, and is dominated by a small number of multinational companies. Barriers to entry are high, and planning is relatively long term because of lead times between order and delivery and planning and sales (Pettigrew, 1985). The industry, however, has been subject to cyclical oscillations because of its interlocking character and principal markets – for example cars (rubber and plastics), agriculture (fertilizers) and housing (textiles and paint) – and the glut-shortage pattern of the market caused by economies of scale and capital intensity (Pettigrew, 1985, p. 61). In the 1980s, as chemicals evolved into a mature industry, and with rising energy costs and environmental factors, there was some contraction. Since much of the product is exported, profits can be heavily influenced by movements in exchange rates. Overall, then, chemicals is an industry conducive to long-term strategic management in human resource matters, as for much else.

The focus on the chemical industry is also appropriate since it is often seen in the literature as a good example of the ways in which changing technology and market situations have enhanced the requirements for a skilled, flexible and motivated workforce. In particular, it has been argued that there is greater opportunity or potential for Employee Involvement (EI) in a capital-intensive process industry (Buchanan, 1986: Marchington and Parker, 1988). There are several reasons for this. The technology employed, especially for process operations, is appropriate for the development of team working and job rotation if management desire this. The type of people employed are increasingly of a higher educational level, they possess strong diagnostic skills, and are often both expected and more inclined to offer ideas for improvements via Total Quality Management (TQM) or quality circle-type initiatives. The average length of service in these companies tends to be high due to strong internal labour markets and firm-specific skills, which in turn encourage a greater employee demand for information from management about future plans and policies. There is also an obvious need for continuity of production because of the extremely high costs incurred by interruptions and start-up, such that good employee relations and a high level of trust are sought by employers, thus providing a rationale for the use of bodies such as Joint Consultative Committees (JCCs) to allow representatives to express views in advance. Furthermore, investment decisions and implementation timescales tend to be longer in process industries, offering greater opportunity for consultation. Thus, given the nature of manual jobs in these industries, especially in firms with long-batch or continuous-process technology, there is more potential time to devote to EI, whether this is team briefing or TQM meetings (which can be planned for periods of downtime such as for cleaning or planned maintenance) or; allowing representatives to attend JCC meetings or other subcommittees.

These structural factors provide an opportunity to develop EI. What translated this into reality at 'Scotchem' (a pseudonym) – the plant of Multi-chem at which this research was undertaken – were greater product market pressures and the management's growing awareness of the need to harness employee commitment to gain competitive advantage. These external pressures 'triggered' (Pettigrew and Whipp, 1991) a management review of its entire approach to employee relations and sent them off to the 'ideas market' in search of new recipes for competitive HRM. This phenomenon can be seen in two **waves**. First, in the early 1980s, when the continued operation of the plant was in serious jeopardy, the changes were regarded as a temporary truce with acceptance of critical changes held together by the immediate and crucial aim of survival. Second, in the late 1980s, the proposed changes formed part of a much broader and, in a sense, less 'urgent' cultural change initiative. This was the 'last piece in the jigsaw' following on from the working through of sustained strategic and organizational change, aimed at putting the employment relationships on a new and different long-term footing. This two-stage pattern of experience can be broadly seen as reflecting a development from a 'fear factor' in the early 1980s (Metcalf, 1989) or what Cressey *et al.* (1985) term 'lifeboat democracy', where the emphasis was on compliance with short-term 'imperatives', to an attempt to develop a more fully cooperative relationship where 'empowerment' and commitment were seen as central to the new way of working. As such the company may reflect changing emphases which are far from unique in terms of employer objectives and methods in employment relations.

The notion of waves as an analytical tool in the examination of managerial EI strategies has been discussed at length elsewhere, and it is argued that this concept is acutely sensitive to the diversity found in these practices in different organizations (Marchington *et al.*, 1992). The waves concept allows for a more discriminating analysis of the centrality and prominence of different forms of EI reflecting different timescales and characteristics within organizations. While the popular notion of cycles of control (Ramsay, 1977; Ackers *et al.*, 1992) implies some sort of repetition over time, the waves idea allows not only for reruns, but also for quite varied patterns of involvement in different workplaces. Of course previous waves may not disappear, and indeed can continue to co-exist with (or contradict) one another over a period of time.

While the waves concept was developed largely to refine the analysis of varied contemporary forms of EI, it is capable of being utilized for other areas of industrial relations as well. We believe that the idea can help link together what are seen in the literature as quite distinct concepts, namely those of lifeboat democracy and empowerment. The former term was used to characterize some employers' greater readiness to 'involve' employees, at least via downward communications exercises, at times when the organization was confronted by severe market contraction (Cressey *et al.*, 1985). In essence, this concerns a temporary but urgent alignment of complementary goals, namely those of survival and job maintenance, although the extent of employee influence is likely to be quite limited. The notion of empowerment has rather longer term and possibly more creative connotations, and is associated with the more recent quality management and world class manufacturing literature (Oakland, 1989; Schonberger, 1990; Wilkinson *et al.*, 1992). According to this, workers have or are 'given' the power to do things themselves. According to Schonberger: 'We want "take charge" employees who will make recommendations and decisions when they have the information and expertise to do so' (Schonberger, 1990, p. 94). The team-working literature makes less grand claims but stresses working without direct supervision and task variety with jobs often rotated on a daily basis (Buchanan, 1986, pp. 71–2).

Of course, in practice, the waves may be more 'ragged' than the formalized programmes of change might imply, and there may be considerable operational deviation from management strategy. Central to understanding how policies are implemented is the distinction drawn by Brewster *et al.* (1983) between espoused and operational policy. Espoused policy is seen as 'the summation of the proposals, objectives and standards that top level management hold or state they hold for establishing the organization's approach to its employees' (p. 63). However, operational policy is the 'way senior management are seen to order industrial relations priorities *vis-à-vis* those of other policies'. Line managers and employees are generally regarded as following the operational policy. This distinction is particularly pertinent to large complex organizations such as Multichem, where it mingles with the plurality of interest groups, to complicate further the change process.

Divergences between espoused and operational policies can explain to some extent why programmes may fail to deliver these objectives. There may also be 'technical' difficulties which include inadequate resource support or a lack of training, for example. Moreover, there may also be more fundamental problems relating to the different conceptions of managers and workforces as to what EI is about. Managers may regard EI as a simple management tool (like any other); however, workforces almost invariably interpret, evaluate and react towards managerial initiatives and changes, and in their own way 'audit' their introduction and operation. Thus, while workers or their representatives may find it difficult to challenge the 'logic' of management action in principle, at the point of production their reactions will be more varied (Roberts and Wilkinson, 1991). These points take us back to the key processual issues first raised in Chapters 1 and 2 of this book, and so the case study has a particular importance for the insights it offers into the nature of the strategic management process.

The Multichem case study

This case study is presented as an unfolding series of events, covering the 1980s. Using the 'waves' concept, analysis of those events occurs within the body of the case study itself, also on a continuous basis. Following the conclusion of the study (p. 105), we then identify and discuss overall learning points related to wider HRM concepts and issues.

The structure of the case study is as follows. First, we examine the background to both phases of development, describing the company and existing work organization. We then discuss the experiences of the 1980s and how these evolved into a more fundamental attempt to refashion the employment relationship. We also examine the thinking behind this, the processes involved and how the actors perceived the changes. Finally, we discuss the intended future of these initiatives.

☐ *Scotchem: markets, technology and employee relations*

Multichem (a pseudonym) is a large European-owned multinational company with interests throughout the chemical industry. At the time of the study, it employed nearly 7000 people in Britain across eight different divisions, with sites located in various parts of the country. (Since that time, however, the number of divisions has been reduced as some parts of the business have been sold off to concentrate resources on a few core, high-added-value activities.) 'Scotchem' still remains within the portfolio of Multichem, whose business now focuses on pharmaceuticals, pigments, dyestuffs and agrochemicals. There is now a much greater product synergy between the different parts of the company, and the employer is well known for its emphasis on quality and tightly controlled technical systems.

☐ *Multichem: corporate values and management styles*

Multichem has been characterized as a forward-thinking employer, open and dynamic in its style and approach to the management of people. Following a wide-ranging report by a large American firm of management consultants in the late 1960s, the company reorganized its activities and published a set of corporate principles which have since been adopted by all the divisions. The corporate principles refer not only to business objectives and share-holders, but also to the organization's commitment to its employees, the community, customers and the environment. The section on employees occupies the most space in the booklet which is issued to all staff, and in this there is great stress on concepts such as teamworking, internal labour markets, promotion, participation and communication, and training and welfare. In particular, the booklet states that:

- we will strive to create an atmosphere conducive at all levels to the effective teamwork which is of great importance for the success of the company,
- promotions will be made as far as possible from within the company,
- we will encourage participation in decision-making within the scope of an employee's responsibilities,
- we will ensure that each employee receives all relevant information

necessary for the performance of duties and an understanding of how these relate to the company as a whole,

■ we will provide for the possibility of developing the potential of employees by means of training, education, job rotation and performance appraisal,

■ we treat employees fairly and with dignity.

Two further points ought to be made about these corporate principles: both have relevance to the discussion of 'mission' in Chapter 2. First, although it is now widespread for employers to commit motherhood statements to paper and disseminate them to employees, this was relatively unusual in the early 1970s, and it serves to illustrate the way in which senior managers in Multichem have seen employee relations for a long time. Second, these types of documents are often more notable for their breach rather than their observance, but it does appear to be taken seriously at Multichem; research undertaken at various sites within the group indicates that this philosophy has been widely put into effect, and human resource managers at establishment level regularly refer to these principles in discussions.

Management styles across the divisions also bear many similarities, despite the fact that there are differences in immediate product market pressures, sizes of establishment and workforce composition. To some extent, this is brought about by a policy of training managers (and potential high-flyers) on the same programmes, and to the practice of moving senior managers (principally in line and technical positions) between sites so as to increase their experience and introduce new ideas. Indeed, the managing director at Scotchem at the time of the study had been brought in from another division, and returned to head office several years later. At each of the sites where our research has been conducted over the last decade, a number of senior managers have been imported from mainland Europe, again showing the influence of the parent company and head office over affairs within the divisions. In the same vein, the human resource managers from different divisions meet together on a regular basis, under the auspices of a specialist manager from the UK headquarters, and there is close informal contact between personnel people at the more heavily unionized sites to compare notes and initiatives.

■ HRM at Multichem in the 1980s

The industrial relations and HRM changes which took place across the company in the 1970s also took a similar course during the 1980s. Multichem as a whole embarked upon a 'turnaround' programme in the late 1970s, basically requiring each of the divisions to produce a plan for survival through the next decade. It was left to each division to prepare its own programme for change, or even to suggest that it should be closed down. The initiatives which were developed at Scotchem (analysed later in this case study) have many similarities with those which were introduced at 'Ichem' (a sister establishment in Northwest England, whose experiences have been described in Marchington and Parker, 1990, pp. 105–28). At Ichem, the turnaround resulted in major job losses by voluntary severance, a major restructuring of operations, the introduction of new methods of working, and a massive increase in benefits for those who remained in work (such as higher pay levels, harmonization of conditions, the removal of clocking-on and -off and a new employment security deal). The major employee involvement initiatives of the period were the introduction of a modified system of team-briefing in the early 1980s, followed by a TQM initiative in the latter part of the decade.

This of course, raises the question of 'fit', first discussed in relation to HRM strategies in Chapter 2. The links between a parent company and its subsidiaries are something often left unanalysed in the HRM literature, but the experiences at Scotchem were mirrored in another company – Freightco – where we have recently undertaken a study of TQM. This organization is part of a French-owned multinational company, which opened up a UK business in 1981 under the control of the man who is still general manager. He stimulated the quality initiative in the latter part of the 1980s, arguing that a structured and formalized approach was needed to improve competitive advantage. The parent company had issued a logistics charter in 1987, but there was no obligation on Freightco to implement any of these ideas. However, two years later, after noticing continual references to BS 5750 (the universal British quality standard), he hired consultants, and the path to registration commenced with a programme entitled 'The Quality Challenge'. He is still the driving force behind the quality initiative and he plays an active part as its champion, chairing the steering committee and continually persuading staff of its merits.

However, it would be incorrect to assume from these events that the corporate headquarters imposes a centralized regime over HRM practices in the various divisions of Multichem. While a number of sites recognize trade unions and have high levels of union membership among manual workers, some do not, but offer similar levels and kinds of benefits to employees without the provision for collective bargaining. Equally, some sites are rather more advanced in terms of quality initiatives, and there are different rates of progress towards harmonization. Even among the sites which recognize and deal with trade unions, the relationships between managers and shop stewards varied considerably: at one site there had been moves to marginalize the convenor because management did not feel that he represented membership opinion, whereas at another relations between the head of human resources and the convenor were being strengthened; the situation at Scotchem was somewhere in between these two. On the one occasion during the 1980s when headquarters had tried to take a more proactive stance over pay negotiations, there had been recriminations after the event as the divisions reasserted their independence and made it clear that they would not be bound by future policy on this matter. In one sense, it was hardly surprising that the divisions were so strong, given the numbers of staff employed in human resources there compared with the skeleton team at head office. Relationships between the centre and the divisions appeared to be relatively equal, a view which has since been confirmed by other high-level contacts within Multichem; the search for legitimacy is clearly a two-way process, as the personnel manager at Ichem illustrated when assessing one of the head office team: 'He's our kind of man, he's all right, he knows what it's all about.' This therefore sets the scene for the detailed analysis of Scotchem which follows, hopefully illustrating the complexity of linkages and lines of command between head office and manufacturing sites in a multiplant organization.

■ The Scotchem site

The site which forms the basis of this article is located on an industrial estate in Scotland and produces pigments on a bulk commodity basis. The site employed approximately 780 staff in 1990, a little more than half the number which worked at the site at the end of the 1970s, although production has more than doubled over the period. Almost all the manual workforce is made up of men. Labour turnover there is low, partly because of high unemployment in the area. Many blue-collar workers have built up considerable service at the firm, a large number having started there in the mid-1960s. As anticipated in the introduction, the long-service profile is one of the problems management faces in attempting to alter the deep-rooted workplace culture.

There are several plants on the Scotchem site. It is particularly notable that plants producing an identical product vary widely in the demands placed upon the workforce because of different technologies. The old units are essentially manually controlled with men charging the machines, man-handling drums and standing at the filling points. In contrast, the new dry grinding unit, for example, is a computer-driven plant with a built-in system for dealing with dust explosions, which provides a cleaner environment for operators through the use of new material-handling techniques which entail no contact with the product. The unit is controlled by operators inputting information to the computer from a terminal within the control room or via local operator panels within the plant. There is some manual work (such as forklift trucks and bag handling) although the latter process is shortly to be automated.

Technology is not, however, the only reason for differences in work organization. For example, in the newer plants, operators are encouraged to rotate tasks among themselves and complete their own worksheets, rather than having work allocated. This dichotomy between old and new is replicated through the other units. However, despite the broad differences outlined there are also similarities. In most units there is a wide range of tasks and even the most automated of these require some manual labour. Equally, the wide range of tasks has facilitated job rotation. The new units require less staff, and include less manual work, but at the same time they require greater knowledge of processes and greater teamwork, thus making demands on social skills (Buchanan and Besant, 1985), and creating greater opportunities for EI.

With regard to union organization, there are three bargaining units at the site. The first comprises the management committee and those reporting to them, a group of staff which is largely non-union. The second unit comprises clerical, technical and supervisory staff, and belongs to MSF, which also has representation rights for the first group. The third unit is the blue-collar group covering both process and craft employees represented by the TGWU, AEU and EETPU. Membership is 100% in the last group and high in the second group. The unions are well organized and there are 3 convenors and over 20 shop stewards who meet as a group on a quarterly basis. Hence, the unions form an important interest group regarding any developments in HRM.

However, this snapshot picture of the current situation both tends to obscure the dynamics of the changing patterns and processes, and says little about how change has been achieved via a series of waves. In the next section we discuss the first wave of change.

■ The first wave of change – crisis and adjustment in the early 1980s

Up to the early 1980s the site was essentially a production manufacturing facility for the company, with a minor responsibility for research. There was no contact with external customers. These characteristics were regarded as a prominent cause of the plight of the site in the early 1980s, which had become simply too isolated from business requirements. After steady business growth in the 1960s and 1970s it was felt to be grossly overmanned by this period, as indeed was the company as a whole. With considerable losses accumulating, corporate management perceived three options:

(1) To close down the site.

(2) To rationalize production, maintaining no more than 200 staff in key plants. However, this was regarded as being no more than a short-term palliative as it was felt unlikely that customers would remain if only a small product range was offered.

(3) To restructure the business. This was the strategy eventually chosen by senior management at the site, and subsequently approved by UK head office.

Although the need to maintain a full portfolio of products restricted rationalization, Scotchem stripped out all non-essential operations; some buildings were closed down and blocked up (to avoid paying rates), some were bulldozed and a number of plants mothballed. The number of employees were reduced from over 1200 (1980) to around 700 over an 18 month period, principally via voluntary severance – although there were some compulsory redundancies for white-collar staff. The relationship with head office was restructured, with Scotchem becoming more consumer-oriented and given international marketing responsibilities for its principal products. Consequently, this first phase was characterized by a 'lifeboat democracy' or 'hard times' approach to HRM and EI.

The company began by providing detailed financial commentaries to all employees – information which had not been previously available even to some managerial staff. Trade unions cooperated in changes to working practices. However, this involvement did not extend to participation in the decision-making process, and the authoritarian nature of change in this period is readily acknowledged by senior managers. Cooperation was attributed to what the managing director referred to as the 'green monster' effect: employees were simply fearful for their jobs and involvement was a tool to facilitate employee understanding of changes taking place. As one manager said, 'We've moved away from "you'll do this" to "this is why you'll do this".' This is perhaps half-way between the notion of 'lifeboat authoritarianism' and 'lifeboat democracy' described by Cressey *et al.* (1985). The 'turnaround project' was seen as a great success, with profits returning in 1984. There was a substantial investment of £40 m over two years in new technology, including the introduction of new units and more sophisticated computer control operations.

While the Scotchem plant had never been strike prone, it is evident from recent developments and observations from all sides that the 'fear factor' and changes in relative power did affect the way relationships developed.

Regional traditions have been an important influence, many referring to the 'local disease', with the protection of jobs being a key issue pursued via some strict demarcation. Thus skill issues have been central to industrial relations at Scotchem, with craft unions forming the 'labour aristocracy' but whose pay influence has come under threat in recent years and whose differentials have been eroded. However, the last major dispute took place in the mid-1970s. The relationship since then has been described as more 'stubborn' than 'aggressive' and there was general recognition from trade unions that Scotchem was a good employer. One union representative referred to a 'carefully cultivated paternalistic management approach' and pointed out that even in the bleakest days of the early 1980s, Scotchem had never forced the pace even when they were 99% certain of achieving it. During these days many workers were sent home on full pay and a road-building programme was undertaken on the site so as to avoid redundancy.

Employees were well aware of the fate of their colleagues who went to work for more money at a nearby car plant but were soon laid off.

Nevertheless, despite these feelings, the refashioned relationship of the early 1980s owed more to fear and a realistic appraisal by shop stewards of their relative weakness, rather than a greater degree of trust (see also p. 50). Thus one senior manager attributed the basis of change to 70% awareness of 'what's going on outside' and 30% to better trust. Certainly, some outcomes changed considerably. By now 10% of workers at Scotchem were temporary – a move which the unions would have blocked in the 1970s. In addition, the number of minor disputes and grievances had dropped dramatically from the 1970s and unions no longer used these as a lever to negotiate over wider issues. 'New realism' appeared to have taken root. In this respect, the path towards the new HRM policy had been cleared by those changes in the economic and political environment which had weakened the role of trade unions. However, as we shall see later, weakened trade unions in no way guarantee greater employee commitment on management terms.

■ The second wave of change – refashioning the employment relationship through The Way Ahead programme

Origins   The origins of the programme to initiate cultural change can be found in the turnaround project, during which much greater information was disseminated to the workforce. This was lifeboat communication in its simplest form. However, as senior managers pointed out, 'it was not easy to get off the tiger' once clearer waters had been reached. Hence the ideas of full information and more open management could not immediately be abandoned, nor did management regard it as desirable to do so. The turnaround project had achieved its aims in substantially reducing costs, building new units, revamping the organizational structure and attaining production targets. However, the people element was seen as the final piece in the jigsaw, building on the limited initiative of the early 1980s. Furthermore, it was felt that recent investment demanded new approaches to work, as did the mature nature of the market. Thus, it was argued that differentiation and competitive advantage were to be achieved by people, rather than technology and capital investment, which were easily replicated. There was much talk of changing culture; employees were regarded as 'sleepy'. The aim was to create a self-motivated better educated workforce, with operators no longer regarded as a 'pair of hands'. Management felt that this could not be achieved by a single step forward but through a long-term evolutionary approach.

Beginnings   The managing director was the key actor in terms of the development of this programme and was very critical of Anglo-American approaches in treating staff as a variable cost. He was both the architect and the stimulus behind The Way Ahead initiative, which was introduced via the MD's annual presentation on business performance to all staff in 1987. He talked of the need for a 'vector' as a vehicle to achieve change, a cultural change programme designed to show employees that the old way of doing things had severe limitations. The Way Ahead approach was essentially contingent: the autocratic style of the early 1980s was seen to have been appropriate for that particular set of circumstances and now a different style was regarded as more relevant.

Steering group   The first reactions of the unions to a new way forward were of apprehension and reluctance to change. Union representatives attended an off-site meeting with senior management to discuss the key issue of little trust which had been amply demonstrated by the bitter negotiations in 1987. A central theme of The Way Ahead was therefore greater openness between management, unions and employees, and it was in this spirit that managers gave the union a folder containing 'the business plan'. This was received initially with some apprehension by the union representatives, who were surprised to find it was only a blank sheet of paper. It was a way of saying 'we want your input', said the personnel manager. The most important issues which were raised included status differences, staff fears and interunion rivalry. A steering group was established, consisting of senior management and union representatives, to discuss (not negotiate) The Way Ahead and this met monthly. However, in the process of winning union 'hearts and minds', middle management felt 'short-circuited' and the unions were uncomfortable in discussing matters which did not result in immediate action.

Six working parties were set up to cater for the need for action, the involvement of middle management and the need to have 'champions'. These discussed shifts, flexibility, multiskilling, single status and other key issues. As one manager put it, this was a method of throwing 'big stones in the pond to see what ripples would come back'. However, because the working parties were made up of representatives from each union group in addition to managers, the different aspirations of the unions and an unwillingness to compromise meant progress was slow.

Mission statement and cascades   A mission statement was distributed to all employees explaining the Scotchem vision. However, it became apparent that this was a premature move as employees had yet to understand the message, and the consultants who had been brought in argued that the programme had simply put 'the cart before the horse' in that working parties had examined areas for change but not *why* changes were being made. Consequently, acceptance was not easily achieved. Furthermore, the shopfloor employees who were expected to change had been entirely left out of the process. The absence of 'crisis' also meant a less receptive workforce. Finally, despite all the activity, there remained a lack of awareness of what Scotchem was attempting to achieve. Already, we can see how far the complex reality of human resources change departs from the simplistic rhetoric of the mission statement, and as has already been noted in Chapters 1 and 2, alters the formally intended course of strategy.

This led to the cascade which started with the management committee and went down through the organization from April 1989. Each session took several hours and attempted to explain management thinking, The Way Ahead and the mission statement as tools to achieve company goals. This was the first time ordinary employees had been informed about and involved, in any real sense, in management thinking. These sessions emphasized quality, customer satisfaction, cost control and new products, and the link between business strategy and the specific departments. The overall package was designed to 'create pride in what we do' and to demonstrate that 'people are the most important factor'. It was emphasized that people should be treated as a resource with managers occupying a supportive rather than directive role, summed up in the term 'moving from cops to being coaches'. Hence training, teamwork, communication and involvement were highlighted (see Chapter 7 for a similar communication strategy in the BET case). Employees generally regarded the cascade as positive, although supervisors and the quality control function were concerned about their future. Furthermore, the shift from the steering group and the working parties to the cascade led to some union fears that managers had simply taken over the process.

The early optimism of the programme diminished when it ran into a number of difficulties with the second cascade and its aftermath. First, because of production pressures and holiday problems, the gap between the two cascades, in some cases seven to eight months, meant the early impetus was lost. However, expectations had been built up and there was growing scepticism about management's commitment to change. The second cascade was designed to produce action plans for each department in an attempt to achieve there what had been achieved in the division as a whole, namely, responsibility for managing their own affairs. This too ran into difficulties when there was no flood of response to the second cascade and managers were therefore left with the choice of either doing nothing or throwing 'logs on the fire' themselves. This led to union concern that the cascade was not consultation but manipulation. In one unit there had been success in setting objectives for individual departments and the production of action plans, although managers complained that most of the worker suggestions were simply things for managers to do. Nevertheless, despite numerous gripes, the *process* of involvement was regarded as very useful, in that work groups met with their supervisors and better communication resulted.

The testbeds The philosophy of The Way Ahead was first to be applied in two new production units which would, in effect, provide a testing ground for these ideas. In this light a totally new approach to setting up the new units was taken; whereas previously Scotchem had simply transferred people and given them new job titles, a vigorous selection procedure now took place (with the emphasis on interpersonal skills rather than just technical ability) along with substantial training which included a six-week full-time programme dealing with problem-solving skills, product knowledge and team-working. This was designed to treat each operator as a person and encourage them not to see their job in narrow terms, but to take on and solve problems themselves rather than immediately passing responsibility to their supervisor. The emphasis on the 'team' was reflected in supervisors being renamed as team leaders (that is, from cops to coaches) and given more responsibility in hiring, firing, training and discipline. Team spirit was reinforced outside work by social functions and within the workplace by changing the shift pattern of the workers to that of their team leaders, that is from five shifts to four-and-a-half shifts, with extra hours accumulated and used for training.

The application of these ideas in the new units was designed to promote the change management desired, and it was hoped that a successful operation would produce a ground-swell in favour of applying such ideas elsewhere. In practice, however, the plan ran into a number of problems. First, the training finished by April 1989 but the new plant was not ready until July: this meant frustrated expectations among employees. Second, there was enormous production pressure on the new units (political and economic changes in Europe leading to a big demand for pigments) and output therefore was the driving force. Third, this combined with start-up difficulties, especially with software problems and the plants not running close to design. Finally, the 'blaze of glory' became something of a damp squib. Some felt the training programme was too good: 'it got them going so they felt 10 feet high but they came down to earth with a bump'. In one unit operators expected a 'wonderful new plant' but instead ended up using 'a big hose and a shovel'. In another, promoted as a clean plant, dust problems arose. Senior management felt those on the line had been incapable of handling these morale problems. Regular meetings planned as part of the new concept were abandoned because of lack of time and analytical problem-solving was never used. 'Fire-fighting' became the norm and workers saw themselves as being blamed for the problems. There was also some tension between the workers in the new units (mostly young and with craft skills) and those in the older units. The result of all this was that some of these workers even began to apply for jobs in the older units, and the 'flagships' appeared to be in serious trouble. Some of these problems reflect a failure to commit the necessary resources and political determination to carry through such an ambitious change programme.

In this respect, truly strategic HRM requires both the resources and senior management will at the implementation stage.

□ **Impact of The Way Ahead – towards human resources management**

So far, we have examined the activity surrounding The Way Ahead. We now examine its impact on the attitudes of middle management and supervisors, unions and workers.

Middle management and supervisors   The key issues in relation to this group were the perceived impact on their jobs and their doubts concerning both the philosophy and operation of the new approach. Thus, it was quite clear that many felt threatened by the changes in role and style which were being introduced: the well-established view was that 'bosses are bosses and kick ass'. There was also concern about job prospects if the traditional charge-hand role was eroded. In broad terms, there was objection both to the actual implementation of the programme and more significantly to its underlying philosophy. In regard to the first, supervisors felt that the delay between the two cascades, the length of the programme (almost two years) and the lack of specific changes had undermined its credibility and reduced trust with the result that 'people think it's a cosmetic exercise'. More fundamentally, they had doubts regarding the philosophy of the programme. Thus there was considerable hostility to the senior management's vision of The Way Ahead, in particular the manner with which they saw senior managers 'eulogizing' the workforce. As a personnel manager acknowledged, supervisors are a good deal less idealistic: 'they feel a branding iron is a more suitable instrument to work with than any concept of employee involvement'.

This was a view strongly held by supervisors pointing to the 'hairy arsed culture' (anecdotes of workers urinating in each others' tea mugs). Supervisors themselves were seen as the 'muscular type not necessarily with fine feelings' and managers acknowledged that they operated in a 'pretty basic and brutal context'. Supervisors felt they ran a tight ship and were not happy at having to devote time pandering to a 'long haired idealistic view of workers'. Given their perception that workers only wanted to 'take, take, take', their apprehension that The Way Ahead was likely to be construed as 'soft management' was understandable. This was evident in their opposition to the removal of the double-clocking system (clocks at both site and plant) as they argued that an earlier system had been replaced by the current one because of abuse. Given this context, supervisors were keen for a 'hard' element to be in the message; thus 'we're going softly, softly, but we need the big sticks to come out as well'. Others claimed that meticulous checking and attention to detail was 'a foreign trait which won't operate here – it's not British'.

Union view   There was considerable ambiguity in union ranks regarding The Way Ahead programme. On the one hand, the union representatives were anxious that the programme might change employee attitudes, however they were also aware that if workers were happy with developments, this left the unions in a strange position. The unions' dilemma was that they found it difficult to challenge the logic of management's programme, and indeed saw many developments as benefiting individuals in the long run, but at the same time saw the possibility of a clear diminution in the union's role in the company. The trade union variable illustrates well the true complexity of managing change in a highly pluralistic setting.

Management believed there was now greater trust, which could be clearly illustrated through an examination of the formal management–union monthly meetings which, in theory, were between the three main unions (TGWU, AEU and MSF) and management, and comprised both negotiation and consultation. Thus the TGWU–management meeting was described by managers as being characterized by a high degree of trust, this itself being reflected by less frequent and shorter meetings. This was attributed by managers to there being less contentious business to be discussed – unions no longer seeing agenda issues as a sign of virility and hence not feeling a sense of failure if there were few items to discuss – and because other mechanisms/channels, especially The Way Ahead and also a monthly *aide-mémoire* slide package, were attracting material, previously the preserve of these meetings. Managers agreed that the volume of material had diminished over the years, and while this could be attributed to political and economic changes, it was also the result of the drawing together of management and unions at the behest of management. Managers pointed to changes in behaviour over the annual pay negotiations as further evidence of higher trust in management–union relations. In the mid-1980s the structure of negotiations had changed, with one set of negotiations covering clerical, process and craft workers rather than as hitherto, three sets of negotiations. Moreover, due to The Way Ahead programme and the creation of more open relations, negotiations in the late 1980s were over in less than a day, settlement being facilitated by the range of information provided on competition, exchange rates, comparative pay settlements and other financial data.

However, that is not to say that the transition had been easy or that the unions were comfortable with the changes. In fact complaints regularly surfaced concerning the nonattendance of senior managers at these committees:

> Their absence creates a sense of loss of esteem within the committee. Whilst recently we have no earth shaking matters to discuss, the lack of a senior management presence gives our members the feeling that the monthly meetings are only concerned with small talk. This, allied

> to the fact that managers appear to want to talk directly to members
> rather than through the stewards, tends to demean the role of the
> stewards committee (convenor, minutes).

This example reinforces the view that real tangible senior management
commitment is important, if talk of valuing the human resource and
involving the workforce is to be taken seriously by line managers and
workers.

This picture of a move towards greater trust relations needs to be
qualified. First, in relation to pay negotiations, one reason for the much
less protracted negotiations was related to the introduction of a bonus
scheme in 1988 which provided a local payment based on site contribution to divisional performance. The calculation was a complex one
(needing a Philadelphia lawyer to understand it, according to the unions)
but in practice it reduced the union role in pay negotiations to discussing
inflation plus the going rate. Thus as one steward complained: 'There
is nothing left to negotiate about.' Second, there was considerable
concern over union by-passing, via the communications sponsored by
The Way Ahead and the more proactive role taken by supervisors.
Furthermore, the nature of consultation was also questioned. One
convenor complained that:

> We have comments from managers about feedback on The Way Ahead
> which look and sound as though they had come from members. This
> is not the case. They have sometimes come from supervisors and other
> points are from the manager himself. We then find that managers are
> implementing the changes on our people.

Third, the relationship was much less good with the craft unions, who
felt their traditional superiority was not given sufficient recognition.

Employee view   Overall, while the unions appeared to recognize the need for
change and the positive aspects of management strategy, the stewards'
concern over their future role was further complicated by the attitudes
of their constituents. One steward argued that while the unions were
well aware of the 'big picture', referring to the recent events at Dundee
(that is, the loss of the proposed Ford plant), workers in the region were
'isolationists', suspicious of anyone who appeared to get on with
management, suspecting collaboration. This fundamental distrust was
based on 'people being divided into bears (workers) and gaffers (management), and the bears don't trust the gaffers'.

Nevertheless, when asked to take a broad view of employee involvement and communications compared with the situation in 1985, over
80% claimed it had improved, including over a third who said it was
much better. Thus in terms of basic structures of communication and
transmission of information the effect was positive, although this may
have been because of lower expectations. In contrast, The Way Ahead,

with its ambitious agenda of transforming the employment relationship, met with considerable scepticism among the workforce. According to stewards, The Way Ahead 'had not yet converted anybody', workers were telling them 'a whole different story', and 'the biggest customer of The Way Ahead was management'. In our small survey of shopfloor opinion most respondents felt that management was interested in employee involvement solely to increase efficiency, while several others felt it was to 'get people to work harder'. However, there were also some very suspicious comments, including views that such schemes were to 'bring on lazy workers' and that one had to 'look up management's sleeves' to find the real reason.

In our survey, only a minority felt it offered more opportunity for individual advancement. There was no consensus as to whether it enabled individuals to contribute more to company success, promised greater job security, or led to managers being more interested in what the workforce had to say. Not surprisingly, perhaps most saw it as too vague. Clearly, the programme had fallen short of expectations. The shopfloor view was that all the benefits – for example, the tapping of shopfloor expertise – went to management. Thus 'what's in it for me?' was a central concern and the lack of specific benefits for shopfloor staff meant a degree of indifference as to the ongoing discussions. As one steward put it: 'the workers were all fired up with the concept of getting not giving', and if there was no money to be had 'people like to be left alone'. Thus workers were dubious about the reciprocity and mutual benefits which were claimed for The Way Ahead. Once more, this suggests that to succeed, HRM must be truly strategic, taking an integrated approach to all those issues which enter its frame, including the detailed consideration of remuneration policies.

Future developments   The view from the top management was that 'trust' was the key to the future. To reinforce this there was an undertaking from the managing director that jobs would not be lost as a result of The Way Ahead. A very long-term view was being taken, illustrated by statements such as: 'We're looking 20 years on and not next month or next year.' 'We don't need to maximize profits in the short run.' Moreover, it was a strongly held view of senior management that Scotchem did not want to 'impose a solution but to redefine a relationship'. Thus it was vital to achieve consensus and common ground so people could feel they owned the process and 'they would all pull together on the same line'. Given this long-term approach, slow progress was not necessarily a failure, although one manager complained that: 'The only horizon they know is the one on the holiday brochure.'

However, senior management felt there was thus no point being 'starry eyed' about events. Staff acceptance of change would clearly temper management actions. Nevertheless, they appreciated to some extent the views of middle management that to keep momentum going 'something must happen'. Thus while senior management did not want simply to 'throw them goodies' – an approach which was attributed to other chemical companies – an 'act of faith' had to be shown. It was acknowledged that workers needed something tangible 'to feel, to see, to touch', relating the broad process of change to a reference point at the workplace. Thus some short-term gains needed to be seen by the workforce.

Consequently, the focus turned to 'looking for something viable to do' and 'creating the right splash' in terms of affordability and impact. Management did not want The Way Ahead to be seen as a 'block of things' to be attained but to be viewed more broadly as about new approaches and attitudes. However, there were some areas where changes could be made. Change would be facilitated by the feedback or the cascade, in that it was possible to pick out what managers wanted and claim support of the workforce. Under consideration was the introduction of single status (in particular abolishing clocking practices), changing shift patterns to align operator and team-leader working hours (and hence emphasize teamwork), the development of personal assessment (a form of appraisal without pay attached) and multiskilling (workers to have a prime trade and an additional skill). All of these had industrial relations implications: changing shift patterns and working hours raised the issue of pay; clocking was supported by one union on safety grounds: multiskilling involved craft issues; and personal assessment had to be sold as developmental rather than control or pay related.

Learning points from the case study

What does the Scotchem experience tell us about the process of implementing strategic HRM in a large, international firm? Three general themes are explored here: the concept of external triggers leading to waves of human resource innovation; the importance of organizational politics in large complex organizations; and the uncertainty of success. These serve to caution us against Olympian conceptions of strategic HRM wherein the executive 'Gods' bring their visions down to the mere mortals and usher in a new world order overnight.

Triggers to HRM innovation and strategy

First we can address the notion of managerially led waves of change and development within the organization. The first wave can be seen as something of a short, sharp shock, aimed at improving industrial relations as part of the turnaround project. The emphasis was concerned with improving the flow of information down the hierarchy from managers to their employees with the objective of enhancing employee awareness of business pressure. In contrast, the second wave was a longer term approach, perhaps driven more by HRM considerations, with the notion of employees as a source of competitive advantage. Thus the emphasis was on fundamentally adjusting the way employees worked, with changes in the nature of work, with the provision of ideas up the hierarchy, and contributions from employees which could improve the substance of decision-making as well as enhance its legitimacy.

The links between the two waves are important particularly in relation to the concept of the strategic management of people. We have argued that there was indeed continuity between these two quite different waves. Such links between the wave of involvement in the early 1980s and of the late 1980s have been given little attention in the academic literature. Typical of the analyses of the early 1980s is Cressey *et al.*'s (1985) focus on lifeboat democracy. More recent studies (for example, Gearey, 1992) have examined team-working and more positive forms of involvement, but these links are not addressed. This may be because they are seen as quite distinct forms of involvement. But while this may be true it does not mean there are no connections between them.

In the case of Scotchem, it would be wrong to suggest that the first wave was conceived with the second already in mind. However, it could be argued that the first wave was a necessary condition for the second, in that the former – via more limited ambitions – laid the foundations in terms of introducing basic communications structures and signalling a change in management style. It could be seen as the bottom step of an 'escalator of involvement' (Marchington *et al.*, 1992). This evolved into a process more firmly rooted in management strategy as part of a resource-based approach to managing staff which was seen as integral to achieving competitive advantage. The first and second waves could co-exist because they were complementary rather than in competition with each other.

Organizational politics and their impact on strategic management

Second, we have observed ambiguities and conflicts among the key actors in the process. While senior management strongly supported The Way Ahead programme, middle management and supervisors were much less enthusiastic. Thus, a theme of this case has been the clear gap between senior managers' vision of the future and the attitudes of middle management and supervisors. This is not simply the gap between espoused and operational policy (Brewster *et al.*, 1983) but, more fundamentally, their conflicting views as to the appropriateness of the espoused policy. It appears in this case that middle management were implementing (although not in a committed fashion) policies which they regarded as neither desirable nor practical.

Among the unions there was also ambiguity. Changes over the course of the 1980s have quite clearly led to a diminution of the union role despite the resilience of industrial relations institutions. Thus alternative channels of information were being utilized in The Way Ahead, and information previously communicated through union channels alone was now being disseminated directly to the workforce as a whole; while the unions had acted as the major conduit of information in the 1970s this was no longer the case, although it is also true to say that the range of information which management now made available was much wider. The bonus scheme had effectively reduced the union negotiating role, and prospective changes including the introduction of personal assessment seemed likely to continue this. The unions were ambivalent in their attitude to many of these changes. In principle, they saw many of the changes as beneficial for employees, although they were concerned at the implications for the union. However, in practice, in terms of implementation, the unions' attitude can be described as one of watchful scepticism/cautious antagonism, particularly in relation to the manner in which management claimed to have achieved consensus.

HRM – transformation or evolution?

Finally, we have observed in this practical example what was noted at a theoretical level in Chapter 3: the limited success thus far of recent attempts to achieve a fundamental transformation in employee relations. In relation to the workforce generally, there appeared little evidence of any fundamental change of attitude, which supports the conclusions of Kelly and Kelly (1991) and Guest and Dewe (1991). Yet the conditions appeared potentially fruitful. The role of the managing director in the transformation of Scotchem was a crucial one and was more akin to American accounts of HRM and change than those found in the United Kingdom. However, his very centrality – the only person you can trust, according to the unions – also points to the fragility of change and the development of 'high-trust' relations, with both managers and unions apprehensive as to what his departure would do to the programme. Moreover, unlike other cases, which have involved the use of a single employee involvement technique which seemed unlikely by itself to transform industrial relations, here we have a wide-ranging programme of change. As the world's leading pigments producer, Scotchem has had the luxury of time in refashioning relationships and making changes; senior managers have appeared relatively unconcerned with the slow progress of The Way Ahead (although middle management have a rather different view) and have been happy to employ a long-term strategy of setting up 'testbeds' and filtering the feedback from the cascade to build up an apparent or real ground-swell for change which does not appear to be directed from the top. Clearly, the programme rests on the assumption that this will be forthcoming. If this is not the case, management may feel they need to proceed with the programme without the consensus upon which The Way Ahead philosophy is based.

Conclusion

The key lesson from this case study confirms the theoretical stance which was developed in Chapter 2; namely that the process of strategic HRM is complicated and problematic, especially in a large complex organization. First, and in tune with Scotchem's reputation as a human resources trendsetter, The Way Ahead programme did benefit from a highly positive context: a relatively long-term and strategic approach, senior management commitment, financial resources and a policy of no redundancy. The fact that success none the less remained problematic is testimony to the force of other obstacles to strategic change in large international organizations. In this respect, age or maturity, and cultural depth means no 'quick fix' or sudden turnaround is possible. In short, it takes more than a fleeting visit from a charismatic 'superboss' to change the direction of firms such as Scotchem. Second is the reality of pluralism: it ensures that there are differing perspectives between the various levels and functions of management as well as between the top management 'mission' and the aspirations of ordinary employees. While the power of the trade unions declined at Scotchem, this did not lead workers to embrace management proposals uncritically. Rather they viewed them half with cynicism – as another passing fad with little meaning for their working lives – and half with apprehension as an unsettling worry. Finally, the Scotchem case shows how employee involvement initiatives may only be partially successful in achieving their aims.

Note

1. The data upon which this chapter is based was collected with the financial assistance of a two-year research grant from the Department of Employment on a project entitled 'New Developments in Employee Involvement'. We are grateful for its support and assistance and a fuller version of the overall findings can be found in Marchington *et al.* (1992). The views expressed here are entirely those of the authors and do not necessarily represent those of the funding organization.
2. The Scotchem case has been the subject of an article in *Personnel Review*, **22**(2), 1993, pp. 22–33, entitled 'Refashioning the employment relationship: the experience of a chemical company over the last decade'.

5

Strategies for human resource management: challenges in smaller and entrepreneurial organizations

John Ritchie

By the end of this chapter the reader will:

1. clearly recognize, and specifically differentiate between, the different organizational forms that smaller and entrepreneurial organizations take, and the 'market' for human resource management that each represents;

2. understand their respective individual strategic and human resource profiles and how these compare;

3. appreciate the likely problems that interventionists encounter when diagnosing and developing their human resource potential.

Introduction: HRM in smaller organizations

Smaller firms have rarely figured highly upon most professional human resource agendas. By the same token, human resources have rarely figured highly upon such firms' managerial agendas either. One school of thought saw little real reason why they should be given prominence: in this view smaller firms were new model employers, inherently high-involvement organizations whose performance rested upon 'naturally' close and harmonious working relationships. In contrast, another school maintained that smaller firms were *not* often good 'model' employers, nor inherently high-involvement organizations, nor even, when properly measured, particularly exceptional new 'job generators' (Storey and Johnson, 1987). Instead they could often appear more like personal fiefdoms, paternalistic homesteads, backstreet workshops, temporary employment stopgaps, oppressive sweat-shops, and generally less desirable workplaces.

Interested practitioners looking towards other state-of-the-art literature for further help and guidance could well find this inconclusive too. After all, for some time neither business strategy, nor HRM, nor smaller businesses themselves mutually embraced (Arthur and Hendry, 1990). Rather, each went its own way, failing to realize their common interests or to benefit each other accordingly. Not only did business strategists rarely descend into real live small business territory: many such firms rarely articulated their business strategies anyway. And since neither regarded human resources very highly, important questions about their strategic intent were left unanswered.

The purpose of this chapter is therefore to put human resources into the picture by working through differing preconceptions about smaller businesses; further differentiating between these firms themselves; seeing what 'markets' for specialist human resource input then result; understanding how different firms craft their strategies in their own particular way; and then compiling their respective human resources profiles to see how these organizations operate now, and where, if at all, their performance might change.

Differentiating smaller and entrepreneurial firms

Wider cultural images of these firms vary considerably (Ritchie, 1986a, 1991) so, in the grip of popular, if ill conceived, and frequently one-sided comparisons with 'large firms' – themselves stereotypically regarded like great crunching 'machine bureaucracies' – there are many simplistic assertions about smaller firms which hardly recognize crucial differences between them, with the result that misleading ideas about the small firm and entrepreneur abound. More difficult still, in disputing that small firms are only 'little big firms', some would-be entrepreneurial evangelists make the reverse error, reducing larger businesses into 'big little firms' instead. Governments compound this confusion when informing doctors, dentists, headmasters and similar specialists that hospitals, schools and supporting services could run better if they were like smaller business too (Kelly, 1991). Given the problem of deciphering who and what smaller businesses really are, human resource specialists may therefore find it difficult to differentiate closely between such firms, particularly when they lack suitable defining frames and back-up data and experience.

How many smaller firms now exist? Who, and how many, do they employ? In general terms, the number of individual British company registrations may have increased while the average number of employees per firm declined, with additional 'job generation' expectations tailing off too (Storey and Johnson, 1990). However, 'small' firms are not easily defined, and even straightforward measures like workforce numbers become supplemented with others associated with balance sheet status, business turnover, total remuneration, client range, and so on. As regards the official maximum numbers employed, just looking at the EC shows a 'small' firm might typically employ anywhere between 9 and 10 in Greece and Portugal, and up to 200 in UK manufacturing. Also in gathering such data, many countries apply different criteria, so that some include certain categories of worker (like those with full-time employment), but not others (like apprentices and trainees). Moreover, 'whilst every EEC country has an empirical concept of SME's, none has a legal concept relevant for labour purposes' (Commission of the European Communities, 1988).

Acknowledging that 'there is no official definition' of what constitutes the smaller firm in the United Kingdom, the Department of Employment's own review (1989) quoted research highlighting continuing turbulence among VAT (sales tax) registered businesses in particular (1 650 000 new registrations, and 1 365 000 deregistrations, between 1979 and 1986) – figures which excluded all the many nonregistered businesses. As well as being unevenly distributed across regions and sectors, such firms vary considerably in employment-size band terms too. For official purposes, and including the self-employed, there were an estimated 2.5 million such businesses in the United Kingdom at the end of 1986. Of these, no less than 96% were estimated to employ fewer than 20 people, while less than half of one per cent employed 200 or more. Outstandingly, nearly two-thirds consisted of only one or two people, and three-quarters of the rest employed ten or fewer. In addition, some estimate that under 10% of all employers of between 1 and 21 people and self-employed workers were manufacturers. Other research claims that, out of every 100 small firms, the fastest growing *four* firms will create half the jobs in the group over a decade (Storey, 1987). Whatever the margin for error over the precise figures concerned, this clearly has major human resource implications. In particular, there would seem to be many such firms where specialized human resource support hardly looks viable. To see just where it might actually fit, one should therefore first differentiate between these firms themselves, and then identify the most appropriate employers among them as shown in Figure 5.1.

The many newer **micro-firms** of recent years are, by themselves, usually miniscule employers either immersed in, or not much different from, their original organizational starting state. Most only grow relatively slowly, and very few ever grow rapidly (Hakim, 1989). Moreover growing **founder firms** are not perpetually expanding, but often reach critical size thresholds, beyond which they risk becoming managerially overextended. Much growth actually occurs during specific phases, followed by others where they consolidate. Once overextended, many founders struggle thereafter, and would sooner their firms stabilize than grow again. Having persisted for 20 plus years, however, mature founder firms develop different profiles, and face renewal and succession problems accordingly.

Second order **entrepreneurial firms** are not averagely growing founder firms; neither are they immediately recognizable from their original starting state. Many will not have stayed purely small firms, in employment terms anyway, for very long. Some could well acquire and absorb other small firms before they make their final breakthrough. Still others could well become pathfinders within their chosen spheres, whether for what they make and sell, how they continue to innovate, the way they do business, and so on.

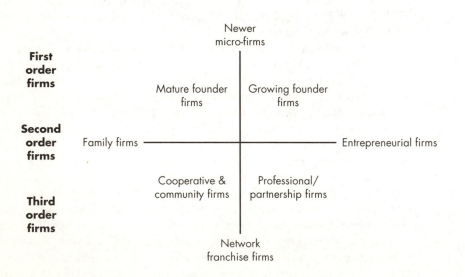

Figure 5.1 *Smaller firm typology*.

By contrast, fully fledged **family firms** could look towards something else, perhaps perpetuating family control, maintaining independence, continuing known traditions, or something similar (see Dailey and Reuschling, 1979). Such 'familism' remains important wherever smaller businesses are concerned, not just in Europe and North America, but among fast-rising Pacific Rim societies in particular (Redding, 1990).

Otherwise, quite another sector has taken shape here, one where third order **cooperatives** and **community businesses**, for example, enable tiny socio-organizational experiments to take place (Anheier and Seibel, 1990; LAURA, 1990). Many so-called **professional partnership firms** – accountants, lawyers, architects, designers, and so on – are found here, having arguably become more like small businesses too, along with **franchise firms**. As such, these third order firms are not particularly numerous, and hardly constitute major employers, but their profiles show important differences.

Markets for HRM among smaller firms compared

Before describing the characteristic employment relationships of each particular type of firm, it is necessary to appreciate the overall significance of smaller firms as employers and what this implies for the market for HRM among such firms.

Being such miniscule employers, few micro-firms see its relevance for them. By joining together, pooling resources, and undergoing mutual training, slow-growth founder firms might just raise their awareness however. In some respects this was precisely what the Training Agency originally intended with their Business Enterprise Training 'option' schemes which, further funded through the TECs, might interest human resource consultants too (Smith, 1990). As regards their own specialist power and influence, such consultants still appear pretty marginal among most growing firms, even the fastest growing of which rarely search far for new managers (Storey, 1987), though option schemes like these could ease consultant entry. This process differs from gaining entry into mature founder firms where sensitive issues to do with retirement, succession and the continuity or disposal or the business could, as Boswell (1973) predicted, increase other defences towards outsiders. Other difficulties arise among fully fledged family firms too where, as we shall see, the classic literature emphasizes how emotionally tied family and business sometimes become (Levinson, 1983).

While not always small, family firms remain very distinctive organizations, as much social institutions as businesses *per se*. For this, as well as for other reasons, many hardly persist into/beyond their third generation. By contrast, genuinely fast-grown, pathfinding entrepreneurial firms employ rather more formal policies, corporate plans and organizational structures, but the way these actually take effect varies considerably. For example, certain entrepreneurs ritually bypass these formalities, making such organizations look more like personal fiefdoms than anything else (De Vries and Miller, 1987; Collins and Moore, 1964, 1970). For that reason, incoming human resource specialists find them attractive in terms of seeing development opportunities ahead, yet perplexing when they set about realizing such. By contrast, many third order firms never make important business breakthroughs, yet differ considerably regarding human resource issues. For example, cooperatives and community businesses – often founded with employment and training purposes in mind – may respect these matters more than most, and have specialist support agencies for help and guidance. Then again, small professional practices often assign responsibility for such issues to senior/managing partners – who will also have other obligations – instead (Arkin, 1991).

The significance of human resource issues varies considerably among franchise firms too. Whereas some pay considerable attention to selecting, training and developing the necessary staff under some quasi-corporate ethos, others stay confined within their chosen business sphere alone, and leave other issues alone. Finally, if one counts certain larger firm spin-offs and spin-outs under this heading, then human resource inputs could increase their 'intrapreneurial' prestige.

Strategically, all this creates two major issues for human resource specialists themselves. The first concerns the likely demand, together with real potential need, for them to input into, or help make more general policy about, firms like these. The second concerns how such demand and/or need is most appropriately supplied, given their particular knowledge and skills.

Looking at comparisons between the different kinds of smaller firms and at what quoted statistics reveal, demand for human resource specialists could remain pretty limited, given that many firms employ very few people, or do not see/rank their employment problems as very important anyway.

These considerations apart, only certain types of small firm ever register much demand for human resource specialists, just as relatively few ever account for significant additional employment. Moreover, as we shall see, having a need can be different from acknowledging it: some small business-people appear reluctant to recognize employee development problems and potential (Scase and Goffee, 1987). Consequently, the real need for human resource input may become either rather more than, or somehow rather different from, anything presently demanded. Such needs are not easily diagnosed; this might mean overcoming founder and/or family defensiveness about raising these matters. Accessing their chosen workforces might prove problematic too. Either way, the mode in which human resource inputs are supplied and delivered is particularly important in this respect. Apart from some fast-growing founder/pathfinding entrepreneurial firms, few will probably have regular in-house expertise. As regards owners and managers, periodic exposure through education, training, peer tutoring and consultancy might appear appropriate, but their workforces' situation remains unclear, though better mutual training alliances could help.

So what is the human resource marketplace actually signalling here? *Demand* for specialized human resource support will probably stay limited as before; however the *need* for such support could well have been played down. Meanwhile, interested practitioners face the rising challenge of finding more appropriate ways of supplying and delivering their services. Consequently, they might need to boost their 'expert power' before they really impress, rather than vaguely hope they will carry some influence over from outside, particularly into ongoing strategy-making.

Smaller firm strategy-making

Orthodox strategic theorizing may not help incoming practitioners deal with firms like these. Not only have many business strategists deliberately neglected such firms, but many firms themselves rarely formally articulate their working strategies anyway. Since 'few strategic planning tools can be directly applied to smaller business' in this respect (Curtis, 1983), new ways of thinking about strategy are necessary before what might actually happen becomes clear (as has been discussed in Chapter 1). The relative absence of highly formalized competitive analyses, mission statements, corporate objectives, long-term corporate plans, and suchlike does not necessarily mean they have no action strategy. As Mintzberg (1989, 1990a,b) argued, those who can only see strategy like some grand 'design' covering all contingencies with high profile planning will rarely find much supporting evidence among firms like these. In many ways their working strategies are more modest, subtle and emergent precisely because they rely more upon active involvement, personal judgement and mutual understandings than anything else.

In short, many such firms more often interpersonally 'craft' than impersonally 'design' their working strategies, and even then they show some important differences between one another within this preferred crafting mode, as illustrated in Figure 5.2.

Important though they are, the significance of these differences should not be exaggerated. In many respects they are more differences of accent than of anything else. Take the personal strategy crafting mode for example. This will occur among most human organizations regardless of size and scale. But for most micro-firms, being tiny employers where founder and firm appear almost indivisible, the personal meaning of any strategy counts more than anywhere else. Given the difficulty of seeing the business behind the person, as it were, any human resource input is probably best delivered firstly among close, personal, one-to-one lines. An example of this is the HMH Sheetmetal case study in Part 3.

Should some such firms ever transform themselves into truly entrepreneurial businesses, one might expect 'personalization' to give way to more formally **businesslike strategy-making**. In practice, few ever make this quantum leap, leaving many lesser growing founder firms somewhere in the middle, resorting to 'mixed mode' strategy crafting. If only because other powerful interests outside, such as large customers and banks, expect them to become more businesslike, many such firms may well start to become more strategically intent, and begin formalizing their business plans. However, many founders hanker for close personal control, and remain reluctant to delegate genuine authority for putting plans into effect (Stanworth and Curran, 1973). Any resulting mixed mode crafting (part personally willed/ part formally planned) may then accentuate those strategic tensions and imbalances which constrain both the realization of their original growth plans and/or the maintenance of close personal control.

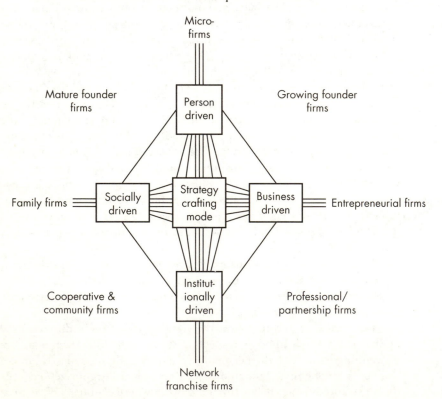

Figure 5.2 Smaller firm strategy crafting modes.

Other difficulties afflict more mature founder firms: their original founders crave perpetual control, while the lack of any immediate family successor can paralyse longer term strategy-making altogether (Christensen, 1953). If they do eventually become fully fledged family firms, such founders' original direct personal influence might gradually recede, and **socialized strategy crafting** take its place, involving other family members, relatives and/or kin. Unless they develop appropriate interpersonal relationships with these close-knit family groups – and certain individuals among their workforce may still subconsciously regard themselves like extended family members too (Miller and Rice, 1967) – many would-be managers and consultants could find that being too formally businesslike increases anxiety over proposed changes (Leach, 1991).

Interested practitioners could well find the Morgan Motor Company case described by Harvey-Jones (1990) in his *Troubleshooter* book and television series instructive in this respect. This long-established, wholly family-owned firm, founded in 1910, assembled uniquely valued cars, under the control of a seven-person board, four of whom were family related. Both they – and some of their workforce – appeared to find Harvey-Jones' business-first approach difficult to take. Despite his evident frustrations, Harvey-Jones the consultant still found 'difficulty letting go', and feared he was 'so conditioned by low expectations' thereafter that he was 'grateful for almost any change that is proposed' to raise its business profile. Meanwhile his managerial clients appeared rather shocked and hurt about this whole approach towards the firm they regarded much like a social institution.

All told, then, there is no 'one best way' to go about crafting strategies among smaller firms, except to recognize that simply following ill-customized corporate approaches imported from larger firms outside will not necessarily work to good effect. Interventionists therefore need quickly to grasp the essence of each firm's organizational character from some overarching frame of knowledge about small firm employment relationships generally.

Smaller firm employment relationships as potential human resource problems

So far we have dealt more with management issues than anything else. Once they reach inside towards their respective workforces, human resource specialists face different problems again. For some time the smaller firm employees' situation has been submerged under duvet concepts like 'small is beautiful'. Any idea that these firms are the epitome of 'good' (roughly translated as highly disciplined, obedient and conflict-free) employer–employee relationships does not necessarily hold however. In 1971, the Bolton committee took very little evidence from small firm employees themselves when claiming that:

> In many respects the small firm provides a better environment for the employee than is possible in most large firms. Although physical working conditions may sometimes be inferior in small firms, most people prefer to work in a small group where communications present fewer problems: the employees in the small firm can easily see the relation between what they are doing and the objectives and performance of the firm as a whole. Where management is more direct and flexible working rules can be varied to suit the individual. . . . No doubt mainly as a result of this, the turnover of staff in small firms is very low and strikes and other kinds of industrial dispute are relatively infrequent.
>
> (HMSO, 1971)

Even at face value such claims look rather unlikely. To be highly dependent upon one or two powerful owner–authority figures, and to work in poorer physical conditions, often for less pay and benefits than elsewhere, with very limited promotion prospects and other hidden barriers to transferring back into large firms outside, hardly suggests 'small is beautiful'. Since then work like Curran (1987), Rainnie (1989) and Goss (1991) has challenged this overidealized picture while showing how much more varied and volatile most small firm employment relationships really are.

In the first instance the research message is that:

> . . . management policy in small firms is often not formulated in a self-conscious pattern, and that informal routinization plays a large part in the day-to-day running of firms. This is particularly true in the area of labour relations. The dominant approach is one that stresses that as long as the workers are working there is no problem. There was little evidence generally of preplanning in order to avoid potential problems.
>
> (Scott *et al.*, 1989)

A picture of unpredictable management practices and indifference towards human resource development commonly prevails. As well as being loosely organized around a few powerful individuals, many such firms use few employment procedures, and often lack awareness of relevant employment legislation. Some maintain stereotypical beliefs about the 'right type' of worker for them while lamenting the inevitable recruitment problems that result. Certain newer firms apart, some hardly train their incoming workers, least of all upon newer technology, while appraisal and development pose problems too. Many owner–managers remain convinced everything would still work well were it not for the occasional 'misfit' or 'troublemaker' who slips through their net. In consequence, many continue 'churning' through their employees, who frequently include people drawn from various lower paid, ethnic minority, and other disadvantaged groups, whom these employment practices further 'casualize', particularly during cutbacks and recession. As so often with smaller firms, bottom-line survival, or just making do, does not leave very much scope for anything that does not give some quick material payback.

Yet the chances of their circumventing these problems by attracting suitably trained individuals from outside and using them well does not look very promising either. As Bosworth (1989) observes:

> Small firms are less able/willing to attract high-quality personnel, although there is a tendency for the small business owner–manager to underestimate the quality of his existing workforce. . . . Small firms not only begin with a lower-quality base, but they are also disadvantaged in their ability to carry out training programmes. They undertake less training per employee and it seems likely that, pound for pound, the training is less productive than in larger firms. The small firm is also forced to make more use of external sources which seem likely to have a lower 'firm-specific' content. The net result is that the training does not 'lock' the employee within the small firm, and thus lowers the return to training.

The form and value of training nevertheless varies considerably between different trade and industrial sectors. In fashion and design, for example, one preferred route for rising young staff is to work alongside key founder figures, as if the 'training' thus imparted anchors their studies, and accelerates their future careers. Away from the leading fashion centres, one particular high-fashion company deliberately recruited well-qualified young designers virtually straight from college, not expecting them to stay and build long-term careers there. Such staff worked very closely with its founder in a routine of making one prototype high-fashion garment each day in an exacting way which simultaneously fascinated and exhausted them. Through time it was informally expected that these incomers would regularly join, produce, then look to leave, either to work upon their own specialist ventures or go elsewhere, once they were fully 'trained'. Despite what this training cost, its founder believed this helped create a network of fashion designers nearby with whom he could periodically intertrade later on.

Contrast this with the difficult training problems encountered in the building and construction sector, where working 'the lump' has long created particular difficulties. Here, while the number of self-employed has grown appreciably, and the relative proportion of those employed elsewhere declined, the increasing number of smaller firms and traders does not necessarily signify upsurgent 'enterprise' *per se*, and may have exacerbated problems of training to meet growing and challenging skill needs instead.

While not exactly universal, this undisguised **minimalist approach** towards employee training and development might appear short-sighted, except that the basic dependency of some such firms within industries like this (see Ball, 1988) makes many owner–managers believe they have little choice other than to perpetuate this approach. From their employees' viewpoint, particularly regarding the rewards and benefits others elsewhere enjoy, smaller firms can appear pretty risky choices. Evidence from the United States furthermore suggests that:

> On average, going to work for a larger employer pays, and pays very well
> . . . indirect evidence fails to confirm that there are unmeasured benefits
> from working in a small business that leave workers as happy as they might
> be in large businesses. Whether one looks at quit rates as a sign of job
> dissatisfaction or the number of applicants per vacancy as an indicator of
> desirable jobs, the total package of wages, benefits and working conditions
> appears to be better in large firms.
>
> (Brown *et al.*, 1990)

If these conditions prevail across the United States, which some regard as
their model 'enterprise society', then questions arise about whether Japan,
sometimes called another 'nation of small businesses', is any different in this
respect. On closer examination, something like 80% of its nonagricultural
workforce may work in firms employing anywhere up to 300 people, but these
firms are locked into very much bigger industrial and company structures
than themselves. So, while surrounding large firms appear more prestigious,
and maintain lifetime employment systems for their own 'core' employees,
they also heavily patronize and, in effect, materially obligate several tiers of
smaller firm subcontractors to follow their lead. Not surprisingly, these
smaller firms cannot offer comparable employment conditions, and variously
pay less, give fewer benefits, and employ somewhat older, more part-time,
and more female workers than their larger patrons, on whom they ultimately
depend (Chalmers, 1989).

Other variations arise within Korea, Singapore, Taiwan, Hong Kong
and with the overseas Chinese family business at large (see Whitley, 1991).
While Western values ideally see families as enhancing individuality, Chinese
values imply individuals should subordinate themselves to, and do everything
to enhance, their own family standing, which counts for more than anything
particular organizations and occupation ever stand for. Thus:

> For the Overseas Chinese, their normal and representative form of organiza-
> tion, although classifiable as a family business, is a family business of a
> special kind. Other family businesses do not have Confucianism provid-
> ing vertical stable order, do not have the particularly Chinese form of
> paternalism based in long-standing patrimonial tradition, do not have trust
> bonds reinforced by Chinese versions of obligation and reciprocity, do not
> have the same psychological dependencies, do not have the intensity of
> identity with family accentuated by experience of Chinese social history
>
> (Redding, 1990)

Since 'there is no indigenous text books, no recognizable management
theory, and the Western text books hardly penetrate at all' here this 'home
made' approach to human resources might have worked well for some under
these unusual circumstances. But, semi-unique though they are, Chinese
family businesses still inhibit employees, while incoming managers must
subordinate themselves to owning family interests before being trusted to
exercise authority in their name (Redding, 1986).

To summarize, while smaller firm employment relationships appear very diverse, many firms are such miniscule employers that these relationships rarely bother them, while others fear that employing many more people will only weaken their personal control. To really explore these relationships further means tapping into how both owners *and* employers see each other's actions and interests being dealt with. Such understandings are not improved by contrived comparisons with much larger firms; what is essential is to differentiate *between* smaller firms.

Human resource strategies for smaller organizations

If the human resource specialist is to think strategically about the needs of small and entrepreneurial firms, it is important not to become overinvolved in the detailed minutiae of employee attraction, selection methods, training schemes, job design, reward and control systems. Instead, the aim should be to envisage how these fit together into distinct HRM profiles for each type of firm, using a typology similar perhaps to that shown on p. 114.

Front-line micro/founder firms

In profile these appear as in Table 5.1. Most **micro-firms** leave little scope for human resource interventions. Individually, they need few, if any, employees, whom they select very personally. Once employed, individuals work somewhat informally, maybe without explicit contracts or job descriptions, performing whatever tasks come their way. Given that continuity of work remains uncertain, rewards vary, so insecurity is never far away. Being younger, volatile firms, their working cultures also fluctuate more than most. As a result, many frequently continue 'churning' employees until they either stabilize, or start growing into something else.

Education and training may possibly increase human resource awareness in such firms. Native feedback from fellow course members helps owners focus upon these issues. Ritchie and Gibb (1982) describe one major field experiment organized through Durham University Business School which brought large numbers of aspiring founders together. They were offered choices of advisory, counselling and training sessions, dealing first with how they would organize themselves for business and then how they would employ others. Such personally customized events can help some anticipate, and start planning for, possible problems in this respect (see also Gill, 1985).

Table 5.1 *Micro/founder firm profiles*

	Newer micro-firms	Growing founder firms	Mature founder firms
Employee entry channels	Highly personal and individual	Interacting networks	Tried and tested networks
Work structure	Minimally formalized	Pending formalization	Internalized along 'proven' lines
Task performance	Initially improvised	Expanded beyond original expectations	Contained within recognized parameters
Reward system	Modest and uncertain	Additionality expected	Regularity expected
Working culture	Liable to flux	Self-sustaining	Self-preserving
Retention and development problem	Liable to employee 'churning'	Further organizational stress with employee burnout/dropout and so on	Underplanned succession and/or fadeout ahead

---

CASE STUDY: *Employment strategies for a small coal mine*

The case of one intending small coal-mine owner illustrates this well. Wanting to assert his independence following various career switches, his first plans regarded employing others as very simple and unproblematic. He would just select capable individual mineworkers on the basis of close personal and local knowledge and, for apparently reasonable pay and rewards, they would then simply perform whatever tasks were necessary, without having any further aspirations. On being made acquainted with the classic studies of autonomous group working in nearby collieries (Trist *et al.*, 1963) his ideas soon changed. Finding that such groups could become more economic as well as personally satisfying to work in, he developed quite another organizational strategy and changed his whole way of thinking about how to manage employees.

Such cases are probably exceptional. While small business education and training has expanded considerably, it is difficult to determine its overall effects, let alone whether human resources play any great role (Curran and Stanworth, 1989; Kirby, 1990).

By comparison, growing founder firm profiles suggest these firms interact more with the outside when attracting and selecting employees. So long as they are growing they can keep the formal structuring of tasks and jobs on hold until they see where their business stands. Clearly, many will then arrive somewhere different from where they expected, implying that they need to learn to change throughout this phase. More than the business alone expands through this process: so too can employees' hopes and expectations of rewards and benefits, along with organizational stress, sometimes making a degree of disappointment, burnout and dropout look inevitable. But while increasing turnover, profits, market breakthroughs, or product development are usually taken as showing the business is really on its way, rarely have human resource achievements become equally well known and reported.

CASE STUDY: *Survival Aids Ltd*

The case of Survival Aids Ltd, a Cumbrian-based survival equipment whole-saler and retailer, appears quite exceptional. One of the new micro-firms in Gibb and Ritchie's original study, this was founded by Nicholas Steven on leaving active military service in 1979, and soon passed through the start-up learning loop towards greater growth. Right from the outset its founder was well disposed towards human resource type thinking, describing this as a 'Theory Y' company, investing in both his own and others' training and development to build the organization.

By current criteria, bearing in mind the few firms which extend this far, Survival Aids did well to reach a £4 000 000 + turnover from its pioneer-ing efforts by 1989, by which time it employed over 40 people and distri-buted products across over 60 different countries. Equally important, for its founder's purposes anyway, was its native organizational character, and how well its own employees regarded it. To help this along, some subordinates did role-swaps with him as founder and managing director, giving particular attention to employee selection, teamworking and open communication about company performance. As back-up reward system, its founder installed detailed employee profit-sharing, thereby spreading any resulting benefits more widely than most. All told, this represented the fruition of an unwritten longer term strategy that assumed human resourcefulness would itself bring about sustainable business growth.

In talks and discussions with other fellow growth firm founders outside, Nicholas Steven encountered some doubts about this approach, but still sustained it while growth continued. What was much less discussed, but eventually proved more telling, was how such founders would sustain themselves after this growth phase. In the event, Nicholas Steven himself experienced increasing burnout and fading interest, resulting in his later selling up and moving back into another ethical 'start-up and grow' type situation elsewhere.

Whatever formal accountings show, the very way some small firms grow carries certain human costs with it, and their subsequent organizational condition very often reflects this, as those who unknowingly acquire them from outside frequently discover (De Vries, 1985). Should they take these costs upon themselves, other founders like Nicholas Steven could well withdraw too, and maybe recharge themselves elsewhere. Certainly this would not surprise observers like De Vries (1980) who maintains:

> Although the entrepreneur in the initial stage of development of the enterprise might have had the ability to inspire his subordinates, the mere fact of growth has complicated this process. His aversion to structure, his preference for personalized relationships, and his reluctance to accept constructive criticism make growth, with its implicit need for a more sophisticated infra and superstructure and greater decentralization, increasingly difficult to handle. Hoarding of information, inconsistencies in day-to-day interpretation of company policies, playing of favourites, and refusal to let people know where they really stand does not contribute to an efficient and effective organization. If this pattern becomes predominant and prevails, few capable subordinates will remain in the organization; the ones left will usually be of a mediocre calibre, spending a great part of their effort on political infighting. It is the absence of actual responsibility with authority which causes capable people to leave while the yes-men – individuals who do not really challenge the entrepreneur's authority – will stay on.

Founders like Nicholas Steven would probably sooner leave rather than let this occur. Given the hasty rash of start-ups and expansion inducements that arose during the 1980s, it is nevertheless possible that these human costs will make themselves more fully felt during the 1990s.

Following the De Vries scenario, those incoming human resource specialists who first visualize good opportunities ahead could soon find many such firms more difficult, frustrating and disappointing than they first anticipated. Otherwise, hitherto unprecedented problems to do with burnout, fadeout and disappointment could leave their mark unless these are confronted earlier, and more effectively.

Despite rising problems, some pundits continue to lavish disproportionate time and attention upon newer high-technology ventures, as if these were some special subset of small-growth firms at large. However, not much is really known about their particular human resource strategies save continuing predictions that managing specialist knowledge 'professionals' requires somewhat different approaches (see, for example, Katz, 1988).

For many small firms, growth occurs during, and sometimes only between, particular phases of development, and never becomes the hoped-for perpetual state. What exactly happens when the novelty, excitement, tests, challenges and rewards this engenders finally fade, has not really attracted much attention. Yet, ironically enough, this is just where small business management education first came in, for example with classic studies of the difficulties of succeeding founder figures, like that by Christensen (1953). Once again, this suggests that new and growing firms can easily become over-generalized models, not really appropriate for understanding the challenges mature-turned-family firms face.

Beyond small business alone, some maturity problems extend right across two-thirds of Western industry now. Not only that, this condition ideally requires, though does not always beget, inventive strategic thinking about the way forward (Harrigan, 1988). It is further suggested that, particularly when they have contrasting experiences beforehand, many managers first find maturity (and possible decline) difficult to take, and too disappointing and depressing to confront. In failing to recognize even the onset of such maturity, they vainly hope that 'something will turn up' so as to restore the previous *status quo* as soon and as painlessly as possible. Maybe some plateaued small firms are the most predictable casualties of them all, and though the stigma of 'failure' stalks this whole sector (Scott and Ritchie, 1984), the very age and future intentions of many founders mean that their firms may never even reach maturity, although those that do could soon require more attention.

Second order entrepreneurial and family firms

What of genuinely entrepreneurial firms? (See Table 5.2.) Are they really that different? So different that they start looking more like larger organizations? As regards human resources, they may well start formalizing recruitment and selection procedures, and even look towards appointing full-time human resource specialists too, but will this necessarily change their original entrepreneurial style? A style which, being actively interventionist, can frequently short-circuit their subordinate managers' authority, whatever their formal structures suggest. On being bypassed like this, these can easily turn into quasi-structures, and therefore unreliable guides to action, like the dramatic working cultures they help perpetuate (De Vries and Miller, 1984, 1987). By sometimes imposing their highly personalised wishes, occasionally irrespective of organizational needs, entrepreneurs actually escalate internal differences and conflicts, while appearing nearly blind to the costs, at least until more 'professional management' overhauls them (Flamholtz, 1990).

Table 5.2 Entrepreneurial and family firm profiles

	Entrepreneurial firms	Family firms
Employee entry channels	More selection formalities observed	Selection socially circumscribed
Work structuring	Quasi-hierarchical with continued entrepreneurial bypassing	'Heirarchy' and custom weigh against prescribed hierarchical routine
Task performance	Waves of routine and radical change	Mutually expected regularities with 'one off' changes
Reward system	Fluctuates with waves of change	Certain constants sought
Working culture	Upsurgent and dramatic	Customary and settled
Retention and development problem	Opportunism and politics may override other organizational imperatives	Further continuity and succession still socially obliged and/or dependent

CASE STUDY: *The overexpanding engineering firm*

One case that illustrates these emerging problems well concerns the new component supplying subsidiary of an expanding British engineering firm. This firm had been founded by an archetypal entrepreneur with a very self-dramatized management style. Its new subsidiary was launched in a new greenfield site with an entirely new management team. This team was thought to represent the type of 'professional' management the firm would need for its next stage of development.

In their original plans the team believed they could best manage through a formalized personnel and industrial relations 'constitution' agreed among all relevant parties and very different from anything at base. Very soon, however, they found themselves unsure about the founder's strategic intentions, and frustrated and overawed with his self-dramatizing management style and its divisive and disturbing effects upon others. Feeling increasingly compromised, their position became even less tenable when full operations began, the incoming workforce suspecting they were mere 'straw bosses'.

Subsequent organizational learning was constrained around this power and authority issue and, given the resulting destabilization, little human resource development actually took place. Thus managers either withdrew, or became preoccupied with self-survival, discarding their original plans and aspirations while denying and minimizing associated conflicts. Ironically, only after being sold to another entrepreneur nearby did this venture finally prosper, while crises at base forced other changes, and organic growth gave way to consolidation and joint venturing in due course.

Like their entrepreneurial counterparts, certain fully fledged **family firms** are not necessarily small scale, yet networks still show extraordinary resilience. By retaining considerable influence over whoever takes the leading role, they reinforce the belief that there are 'reserved seats' for family and kin whatever their true managerial ability. Put another way, 'heirarchy' still dominates, even though the formal hierarchy suggests otherwise. Yet that is not always, or even necessarily, the case. Otherwise, regular tasks take precedence but, despite their outwardly settled working cultures, interventionists need to be wary of how deeply disturbing underlying family conflicts can be (Levinson, 1971).

CASE STUDY: *Diana Company*

De Vries and Miller (1984) provide an unusually deep and revealing clinical case history which illustrates much about family business dynamics. It concerns a high-quality lingerie manufacturer called the Diana Company which the Adams family had owned for more than 50 years since its legendary 'old tyrant' founder began operations. Since its early struggles, it had matured and settled, yet sales and profits were still erratic when, following the threatened resignation of one family member, his successors sought consultant advice about recurrent sales and marketing difficulties.

While the consultants concerned soon identified particular problems, they also suspected the somewhat deeper and more complex causes which De Vries and Miller then pursued. As clinicians they went beyond the firm's vague organizational structuring and managerial confusion in that respect. They also diagnosed malignant conflicts over, and some hoarding of, certain successors' power; feelings that management was like being continually 'under siege'; chronic mistrust and suspicion of certain others; manipulative labour relations dealings, and so on. Not that these were readily recognized and acknowledged for what they were; rather, they were smothered and submerged under euphemistic sentiments about being 'a big happy football team' instead.

As process consultants, De Vries and Miller gradually brought these deeper discrepancies and contradictions into more open focus, and attempted to help others work them through in the hope that lasting organizational change could take place. Such change included redesigning the organizational structure, and redefining work roles where appropriate, while developing middle management and altering selection and training practices accordingly. While not entirely successful – few such interventions ever are – a degree of business recovery then took place, and other sensitive problems were better addressed correspondingly.

Possibly there is more specialized expertise with family business interventions in the United States than in the United Kingdom however. Texts like Dyer (1986) therefore offer well-tailored guidance here. Otherwise, the family firm probably remains more important than is sometimes realized, not just in certain European countries like Italy for example, but elsewhere around the Pacific Rim too.

Third order franchise, professional and community–voluntary firms

Despite being unevenly distributed across the EC, **franchising** (see Table 5.3) now appears more important in the United Kingdom where the British Franchise Association estimated that 183 600 people were 'gainfully employed' in 1990 compared with 185 000 in 1989, nearly 60% being full-time employees. Well-known breweries and oil companies, as well as others like Singer, General Motors and Coca-Cola all helped put franchising on the map, but it remains basically small business based, although the likes of the Body Shop, Holiday Inns, and Prontaprint and Fastframe are household names.

Behind the scenes the actual form franchises take have changed too. Once this denoted the granting of concessions to trade in some particular area, product or service. Now it extends to so-called job franchises (such as house cleaning), business franchises (such as office services) and investment franchises (such as hotels) too. For public purposes, franchiser and franchisee are regarded as partners, but differences over power and control still pose important issues. Some therefore make very different use of selection and training techniques to suit their own particular purposes. Certain high-profile franchisers, for example, use more sophisticated techniques for screening potential franchisees, and specify detailed employee training programmes for those they choose, yet they also seek such close control that they leave the franchisees little room for manoeuvre. In consequence, some would

Table 5.3 Partnership, franchise and community – cooperative firm profiles

	Professional/ partnership firms	Franchise firms	Cooperative and community firms
Employee entry channels	Regulated network	Structured network	Informal group network
Work structuring	Professional formalities observed	Replicates standard pattern	Overlapping operation and management
Task performance	Regularized	Programmed	Experimental
Reward system	Stratified	Contracted	Equalized
Working culture	Status-bound	Negotiated	Mutualized
Retention and development problem	Sustaining competitive and institutional capability	Churning obscures problem itself	Managing group dissent and in-group processess

regard McDonalds, for example, as an archetypal machine bureaucracy, where the more original and challenging tasks are held over for its own central staff, while its retail outlet routines restrict other employees (Morgan, 1989).

On the other hand, much smaller, often less rigorously structured companies may grow by franchising their operations. Their reasons might include making best use of the skills and expertize of their existing staff, who could easily become overstretched should they continue expanding from the grass roots instead. Thus, one small London-based vehicle cleaning company was so fearful of overstretching its existing staff that, coupled with problems over selecting and retaining newcomers, it seemed more attractive to continue growing through franchising its operations. For a specified downpayment and percentage of turnover it provided franchisees with equipment, administrative support and detailed training consistent with what its 160 page training manual prescribed.

CASE STUDY: *Benetton*

In some respects the unique fashion and clothing network built around Benetton in Italy illustrates issues of small firm 'flexibility' within larger industrial structures particularly well. An example of family entrepreneurship, Benetton was founded in 1965 and developed this network so effectively that, by the late 1980s, it had an 'inside' workforce of around 1600, with 15–20 000 'outside'. More particularly, it achieved much of this expansion by subcontracting production (to the extent that some 300 small firms arguably contributed nearly 70% of total value added) and franchised retail distribution, such outlets being wholly tied into Benetton alone.

Both design and production made considerable use of new technology and, while little unionized, there were originally agreements that 'inside' and 'outside' workforces should receive comparable rewards. Similarly, highly standardized Benetton retail outlets carried minimal stock, but maintained close information links with the centre, so that, in effect, both 'just-in-time' production and selling were brought together (Belussi, 1989). However, there is another face to this much-glamorized fashionwear industry, one that sees many downstream operators struggling to survive, creating poor conditions for HRM accordingly.

Small professional partnership firms also operate within regulatory networks. As regards the structuring of their work, certain formalities surround the status of partners and professionals particularly. While client needs may differ, the way practitioners handle such work becomes more regular, through standardized documents and procedures for example.

Inside such firms professionals and support staff have different status and reward systems, while secretarial and clerical staff typically identify more with individual partners than the firm itself. Continued professional updating, and maintaining parity with other firms outside, nevertheless present increasing problems for these businesses with rather different consulting challenges accordingly (Gray, 1987).

Likewise, **cooperative and community–voluntary 'firms'**, if we may call them that, are surprisingly numerous and distinctive, not merely in the United Kingdom alone. Founded through informal group networks, they sometimes galvanize into wider social movements. From the human resource viewpoint, it is an advantage to be sympathetic to, and well situated within, these networks and supportive of their wider aims, otherwise their essential informality – and maybe conviviality – is not always easily appreciated from outside. Once inside, many play up their basic voluntariness, while playing down the need for organization and management, as if these were mutually incompatible (Handy, 1988). For that reason, interventionists need to be sensitive towards how they regard, and personally represent, proposed organizational and management changes, even though prolonged experience of 'radical failure' has made some insiders call for greater receptivity towards such (Landry *et al.*, 1985).

In such organizations many members would prefer that their everyday operations and management were indivisible. Particularly during the early stages, the tasks members perform have close personal meanings for them which, by way of contrast, play down administration and management. The real question is how long such a state of affairs can continue, for both timing and manner as well as content of any intervention appear crucial. In some circumstances, further success brings new problems which might force this issue, as when certain cooperatives 'dilute' their original membership with conventional employees, putting equal status and reward systems under pressure. This could bring into focus the problem of retaining and developing membership about which human resource specialists – or others claiming such skill – might then be consulted.

Many outsiders remain dismissive about cooperatives' potential and performance. While many voluntary organizations could well feel threatened by this, it is worthwhile recalling that currently esteemed organizations like building societies once sprang from these roots, while cooperatives helped pioneer today's wholefood revolution in the face of much doubt and resistance.

As regards cooperatives, the literature expresses some concern about possible mid-term 'degeneration' from 'democratic' into more 'hierarchic' management control which human resource specialists need to be wary of, in case they are suspected of helping bring this about. Some nevertheless call for closer auditing of 'returns to labour', or how well members' interests and objectives are actually met, though low pay, multiple-skill demands, role conflicts and doubtful regard for 'outsiders' could bar the way for more 'professional' management help.

As with other micro-firms at large, human resource specialists could well find education and training – often highly valued among these networks – enable them to intervene more effectively here. Community businesses – locally mounted ventures that provide simple services which might employ disadvantaged people from poor neighbourhoods – have benefited from this (Ritchie, 1986b). Otherwise, voluntary organizations face increasing problems ahead. Acknowledging that other management thinking rarely recognizes this sector, Butler and Wilson (1990) maintain that here:

> Strategic survival and the continued regeneration of organization have become primary issues and, in order to achieve these, questions of organization design and of management style have come to dominate the managerial agenda.

Given that the entry of 'professional' managers often 'seems to bring about an almost inevitable clash of values' with other staff, an innovative approach may be necessary to bring about worthwhile changes.

CASE STUDY: *Traidcraft*

The case of Traidcraft Ltd is heartening in this respect. 'People before profit'. 'Justice in trade'. Evocative slogans both. But are they really translatable into practice? Traidcraft believed so. In 1990, from its main organizational base in Gateshead, it achieved a £5.4 million turnover, and grew to employ 150 people directly, and more indirectly, over an 11-year period by providing outlets which gave work for, and returned part of the resulting economic benefit to, families from some of the world's poorest countries.

Drawing on its strong religious roots, this venture continually explored and experimented with its own organization throughout this time. Working through close-knit informal networks, it gave many the opportunity to shape its management, equalized common differences in status and rewards, and created its own mutually supportive working culture, surprising many by its quiet successes.

Conclusion

We have seen that there are vast numbers of smaller businesses in parts of Europe, the United States and the Pacific Rim, and growing numbers in the United Kingdom too, but relatively few pathbreaking entrepreneurial ones. One should not be overwhelmed by their sheer numbers, but should clearly differentiate between the main *types* of small firm now emerging, since each has its own preferred approach to strategy-making, and its own individual human resource profile. As potential minimarkets for HRM interventions, smaller firms differ greatly from each other, not least concerning whether they will even consider 'human resource strategy' let alone apply it. Even where they employ reasonably significant numbers of people – and, statistically anyway, many never really will – they hardly contemplate formalizing their working strategies, still less integrating human resource development plans into them.

When it occurs, most strategy-making usually takes more subtle, personalized forms among few key actors, whom human resource specialists must personally influence accordingly. Even then, few individual firms will ordinarily request such help because their owners cannot see any great role for HRM. However, with a new generation of smaller businesses coming forward, together with other means of support, HRM specialists could eventually make more headway than before, provided they anticipate and resolve certain continuing problems (Curran and Blackburn, 1991).

Just gaining better access into the more responsive firms is difficult enough. Given how apparently ignorant, reticent or defensive some owners feel about these issues, incoming specialists may first find it difficult to build up a satisfactory portfolio of individual firms without investing considerable time and effort in research and development themselves. Meanwhile, as if this were not enough, they could still find that outside pressures, plus the harsh imperatives of short-term survival, leave limited room for manoeuvre.

For that reason they should perhaps first specialize with certain particular types of firm and associated networks, concentrating attention and developing expertise rather than spreading themselves widely and thinly. While being trained and experienced outside the smaller firm sector has its advantages (Gibb, 1990) the downside soon emerges when specialists assume that what sufficed elsewhere will automatically carry over into firms like these. It is not a matter of smaller firms being more 'beautiful'; it is that they are different, as much from each other as from their larger counterparts. Good interventionists clearly recognize this.

By the same token, any attempt to make smaller businesses look more like new model organizations and employers, of a kind that larger firms outside might usefully copy and imitate, with their personnel and human resource specialists encouraged to 'become entrepreneurs, but entrepreneurs with a human face' (Armstrong, 1989), looks pretty fanciful too. Pathfinders though they originally are, genuinely entrepreneurial firms are few and rare, and are frequently very different from many smaller firms surrounding them. Moreover, recent events show how dramatically these destabilize and disintegrate. Miller (1990) emphasizes how nominally 'excellent' companies eventually bring about their own downfall in several different ways, showing how transient organizational fashions turn out to be.

To realize the full potential of HRM it may be necessary to look beyond the individual small firms. In many respects this is the necessary, but not sufficient, condition for such development (Hendry, 1991). Only when more such firms collaborate for this particular purpose, and more public and corporate programmes enable them to do so, are the full conditions likely to be met, and then some dramatic changes could follow.

6

Industrial relations, employment relations and strategic human resource management

David Bright

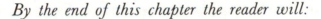

By the end of this chapter the reader will:

1. understand the place of industrial relations and employment relations management within a wider approach to the management of human resources;

2. understand the major current issues in industrial and employment relations;

3. have an awareness of the value of a developed strategy for industrial relations and employment relations;

4. have an awareness of the type of elements which make up such strategies.

This chapter considers industrial relations and employment relations in contemporary business organizations. It examines current practices and analyses the role of industrial relations and employment relations management within an HRM strategy.

The nature of industrial relations, employment relations and human resource management

Industrial relations

While the study of **industrial relations** can be traced back to the nineteenth century and beyond, the emergence of a subject area of note under this title is generally linked to the work of Dunlop (1958) and to the publications of the so-called Oxford school of Flanders, Clegg, McCarthy and Fox in the 1960s (Flanders, 1969).

Since the 1960s a welter of literature has emerged, with the result that although the subject material is essentially hybrid it has become a well-established area of study in universities, both new and old, business schools and colleges of all kinds, as well as in a myriad of company in-house training courses. A considerable amount of intellectual effort was expounded in the 1960s and 1970s in an attempt to provide a rigorous definition of the discipline of industrial relations and of its subject matter (Blain and Gennard, 1970; Flanders, 1969; Margerison, 1969), though more recent research effort appears to accept as a working framework a wide interpretation of what industrial relations is about. Your author is no exception to this latter school of thought, believing that what we have come to understand as 'industrial relations' is an eclectic series of attitudes, practices and forms of behaviour related to working processes and rewards in the business organization and in wider industrial society.

The central theme in the study and the practice of industrial relations is one of interaction between the employer and the workforce in which collective behaviour is channelled through the workings of trade unions. It is held to be a bilateral process of rule-making and rule-changing in which management and trade unions play key roles.

Industrial relations, therefore, has traditionally required employers and trade unions to deal collectively with each other through the media of collective bargaining, procedural norms, consultation and consideration. Dealings exist at both the industry level and the level of the firm, with the latter becoming increasingly important in the years since 1945.

Numerically, at least, the apotheosis of this type of collective regulation can be seen to be associated with the late 1960s and 1970s. In 1979 trade union membership in the United Kingdom was 13.5 million, representing some 55% of the working population. Some 5.5 million of these trade unionists worked in 'closed shops' in which membership was a term of the employment contract. Since that year, however, union power and membership have been in decline due to a combination of economic recession, structural change, political and legislative developments and, possibly, social attitudes. This having been said, trade unions are still recognized by thousands of employers and are still an important force in the majority of large workplaces. Consequently, very many employers seeking to change their practices and move towards an HRM approach have to give critical consideration to the role and reaction of the union machine. (For a recent study see Blyton and Turnbull, 1992, Part III.)

Employment relations

At the same time, it should be noted that a number of medium- and large-sized businesses do not recognize trade unions these days, nor do the vast majority of small companies. They all, however, must manage issues concerned with staff and conditions of employment. Such businesses often use the term **employment relations** to describe the scope and nature of these issues. Additionally, as will be described in this chapter, a number of organizations that recognize unions have worked in the last decade or so to change their approach in this regard, thus moving from an industrial relations perspective to one more akin to employment relations. Employment relations-related practices recognize the need to work constructively with the workforce to achieve their understanding of corporate objectives and working practices. Employment relations also reflects the fact that organizations are pluralist systems (as discussed in Chapters 1 and 2) and that manifestations of conflict of interest are natural. The approaches differ, however, with regard to the role given to union activity and the channels of communication developed by management to facilitate the management of staff.

Put simplistically, in industrial relations the predominant emphasis is concerned with management – union relations and how these impact upon staff; in employment relations the major emphasis is given to management–employee relations.

Strategic human resource management

In adopting a strategic approach to HRM we are concerned with the ability of the business to manage its people-related activities effectively, to mesh these together and to facilitate human resource activities supporting the corporate objectives. Sisson (1989) suggests that HRM features include stress on the integration of personnel policies, giving line management key personnel responsibilities, a shift in emphasis from collectivism to individualism, and a desire for employee commitment and 'ownership'.

Management have a key role in setting the relevant human resource objectives, making sure that all subset objectives are congruent and feasible and changing approaches and practices where necessary. Thus any organization wishing to move to a more holistic approach to the management of its human resources needs to consider how the existing in-house system of industrial relations or employment relations will fit in and in what areas changes will be necessary to achieve the desired dovetailing.

In this chapter much of the consideration of HRM addresses the field of industrial relations and the role of unions within it. This discussion is set against a backcloth of HRM strategy and considers developments that have taken place in actual companies to allow industrial relations to become part of an HRM approach and also how such developments *might* take place in businesses which are seeking to change their current approach.

Many of the issues under discussion also apply to a company using employment relations techniques, with the major qualification that negotiating change with unions in this situation might take on a different flavour or, for many businesses, may not be necessary at all.

In simple terms, if transition along HRM lines can be achieved in a union-organized business, it can certainly also be achieved in a business where management–employee relations is pre-eminent.

The management function related to the conduct of industrial relations

In Chapter 2 an examination of the differences and similarities between HRM and traditional personnel management was set out. In essence, it was argued that HRM is a more holistic concept, linking together strands of management in order to help achieve the overall objectives of the business.

Industrial relations is one such strand. There is, however, one clear difference between industrial relations and the other strands cited and it is, as already stated, that industrial relations involves a degree of bilateral decision-making not present elsewhere, with management dealing across the bargaining table and in consultation with elected representatives of the workforce organized through the unions.

There are approximately 300 unions in the United Kingdom, far more than in other European countries. Their organizational genesis and logic are varied. Some have emerged around craft groupings, some around sectors of industry, and others are more general in coverage and tradition, looking after a wide range of workers from a variety of industries. While the recession of the 1980s and 1990s was hard on the unions (they lost over three million members), they still number some 36% of the British workforce in their ranks and they therefore cannot be ignored by management.

It should be noted at this juncture that the pattern of organization of British unions is not mirrored in other countries. While each country has an inevitable degree of uniqueness, the United Kingdom appears to be more heterogeneous in terms of forms of organization than most. In West Germany, post-war reconstruction resulted in the creation of some 16 industrial-based unions; a similar structural pattern exists in France. In Japan it is usual to find unions based around particular business corporations, while in Italy it is more common to find unions linked to particular political parties (Bean, 1989).

It is noteworthy, however, that in recent years the old pattern of unionism has changed to an extent in the United Kingdom as single-union agreements and large mergers creating super-unions, such as Unison, has meant that traditional recruitment territories and areas of influence have become of less relevance than in the past.

If we look back through the last decade in the United Kingdom and in the rest of Europe we can readily see that the 1980s and early 1990s were associated with very difficult trading conditions and consequently high levels of unemployment, with the situation in the United Kingdom being worse than in most Western European economies. Such a climate and the commercial pressures it produced forced many business organizations to examine closely their operating methods, with the watchword throughout being increased cost-effectiveness. From such examination came a greater concern for improvement in manufacturing or service quality and productivity, and correspondingly a greater degree of interest was shown by employers in the cost-effective management of industrial relations, often within a stated HRM approach.

Indicators of such cost effectiveness are recognized by Chris Brewster (1989) and others (Purcell and Sisson, 1984; Armstrong, 1987; Guest, 1987; Marchington, 1989) evincing an overriding concern to ensure that the right kind of people, not necessarily employees, are available only when needed and at the least possible cost.

This thinking demonstrates a straightforward and preoccupation with managing the labour resource in a way supportive of production and integrated with other people-related activities, such as recruitment and training:

> They [HRM managers] began to develop criteria of cost control, of flexibility and amenability from their employees and the most productive use of the workforce. The touchstone became cost-effectiveness; the cost-effective use of the human resource.
>
> (Brewster, 1989, p. 83)

To realize this type of objective in a greenfield site operation where a business is set up from scratch, will probably not prove to be too difficult. Thus when Nissan (GB) set up their operation in Sunderland, it developed a system of group working and decision-making which was tailored to match its Just In Time (JIT) system of production.

In JIT working, the organization operates with minimum levels of stocks at either end of the production process, relying on accurate forecasting and flexible working practices for support. The system is well grounded in the United States in companies such as Coca-Cola, IBM and now, to an extent, Ford Motors. It has also been regularly utilized by Japanese undertakings globally.

In a brownfield (or pre-existing) operation, however, to achieve such a change in the nature of industrial relations will undoubtedly be a much more complex task, and a more challenging prospect for management and unions alike. Some of the issues involved are inherent in the following short case study.

CASE STUDY: *Local bargaining in UK TV companies*

In 1988 the television companies which operate the independent channels in the United Kingdom terminated national bargaining with the unions. The companies felt that national bargaining was outdated and was proving expensive, particularly through what was known as the 'golden hours' agreement in which high premium payments were made for hours worked. Since the ending of national bargaining the companies have either concluded agreements with the unions locally or are in the process of doing so. The following issues have been central to these negotiations:

- Agreed staffing levels have been reduced.
- Long-standing working hours agreements have been amended, giving management greater discretion in how work is organized and reducing the need for overtime payments.
- Multiskilling has been introduced. This has broken down some traditional job boundaries.

To manage change smoothly is never easy, but to manage industrial relations change, where this might involve a shift in culture as well as practices, is particularly difficult. Management have, however, benefited from the recent economic recession in two ways when seeking to introduce such changes.

First, just as the economic downturn forced many employers to examine critically what they did in order to ensure the survival of the business, the haemorrhage of membership through redundancies encouraged the unions to adapt and work more closely with management in an attempt to protect more jobs from being lost. This became an element of the 'new realism' applied to union behaviour. It led, as we will see later, to changes in working numbers, working practices and an overall increase in flexibility.

The second way in which management could be seen to 'benefit' from the conditions of recession was through the shift in the amount of bargaining power they possessed. Bargaining power is a nebulous concept but a very real practical issue: it is the ability of one party to persuade, encourage, negotiate or coerce another party into agreeing to something that did not fully accord with the initial stance of that party.

Bargaining power in industrial relations is directly related to the state of the labour market in a particular area. In times of high employment, unions enjoy a powerful position and are able to utilize this to achieve high money wage settlements and other related benefits. At times of recession, which was generally the situation in much of Europe and America throughout the late 1970s to 1990s, demand for labour runs down, union power diminishes in tandem and management power increases accordingly. Thus, the ability of management to introduce a more cost-effective set of industrial relations policies and practices increased across Europe and particularly in the United Kingdom insofar as the unions' ability effectively to oppose change was reduced. This is borne out by the data on trends on industrial disputes set out in Appendix A.

A further factor which has served to increase managerial power in the late 1980s and 1990s in the United Kingdom has been the Conservative government's use of statute law to control key aspects of union activities and employees' rights. Between 1979 and 1993 the Royal Assent was given to eight major pieces of employment legislation. In addition, there was the emergence of a number of rule and regulatory changes. The result of both of these developments was a very considerable increase in the application of law to the workplace and dramatic changes in the law affecting the closed shop and in matters of industrial action. A further bill is currently (1993) progressing through Parliament.

The government's objectives during the period have, however, been more wide-ranging than the simple control of the unions' ability to engage in industrial action. These objectives have included:

- the removal of what were considered 'unnecessary' modes of intrusion into the operation of the marketplace in matters of wage-fixing;

- the removal or limitation of certain areas of employment protection from small businesses as a measure of encouraging the growth of 'enterprise';

- assistance for the emergence of more flexible employing organizations through the curtailment of areas of employment protection, such as the qualifying period for unfair dismissal applications;

- help in making the unions more responsive to the wishes of the majority of their members;

- limiting the ability of unions and their members to take lawful and effective industrial action.

Even in a brownfield operation, therefore, management can be in a reasonable strategic position to re-examine the nature and quality of the industrial relations existing in their workplaces and begin the process of reshaping these where necessary to fit into a wider HRM philosophy and programme.

What are cost-effective industrial relations and employment relations?

If industrial relations or employment relations are to fit within an overall HRM strategy they have to be managed. This is axiomatic, and yet it would not be too unkind to say that some employers have only recently realized this. To do this there should be a set of objectives related to the theme of cost-effectiveness, a style of management which embraces these, and a series of practices designed to be fluid and supportive of the overall business objectives.

We can now examine the role of the first two of these before considering some of the practices relevant to the achievement of cost-effective industrial relations.

Management objectives

Objectives can and do vary depending on the particular nature of the organization, so that a welfare organization might be less overt in its desire for cost-effectiveness than a commercial organization. It is unlikely, however, given the limited resourcing which occurs in most, if not all, countries, that even welfare organizations such as health bodies or educational bodies can afford to ignore the potential benefits accruing from increased cost-effectiveness.

Any organization which embarks on an HRM programme will need to set out the related sets of activity which it deems relevant to this programme and consider the objectives which should apply to them. So, for example, a company could set down as industrial relations objectives some of the following:

- harmonious working arrangements between the management, the unions and the workforce;

- optimal labour flexibility;

- the establishment of procedures which allow for grievances to be settled and disputes to be avoided;

- a commitment of all parties to high productivity, quality and profitability;

- an open policy for the dissemination of information to the workforce and from the workforce to management.

In an increasing number of employing organizations the basic objectives are fleshed out and publicized to the workforce in the form of a mission statement which can be discussed at different stages of implementation by the workforce before being distributed and put into practice.

Management style

It is impossible to talk with a high degree of accuracy about actual management styles. There are probably as many styles as there are managers! It is possible, however, to talk about 'ideal types' of management style. Indeed, to understand the purpose behind industrial relations strategies we need to understand the overall approach of the managers behind the development and implementation of these practices.

For many commentators, consideration of managerial style begins with the work of Alan Fox in the 1960s (Fox, 1969). Fox argued that two key managerial perspectives could be identified, respectively, the unitary and pluralistic. In the former perspective, management saw the goals of the organization as congruent, regardless of the position of the individual within it. Here, industrial conflict was avoidable and unnecessary:

> So far as employers and managers themselves are concerned, the analogy can be refined a little. The vision is closest to the professional football team, for here, combined with the team structure and its associated loyalties, one finds a substantial measure of managerial prerogative at the top in the persons of the manager, trainer, and board members. Team spirit and undivided management authority co-exist to the benefit of all.
>
> (Fox, 1969, p. 392)

The second frame of reference, the pluralistic, recognized that there was not one overriding consensual objective but a series (plurality) of objectives representing the interests of sectional groups:

> The full acceptance of the notion that an industrial organisation is made up of sectional groups with divergent interests involves also a full acceptance of the fact that degree of common purpose which can exist in industry is only of a very limited nature.
>
> (Fox, 1969, p. 393)

The acceptance of the spirit of pluralism was a feature of the thinking adopted by many employers in the 1970s and early 1980s. On the shop-floor and in the office, personnel specialists recognized, among other things: the role of the union, both officially and unofficially; the need for negotiation over a wide range of substantive and procedural matters; and the need to trade money for change rather than to expect it normatively from the workforce.

While pluralism as a concept can be given form in a number of interest groups, a number of commentators and, no doubt, more than a few managers, believed that for the more important issues, the interest groups were reduced to two: the management and the union. This is industrial relations thinking at its most basic.

> Trade unions are seen as the legitimate representative of labour and conflicts arising from the clash of interests are resolved, if possible, by bargaining and compromise, and if not, by the application of overt power. The need for mutually agreed solutions to conflictual issues is thus elevated as the central function of industrial relations through the institutionalization of conflict.
>
> (Purcell and Sisson, 1983, p. 113)

The unitary and pluralistic are by no means the only managerial frameworks (Palmer, 1987), but they have, perhaps, received the most attention. They are also capable of refinement and subdivision. Fox, in the 1970s, proffered a significant refinement of his thinking, arguing that even an application of a pluralistic *modus operandi* was, in fact, a unitary practice because of its acceptance of mutual existence rather than conquest (Fox, 1973). Interesting as this observation is, it does not alter the fact that pluralism and, in particular, the legitimacy of the union bargaining role became both ideologically and practically accepted by many employers through their personnel specialists in the years from 1966 until the early 1980s when new variants became more noticeable.

Employment relations thinking recognizes that a number of stakeholders exist in any organization, but the relevant practices play down the important role given to the unions in traditional industrial relations. Its style can, perhaps, be illustrated by the round table of consultation more than by the oblong table of industrial relations negotiation. Human resource management thinking takes this approach further by recognizing the concept of the stakeholder, but aiming to harness any differing interests strategically so that the overall business objectives are supported rather than being potentially impeded. Within this approach the role of the unions is somewhat less central than in traditional industrial relations thinking.

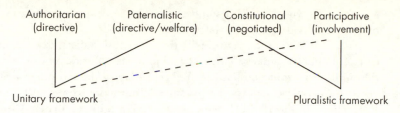

Figure 6.1 *Managerial styles (based on Poole, 1986).*

One rather simple depiction of the typical variants in style is seen in Figure 6.1. The authoritarian style is one where management rule by diktat. It would be unusual to find a union recognized in such an undertaking. Examples of a pure kind are not common, though Rainnie (1989) describes one or two in his study of small businesses, and other writers have cited the famous 1976 stoppage at the Grunwick photoprocessing plant as a reaction to such managerial autocracy (Rogaly, 1977).

The paternalistic style also embraces the unitary framework but is a softer expression of it. Here the employer adopts a more caring approach to his employees, utilizing a range of welfare and other benefits such as health care, good pensions and working conditions to create and cement a bond between the organization and the worker. This approach in its more traditional form tended to look inimically on union recognition also. In its pure form such a perspective could be seen historically in a number of US organizations, some building societies and some family-run businesses.

In recent years such an approach may well have been more complex and Purcell and Sisson utilize Fox's term 'sophisticated paternalists' to describe a more modern variation:

> Most of these enterprises but not all of them refuse to recognise trade unions. Their outward stance – certainly toward their employees – is essentially unitary. That is why they are grouped with the paternalists. But there is a crucial difference. The sophisticated paternalists do not take it for granted that their employees accept the company's objectives or automatically legitimise management decision-making; they spend considerable time and resources in ensuring that their employees have the right approach. Recruitment, selection, training, counselling, high pay and fringe benefits – these and other personnel policies are used to ensure that individual aspirations are mostly satisfied, that collective action is seen as unnecessary and inappropriate.
>
> (Purcell and Sisson, 1983, p. 114)

Examples of organizations espousing this type of approach could include some other US multinationals, such as Black and Decker, IBM and Kodak, and some long-standing UK employers including many large retailers. Such an approach would fit with some of those organizations preferring employment relations to an industrial relations approach.

The third group in Figure 6.1, the constitutionalists, gives considerable constitutional legitimacy to the role and practices of trade unions. Here again, the pure form would be hard to find nowadays. Though other writers have cited the American experience since President Roosevelt's New Deal Programme of the 1930s (Kochan *et al.*, 1986), a looser British variation has been well established since 1945, where employers recognize that certain rules and decisions will be made bilaterally, involving at least one but more typically a few unions. In the 1960s and 1970s such employers were well represented in the engineering industry and, particularly, in the motor manufacturing sectors of the economy.

Finally, we can consider the participative group of organizations, which contain some of the newer British greenfield site operations such as Coca-Cola/Schweppes, Nissan and Sanyo. They recognise trade unions and, to an extent, encourage their growth. Such organizations, however, see industrial relations as something in which the union machinery is involved but does not have a monopoly in terms of employee representation. Thus, systems of consultation and negotiation are constructed which involve different groups of employees and have roles for employee representatives rather than just shop stewards or full-time trade union officers. There may be a single union agreement but membership is not compulsory. In other words, the business recognizes just one union for all of its staff but does not pressurize them to join (which would now, in any event, be unlawful).

Such companies often utilize a vehicle such as a company council to formalize their industrial relations proceedings, where the flavour is very much the round table approach (Walton and McKersie's integrative bargaining, 1985). Komatsu has a company council which sits around a large round table for its meetings. Sanyo has a Sanyo Members Advisory Board, and Coca-Cola/Schweppes has a site council.

In this last type of approach HRM thinking would be at home. The organization understands that conflict of interest is natural – people problems will ensue even in the best run businesses. The approach, however, is to manage these problems effectively, partly by having the right sort of staff and the right working practices, but also by having a system of representation and, in particular, a system of communication which allow problems to be aired and solved at an early stage.

Consider the following case study based on extracts of the company council objectives for a major company.

CASE STUDY: *The objectives of the Council*

Under the terms of the Agreement between the company and the union, a Site Council is to be established with the aim of promoting effective communication and harmonious relations between the Company, its employees and the Union. It is intended that the Site Council will be an effective forum in which elected representatives of employees can discuss with representatives of the Company those matters which directly affect them. In so doing it is recognized that all concerned have a mutual interest in ensuring the prosperity of all employees. It is intended that the Council may discuss the following matters:

1. The Company's business, for example, quality, production levels, market share, profitability and investment, and in such matters will be a consultative forum.

2. Matters referred to it under the terms of the Procedure Agreement.

3. All negotiations on salaries and terms and conditions of employment for employees whose job titles are designated in Appendix 4. These will be conducted solely by separate meetings of the Council.

What such policies suggest is that industrial relations management recognizes the following:

- the contribution made by good industrial relations to the achievement of business objectives;

- the need to be proactive in the management of industrial relations; and

- the importance of an industrial relations strategy – of planning rather than fire-fighting.

In Figure 6.1 we considered one way of classifying management styles. Adherents of the pure traditional and paternalistic frameworks would probably be uninterested in achieving a change in the cost-effectiveness of their industrial relations, for the simple reason that by adhering to such an approach they would believe that they had already achieved all that was possible. It is in the other positions that management might well come to the conclusion that industrial relations can and should be more effectively managed. This is particularly likely with those organizations which have traditionally handled industrial relations in an *ad hoc* way.

As well as some changes in processes, such movements could well involve a shift in emphasis. As Sisson notes:

> The main emphasis is on management–employee relations rather than on management–trade union relations; and the objective is to maximise the commitment of employees through the adoption of organic and developed structures in which the individual is encouraged to develop the habits of self-discipline and initiative.
>
> (Sisson, 1989, p. 31)

Going down such a path might result in an organization moving steadily down to the participative end of the spectrum with emphasis on employees rather than unions; on communication; and on involvement in decision-making through greater joint consultation. This will not necessarily result in a marginalization of collective bargaining, rather the construction of a powerful adjunct to it (Marchington, 1989).

In the following section we will examine some of the developments in practices associated with cost-effective industrial relations and employment relations.

Industrial relations and employment relations strategies

A strategy is a campaign plan focusing on various approaches, issues and practices. If a manager is to have an industrial relations strategy the following areas should be carefully considered:

- recruitment patterns
- rewards and working systems
- communication systems (information flow)

Recruitment patterns

The importance of the right type of workforce is self-evident to any organization wishing to achieve its objectives. While this topic is dealt with in detail in Chapter 9, a number of issues related to it are central to industrial relations management and are thus mentioned here.

It is axiomatic that the type of workforce composition can affect the tenor of industrial relations. Certainly, it has been suggested with regard to greenfield site operations that a number of organizations recruited a sizeable proportion of their staff directly from the ranks of school leavers, as this allowed the organizations to inculcate shared values more easily, in that such new workers had no experience of other work cultures and union practices to draw upon. This was the case, for example, with NSK Bearings in the north-east of England for whom 70% of the start-up labour force were school leavers. Other organizations, while being careful about their recruitment practices, have not relied to the same extent on school leavers. Indeed, given the increasing requirement for technological skill and familiarity, some industrial experience has been a selection requirement for many jobs in companies like Komatsu, Nissan and Coca-Cola/Schweppes, though school leavers tend to be highly sought after in less technically intensive organizations like the retail and financial services sectors of the economy.

William Brown considers that the 1980s, unlike earlier decades, has been dominated by the employers' search for increased efficiency through flexibility (Brown, 1989). Such a trend achieved increased popularity with the publication in 1984 of Atkinson's ideas on the 'flexible firm' (Atkinson, 1984). In this, organizations were seen to be developing increased effectiveness through three areas:

- numerical flexibility in matters of employment contracts and working time,
- functional flexibility in working practices and skill levels, and
- financial flexibility in reward systems.

While Atkinson's model is generally regarded as an ideal rather than an actual form, it is evident that many business organizations, in both public and private sectors, have increased their flexibility in all three modes. The impact of this can be seen in the increases in productivity achieved in the United Kingdom in the 1980s compared to other industrialized countries.

Numerical flexibility involves using staff on different types of contracts and for different time-periods. Part-time employment is now quite prevalent, as is the use of subcontract labour for a variety of tasks, ranging from security to catering. It is also quite common for employers to retain a proportion of their workforce on fixed-term temporary contracts which may or may not be renewed, depending on the state of the market and/or the capability of the employee. Examination of the 1991 Labour Force Survey indicates that 1 453 000 people work on a temporary basis (5.8% of the workforce). This figure has increased steadily through the last decade, with 58% of these workers being female.

Such variety can give management greater control of staff numbers and deployment and can ease their industrial relations problems at times of staff reductions. It should be noted, however, that greater use of such numerical flexibility appears to be associated more with brownfield operations than with new start-ups.

As we move through the last decade of the century, British employers are operating against an employment backcloth characterized by:

- a large service sector component with manufacturing industry now representing only 23% of all jobs;
- an increasing proportion of female employees;
- a decline in young people entering the marketplace; and
- general recession with pockets of particularly high unemployment.

At the same time employers are taking more care than ever before to get their recruitment and development practices correct for the needs of the business, as Chapter 9 demonstrates.

Rewards and working systems

Collective bargaining as a practice dates back in some form or other to the emergence of the factory as a system of production. It is also an inevitable reflection of the growth pattern of trade unions. The pattern became centralized in the years surrounding the First World War, largely as a consequence of government policies for managing the economy. Relatedly, the reports of the Whitley committee, published in 1917, recommended the establishment of more widespread industry-type bargaining through a system of joint industrial councils in the private sector and similar bodies for areas of the public sector, such as the Health Service.

Looking back, it appears that while the system had its successes and while a number of joint industrial councils still operate today, much of the pre-eminence of this type of bargaining in matters of wage-fixing had been significantly reduced by the end of the 1950s as companies and trade unions participated in what some observers saw as a 'drift of earnings away from wage rates and the growing ineffectiveness of disputes machinery' (Donovan Report, 1968). Indeed, the economic and industrial relations consequences of this earnings drift were seen by the Donovan Commission as one of its major areas of concern, leading to the key recommendation that company directors should undertake reviews of the quality of industrial relations practices in their organizations, looking among other things at:

- collective bargaining machinery
- grievance procedures
- recognition of the role of the shop steward
- redundancy agreements
- disciplinary procedures
- joint discussions on matters of safety.

The report's recommendations on bargaining structure, coming at a time of comparative full employment and increasing company size, were persuasive for many employers, and the 1970s saw the development of a new degree of corporatism in bargaining, with company-wide policies and single-employer bargaining structures becoming far more widespread.

As analysis of a 1980 workplace survey noted:

> The most striking finding (of this chapter) has been that of the rise in significance of single-employer bargaining for manual workers.
>
> (Brown, 1981, p. 24)

There is no doubt that a mini-revolution has taken place in the nature of reward schemes and working practices in recent years with management seeking and often succeeding in designing very high levels of flexibility into them. In particular, three developments should be noted. These are: the increased functional flexibility of skills and working arrangements; the application of performance-related pay and profit bonuses; and the growth of employee share ownership. These can be examined in turn.

Increased **functional flexibility** can be achieved in a number of ways: by improving the skill level of key staff (multiskilling); by extending the range of tasks performed by workgroups; and by negotiating the removal of lines of job demarcation with the trade unions. The object behind these steps is that of developing a more fluid, skilled and (often) reduced workforce.

Thus, for example, comes the following extract from the Nissan (GB) working agreement:

> To ensure the fullest use of facilities and manpower there will be complete flexibility and mobility of employees.
>
> It is agreed that changes in technology, process and practices will be introduced and that such changes will affect both productivity and manning levels.
>
> To undertake such flexibility and change employees will undertake training for all work as required by the company.
>
> (Wickens, 1987)

At an older plant, Colgate-Palmolive in Salford, management and unions agreed a series of key working changes as a part of the 1988–89 pay agreement. For agreeing to these changes the workforce received an additional 3.72% of pay. The principles that management wished to achieve included:

> the removal of artificial demarcations between crafts, subject to individual capability and safety requirements;
>
> co-operation within the consultative process to establish training programmes to enhance craft skills; and
>
> co-operation with the implementation of the training programmes.
>
> (Industrial Relations Review and Report, 1989b)

Many such agreements appeared in the 1980s and early 1990s in the United Kingdom and across the rest of Europe. A number of agreements of this kind were based on the particular plant or workplace but some are industry-wide, such as the 1983 agreement between the British Printing Industry Federation and the print union SOGAT, which included clauses on limiting demarcation in the workplace, local deals on hours and shift patterns, and a guarantee of no redundancies arising out of changed working practices.

As well as increasing operating efficiency, functional flexibility can help management achieve other benefits in the area of industrial relations and HRM:

- It can work to increase the notion of goal consensus and 'soften' some of the sharper edges of pluralism.

- It can be used in tandem with a harmonization programme to achieve a 'single status' workforce.

- It can help improve communication channels.

The further area of flexibility relating to reward and working systems is that of pay and, in particular, trends in the last few years which have seen the introduction of more individualism (Brewster, 1989) in matters of pay distribution, often through the vehicle of performance or merit-related pay. Brown sees the successful management of pay as a situation in which:

> . . . an organization requires an internal structure of rewards that is consistent and acceptable to those covered and that if this is achieved the level of rewards need only be kept roughly comparable with those provided by other employers.
>
> (Brown, 1989, p. 267)

Within this statement Brown is linking three issues: equity as perceived by the workforce, the concept of some sort of 'going rate', and the workplace. These issues are vital to the successful management of pay and they will be dealt with in some detail in Chapter 11. They need, however, some discussion here also. When a union submits a pay claim a number of elements may be cited in support. These may include:

- the rate of price inflation,
- the level of company profits,
- payment for increases in flexibility and productivity,
- the national or industry 'going rate',
- reference back to a base year for catching up, and
- comparisons with other groups in the workplace.

While it is true to say that many union negotiators still regularly use notions of the 'going rate' in their claims in the 1990s, one of the trends of pay bargaining in the last decade has been the increased focus by management on the ability or inability of the organization to pay. This trend has often been accompanied by another, related one, the further decentralization of the bargaining structures to which we alluded earlier. Brewster explains the rationale behind these trends thus:

> Prior to the 1980s it would have seemed idiosyncratic to write so much about managerial policies in industrial relations with so little mention of trade unions. That it is relevant to do so now reflects another key element of cost-effective strategies: managerial attempts to individualize and localize industrial relations. The rationale for such policies is to avoid the errors of the past.
>
> (Brewster, 1989, p. 87)

Brewster is referring here to the involvement of external union officials and external comparisons in traditional wage bargaining. What management have been seeking to do by localizing bargaining is to create a bargaining mode which is more responsive in general and, in particular, relates to:

- company profitability,
- local labour markets, and
- different product market conditions.

Additionally, localized bargaining allows management to negotiate more easily on matters of flexibility and should assist the development of shared values between the workforce and management. Local bargaining is also of relevance should an industrial dispute emerge, as under the various employment acts of the 1980s, lawful industrial action can only be taken against the employees' own employer, with picketing protection being similarly limited to 'at or near the workers' own place of work'. Strands of localized bargaining have appeared in the United Kingdom in all types of organizations from Courtaulds to British Steel as well as in many parts of the public sector. ACAS, among many commentators, feel that in the United Kingdom, at least, this trend is here to stay:

> Many organisations which survived the traumatic years of the early 1980s began to move away from centralised collective bargaining to arrangements which, they felt, could allow pay and terms and conditions to be matched more closely to the circumstances of their particular companies. Similarly, larger organisations which had previously relied on company-wide bargaining often moved to arrangements centred on divisions, plants and even departments.
>
> (ACAS, 1989, p. 11)

What such managements have been able to do, therefore, is to persuade union negotiators and workforces alike that the local level is the sensible level and that local pay systems can be fair and valuable.

Management have also, in a sizeable number of organizations, persuaded their workforces that the traditional 'across the board' pay agreement was outmoded and that paying more for greater skill, effort and competence was sensible and fair. For many union officers such an argument is not immediately persuasive, breaking away, as it does, from one of the Webbs' founding principles of unionism, 'the common rule' (Webb and Webb, 1920). Nevertheless, a combination of management proactivity and their recently increased bargaining power saw the implementation of **performance-related pay systems** in a wide range of organizations by the end of the 1980s. Such schemes are often linked to formal systems of appraisal, as in the National and Provincial Building Society. In their agreement the amount of the payroll 'pot' was to be decided through negotiation with the recognized union. Each member of staff would be appraised formally by his or her manager and the actual amount of increase given to the worker was decided via the application of a matrix to the result of the appraisal and the pre-existing position of the employee on the salary band for their job. Such a system allows management some degree of flexibility in rewarding staff but at the same time the matrix provides a minimum level of increase. Thus, for example, a worker appraised as 'fully competent' could receive, say, between 9% and 12% but would *have* to receive at least a 9% increase.

A survey of organizations using performance-related pay in 1989 (Industrial Relations Review and Report, 1989a, p. 2) suggests at least 10 reasons for its introduction:

- improving performance
- changing corporate culture
- responding to skill shortages
- replacing outmoded pay structures
- offering employees the chance to earn more money
- reducing collective bargaining strength
- lowering employees' pay expectations
- making managers manage
- responding to political initiatives
- keeping up with the competition.

The Woolwich Building Society negotiated a two-stage pay increase with its in-house union in October 1989 to run until April 1991. As well as an across the board increase, a further 4% of the payroll was to be distributed on a performance basis following appraisals.

Data from a 1988 survey by ACAS demonstrates that performance-related pay is now spread well beyond the financial services sector. From a survey of 664 managers from a wide variety of industries they note:

> About a third of respondents had merit pay schemes, with three quarters covering non-manuals only and about a fifth covering both manuals and non-manuals. The incidence of merit payments is reported to have increased by 25% over the last three years with most of the growth taking place in the service sector.
>
> (ACAS, 1988, p. 7)

This type of payment policy is now well established in American companies like Ford, in Canadian ones such as Massey-Ferguson and in many European ones.

As can be seen in Chapter 11, recent years have seen some **growth in profit bonuses and in share ownership** by employees. These schemes can also serve to increase links between the management and the workforce and could aid the process of goal congruency. They appear to have particular relevance for attempts to cement a lasting relationship between the individual and the business, in that the former is seen to benefit directly and financially from the performance of the latter. For this reason such schemes are worth considering by managers seeking to improve the quality of industrial relations and workplace relationships in the longer term.

Communication systems

The achievement of good communications should always be of the highest importance in matters of HRM and the topic is discussed in detail in Chapter 7. Industrial relations is, of course, no exception to this axiom. As management have been seeking to inculcate or develop changes in practices, communication systems have, in many organizations, been reviewed and redesigned.

This has been done in a variety of ways. Some systems are merely one-way dissemination vehicles, such as the typical models of team briefing, in which small groups are briefed regularly about production and other related matters. Other systems allow for a two-way process with ideas and problems emanating both from the workforce to management and vice versa. Built into both types of system is a concern for production or service quality, with strong emphasis being placed on getting the product or service right from the outset, rather than inspecting for poor quality at a later stage. Thus, communication mechanisms can be used as part of a wider scheme for the management of quality, known in some organizations as total quality management or total quality product.

As with many other elements of an industrial relations or HRM strategy, effective communication schemes can often possess wider benefits for the organization beyond job quality:

- They can encourage initiative.
- They can demonstrate that all employees have ideas and are worth listening to.
- They can be used to promote single-status staffing.
- They can be of assistance in identifying talent for future development.

See, for example, the benefits cited by Lucas Industries (Industrial Relations Review and Report, 1989d, pp. 6–8) for their employee suggestion scheme, a further facet of communication:

> It improves morale
>   upward communication
>   team-work
>   identifies areas for improvement
>   improves customer relations
>   company's health and safety performance and results in
>   output improvement
>   (Extract from Lucas Industries Scheme)

There is a further advantage in effective management communications, which might not be particularly overtly stated by managers but is very real nevertheless. Where companies recognize trade unions (about 36% of the British workforce are members) it has often been the case that the union channels of communication via shop stewards and representatives have been most effective. Many managers can cite examples of finding out the decisions of senior management by talking to shop stewards. In such situations senior management had, in a *de facto* way, handed over responsibility for industrial relations communication to the union. Apart from the fact that such senior managers were failing to do their job properly, it was also possible that the interpretation of policy or events as conveyed by the union machinery would not be the same interpretation as viewed by management. No doubt aided by the favourable level of bargaining power accruing to them in the 1980s and early 1990s, many managements have been keen to build up new types of communication systems to enable them to communicate directly with their employees, rather than just with the union officers.

CASE STUDY: *BT's approach to communications (see also Industrial Relations Review and Report, 1989c)*

BT (UK) is one of four divisions of British Telecom. It has 207 000 employees. Following a 1986 attitude survey of its staff, the organization became very concerned about the quality of its communications. To improve the situation it has given a high priority to effective communication channels. It has set up an employee communications unit (ECU) to coordinate the initiative. The ECU is keen to develop good practice and is utilizing a series of guidelines for use with these channels. The channels include:

- attitude surveys
- team briefings/meetings

- the 'open line' facility
- the 'walking the job' initiative
- use of videos
- publications
- direct mail
- training

Conclusion

Although this chapter has been concerned in the main with industrial relations in the organization, little has been said about British trade unions. This does not mean that the unions should be ignored. They have had a miserable last few years, seeing their membership fall by nearly 4 million from the 1979 peak of 13.5 million. They have had to live with what they see as a virulently anti-union government and have had most of the legal freedoms they enjoyed radically constrained by legislation. Nevertheless, the unions are still here. Several TUC unions have now developed a softer image to attract and retain new types of member, where the emphasis is on financial benefits and welfare rather than on policies. By 1993 their membership haemorrhage has slowed somewhat. They are more popular in opinion polls than they have been for years, and even in years where management have enjoyed a strong position there is little evidence of de-recognition (Claydon, 1989).

It is likely that for many organizations industrial relations for the rest of the 1990s will still mean dealing with trade unions and trade union members. Thus, management would be well advised to negotiate constructively with unions rather than attempt to discount them.

The way management seek to manage will depend to a significant degree on their objectives and their style. It is the case, of course, that the style of industrial relations management of the 1990s will be varied, as at any time, but it is likely that many organizations will seek to adopt styles and practices more akin to what has been referred to as the 'participative' rather than the pure 'constitutional', particularly where the industrial relations activities are seen as part of wider strategic approaches to HRM.

In this case management will seek to dilute the pure type of 'constitutionalism' by bringing in practices which represent more integrative rather than distributive modes of dealing. Local flexibility bargaining, good two-way communication systems and financial rewards tied to effort can all help to do this. At the same time all of these areas must be linked to recruitment and development.

It is likely that management will increasingly recognize the importance of trying to achieve cost-effective industrial relations by planning, by determining objectives and by the development of a medium- to long-term strategy. In the last few years, we have seen industrial relations managed more effectively in employer terms in many organizations. The concept of cost-effectiveness has been articulated as a key objective. We have examined the elements that go towards the achievement of this goal and have linked these to a wider, more embracing policy for HRM.

However, it should be remembered that while many aspects of industrial relations have tended to be culturally specific in that they are particular to one country, other trends might serve to loosen this over time. For example, as has already been seen in Chapter 3, in a single European market with its interchange of employees and organizations, such differences could well become less noticeable in attitude and practices. This will also be affected by the continual transnational investment patterns of big corporations, be they American, Japanese or European. One early signpost of this harmonization will be the impact of the European Social Charter on employers and employees in member states in 1993 onwards.

Good industrial relations has always been important to management and employees alike. It is likely that its importance has never been higher to those organizations seeking to achieve more cost-effective working systems and a more strategic, integrative approach to HRM.

PART 2

Human Resource Strategies in the Workplace

7 Communicating organizational vision, goals and human resource strategy

8 Achieving equality of treatment and opportunity in the workplace

9 The strategic management of recruitment and selection

10 Performance management: its role and methods in human resource strategy

11 Choosing and using relevant financial reward systems

12 Developing people – for whose bottom line?

7

Communicating organizational vision, goals and human resource strategy

Stephen Pain

By the end of this chapter the reader will:

1. understand how communication techniques can support the strategy development process;

2. understand how effective two-way communications can help to make strategy 'happen' and to achieve commitment of employees to the human resource mission and goals;

3. be able to identify ways in which communication processes can facilitate and help to secure organizational change.

Communicating the organizational vision and goals

In Chapters 1 and 2 the issues involved in developing an overall vision, mission and strategy for an organization and of producing a human resource strategy aligned with business goals, were identified and analysed. It will by now be clear that if organizations are to survive in increasingly unstable environments, they must have a clear view of what business they are and should be in and of the major organizational pressure points related to delivering to their customers what they have promised.

The main message of this chapter is that a mission statement is only an initial step towards achieving the organization's vision and goals. In the same way, formulating human resource mission and strategy is but the start of a long process in which success will depend, *inter alia*, on the communication of that strategy to everyone in the business in such a way as to ensure that its implications at the levels of units, teams and individuals are fully understood, accepted and acted upon. People must be able to see, also, that human resource strategy and plans are feasible given the internal organizational environment within which they have to operate – the structure and culture which will either release or inhibit people's commitment, effort and performance. Of course, communication activity is a support function: it cannot of itself achieve organizational goals, but the principles and techniques it utilizes can be mobilized to secure support among employees for those goals, and can also provide important feedback information upon which future policies and strategies can in turn be based.

Reconciling organizational and individual needs

One of the main issues in communication strategy is how to discover and reconcile the needs and goals of the corporate organization on the one hand and of groups and individuals within it on the other, This, of course, is a core part of management's function:

> Getting employee communication right – that is, making it effective for both the organization and for its employees – means doing a number of things well and doing them simultaneously. That is why many people working in this field are now talking of employee communication as an integral part of the management process.
>
> (Arnott, 1987)

Management's communication task encompasses the need to ensure that information is received by managers as well as being transmitted by them:

> It is unfair to expect a company's personnel to become more creative and generate more ideas if the organization is unable or unwilling to provide a facilitating communication system. . . . Ideas are like gold dust and if the system is incapable of catching each one of them and evaluating them, the organization is the loser.
>
> (Majaro, 1988)

It is not the job of management to generate all the ideas about mission, goals and strategies, or to interpret their communication task as one of passing on the message. They must set up the kind of two-way communications systems and procedures that will ensure that people can question and give their own reactions to those ideas, and that ultimately their ideas can be translated into working reality.

Arnott shows, at a conceptual level, the importance of using similarities and differences between organizational and individual needs to guide communications strategy in the workplace. Bringing about a closer integration of the individual and the workplace is one of the greatest challenges facing human resource professionals.

The concept of ownership

If we accept the validity of Drucker's point (1989) that whatever gives access to livelihood, status and position in society can be considered as 'property' to which rights are attached, then the concept of **ownership** suggests a range of criteria for assessing how far the needs and interests of each party to the employment contract are being or can be met. Thus for an individual employee, one way of assessing how 'good' is a particular employer would be for that employee to ask: 'How much can I own? How much am I allowed to own?' Answers may be found in the extent to which they can participate in the company's share option scheme – thus enabling them to own part of the business; in the kind of decisions they are allowed to make, and the extent and nature of authority they are given; in how far they are enabled to 'take a good idea and run with it'; and on how far they will be recognized for the ownership of particular projects and rewarded accordingly (an issue which is surfacing in many performance-related pay schemes where rewards go to individuals rather than to the whole team that 'owns' a project, or to the manager of those whose effort has ensured the achievement of a unit's targets but not to those employees themselves (see Chapter 6)).

So it can be argued that ownership, in this widest sense, is a key to motivation, and therefore an issue that must be of major concern in any decision about how best to communicate strategy to people and win their commitment to it.

The concept of the good employer

There is another dimension to individual needs: that of ethics, and the concept of the responsible company and the **good employer**. One of the emerging themes in HRM literature is that of corporate citizenship, a subtle change in organizational climate generally from 'profit no matter what' to 'profit with a conscience'. Although the whole notion is more advanced in the United States than in the United Kingdom, corporate responsibility to the customer, to the supplier, to employees and their families, to the potential recruit, to competitors (as the BA versus Branson case in 1993, referred to in Chapter 2, demonstrated), and to the local, national, or even global community is increasingly on the boardroom agenda. That it is there is clear recognition that such issues can have serious implications for the image and profitability of the business; and that conscious development of networking with key internal and external stakeholders in the business is 'good for business' but can only work if it recognizes the major concerns of those stakeholders. Thus a board may now have to pay particular attention to questions such as: 'What does it mean to be an equal opportunity employer?' (Chapter 8); 'How much, if anything, do we invest in developing greener technologies to protect the environment? How much and what kind of contribution do we make to local communities? How far do we go in providing welfare facilities for our employees?'

In a growing number of organizations, especially those international and global companies whose operations have in so many ways profound effects on the physical and social environment with which they interact, the human resource director must consider how HRM mission, goals and strategy can accommodate in measurable ways the concept of the responsible company and the good employer. Moreover, the employer must not just be good by his or her own definition, but must be seen to be 'good' by the fragmented communities within and outside the organization through which and in which it operates, recruits and promotes.

As Chapter 9 shows, recruitment is an area of HRM which is particularly vulnerable to pressures from society. It is also one where communications can help to identify what it is that constitutes a good employer for different communities, and to promote the organization in that light. One of the UK's major employers, BET, the specialist services company, is well aware of the need to be seen externally as well as internally as a good employer. BET has many businesses which operate in many different markets. Its ability, therefore, to attract, motivate and retain people who have the skills the company needs depends on an understanding of precisely what is important to those working in particular industry segments. Only then can relevant recruitment policies be devised, and their likely impact on other areas of HRM such as reward systems and training and development policies be carefully assessed.

CASE STUDY: *Defining the characteristics of the 'good employer' at BET*

■ **Background**

BET needs to be able to identify what exactly it is that, for employees in its different businesses – or indeed at different levels and in different parts of each business – would make BET appear a 'good employer'. The human resource professional must therefore create opportunities for employees to contribute their views on the matter, and actively involve them in the process.

■ **Identifying the characteristics**

The process can in theory take many forms: for example, informal meetings with employees, group discussions, structured questionnaires. The aim in every case is to find out much more about the employees who are attracted to and work in various parts of the company.

At BET, research encompassing all these methods was carried out among employees in its employment services business (BET Personnel Services). In the following figures, the shaded areas represent the views of those employees; the solid areas represent statistical averages in similar businesses collected by the external research specialist across a range of similar businesses.

In Figure 7.1, the factors shown are those assessed by the employees as most important to them in their current jobs. Note, for the BET employees, the importance of opportunities for advancement; of pay; and of an interesting and enjoyable job. Note also how many of the factors relate to management style rather than to policies, systems or procedures, and how employees valued praise, recognition for effort and a feeling of accomplishment. Contrast with these the relatively low rating – especially compared with industry norms – for job security, a factor which management often assumes is all-important.

Looking at Figure 7.2, despite the fact that many of those working in employment services are female, the findings challenge widely held assumptions about the kind of fringe benefits women most desire. Those traditionally associated with working women scored very low indeed, with opportunities for job sharing scraping in with only 1% and the provision of creches and

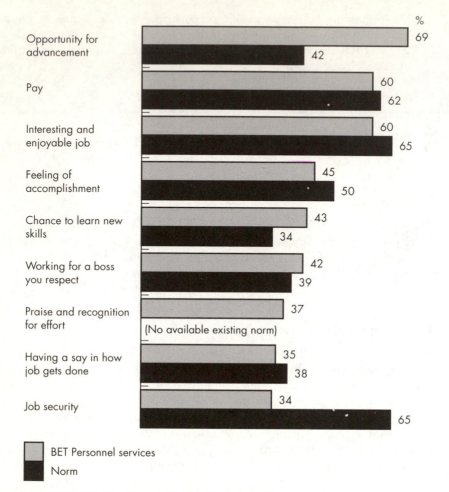

%

Opportunity for advancement	69 / 42
Pay	60 / 62
Interesting and enjoyable job	60 / 65
Feeling of accomplishment	45 / 50
Chance to learn new skills	43 / 34
Working for a boss you respect	42 / 39
Praise and recognition for effort	37 / (No available existing norm)
Having a say in how job gets done	35 / 38
Job security	34 / 65

☐ BET Personnel services
■ Norm

Figure 7.1 *Most important factors in a job.*

other facilities also given little importance, On the other hand, in this fast-moving sales environment, the most valued fringe benefits are incentives and immediate rewards such as bonus schemes, praise for a job well done, and other forms of recognition and lifestyle benefits.

All these insights are confirmed in Figure 7.3, where respondents were asked to provide a list, unprompted, of what it was that, to them, typified a 'good employer'. Highest on the list came the provision of career opportunities, followed closely by fair pay, and then by good training.

Such employee profiling has limited value unless done in the context of a comparative exercise. In this case research also identified that the profile of women working in employment services was very different from, say,

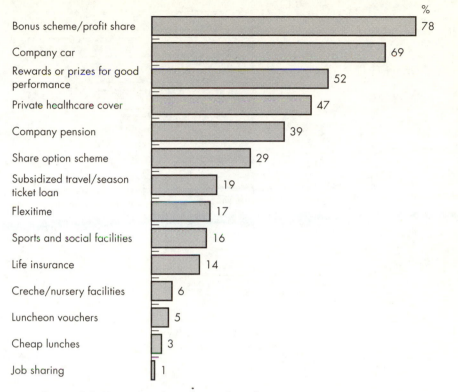

Bonus scheme/profit share — 78
Company car — 69
Rewards or prizes for good performance — 52
Private healthcare cover — 47
Company pension — 39
Share option scheme — 29
Subsidized travel/season ticket loan — 19
Flexitime — 17
Sports and social facilities — 16
Life insurance — 14
Creche/nursery facilities — 6
Luncheon vouchers — 5
Cheap lunches — 3
Job sharing — 1

Figure 7.2 *Most important fringe benefits*.

that of women working in ICS's Model Branch. For instance, women in employment services were mainly young pre-marrieds who enjoyed the pace and opportunity for advancement that a high-pressure sales environment can offer. Not surprisingly, therefore, they seemed most motivated by instant reward for success in the form of incentives and bonuses.

This case study demonstrates the value of involving employees actively in a communication exercise whose aim is to elicit their views and perceptions about an issue of crucial importance to the company – what seem to be the characteristics it should develop in order to be perceived in its typical labour market as a good employer. The data also enabled the identification of the kind of human resource policies that BET, as a good employer, would need to implement on recruitment, deployment and organization of people and on their training, development and rewards.

Many of the initiatives that are inspired by employees as a result of this kind of communications exercise can often be introduced at little or no cost to the company in terms of improved systems or facilities; but they do have

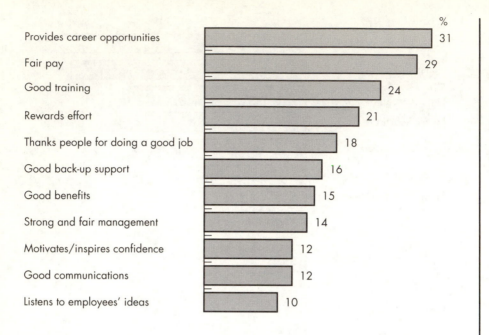

%

Provides career opportunities 31
Fair pay 29
Good training 24
Rewards effort 21
Thanks people for doing a good job 18
Good back-up support 16
Good benefits 15
Strong and fair management 14
Motivates/inspires confidence 12
Good communications 12
Listens to employees' ideas 10

Figure 7.3 *What constitutes a good employer?*

clear implications for management style and behaviour, as well as for reward strategies, and those implications need to be carefully considered.

To summarize the issues so far raised in this section about the reconciliation of organizational and individual needs:

- There must be two-way communications systems and procedures in place that will ensure that corporate goals and the strategies to which they give rise take adequately into account the needs and interests of individuals in the workplace.

- The tensions inherent in the rapidly changing nature of the employment relationship in many organizations must be identified so that appropriate human resource strategies are implemented to tackle them with outcomes viewed as positive by individuals as well as by the organization.

- The concepts of job property rights and of the good employer must be taken into account in human resource strategy.

- Human resource policies will increasingly be needed that will convincingly demonstrate the company's acceptance of its social responsibilities to its internal and external communities, stakeholders and competitors.

Reconciling needs and goals in the decentralized organization

What many see as a new age of individualism, bringing with it a need to adapt to a great diversity of values, expectations and demands, places a burden on any organization, particularly one that is large and/or complex in its mission and tasks. At any one time such an organization will comprise a diversity of occupations, backgrounds and skills in the service of a variety of customers who are often in different industry sectors and geographical locations. There may, in addition, be intranational and international cultural differences, preferences, styles and motivations – in fact, so many variables that it is unlikely that, collectively, the organization can manage them effectively. Yet if the organization fails to create an environment which is receptive to those differences, particularly at the individual level, it is likely that individuals will either leave or withdraw any but minimal effort, perceiving that in real terms they have no ownership of anything they value.

Nowhere are these kinds of differences and pressures more clearly illustrated than in the decentralized organization (see Chapters 2 and 4), where in addition the strategies of individual business units may have to be different in kind from the general push of strategy at the centre (Miller, 1989; Purcell, 1989). Nowhere is it clearer that the concept of organizational unity must give way to the concept of organizational pluralism. But how?

The significance of the issues we are now discussing is that, as the Multichem case study in Chapter 4 strikingly illustrated, there *is* a pluralist dynamic, and that it is driven most strongly at the level of business units in the decentralized organization by pressures from business strategy, from employees, and from the market. In order to maximize performance the centre must accept that it needs to give up control in one sense in order to maintain control in another – the conundrum of 'tight/loose' already discussed in Chapters 1 and 2. The centre must therefore address the issue of what, collectively, it wants to 'own' before it can start to communicate business and human resource strategy across the organization. This means finding answers to questions such as:

- What business are we, should we, be in?
- Is senior management really willing to change and to make the changes needed in order to achieve that goal?
- What is the most appropriate form of organizational structure, and how can it best be differentiated to suit the needs and strategies of the units?
- Which functions should be carried out at the centre, and which at the level of the business units?
- What are the main pressures, at that level, on managers, on teams, and on individuals and what, therefore, are their main preoccupations in the workplace?

- What should our HRM strategy and policies be to support the goals of the changing organization, and how can they be communicated in order to secure effective implementation in the workplace?

To create the environment that can cope with the organized fragmentation that is required by decentralization, the centre must position itself as enabler not autocrat, as support function as well as control function. In the language of post-modernism (Clegg, 1990), although expressing in simplistic terms what is in reality a profoundly complex set of organizational processes, the centre must seek to encourage networks which can exist independently of the centre. As long as the network is active, credible and fed continually with the kind of messages that express the needs and goals of the centre in a language most relevant to the needs and goals of the units, so will those message be received, understood, and acted upon.

This means that local managers must have the authority to act in the way they think fit, since they are closest to changes in markets, customer demands and the labour markets from which they draw their employees. That leaves the centre with a clutch of enabling roles and with the task of formulating and communicating overall organization strategy in ways that will ensure its effective implementation at unit levels. Many organizations have already experienced this shift of direct responsibility for the running of the business to a wide group of competent managers, most notably some of the retail banks in the United Kingdom where accountability has been pushed further down the line to branch manager level and the culture is in the process of being changed from one which is procedure driven to one which is entrepreneurial, However, the processes involved are, as already noted and as explained in detail in Clegg (1990), immensely complicated: decentralization may be pushed too far, with the result that, rather than a satisfactory balance between 'tight' and 'loose' being found, there is (as has already been identified in Chapter 2) a damaging drift of units away from any meaningful relationship with the centre. At that point the centre may panic, draw in its power and resources, and reverse the decentralizing process. Then, if not long before then, communication can do little if anything to resolve the self-evident conflict in needs and issues of ownership between the corporate body and its constituent elements.

The following case study explains how BET tackled the problem of heightening awareness of the company as a whole in a decentralized business and how it communicated its corporate strategy to its widely dispersed workforces. The study lacks the analytical depth of the Multichem case study in Chapter 4; however, its purpose is different. It simply seeks to explain the rationale behind the company's communication strategy at different points in time, and the communication methods it used, thus illustrating some of the theoretical points made so far in this chapter.

CASE STUDY: *Communicating corporate strategy at BET*

■ BET: Vision, mission and strategy

BET has singlemindedly pursued its vision of becoming the leading provider of specialist services to industry, commerce, construction and public sectors since the early 1980s. During that time the company has undertaken an extensive acquisition and divestment programme. The transformation has been supported by a vigorous, integrated range of internal communication activities designed to promote BET to its 100 000-plus employees as one company providing a whole range of specialist services under very different but strong trading names.

Once the businesses that BET had identified as crucial to its long-term vision had been acquired, the strategic emphasis shifted to one of making those businesses work, often together, to achieve above-average levels of growth for their respective sector.

This emphasis on organic growth involved an acceleration of certain entrepreneurial principles: restructuring shortened the lines of communication, cross-marketing activity between operating companies was encouraged and rewarded, and networks independent of the centre were facilitated. A new atmosphere of openness characterized communication activity.

■ BET's communication strategy and initiatives

Communication strategy aimed to get across to all BET's stakeholders the message about the possibilities for the support services sector of the economy. It was particularly important to communicate effectively with employees in order to win their understanding and commitment given the very high rate of acquisition and disposal activity. The channels of communication included events, presentations, high visibility of the chief executive at regional meetings and direct contact with managers face to face, a company newspaper, a video, management bulletins, and corporate TV and press advertisements. The channels themselves are not important in strategic terms: what is important are results achieved in relation to the strategic objective, and lessons learned for the future.

Any transformation or reorientation towards a new management style brings with it uncertainty and, commonly, either opposition or at best a 'wait and see' attitude among employees – the 'organizational inertia' already discussed in Chapter 2 and illustrated in Chapter 4. But with a multifaceted programme of two-way communications which included events involving all the BET stakeholders – customers, employees, local communities, investors

– and programmes where people could get personally involved, an environment was being created where contacts could be made and ideas could be shared to a far greater extent than had ever happened before in the company.

■ The management survey

Late in 1989 a management survey was launched at BET – the third such exercise in three years. It was conducted among BET's top 2500 managers in the areas where BET had concentrated the development of its operations: the United Kingdom, continental Europe and North America. One of the main thrusts of business strategy had been to move away from its former conglomerate status and to reposition itself as a clearly identifiable service business. A key aim of the survey was, therefore, how to discover how far managers perceived BET in that way.

The questions managers were asked focused on BET as the parent company: its perceived qualities, identity and capacity for adding value to their own operations. Responses revealed a profound shift in managers, who clearly no longer saw BET as a conglomerate. The responses also identified the importance, in achieving that shift, of the communication programme which involved a major advertising campaign: reaction to that programme and to an associated new corporate identity scheme was positive.

Here, then, were the first signs of the development of a new culture characterized by a real sense of belonging to and active involvement with the changed organization of BET. Financial involvement had already been promoted a few years previously with the introduction of an employee share option scheme. What the 1989 survey revealed was avowed support for a company which was seen as making every effort to give its people a feeling of identification with the parent company and, through that, of status in the particular communities in which they worked. Figures 7.4 and 7.5 show some of the responses made in relation to questions about BET's corporate identity.

For an employee working in a company owned by BET there is a need for identification at two levels: that of the employing and that of the parent company. It was always a priority in BET to promote overall strategy to employees while also preserving among employees the strong trading identities of the indivtual operating subsidiaries to which they belong. The survey revealed positive trends here: there was indeed a strong sense of loyalty and identification with employees' own companies, but there was also a recognition of the benefits of belonging to a much larger organization with its own primary values (Figure 7.5a).

Managers were also aware of the marketing benefits of being part of BET: there were more possibilities perceived for cross-marketing opportunities with businesses within BET and additional credibility when dealing with existing and new customers (Figure 7.5b).

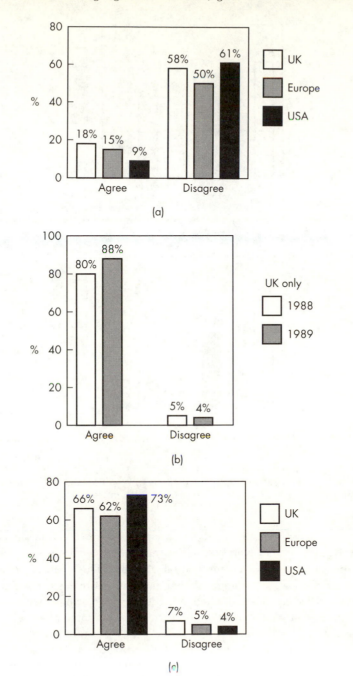

Figure 7.4 *The BET management survey – Part 1: (a) BET is just a conglomerate; (b) BET should continue to advertise to raise its profile with customers; (c) we could make more use of the BET corporate identity.*

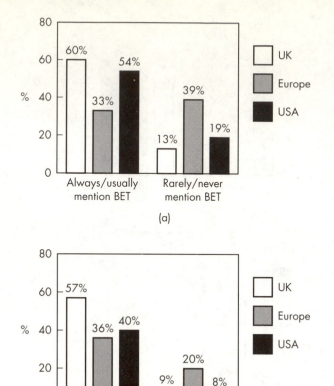

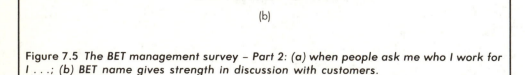

Figure 7.5 *The BET management survey – Part 2: (a) when people ask me who I work for I . . .; (b) BET name gives strength in discussion with customers.*

Looking at attitudes across different countries, those of managers in the United Kingdom and North America appeared generally more positive than those of managers in continental Europe. This seemed to validate BET's communication strategy at that particular time, since it had been specifically directed at the United Kingdom and North America, leaving operations in continental Europe in the main for a later phase of communication activity.

The 1989 survey therefore provided strong evidence that BET was making real progress in its communication aim of creating the perception of a specialist services company and of providing a strong corporate identity or framework within which its companies could operate. Clearly, it had decided what business it was in and had involved its employees in understanding the implications of that for the business as a whole and for their own operations within it.

■   **The challenge of fragmentation**

At this point the communication task became more challenging. Thus far, at corporate level, communication was organized within the context of the organization as a whole. The problems of increasing fragmentation within the business sector had yet to be tackled.

This, together with a switch in strategic emphasis for the organization, signalled a change in its approach to human resource and related communication strategy. Having largely completed the acquisition and disposal programme, the long-term objective now became one of growth. That meant understanding each of the businesses in more detail, particularly in relation to their markets and customers, and the needs, motivations and expectations of the people who are attracted to work in certain industries. Strategy, in these respects, shifted from macro- to micro-preoccupations and embraced what is often referred to as 'internal marketing'.

Management's communication tasks

Whether in the centralized or decentralized organization it is managers who carry the main burden of representing the interests of the business, either geographically or by sector or both, depending on the size and scope of operations. The aim and responsibility of the centre is to educate, train and motivate their managers to live and breathe strategy to the point where, because they truly own it, they believe in it and can communicate it effectively to their people. If they do come to feel that they own the strategy of the organization in this way, and if they can be encouraged and rewarded for acting in ways that underwrite that ownership, they will carry more conviction with their people who, in turn, are therefore more likely to support the strategy. In addition, there is likely to be a greater consistency in strategy and its implementation in the workplace that will help to ensure sustained support. In the case of human resource strategy, this should lead to greater coherence and integration of the various elements of the human resource 'wheel' which, as has already been seen in Chapter 2, appears to be essential to the effective implementation of that strategy throughout the organization.

What, then, are managers' main communication tasks? Management style, behaviour and action are themselves the most telling form of communication, and in that sense communication is a process which need not be costly. It has little to do with marketing and materials, everything to do with the ways in which managers manage. However, to say that communication is simply a matter of a manager doing his or her job is misleading: there must be a clear and accurate knowledge of what that job is, of the overall goals and strategy of the company, of how the manager's operations must fit into and contribute towards the achievement of that strategy, and of the kind of messages that must be communicated – and to whom.

In developing and communicating human resource strategies, the human resource professional – or the manager responsible for that function – must recognize the need to reconcile the interests of individuals, teams and their managers, taking them out of their 'boxes' and helping them to interact as a cohesive unit.

The BET case study throws particular light on the ways in which communication strategy can provide crucial data on whether or not the parent company has successfully managed to overcome some of the problems of 'tight/loose' discussed already in Chapter 2. As the organization as a whole became more decentralized, a similar process was introduced at the business-unit level. Now let us look at one particular process in a BET business unit called Initial Contract Services (ICS), a market leader in the contract cleaning industry. Our aim is to show how, in selected branches within that company, crucial communication tasks of managers and human resource professionals were tackled. The process called Model Branch that was undertaken by ICS in order to address some of the human resource issues impacting on its business demonstrates the complexity of the relationships between individuals and their organization, and shows how a business can actively address the pluralist environment in which it finds it must operate. The case also exemplifies a company attempting to acknowledge and deal with the challenges facing the human resource function already discussed in this chapter.

CASE STUDY: *Model Branch at ICS*

Model Branch is about a process. The home of that process is not in the quality department, the internal communication or internal marketing department, the strategic planning function or indeed in any other discrete part of the company. It embraces all departments and is, at its simplest, good management practice. The key to its success is that it identifies and then uses to its advantage one crucial factor: the development and maintenance of effective personal networks between customers, employees and the communities in which they operate, while it also underwrites that activity by a careful blend of leadership and teamwork.

■ Background to ICS and the cleaning industry

Contract cleaning is a highly fragmented and labour-intensive business. ICS has more than 50 000 employees, most of whom work part-time. It is therefore very much a 'people' business. Most of these people seldom visit an ICS office because they travel each day between home and work location. Many are more likely to identify with the customer whose premises they clean rather than with ICS itself.

■ The Model Branch initiative

Early in 1989, ICS Northern recognized that in order further to improve performance they must look afresh at the way the business was organized. The aim of the Model Branch initiative was to refocus branch operations on the needs of the customer. The initiative concentrated on the key human resource issues of staffing, flexibility and speed of response to customer needs and demands.

In outline, the Model Branch process comprised the following steps:

1. *Presentations to regional managers* on overall business environment and problems peculiar to ICS.

2. *Assignment given to regional managers at locations away from their own office environment* – 'If there were no constraints on costs, people or other resources, how would you organize the business to deliver to the customer the perfect service?'

3. *Presentations to other, less senior, managers* on the Model Branch exercise, in order to ensure their involvement and support, create momentum, and foster a new spirit of openness.

4. A *customer survey* to determine the most important factors for them in the customer/supplier relationship.

5. An *employee survey* to identify why people were attracted to the industry, what motivated them at work, what were the most important factors for them in a job, what qualities did they think characterized 'a good supervisor', and so on.

   Other issues addressed by the research included mode of transport to and from work, ethnic origin of employees, membership of trade unions, and other matters that, again, related directly to their orientation to work, their motivation at work, and their personal preoccupations in the workplace (Figure 7.6), and thus represented issues of direct importance to them. (Contrast this approach with that in the previous case study about BET where the survey concentrated on more abstract concepts such as corporate image.)

6. *Feedback of customer and employee survey results* to participants, using face-to-face presentations supported by video and print materials.

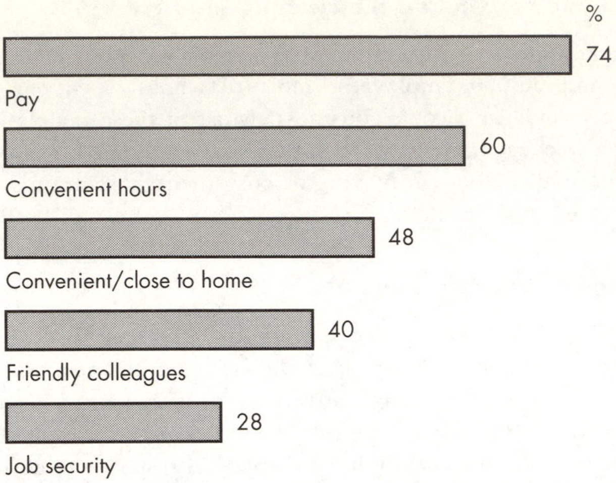

(a)

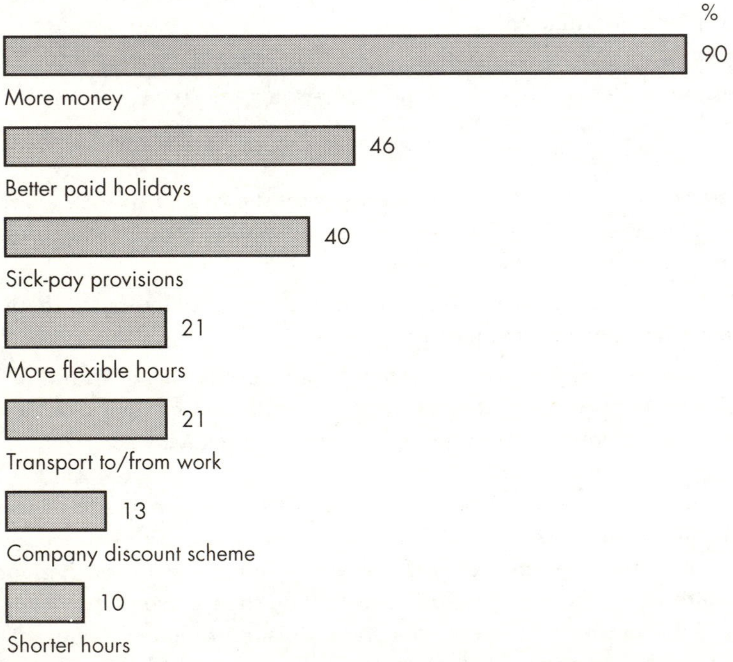

(b)

Figure 7.6 The Model Branch employee survey – Part 1: (a) most important job factors;
(b) factors influencing job change; (c) attitude to work.

%

Proud — 38

Satisfied — 57

Not bothered — 3

Dissatisfied — 2

No answer — 1

(c)

Figure 7.6 cont.

7. *Selection of Model Branches.*

8. *Implementation of proposals* developed by the regional managers' workgroup (see above).

9. *Regular review of Model Branches operations* against key performance indicators.

10. *Extension of good practices* identified during the Model Branch initiative to other branches.

Figure 7.7 indicates the approach taken to eliciting employees' opinions during the Model Branch exercise. It was important that both supervisors and operatives were offered the chance to contribute their views on their jobs, their managers, and their company; the research thereby involved all employees participating in the Model Branch process in identifying the gaps between organizational and individual needs.

One example of how this involvement bore fruit in terms of identifying operational, human resource and communication issues, as well as in shaping future human resource strategies, was in the area of recruitment. Recruitment at ICS depends largely on the personal networks of the supervisor and operatives. Having operatives rate what they saw to be the key characteristics of 'a good supervisor' helped to highlight training needs and appropriate management style, all issues illustrated in Figure 7.7(a–c). Their answers to the biographical and demographic questions in the survey (Figure 7.7d and e) supplied information about the external labour market which could then be fed into decisions about future recruitment strategy.

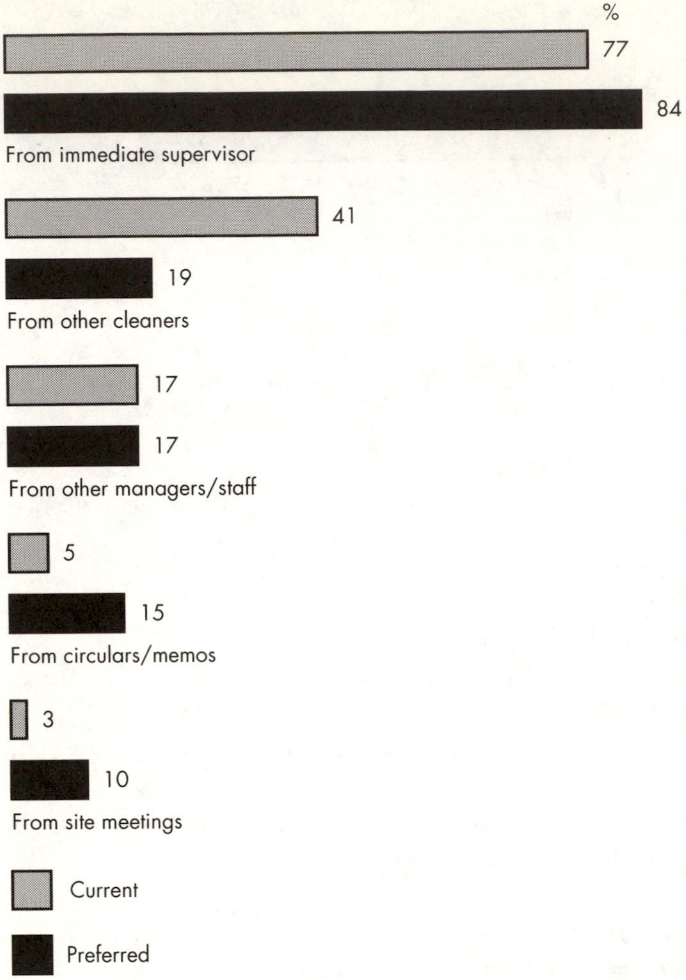

%
77

84

From immediate supervisor

41

19

From other cleaners

17

17

From other managers/staff

5

15

From circulars/memos

3

10

From site meetings

Current

Preferred

(a)

Figure 7.7 The Model Branch employee survey – Part 2: (a) communication channels; (b) feedback on performance; (c) important supervisor qualities; (d) how current job found; (e) recruiting staff.

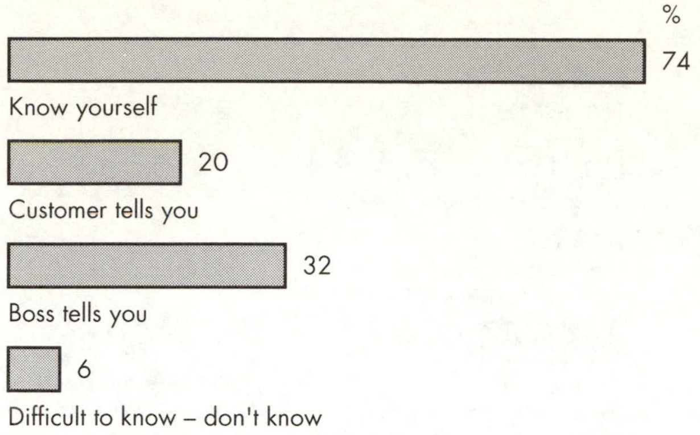

%

74

Know yourself

20

Customer tells you

32

Boss tells you

6

Difficult to know – don't know

(b)

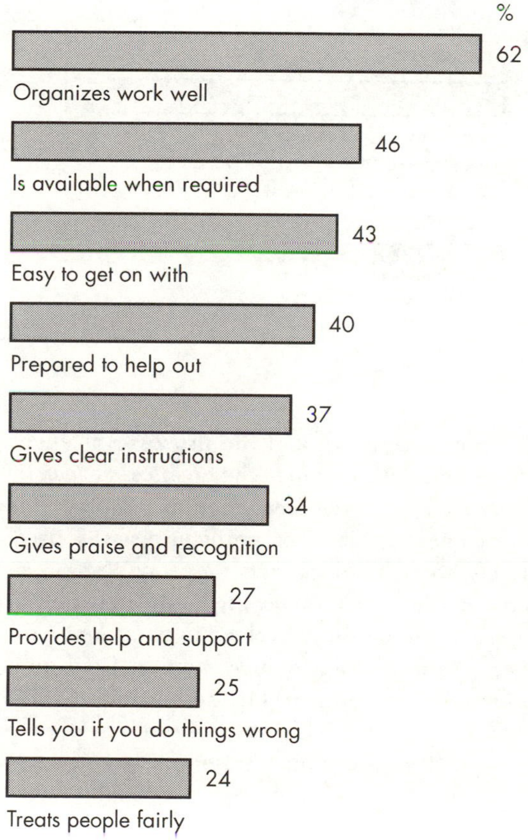

%

62

Organizes work well

46

Is available when required

43

Easy to get on with

40

Prepared to help out

37

Gives clear instructions

34

Gives praise and recognition

27

Provides help and support

25

Tells you if you do things wrong

24

Treats people fairly

(c)

Figure 7.7 cont.

(continued)

%

65
From a friend

9
On contract with other firm

8
From newspaper advertisement

18
Other source

(d)

%

29
Own personal contacts

65
Personal contacts of cleaners

17
Advertisements in newspaper

19
Local job centre

(e)

Figure 7.7 *cont*.

The Model Branch initiative and the processes it envolved were based on the concept of securing ownership of the business at each level – something seen by ICS as crucial in developing genuine employee involvement and commitment to business goals. Communication was used not merely to inform but actively to help to change the way things were done in the company. This did not involve establishing completely new systems; it aimed to encourage employees to become involved in continually redefining systems in order to deliver a better service to the customer. Continuous improvement is a phrase commonly associated with Japanese work practices, but in essence this is what this process is about – the active search by every employee, every day, for better ways of carrying out the job.

> The right size will increasingly be whatever handles most effectively the information needed for task and function.
>
> (Drucker, 1989)

Through the Model Branch process the 'right' size for a branch was fixed at a unit handling a specified amount of turnover. Larger branches would simply comprise two, three, four or more units depending on the volume of business handled. This size was judged 'right' because it would provide the optimum customer contact time for general, operations and service managers which was targeted at a specific number of calls per week, thus enhancing the efficiency of the personal networks which drive the business.

Changes were made to the structure of the branch, the status and titles of individuals, and to working methods; for example, an investment was made in mobile radio communications so that each customer was only a radio call away at any time. What is important here, however, is not the detail of the changes themselves, but the whole process whereby ideas from those directly in contact with customers were used to refocus the organization on customer service. The role of management was to enable the creation of the right environment to achieve that mission, and to continue to support it.

Model Branch is a novel approach to a particular set of organizational problems and challenges. Because processes themselves are continually reviewed and refined, it is unlikely to stand the test of time, and inevitably it will be replaced by alternative approaches. But, as was discussed in Chapter 2, that is how processes should operate: sensitivity, creativity and political skill are qualities vital to the success of strategy, and keeping the momentum going is one of the fundamental issues in bridging the gap between the formulation of human resource strategy and its effective implementation in the workplace.

The main lesson to be learnt from this case study, then, is that business goals and a related human resource strategy can be facilitated in the workplace through an employee communications exercise involving managers which creates a receptive environment; and that within that environment new initiatives and ideas can be encouraged, reviewed and implemented – or discarded – without conflict, in a spirit of teamwork and commonality of interest which will be reflected in the longer term success of the organization. Communication processes thus become a way of developing people and facilitating a 'learning organization' (see Chapter 12).

The impact of organization structure and culture on employee attitudes and performance

We have looked at some of the communication tasks facing managers attempting to ensure the effective implementation of human resource strategies in the workplace. However, as we saw especially in Chapters 1, 2 and 4, the internal organizational environment will be a key determinant of how far any strategies can succeed. Without good 'fit' between business goals and strategy, HRM goals, and strategy, and the structure and culture of the organization, effective performance and productive patterns of organizational development cannot occur.

Let us look at some of the characteristics of what might be called traditional, more mechanistic organization structures and cultures on the one hand, and of more organic, entrepreneurial environments on the other. At this stage, generalizations are inevitable, but the aim of Figure 7.8 is simply to paint a picture for the layperson that is recognizably true to life.

The author observed all these major shifts in emphasis when working with a number of large, UK-based and multinational organizations. They are also well documented in research and literature about the management of uncertainty and the changing nature of organizations (for example, Burns and Stalker, 1961; Buchanan, 1982; Toffler, 1985; Drucker, 1988; Clegg, 1990). Organizations in unpredictable environments need to encourage the continuous formation and reformation of a variety of groupings to deal with a wide range of tasks and problems. The aim is to create, after the inevitable period of resistance of old habits to new orders, an organizational fluidity that leads to a new orientation of the entire workforce. That, in turn, will require new strategies and processes for human resource management and development (see Harrison, 1992, Chapter 21).

In too many organizations the structure chart still impedes effective performance. Therefore the continual review of an organization and the people within it is one of the most important exercises that can be embarked on. However, only if that task is recognized as a strategic challenge requiring the commitment and time of senior management can culture change be handled successfully. With the help of communication processes, such as those at BET and its companies, and the initiatives to which they give rise, it should become possible to identify the kinds of strategies and policies that will reduce the boundaries between individuals and the organization, and to ensure through time that those strategies win the commitment of employees and are effectively implemented in the workplace. Boundary management, as was seen in Chapter 2, is an important task in HRM.

The role of the manager in changing organizational culture and communicating a new HRM strategy

The issues discussed so far in this chapter represent both problems and opportunities for the human resource manager. As has been powerfully

Characteristics of stable, mechanistic systems	Characteristics of dynamic, entrepeneurial systems
Hierarchical	Flat
Autocratic	Team driven
Slow to react	Fast reactive
Hugging of information	Openness
Knowledge	Understanding
Rigidity	Flexibility
Change as 'an event'	Change as 'the norm'
Job definition	Project definition
Written documentation	Face-to-face contact
Efficiency	Effectiveness
Top down	Bottom up
Passive involvement	Active involvement
Loyalty	Mobility
Integration	Fragmentation
Unitary	Pluralistic
Centrality	Locality
Narrow focus	Wide focus
Centrally controlled networks	Locally controlled networks
Managers as dictators	Managers as enablers
Workforce as employees	Workforce as associates
One-way communication	Two-way communication
Hearing	Listening
Sceptism/fear	Trust/confidence
Compartmentalized functions	Integrated functions
People in boxes	**People jumping out of boxes**

Figure 7.8 *Jumping out of boxes*.

demonstrated in Part 1 of this book, it is of course unwise to assume that the handling of these issues is the prerogative of the human resource specialists; they are the responsibility of every manager. The human resource manager, however, can act as catalyst within a team of senior managers who are striving to create a new environment based on new values, new goals, new priorities and new ways of doing things.

In an organization where, as Thomson (1990) points out, the challenge is to manage competing groups with different power relations and different needs, the culture has shifted from one of compartmentalization to one which recognizes that managers, contrary to much popular belief, are not all good at everything but need to be able to marshall a range of different yet complementary skills to get a job done.

In the growing number of situations where the job of manager is no longer based on a complex hierarchy, the manager must become a facilitator, enabler, supporter and maintainer of personal networks. Managers must recognize the capacity of their people and tap into their creativity to drive the organization towards the achievement of its business goals. This requires qualities of perceptiveness, creativity, communication and openness; it also means that the manager must look outside his or her immediate sphere of operation to assess what kind of environment employees are working in, what are the internal and external pressures which may inhibit desired levels of effort and performance, and what is needed to help people to understand their markets, their customers, and the areas of commonality between their own needs and those of the business.

> Employee communication is all about running the organization effectively. It is about making sure people know what needs to be done, understand why it's necessary, feel committed to achieving it, and have a chance to use their own knowledge and skills to do it better if possible.
>
> (Arnott, 1987)

Conclusion

To return to the learning objectives at the start of this chapter, what are the key tasks of communication in facilitating organizational change and in the implementation of human resource mission and strategy in the organization?

- to identify the human issues and problems involved in increasing fragmentation of structure and of groups in an organization;
- to identify significant trends in employee morale, motivation and expectations in the workplace;
- to establish accurately the opinions and ideas of employees and other stakeholders in the business about how best to achieve corporate goals;
- to facilitate a greater responsiveness to employees' interests and ideas, and to identify where there is a need for greater organizational and procedural flexibility;
- to act as a catalyst for change, helping to reconcile the needs of the business with the needs of other key stakeholders;
- to help to create and sustain an environment which is receptive to greater involvement and participation from employees, in order to ensure their maximum 'ownership' of the business and commitment to its strategic objectives.

8

Achieving equality of treatment and opportunity in the workplace

Monica Shaw

By the end of the chapter the reader will:

1. understand some of the main pressures upon organizations to move towards equality and the relevance of equal opportunity policies to strategic HRM;

2. be aware of the contemporary situation in the United Kingdom related to equality in the workplace, and appreciate the differences between declared and real commitment to ensuring equality of treatment and equality in employment;

3. be able to identify environmental factors which influence equal opportunity culture, policies and practices within organizations;

4. appreciate the human resource strategies and practices needed to achieve lasting change related to equality in the workplace.

Equal opportunities and the concept of strategic HRM

> Good equal opportunities is about good management practice; about recruiting, developing and retaining the skills and creative ideas we all so badly need in our organisations. It is about the way we manage our most precious resource – the women and men in our workforce. About the way we interview and assess, the way we train, the way we promote, the way we recognise performance and about the sort of conditions we offer. It is also about the sort of culture and ethos we nurture.
> (Joanna Foster, Chair of the Equal Opportunities Commission, 1989)

One of the central tenets of strategic HRM, as opposed to more traditional personnel management models, is the close fit it advocates between the management of human resources and business strategy. At first sight this might seem unpromising territory for a flowering of equal opportunity policies and practices. For many, the pursuit of equal opportunities is a moral enterprise which has everything to do with redressing wrongs in society and very little to do with a hard-headed business world.

It can be argued that the 'softer' versions of HRM (discussed in Chapter 2) which lay stress on human capability and commitment are more consistent with equal opportunity objectives, but the connection may be very weak. Within the HRM literature the concept 'human' is typically used unproblematically as a generic term which encompasses diversity amongst individuals. Differences between categories of people and the inequalities which have traditionally affected their place in the labour market are rarely discussed. The concept of equal opportunity can also be used in a relatively neutral way to describe the abstract rights of individuals to equal treatment. It only begins to be challenging when it is combined with an analysis of structural inequality and the specific relationship of disadvantaged groups to the labour market. Thus 'soft' versions of HRM need to be combined with 'strong' versions of equal opportunity for innovatory thinking and practice to occur.

It is increasingly argued that equal opportunity strategies are vital to meeting the challenges of demographic and organizational change of the 1990s – a decade in which increasing international competition, against a backcloth of skills shortages, will require innovative approaches to the recruitment and retention of a committed and qualified workforce. Such innovative approaches demand a less generalized notion of 'human' resources and much greater attention to patterns of inequality and barriers to employment for certain groups in society. The potential importance of equal opportunity policy and practice has been most forcibly argued in relation to demographic changes which will increase employer competition for the declining numbers of school leavers during the 1990s and which may open the way for developing the potential of traditionally marginalized groups. It is also widely recognized that employers will have to cope with skills shortages at a time when the need for professional, managerial, scientific and technical skills has never been higher. With the development of the single European market during the 1990s, competition for goods and services will be matched by competition for a quality workforce.

Thus it can be argued that competitive organizations will be those which anticipate and design human resource strategies that recognize the positive value to be gained from equal opportunity policies and practices, not simply as recruitment devices, but as the means for creating the best conditions in which the talents and skills of employees will be retained and flourish. For example some organizations, recognizing the waste of women's skills and potential, are investing in work-based nurseries, career-break schemes, more flexible working conditions and appropriate training, resulting in greater representation of women in middle management positions. As the examples of innovative practice included in this chapter show, strategies like this, which break with traditional employment patterns, work best when they are combined with efforts to overcome hostility and prejudice. Case studies also suggest that a sensitive understanding of the organization and its culture, the formulation of clear and realistic objectives, and education and training for all employees are necessary for achieving change. We should, though, be wary of assuming that the implementation of equal opportunity policies can be described as an entirely rational process. If the results of process research on strategic management uncover 'a more interactive, incremental or emergent process, tempered by learning' (Chapter 1, p. 31), how much more will this be the case in the sensitive area of equal opportunities! Whatever strategies are adopted within the context of particular organizations, it is unlikely that much change will occur unless there is real effort to take an extensive and pervasive approach to the development of equal opportunities, but this will never be a straightforward or easy process.

As much of the research referred to in this chapter indicates, there remains a tendency in many organizations to marginalize equal opportunities, even though in the 1980s there was an impressive increase in the number of organizations describing themselves as equal opportunity employers or more modestly as 'working towards equality'. The reasons for the rather slow progress in putting these principles at the heart of human resource strategy are complex. First, we should be aware that the spread of equal opportunity policies was in large part inspired by legal requirements, and that mere adherence to the law does not necessarily bring about the changes required to tackle the human resource problems of the 1990s. The law provides an important framework but it can lead to protectionist attitudes and defensive personnel practices. Second, it is important to recognize that the development of equality in organizations challenges traditions, threatens powerful interests and confronts deep-seated prejudices. For many employers the 'costs' in confronting the *status quo* might seem too dear.

The underlying philosophy of this chapter is that 'strong' versions of equal opportunity policies and practice should be an integral feature of human resource strategy for the 1990s and beyond, while recognizing that this prescriptive stance belies the complexity of the task. The problems associated with achieving equality in organizations are discussed in the context of equality and the law and inequalities in the labour market in relation to race, ethnicity, disability and age. Special attention is devoted to women's position in paid work, since many analysts predict that the 1990s will be a decade in which women will make great strides towards equality in employment. As will be seen, this will not happen unless organizations recognize their value and develop the proactive strategies which will ensure their contribution.

Equal opportunity policies and practices in the workplace

Human resource strategies for the 1990s require a major shift in thinking about the diversity of human talent and the untapped potential of those whose position in the labour market has traditionally been determined by their membership of certain groups. Women, members of ethnic minorities, those with a disability and people in certain age groups have all been marginalized in relation to education, training and employment. There is a slow recognition that individual potential cuts across membership of such groups and that human talent is wasted in a system built upon discrimination. Equal opportunity policies may be seen as the first step in combating discrimination within organizations, but much depends upon whether they are merely window dressing or whether they are designed to bring about real change.

Formal policy statements and practice

Although some employers will claim to be equal opportunity employers, they may not even have a written statement to back this up. Still others will go no further than developing a formal statement of principle, which although important is only the first step in the process of working towards equality. Formal statements can be difficult to agree, particularly in respect of the disadvantaged groups they purport to cover. I have witnessed much heated debate as to whether sexual orientation and age should be included as nondiscriminatory categories. There may be less resistance to a policy which advocates nondiscriminatory practice on the basis of gender, race or ethnic origin and disability, but none of this can be assumed. The process of formulating a policy statement will inevitably dredge up prejudice and challenge established interests. Most research confirms that however difficult, it is essential to involve employees in discussion at all levels of the organization in policy formulation and development.

Policy statements may either be brief or take the form of a more comprehensive document. Although there are differences in the way that organizations phrase the principle of equality, the basic ingredients are similar, typically referring to employee rights to equal treatment and sometimes including specific reference to employment practices such as recruitment, training and promotion. More important than the wording are the steps taken to enact the policy. Case studies indicate that equal opportunity statements have to be backed by well-formulated strategies for action, commitment from the top of the organization and appropriate structures to involve both staff and management in the process of change. The following case study of the BBC has been suggested as an example of good practice in this respect, in which effective equal opportunity strategies were being developed in the late 1980s:

> The BBC is a good example of an organisation which has fully endorsed a report, asked for by the Board of Governors and Board of Management, which recommended changes which have subsequently been implemented.
> (Straw, 1990, p. 98)

CASE STUDY: *BBC policy statement*

Based on case study material provided by Jane Straw in *Equal Opportunities* (1990) with kind permission from the publishing department of the Institute of Personnel Management.

> The BBC's policies are based on equal opportunity for all. This applies to external recruitment, internal appointments, terms of employment, conditions of service and opportunities for training and promotion, irrespective of sex, marital status, creed, colour, race or ethnic origin, and the BBC is committed to the development and promotion of such equality of opportunity. Staff who believe they have been denied equality of opportunity may pursue their complaint through the appeals and grievances procedures as may be appropriate.

■ Action

The Board of Governors at the BBC acknowledged a lack of progress in relation to earlier policy statements on equality. There followed the appointment of an equal opportunities officer in 1987 and a report which recommended action in raising awareness and training; investing in staff; and monitoring and publicizing results. The structure of the BBC, with a large number of different work bases, required that functions were devolved to directorates. Directorate implementation groups were formed, made up of key decision-makers, including equal opportunities officers to advise and support the equality process. The outcomes were reported in 1989 as promising, with an increased representation of women in managerial grades (although still very few at senior management level), the provision of a work-based nursery, an extended career scheme with the possibility of staff negotiating a five-year break, and an increase in job shares and part-time work (though we should note that part-time employment is not necessarily an equalizing process for women).

The BBC has continued to develop equal opportunity policy and practice. It was among the first organizations to become formally committed to Opportunity 2000, which was launched in October 1990 as a business campaign 'to increase quality and quantity of women's participation in the workforce'. Following the setting of ethnic minority employment targets, accompanied by positive action on recruitment and training in order to achieve them, the BBC announced employment targets for women in 1990 after consultation with senior managers from different directorates. The targets were set to increase further the representation of women in management, from 16% of women in middle management and 10% in senior management in 1990 to 40% of middle and senior management and 30% of senior executive posts by 1996. Progress and reviews of these targets are to be considered annually by the Board. These objectives are to be backed by efforts to make the organization's culture and working arrangements more suited to women employees. The corporate equal opportunities officer suggests that a key strategy in changing culture is the extension of flexible working patterns to men:

> It is important that men as well as women are encouraged to take up any such options such as flexible working arrangements and the BBC is seeking to do this.
>
> (Trynka in *Equal Opportunities Review*, 1992, p. 24)

It will be interesting to chart the success of the BBC's efforts to implement its equal opportunity policies through the 1990s. The television and broad-casting industry has been subject to major restructuring and both the BBC and ITV companies suffered job losses among permanent staff in the early 1990s.

One trend may be for an increasing casualization of labour which will work against the development of equal opportunities. Organizations like the

BBC have to be studied in relation to the wider social and political context in which even 'strong' versions of equal opportunities may be eroded. The BBC at least represents some effort to go beyond what we might call ritualistic responses to equal opportunity and practice.

Ritualistic responses to equal opportunity policy and practice

Formal equal opportunity policies typically enshrine commitment and prescriptions but they often lack clear guidelines about outcomes or processes. An additional problem is that even where effort is expended in translating the policy into practice it may get caught in an overformalized and bureaucratic approach. For example, many organizations pay considerable attention to detailed personnel procedures such as recruitment, selection and monitoring – all of which are important ingredients of good equal opportunity practice, but not in themselves a sufficient means to effect change. Unless these practices are linked to specified outcomes, they will become ritualistic and equality no more than a formality. As Lorraine Paddison commented (1989), making sure that procedures reflect legal requirements, best practice and the needs of particular organizations is clearly important.

> All too often, however, it is an end in itself and the rewritten policies and statistics collected via the monitoring system gather dust on the shelves of personnel and line managers.
>
> (Paddison, 1989)

Without specified outcomes such as targets for a changed composition of the workforce or of its structure (quotas are illegal under the race and sex legislation), personnel procedures can act as a protective device and produce little change. Indeed it can be argued that they become counter-productive:

> Transforming prescriptions into workable policies requires more than the addition of detail, and tightening checks on adherence to bureaucratic procedures is only likely to result in a destructive spiral of ever greater checks and controls followed by more sophisticated avoidance tactics.
>
> (Liff, 1989, p. 32)

Liff suggests extending the objectives of equal opportunity policies and codes of practice to include:

- increasing the understanding of all employees of current inequalities and their causes so as to develop a consensus for change;
- increasing the understanding of those who implement equal opportunity policies of the hopes and fears of all those affected; and

- clearer statements about what are the expected outcomes of particular policies – this would help to reduce the anxiety and hostility generated when intentions are unclear.

If such objectives were included in policy formation and practice it would go some way to recognizing the active processes which are required to break down resistance to change. An educative process which recognizes the sensitivity of the issues and openness about the desired outcomes of equal opportunity policies and practices is clearly an important ingredient for achieving change. At the same time if equal opportunity policies and codes of practice were extended in the way advocated by Liff, they would serve to commit the organization to a fairly comprehensive programme for change. Human resource planning would take on a broader meaning in terms of creating a cultural ethos of equality. Without this, it might be argued that there will be a temptation for employees at all levels of the organization to relegate equal opportunity policies to the back burner. Good intentions may well give way to ritualism and inertia.

Equal opportunity policies and integrated strategies

For policies to work they have to be clearly understood, visible and integrated into the mission of the organization. Initial good practice in this respect may generate further change which serves the interest of the organization in successfully combining equal opportunity goals with business objectives, as the following case study illustrates.

CASE STUDY: British Telecommunications plc

Based on a conference paper by Sue Lewis, presented to the Institute of Personnel Management Annual Conference (1989) by kind permission of the Intellectual Property Department, BT.

BT, looking towards the 1990s and convinced that women were an underutilized resource, developed a strategy to increase the numbers of women in middle management. The approach combined succession planning to identify key people with specially designed training and career planning. The programme was effective in promoting women into management (32% more in the targeted areas than in the untargeted areas), and also spawned other equality initiatives. These included short courses for more junior women, a corporate programme to bridge the women-into-engineering gap, job-sharing schemes, and a further review of childcare policy. In addition, a Women's Network (funded by BT) was formed which attracted 700 members (men and women), holding monthly meetings and developing a newsletter; social events; a job-sharing register; a directory; career planning workshops; and providing networking opportunities through which the concerns of employees could be put to BT. Sue Lewis, Personnel Development Manager, reporting on these developments in 1989, concluded:

> After all these pieces of work and initiatives and strategies it is probably fair to say that many women in the company still feel that BT is not doing much to help them. The numbers are so great (we currently employ 220 000 people) that it will take a long time to have much impact – and we have a long way to go yet.
>
> In short and in my experience, people working in this area need two things above all:
>
> ■ integrated strategies (to overcome hostility/inertia)
>
> ■ *active* commitment from the top
>
> To succeed in the 1990s and beyond, businesses must innovate, and at the same time learn from the best practice of others.
>
> (Lewis, 1989)

The translation of equal opportunity policies into workable and meaningful practice is a difficult process but, as the examples of the BBC and BT suggest, commitment to progress can bring some results. In both cases there is recognition that the desired outcome in terms of human resource strategy (for example, getting more women into management) is not something which can be achieved overnight or in isolation. Rather the organization must be prepared to plan such outcomes in the context of a comprehensive and sensitive approach to equality issues. Much depends on the will and determination to pursue change.

Gaps between policy and practice

Research to date provides rather an uninspiring picture concerning the extent to which equal opportunity practice has developed in organizations, although it is important to exercise caution since we only have a partial picture in what is a relatively new and developing field of enquiry. However, various studies of organizations claiming to be equal opportunity employers suggest a wide gap between policy and practice. For example in 1988, a survey of the 60 largest private sector UK firms, in which 21 responded, showed that all but one had an equality policy and that the majority monitored it regularly. More than half had a procedure for dealing with sexual harassment. However, company practice in relation to tackling women's unequal position in employment was much less in evidence: 27% had job-share schemes, 7% made payments towards childcare and none offered nursery provision:

> If the best employers are ignoring key issues like career breaks, childcare provision and training, then for the majority of women workers employed under inferior terms there is little prospect for equality at work.
>
> (Labour Research, 1988)

In this respect much has been made of the possibilities of attracting women back into paid work by recognizing and making provision for childcare; however innovative strategies seem to be the exception rather than the rule. Highlighted in Europe's Second Action Programme (1986–90) on the promotion of equality for women in work, childcare provision remains variable among member states with a poor record in the United Kingdom. Such provision could include workplace nurseries, nurseries shared between organizations, play schemes to cover school holidays, childminding schemes, allowances to pay for childcare, time off to care for sick children and enhanced maternity schemes. Some employers have risen to the challenge but in general the response has been slow. A survey conducted by HOST Training and Consultancy Service in 1989 found that only 3% of responding employers were providing some form of childcare assistance, although five times as many were considering it, and that current provision was concentrated in financial and business services in Greater London and the South East.

A further HOST survey conducted in 1989 indicated that women in the public sector were much more likely to receive some form of childcare assistance (1 in 8 workplace provision and 1 in 20 other forms). Only 2% of employers in industry and commerce provided some form of workplace childcare and 1% provided childcare allowances (Berry-Lound, 1990). Clearly, the issue of childcare has not yet penetrated human resource strategies in the private sector. Where it exists in any form it is much more likely to cater for the under-fives. Yet it is now well established that inadequate childcare is the most important barrier to women returning to employment (Confederation of British Industry, 1989). Without a dramatic change in the central role women play in society as carers, it is likely that the rising numbers of elderly people will add to their burdens. This will set up further competing pressures with the needs of employers to recruit and retain women. Compared with USA employers who have produced some innovative schemes on elderly care, UK employers have so far done little.

Studies to investigate employer practice in relation to ethnic minorities indicate a similar slow response. One such study conducted in 1989, surveyed the 60 largest UK firms to explore how far the Commission for Racial Equality's 1984 Code of Practice had promoted equality. Only 16 organizations provided a full response and it might be assumed that these represented the best rather than the worst practice. The results suggest that there had been relatively little action to meet the CRE's Code of Practice. Monitoring was not much in evidence, with only four companies able to say what proportion of their workforce was black; half of those responding had a policy on racial harassment but only one company had acted on its racial harassment policy; only three companies offered specific training and only one had offered language training (Labour Research, 1989). A larger study by the CRE similarly showed that knowledge of the code and efforts to implement it were very patchy among organizations (Commission for Racial Equality, 1989). The failure to put policy into practice was also identified in a Sheffield-based survey, where it was found that employers with equal opportunity policies were no more likely to employ members of ethnic minorities than employers without such policies, leading to the conclusion:

> In general it can be concluded that policy management and implementation structures for the translation of policy into practice were a good deal less developed than policies themselves.
>
> (Gibbon, 1989, p. 12)

It is difficult to avoid the interpretation that by the turn of the decade, the 1980s explosion of equal opportunity policies had made very little difference to employment practice. This is perhaps overpessimistic. Further evidence suggests that the translation of policy into practice had been slowly developing in financial, retail and public organizations. Apart from a developing body of case material which supports this view, it has also been confirmed in a survey of 24 organizations which found that the larger organizations in the service sector (employing large numbers of women) had the most developed equal opportunity programmes related to human resource planning and addressed to meeting skills shortages (Cockman *et al.*, 1990). Yet progress in closing the gap between equal opportunity policy and practice is patchy and limited. While there is evidence of increased interest (still mostly cautious) among employers during the early 1990s in a range of schemes which recognize the childcare responsibilities of women employees and provision for more flexible working arrangements, there is little evidence that other disadvantaged groups have been the focus of much innovative practice at all. The gains for women, as will be shown later in this chapter, are relatively small.

In order to consider the development (or lack of it, as the case may be) of equal opportunity policy and practice in organizations it is necessary to consider the wider context of demographic change, of legal requirements and of the structures of inequality in society. This will provide some flesh to the notion of 'strong' versions of equal opportunity as well as indicating the complex issues involved in their development.

The demographic timebomb and employer responses

There are a number of important pressures on organizations to review their current employment practices and to move towards more equitable policies. Pressures for change arise from within the organization as groups of employees become more aware of their rights and make demands; but many would argue that the main impetus for change comes from external factors. In recent years demographic changes have provided the greatest push towards equality in organizations, although it must be admitted that during a recession this issue tends to fade somewhat.

However, it is important for organizations to plan beyond recession, and demographic change must still be faced as a key challenge in recruitment and retention of a skilled labour force.

Demographic change and employer responses

> The importance of equality of opportunity has never been more central to all of us involved in work. . . . In the past, with a plentiful workforce to draw upon, it has been an approach which some organisations have chosen to adopt as part of good professional practice. Yet in the 1990s against a background of demographical change, an understanding and practice of equal opportunities policies is essential if the UK is to meet the demands of an increasingly competitive market, and, indeed, if some organisations are to survive at all.
>
> (Straw, 1990, p. 1)

The demographic changes to which Straw refers have caused a certain amount of concern among employers and debate among experts as to how employers are likely to respond. It has been estimated that in the United Kingdom by the year 2000 there will be 2.3 million more people between 25 and 54 in the labour force and 1.3 million fewer aged under 25 than in 1988. By the turn of the century the 16–24 age group will be 14% below the 1988–89 level (National Economic Development Office, 1989). These demographic changes are typical of most industrialized nations and thus the problem of how employers are to compete for a shrinking younger age group and to adjust to a maturing labour force is one of wide concern (Commission of the European Communities, 1990). Not surprisingly, such concern has brought the question of equality of opportunity for women and other disadvantaged groups to the fore. Pressure is on employers to devise human resource strategies which acknowledge the underutilized potential of older people, those from ethnic minorities, people with disabilities and women. The potential of older women to fill the gap left by younger workers, linked to their increased willingness to join the labour force in the 1980s predominates in the debates. Women accounted for 75% of the growth in the labour force from 1984 to 1990 and it is predicted that this growth will increase to 96% by the year 2001 (LMQR, 1991).

> Whether or not this presents a problem for employers depends entirely upon their ability to do two things: to recognise, and get rid of explicit and implicit discrimination against women, and to recognise and provide for the particular problems facing older women returning to work after a break for child rearing. On past evidence, anyone could be forgiven for being pessimistic on this score.
>
> (Atkinson, 1989, p. 21)

It would seem that employers are now more aware of the changing shape of the labour force but the question remains as to whether they are adopting appropriate strategies for the 1990s. The most pessimistic view is based on the result of some survey evidence which suggests that employers believe that they can buy their way out of trouble by offering competitive wages. Thus it has been argued that there exists:

> . . . a wide gap between an increasing level of awareness within the personnel profession, and a failure to translate this into effective corporate policy initiatives.
>
> (Atkinson, 1989, p. 20)

Alternative survey evidence indicates that considerable effort has been expended in gaining a competitive edge in recruiting young people by a broader range of policies than merely increasing wages and benefits. These include providing youth training, career packages, forging stronger links with education, changing selection systems to place less emphasis on educational qualifications or reducing entry standards. But such strategies may only bring short-term benefits in a competitive labour market:

> . . . in a labour market where many others are following a similar path they need to be supported by other initiatives which reduce dependence on young recruits.
>
> (Parsons, 1990, p. 65)

Where employers have focused their attention on youth recruitment, there is little evidence that this has been targeted at young people from ethnic minorities, even though demographical analysis suggests that they will form an increasing proportion of new labour market entrants (LMQR, 1992). Initiatives which go beyond securing a competitive edge in the white youth labour market become all the more urgent if employers are to recruit increasing numbers of highly skilled workers during the 1990s. Analysis indicates a continued decline in unskilled and manual occupations and an expanding demand for skilled workers, particularly in professional, scientific and technical occupations. Given that women are generally less well qualified, and have work patterns which exclude many of them from training, it would seem that employers might have left it too late and that only a very small minority of women will benefit from innovative strategies to bring them back and to retain them in employment. We will return to this point later in the chapter.

Equality and the legal context

The principle of individual equality

The principle of individual equality, now enshrined in international law, was first articulated in the American Declaration of Independence, 1776, and the French Declaration of Human Rights, 1789. Both were partial in that they were assertions of the rights of white males, however they became important springboards for the development of antislavery, civil rights and feminist movements to claim their right to equal citizenship. Such movements and the many which followed have campaigned for legal changes to achieve equal rights. The concept of equal rights was developed through liberal philosophical and political thought, initially posed in opposition to a social order which defined rights in terms of social position rather than as the inalienable possessions of individuals. The concept of equal opportunity is firmly bedded in this tradition, upholding as it does the ideal of equal treatment. It should be noted that this is a limited conceptualization of equality, since it does not challenge the existing institutions of society, which themselves give rise to inequality, but simply argues for equal access to unequal positions:

> . . . the essence of equal opportunity is that individuals should be judged as individuals according to their merits and not on the basis of a characteristic ascribed to them arbitrarily because they are members of a group.
>
> (Rubenstein, 1986, p. 36)

The problem is that this ideal, based upon notions of justice and fairness, is difficult to achieve because of the deep-rooted inequalities which exist in society. What counts as merit will be judged on the basis of individual achievements such as education and qualifications, but these achievements are in large part determined by membership of certain groups. Thus running alongside the ideal of equal opportunity should be the recognition of disadvantage if the ideal is to mean anything more than an abstract and formal statement of individual right.

Declarations by international bodies have acted as an important spur to the ideals of nondiscriminatory practice in employment, both by framing the general principle of equal rights and by specific attempts to protect the rights of disadvantaged groups. Important among these were the Charter of the United Nations of 1945 and the Declaration of Human Rights of 1948. Within the Declaration of 1948, article 2 established that individuals are entitled to all the rights and freedoms which are set forth in the declaration 'without distinction of any kind, such as race, colour, sex, language, religion, political or other opinions, national or social origin, property, birth or other status'. Attempts have also been made to redress discrimination against certain groups (for example, The United Nations Convention on the Elimination of all forms of Racial Discrimination, 1965) and to develop instruments to counter inequalities in particular areas of life, most notably in relation to employment rights. For example, the ILO Convention 1958, instrument 111, requires that states take measures against discrimination in employment 'on the basis of race, sex, religion, national extraction or social origin'.

European legislation and the equality principle

European legislation has also provided an important context in which member states of the EC have formulated and reformulated equality laws (mainly in relation to women's rights), although here as elsewhere there is considerable variation within nations. Articles 48–51 of the Treaty of Rome establish the right of free movement of workers and prohibit discrimination on grounds of nationality. Article 119 and a number of subsequent directives apply the principle of nondiscrimination on grounds of sex in the context of employment. The equality principle has been described as one of the 'foundations of the community', designed to ensure that member states who implement it are not at an economic disadvantage in comparison with those who do not, and that the living and working conditions of the peoples of the community will be improved. There is little doubt that European initiatives have provided and will continue to provide an important impetus for the development of equality law in all member states so that national legislation can be brought into line with European law. Perhaps more important than this is the climate which European legislation and social action programmes have created for individuals to become more aware of their rights. However, in the light of recent political wrangles about the Maastricht Treaty, and the British government's resistance to the social chapter, it remains to be seen whether the earlier optimism, expressed here, will be justified:

> . . . the social charter brings issues of collective bargaining, worker parti-cipation and equal opportunities back onto the European Agenda. This is good news for Europe's women. . . . We are still hampered by rigid sexual divisions of labour, and by negative assumptions about the worth and value of women and our contribution to production and society. '1992' is an unrepeatable opportunity to improve European women's rights.
>
> (Pillinger, 1989, p. 35)

British equality legislation

The most significant developments in British equality legislation which have influenced organizations to become more concerned with equal opportunities, if only in a defensive sense, are the Sex Discrimination Act 1975; the Race Relations Act 1976; the Equal Pay Act 1970; and the Equal Pay (Amendment) Regulation 1983. There has been no significant additional legal pressure on organizations to increase opportunities for disabled people, their employment rights being covered by the Disabled Persons Acts (Employment) of 1944 and 1958. The provisions of these acts are extremely weak. They have established an employment register for disabled people which is purely voluntary. A conservative estimate would be that only 40% of those eligible to register do so. Apart from two specially reserved occupations – car park attendants and lift attendants – the main regulation on employers of more than 20 people is that they are required to employ a quota of 3% of registered disabled people. The penalty for noncompliance usually takes the form of a small fine and only 10 employers have ever been prosecuted, the last one in 1975 (Barnes, 1992). Not surprisingly, the number of employers meeting their quota is extremely low. In terms of legislation, efforts to overcome the disadvantages experienced by disabled persons falls far short of those designed to combat sex and race discrimination.

The Equal Pay (Amendment) Regulation resulted from proceedings brought against the British government by the European Commission which enforced compliance with Europe's Directive on Equal Pay issued in 1975. Basically this demanded a major change to Britain's Equal Pay Act of 1970, which specified equal pay for women and men for 'like work' or 'equivalent work' but gave no room for claims based upon 'work of equal value' which eventually became included in the amended act to cover jobs which, though different, make similar demands in terms of skill, effort and decision on employees. The significance of this amendment if widely enforced, and which explains the British government's resistance to it, was identified by a study conducted in 1989. This suggested that the continuing gap between women's and men's earnings was explained less by women's concentration in low skill jobs and more by women being paid less for performing work of similar skill to men. This study estimated that if the rule of equal value were applied, women would earn 90% of men's earnings (Bargaining Report, 1990). The latest UK figures from the New Earnings Survey (women earning 79p for every £1 earned by men in April 1992) are evidence of the ineffectiveness of the legislation to counter the effects of occupational segregation where employers can take refuge in the impossibility of finding comparators between 'men's jobs' and 'women's jobs' (Rubery, 1992).

Equal pay legislation has not yet produced a widespread equalization of women's and men's earnings. Industrial tribunal figures continue to show a low success rate. In 1991 only 10 cases were won (Labour Research, 1992).

As many company lawyers would confirm, there are still many loopholes in the law, especially in relation to equal value claims. Once an employee has shown that there are inequalities in pay, the employer has to prove that the criteria for them are not discriminatory: criteria such as qualifications, length of service and experience would not be. In relation to equal value claims, case law has also established that employers may justify different rates on the grounds of market forces. All of this contributes to a position where in spite of European law, the UK gender gap in earnings is one of the widest in Europe (Equal Opportunities Commission, 1992). In the light of the general failure throughout the community to bring about equality in women's earnings, the European Commission is drawing up a memorandum to clarify the 'equal value' concept and to provide guidelines on criteria to be used in job evaluation and job classification. Whether this will promote the cause of equal pay or whether it will spur further inventive ways to circumvent it remains to be seen.

The Sex Discrimination Act 1975 and the Race Relations Act 1976 were designed in tandem to combat discrimination in a number of areas including employment. They have had an important impact upon organizations in respect of legal/personnel procedures because they specifically forbid discrimination in employment in the areas of recruitment; terms of employment; access to promotion, training and transfer; and dismissal. No employer can afford to ignore the legal requirements of the acts although as yet they have not promoted the equalization process which many had hoped that they would. In relation to legislation on sex discrimination, further amendments were made in 1986 to bring British law in line with the EC Equal Treatment directive. These amendments include discrimination in collective agreements and in retirement ages.

Direct and indirect discrimination

Both acts make an important distinction between direct and indirect discrimination in the definition of illegal acts. Direct discrimination is defined as treating a person, on the grounds of sex (this refers to men as well as women and marital status) or race (this refers to colour, race, nationality, citizenship, ethnic or national origins), less favourably than a person of the opposite sex or race is or would be treated in the same circumstances. Indirect discrimination refers to setting requirements or conditions which are loaded against particular groups and where an employer cannot justify them. The concept of indirect discrimination owes much to developments in equality law in the United States. It is aimed at practices which appear on the surface to be fair but which may have unintended discriminatory effects. For example, a tribunal upheld the complaint of a woman who argued that she had suffered indirect discrimination because the post as an executive civil servant for which she had applied had an upper age limit of 28 years. She was supported in her claim that women would be less likely to comply with this age limit because they leave the labour market in their 20s to have children (Price v. Civil Service Commission, 1978).

The acts also cover victimization in order to protect individuals from unfavourable treatment if they pursue a complaint. Thus it would be unlawful to treat a person less favourably than others if they had brought proceedings under the act or if they had given information or evidence in connection with proceedings brought by other employees. In spite of refinements in the definition of discrimination and the protection for individuals, the number of tribunal cases and of successful outcomes remains low (Employment Gazette, 1990). In respect of the Sex Discrimination Act, one analysis of tribunal cases over the period 1976–82 produced the surprising finding that men were using the act far more than women:

> It should come as no surprise that women have declined to make greater use of the law in overcoming discrimination. The combination of inadequate remedies and difficulties of proof appear to have ensured that the Act would only operate on the margins of discrimination in the labour market.
>
> (Hutton, 1984, p. 11).

Enabling features of equal opportunity legislation

There are some important exceptions within the acts to the above regulations. Where there is genuine occupational qualification it is not unlawful to employ a person of a particular race or sex. Examples might be the employment of a black actor for a particular dramatic role or the employment of a woman attendant for a women's changing room in order to meet the requirement of decency or privacy. Of more significance than this are the clauses covering positive action – not to be confused with 'reverse discrimination'.

The provisions for positive action may be exercised by employers, training bodies, trade unions and employers' associations and are intended to provide the opportunity for overcoming some of the obstacles to the under-representation of particular groups in employment. Thus while employers are not required to take positive action, they are enabled to encourage or train members of underrepresented groups in order to help equip them for employment. This does not, of course, make it lawful to discriminate in favour of an underrepresented group at the point of recruitment, promotion, dismissal or in the provision of benefits. However, if employers were to act within the spirit of the law to combine antidiscrimination policies with positive action it could increase employment opportunities for disadvantaged groups. There are some examples of organizations who have provided training opportunities for members of ethnic minorities and women to overcome lack of qualifications or who have made real efforts to target advertisements and information to particular groups. Littlewoods is one such organization which attempts to make vacancies known to members of ethnic minorities by placing advertisements in 'appropriate newspapers and periodicals; and employment agencies experienced in the recruitment of minority groups' (Littlewoods Equal Opportunities (Code of Practice, 1986)).

However, more effort has gone into avoiding the charge of discrimination than it has into making use of the enabling spirit of the legislation. The Commission for Racial Equality and the Equal Opportunities Commission, bodies set up by the acts with powers to promote equality, have expressed deep dissatisfaction with the legislation both because it is not sufficiently coercive and because it is not sufficiently positive. Despite the codes of practice which they have issued to employers to promote compliance with the acts in more proactive way, despite their own powers to support individuals and to bring cases to the courts and despite their investigative role into organizations with a poor record in relation to the law, change has been slow. Both bodies have made recommendations to the secretary of state for changes to strengthen the law. The EOC has called for a new Equal Treatment Act which would replace existing equal pay and sex discrimination legislation and would take into account the standards and provisions of European law. It is likely that European influence will continue to impact upon domestic law as we move through the 1990s, although so far European initiatives have been very weak in respect of race and disability. There is an urgent need for community legislation in both areas. With regard to racial discrimination it is now a matter of concern to the ethnic minorities in the United Kingdom that European law offers them less protection than British law.

The law: a double-edged sword

It might be argued that the law is a double-edged sword in the fight for equality. On the one hand it provides opportunities for contesting discrimination through the courts; on the other it produces a defensive posture in many organizations, their main concern being to tidy up procedures so as to avoid the charge of discrimination. For example, much effort may be spent in covering up loopholes in recruitment practices so as to avoid litigation, without any real change to the pattern of recruitment. However, many would agree that the law is an essential if limited tool in the development of equal opportunities.

As can be seen, constitutional and legal definitions of equality rest upon the basic premise that individuals are entitled to equal treatment whatever their origin or social background. That the law is not more effective in bringing about change is partly a function of the way it is framed and the many problems which individuals find in using it for redress. However, legal solutions can only go so far in combating inequalities which are embedded in all our institutions. Those who find themselves unable to gain access to better paid employment because of a lack of qualifications are unlikely to find a solution in the law, although legislation may help to set a climate in which fairer education and training policies are developed.

Inequalities in the labour market

Employing organizations both reflect the existing inequalities of society and play a major role in reproducing them. A real commitment to equality would mean breaking that cycle and taking a proactive stance against the structures which divide people by gender, race, nationality and class. It would mean challenging discrimination based upon disability, sexual orientation and age. Divisions and processes of discrimination permeate society and profoundly affect a person's equality of opportunity in the workplace. It would be difficult to argue that organizational policies could by themselves produce a more equitable society, but clearly they have an important role to play in breaking the cycle of inequality which affects the individual's employment rights. A brief examination of some features of the current labour market reveals that membership of certain groups fundamentally affects a person's rights to equal opportunity in employment.

Patterns of unemployment among the ethnic minorities, the 'disabled' and the 'old'

One of the most significant divisions in modern industrial society is that created by high levels of unemployment, particularly of long-term unemployment. A detailed discussion of the problems in defining and measuring unemployment cannot be attempted here. My intention is to point to several examples where, imperfect though unemployment statistics are, they reveal the structural inequalities which underlie them.

In the United Kingdom for instance, while there is considerable variation in unemployment rates between ethnic minority groups, further complicated by variations of sex and age, members of ethnic minorities are much more likely to experience unemployment than whites in the population in similar sex and age groups. Overall, during the period 1987–89 the unemployment rate for ethnic minorities was 14% compared with 9% for the white population, this difference reflected in the 16–24 year old age group (Employment Gazette, 1991a). Youth unemployment rates in general are higher than for other age groups – a problem which can be found throughout Europe and which is related to lack of skills and qualifications. The reasons for a higher rate of unemployment among young people from ethnic minorities are complex, including the disadvantages of coming from families where unemployment and low-paid jobs are more common, from living in high unemployment areas and in some cases from their lack of qualifications. Research has shown a high educational participation rate and commitment among young people in ethnic minorities, an investment on their part which remains to be recognized by employers. A commentary on the findings of one such study concludes:

> . . . even after taking account of factors such as attainment and local labour market conditions, the research found that young people from ethnic minorities were more likely to experience both higher rates and longer spells of unemployment. This difference in performance cannot be 'explained' statistically.
>
> (LMQR, 1992)

Statistics on patterns of unemployment among the ethnic minorities are indicative of the way in which inequality is structured in society. To the evident disadvantages which affect the employment opportunities of certain groups must be added the processes of discrimination which erect further barriers. Among those barriers are the policies and practices of educational institutions and employers. Arguably, people with a disability suffer the highest rates of unemployment as a result.

Assessments of levels of unemployment among those with a disability vary according to definitions of disability and estimates of the proportion of people with a disability in the population. Accordingly, the rate has been shown to be as low as 5%, based on those registered as disabled in 1990; and as high as 27% for men and 20% for women in 1989, based on Office of Population Censuses and Surveys (OPCS) data (Floyd, 1991). It is widely agreed that the OPCS statistics are drawn from a more realistic estimate of the numbers of people with a disability in the population than that provided by registration.

There is little doubt that among those with a disability, unemployment is a common experience, often of a prolonged nature. Their marginal position in the labour market reflects widespread exclusionary practices which leads one author to describe them as an underclass (Oliver, 1991). Employer practices towards those with disabilities is typically based on untested assumptions about their suitability and 'fitness' for jobs. Thus it is 'the disabled' who are seen to be the problem and not the disabling attitudes and restrictive environments of organizations which together constitute persistent barriers to their employment opportunities (Barnes, 1992).

Although not so deeply entrenched, similar processes of discrimination against older people are evident during periods when labour supply exceeds demand. In recent years the number of unemployed people aged between 45 and state retirement age has risen and they have experienced longer periods of unemployment than other age groups. For example, in the United Kingdom in 1990, 34% of the older age group had been seeking work for three years compared with 15% of those aged 25–44 and 5% of those aged 16–24 (Employment Gazette, 1991b). Once having been defined as 'old' the disadvantage of that label leads to a deteriorating position in which obtaining employment becomes less and less likely. Studies indicate evidence of increasing age discrimination in advertisements against those over 45, even among firms declaring themselves to be equal opportunities employers (Equal Opportunities Review, 1989). Such discriminatory practices are based on myths and stereotypes of those in middle age as less adaptable and slower to learn new skills.

The above examples of unemployment among ethnic minorities, people with a disability and older people illustrate the different starting points from which they seek to enter paid work and indicate some of the barriers which stand in their way. What we discover when we look beneath statistics is a complex process of marginalization which requires proactive action on the part of employers if it is to be countered. Discrimination based upon membership of certain groups in society will not only lead to exclusion from paid employment of longer or shorter periods; it will also limit the type of paid work available to those jobs which are less well paid, with less opportunity for progression, and with less job security. This pattern is clearly evident when we examine the effects of gender discrimination on women's position in the labour market.

Patterns of employment among women

Women's current status in the labour force echoes a long history of unequal access to education and employment. Some believe that the 1990s will be the time when women break with a past in which they have been undervalued and underutilized in paid work. Opportunity 2000 is a British campaign which seeks to give practical expression to that belief. The problem is whether such a campaign addresses the barriers to equality in the workplace for all women or for only a few. Some argue that its scope is too limited because it is founded on a simplistic analysis of women's inequality in employment (Equal Opportunities Review, 1992). Moreover, past efforts to change women's unequal position in the labour market indicate just how entrenched it is:

> By 1990, a decade and a half will have passed since the adoption of the first community Directive to provide equality of treatment of men and women in the labour market, and the second Community Action Programme for Equal Opportunity for women will have come to an end. Despite these legal and social initiatives, progress in achieving equality has been slow and

women still remain confined to traditional occupations with relatively low
level jobs.

(Commission of the European Communities, 1989, p. 85)

this, despite the fact that more women are in paid work than ever before in
industrial societies and the hope that their increasing participation in the
labour force will plug the gap left by declining numbers of young people. The
1991 Labour Force Survey shows that the number of women in employment
had increased by almost 20% since 1979 (Employment Gazette, 1992).
Women's increased participation yet their marginal position in the labour
market is evident in all industrialized societies, although cultural variations
make for different patterns. For example, France and Britain have similar
high rates of female participation in the labour force but France has a lower
rate of part-time employment among women (Beechey, 1989). Moreover, in
France part-time employees have the same rights as full-time employees
whereas in Britain they do not. However, women's unemployment is higher
in France and they are just as likely to be concentrated in a narrow band of
female occupations. The patterns of gender inequality may not be identical
but broad trends persist.

European statistics reveal that women in the EC countries are mainly
employed in the service sector (73% of the total) and only a minority in
industry (20%). The expansion of the service sector through the 1980s was
accompanied by an increase in part-time jobs in which women, particularly
married women, also predominate. This has had the effect of bringing more
women into the labour force and of 'cushioning' them against unemployment
(at least as officially measured). Recent UK statistics indicate that 82% of
employed women are in service industry jobs compared with 54% of men,
with slightly lower levels of unemployment for women; 7% compared with
9% for men (Employment Gazette, 1992). But as the recession in the early
1990s bit hard there were signs that jobs in the service sector were declining.
If trends like that were to continue, official rates of unemployment among
women would no doubt rise again as they have in the past. The 1991 Labour
Force Survey indicated that women accounted for 43% of employed people
and that two-fifths worked part-time, with 1.89 million working 15 hours or
less per week (Employment Gazette, 1992). There is little employment
security for such workers.

The expansion of women's jobs in the service sector can be seen as a
continuing trend of occupational segregation which establishes certain kinds
of work as women's work, built upon and reproducing gender divisions in
society. Evidence shows that women are overrepresented in lower grade
occupations across a relatively narrow band – clerical work, professions such
as teaching and nursing and personal service jobs. It has been argued that
the growth of part-time jobs in such occupations as cleaning, cooking and
caring work is a new form of organized work specific to women which exploits

their tenuous relation to the labour market (Beechey and Perkins, 1987). It has the effect of confining large numbers of women to low-level employment which runs counter to any aspirations for their future contribution to a skilled labour force:

> The low pay which characterises part-time work and the concentration of women in such work accentuates the segregation already apparent in men's and women's employment patterns, and further confines women to the low skilled, insecure jobs.
>
> (Morris, 1991, p. 77)

Women: a flexible labour force

The above trends suggest that large numbers of women meet the requirements of what has been termed the 'flexible firm' which requires a core of permanent staff and a periphery of workers who provide numerical flexibility (Atkinson, 1984). Although a recurring theme of debates about the labour market in Europe in the 1980s, where there has generally been a growth of what can be termed nonstandard work (such as temporary work, short-term contracts, agency temping, part-time work and self-employment), it is by no means clear whether this will be an enduring feature of the labour market or of human resource strategies. However, it is important to recognize that legal changes, particularly in the United Kingdom in relation to the public sector, push employers in the direction of flexibility. For example, local authorities are required by law to put a range of services out to competitive tendering – typically this leads to redundancies and a worsening of conditions among already disadvantaged groups. Equally, pressures on all organizations to become more efficient may weaken equal opportunity initiatives. For example, recent research into one large retail company identified the trends towards more part-time work (without *pro rata* pay rates and pension rights) and towards temporary contracts. In the same company, the equal opportunities officer's recommendation to improve maternity policy for all employees was ultimately confined, on financial grounds, to middle and senior management (Cockburn, 1991). If the trend towards flexibility were to continue, it would clearly influence the direction and levels of commitment to equality in organizations, in spite of demographic change which some believe will create opportunities for women and other disadvantaged groups:

> Changes in the gender distribution of employment have important consequences for human resource management particularly when they are related to changes in demographic structure. Potential labour shortages in the next century are likely to see employers balancing the need for numerical flexibility with the desire to recruit and retain women workers.
>
> (Bridgeford and Stirling, 1993)

Those who are on the margins are most likely to be left in the cold, even where opportunities for training and career development become more available for core workers. Part-time female employees are those least likely to receive on-the-job training. Peripheral workers might however benefit either by innovative employment schemes which draw them closer to the core (such as opportunities to take up management positions on a part-time or job-share basis) or by the enhancement of employment rights for nonstandard forms of employment. Much depends upon the strategies which employers develop as their response to the changing shape of the labour force.

Equality in the workplace: working for change

Working for equality is a difficult task and one which cannot be ensured merely by having the 'right' policies. Of greater importance is the way in which equality issues are defined and tackled within the specific cultures of organizations in which there will be more or less resistance to the changes envisaged.

The problem of 'ownership' of equal opportunities

When considering who 'owns' equal opportunities in the organization it is important to recognize a possible tension between centralized equal opportunity policies and decentralized and more flexible management, seen by many to be a desirable characteristic of strategic HRM. Many organizations have gone down the path of appointing equal opportunity officers located either in personnel divisions or in specialist units. This has the advantage of giving a higher profile to equal opportunities than would otherwise be the case, but it raises a number of important questions about the place and authority of equal opportunity officers in the management structure of the organization. Research so far indicates that without commitment from board level the task of equal opportunity officers is extremely difficult, if not impossible. However, the will of line managers to enact the policy is just as important. As has been seen in Chapter 3, studies of the development of human resource systems confirm a general trend towards expansion of the line manager's role to include many of the functions which were previously seen as the proper concern of personnel specialists. As such, their awareness of equality issues and commitment to them become even more crucial to the process of change:

> Effective equal opportunity policy and, more importantly, practice will result when we achieve line management 'ownership'. This can only occur by integrating equal opportunity ethos into every aspect of human resource strategy and its local application.
>
> (Mahon, 1989, p. 79)

The problem of competing interests and resistance to change

In order to achieve the integration of equality of opportunity into every aspect of human resource strategy, it is essential to assess the existing culture of an organization. In general there will be resistance to change and, as has been shown, the inequalities which pervade society will be reflected to varying degrees in the attitudes and behaviours of people who work within organizations. Within specific organizations it cannot be assumed that either management or worker attitudes will be uniform. Reasons for resisting change towards equality will vary, just as will motives for supporting change.

Managerial motives for adopting/supporting equal opportunity policies will probably run along a spectrum from moral commitment to defensive compliance to the law to outright resistance. In some cases, as we have seen, management may also be convinced that equal opportunity policies and strategies will ensure the optimum use of available human resources, and in this respect they have focused more on women than on other disadvantaged groups. However, resistance to equality is likely to come from those higher up in the echelons of the organization because they have more to lose. For example, if more women are to enter the higher reaches of management, this requires a change in the traditional distribution of power of men over women in organizations. It also threatens to expose masculine ways of working and demands changes in working relationships. Sexist attitudes and behaviour among senior male managers are still much in evidence and have been cited as among the main factors constraining women's advancement (Hansard Society, 1990).

Few women make it into top managerial positions even in those occupations which are predominantly 'female'. There is some evidence that women have gained ground in lower and middle levels of management but progress is slow. In the United Kingdom it has been estimated that women's advancement in general management positions increased from less than 5% in 1971 to 11% in 1988; and in managerial jobs outside general management from 20% in 1971 to 25% by 1988. However, little change had occurred at the top of organizations where scarcely a women can be found at executive or board level (Hansard Society, 1990). Figures indicating that women hold 4% of middle to senior management positions and 2% of executive posts are probably close to the present position (Hammond, 1992). Research both nationally and internationally confirms that women's progress to higher levels of management is hampered by traditional definitions of gender roles and outdated training and employment policies (Jelnick and Adler, 1988). Without well-formulated human resource strategies to enable women to develop their potential in organizations which are prepared to change their cultures, we are unlikely to see them moving up organizational hierarchies which, in many respects, exclude them. Focusing in isolation on a few 'promising' women is to side-step the equality issue and will generate hostility among women as well as men.

Equal opportunity policies can usher in resistance at all levels of the organization, particularly when they are seen to target certain groups. Indeed, positive action on behalf of selected groups may cause resentment from others. This is not necessarily an argument against positive action as an important strategy in achieving change. For example, the introduction in Leicester City Council for a 'retainer and re-entry' scheme drew criticism from the organization's race relations unit on the grounds that it might be indirectly discriminatory because it would benefit white women more than ethnic minority women. However, analysis of the age distribution of women employees showed that only one-third of white women were under 30 compared with two-thirds of ethnic minority women. On this basis it was possible to argue that the scheme might benefit ethnic minority women more, although they were an underrepresented group and this would require a different remedy (Powell, 1989). This serves to show not only the importance of effective monitoring, but also the delicacy of planning and evaluating changes which may be seen as threatening to the interests and needs of different groups within the workforce.

Conclusion: formulating a strategy for change in the workplace

It has been argued that without a transformation of the power structures in organizations which would mean an equalization process for all, action which advantages particular groups will be divisive (Cockburn, 1991). Others have argued in similar vein that if equality is to permeate the organization it would involve radical changes in the definition and requirements of jobs. For example, more flexible arrangements for all jobs would break down the link between part-time and low-level work and the concept of career as a male preserve (Webb and Liff, 1988).

Whether or not organizations envisage radical change, it is clear that the process of change will be a long one in which it is wise to set objectives within realistic timescales. Transformation of the organization in terms of equality may be considered as part of a long agenda, the short agenda focusing on 'cleaning up' personnel practices (Cockburn, 1991). The most realistic approach is to focus on the steps which must be taken in between, and to formulate strategy in relation to the existing culture of the organization and in terms of specified goals for change. The task for organizations who are convinced that equal opportunities make good business sense is to set their own agendas, which will take them beyond formalistic concerns with personnel procedures and towards a cultural shift.

Evidence from organizations which claim some success in developing innovations in equal opportunities suggests the importance of informed and systematic planning, carefully designed training programmes and effective communication. In a number of cases the use of external consultants has proved valuable. Once an agenda is set it should be subject to regular review to establish levels of awareness of equality issues, potential conflicts, and to make further plans in the light of existing achievements and/or problems. The following case study of the Wellcome Foundation offers examples of strategy and practice which human resource managers and specialists elsewhere could study with benefit for their organizations:

> I cannot stress enough the need to understand your own organisation and culture, and to utilise its strengths. To attempt to impose any set 'methodology' in such a sensitive subject area as this will create resistance and prove counter-productive.
>
> (Tom Mahon, Chair of Wellcome's intersite Equal
> Opportunities Committee, 1989)

CASE STUDY: *Planning for change at Wellcome Foundation*

[Based on an article by Tom Mahon in *Personnel Management* (1989) with kind permission of the *Personnel Management*, monthly magazine of the Institute of Personnel Management.]

In the early 1980s equal opportunity policies had been developed as part of the personnel function to ensure 'good employment policies'. Demographic change and an increasingly competitive international market led the company to plan for a much stronger relationship between human resource planning and equal opportunities. It is suggested that the union, then ASTMS and subsequently MSF, was also instrumental in bringing equality of opportunity for women in the organization to the fore.

- In 1984 produced a policy statement and decided on an in-depth review to be conducted by external consultants. The review made 76 recommendations, including the setting up of a jointly constituted equal opportunity committee (this reflecting earlier discussions which had identified the concern of both the union and staff to develop equal opportunities in the organization).

- Decided to prioritize the 76 recommendations into short-, medium- and long-term timescales.

- In 1986 implemented a number of straightforward personnel practice recommendations; for example, changing application forms so that information on ethnic origin and marital status would be entered on a 'tear off' section, to be torn off before the form is forwarded to managers; amending courses for managers on recruitment and selection and injecting discussion of equal opportunity courses into all workshops, seminars and courses; encouraging women to return to work after childbirth by offering the equivalent of six weeks' basic pay, over and above statutory maternity pay.

- Decided to invest in awareness training developed by external consultants and tailored to Wellcome's needs. This covered the senior management group, all personnel/training teams and employee representatives. Paid particular attention to the need to handle the training in a firm but sensitive style so as to reinforce company commitment to equal opportunity and to secure enthusiasm for personal action plans. The consultants also ran courses to train internal training staff.

- Launched a new internal magazine dedicated to equal opportunity issues, edited by the company's UK equal opportunity coordinator and distributed free with the company house journal. Used the magazine to introduce a sexual harassment policy.

- By 1990 had established initiatives in response to the pressing problem of childcare, including the opening of two nurseries in partnership with other organizations; the setting up of informal networks for working parents; and consideration of paternity leave. Committed to examining career breaks and other forms of parental leave in the following year.

- Added to the agenda, the development of a system for monitoring to inform future policy.

- Identified for future consideration the EOC's aim to enhance the status of part-time work and to achieve pay and nonpay benefits for part-time workers equivalent to full-timers.

Clearly many of these activities are building blocks for the future and we recognise we have much still to do. But we do feel we are improving the profile we present to prospective employees, as well as improving the motivation of our current workforce.

(Mahon, 1989)

Although the findings of much of the research summarized earlier indicate the slow progress of equality programmes on both an international and a national level, some organizations are successfully addressing the human resource problems of the 1990s and developing appropriate 'strong' versions of equal opportunity policies and practices. It is at least possible that these forward-looking organizations are setting a pattern for the future. Without such attempts to break the cycle of inequality, disadvantaged groups will remain an untapped pool of talent during a period when many believe that their contribution to the changing world of work could be crucial.

9

The strategic management of recruitment and selection

Robin Evenden

By the end of this chapter the reader will:

1. understand how selection can contribute effectively to strategic management;

2. understand concepts relating to selection and its interaction with other processes in human resource management;

3. be able to identify selection issues which have strategic implications;

4. have a critical appreciation of a range of selection methods and their practical implications for an organization.

Introduction

The approaches to strategic management were presented in the first chapter of this book. Some macro models, rather like their source discipline of economics, appear to allow no room for real people in their world, let alone HRM. This chapter assumes that strategic goals and the extent to which they are achieved are influenced by people, and that the quality of the contribution of the human resource is in part a function of selection.

Storey (1992) has articulated the distinctive features of HRM, as opposed to traditional personnel management. Two of these underpin the analysis in this chapter of the connections between strategic management, human resource management and selection: the integration of selection, appraisal, development and performance management; and the management of people as a business-oriented process, in the sense that people perform and add value to the organization. Although there may be distinctions between HRM and personnel management in terms of beliefs, assumptions and focus (Storey, 1992), throughout this chapter those professionals labelled 'personnel' are viewed as potential exponents of HRM.

It is misleading to define HRM ideologically as 'new right Thatcherism' intent upon socially engineering an 'enterprise culture' (Blyton and Turnbull, 1992). HRM is instrumental in achieving the strategic goals of an organization, whether they are bottom line and commercial, or related to service or to social responsibility. An instrument which is used to seek the efficient use of all resources and to achieve planned objectives through commitment and involvement is not the philosophical property of either left or right.

The approach taken here involves some theory, conceptualizing the relationship between the organization and its environment. It will also include some description of how organizations use HRM, with cases and illustrations. There will also be prescriptive elements which suggest how organizations and human resource managers can apply analytic devices and methods to review and perform their selection function strategically.

The strategic role of HRM and its implications for selection

Selection is the process of deciding who to move into an organization (recruitment); who to move up (promotion); who to move across (transfer); and who to move out (dismissal). It is about moving people according to judgements about their potential contribution to the organization through job performance. Human resource management uses **job analysis** to identify the kind of personal characteristics needed to perform adequately. They are described in a profile or **person specification,** which is dependent upon the requirements of the job, identified in a **job description** which is influenced by many factors. These include technical content, people content and organizational context, described by Hall (1992) as the intangible resources of know-how, personal relationships and culture.

The resources Hall mentions contribute to the achievement of our strategic goals. If strategic plans are laid, based upon a strategic vision, and if new organizational objectives are set, there will be implications for the human resources required. The management of the strategy and the achievement of its goals is in part up to HRM, which interprets the strategic plan, and makes the intangible become tangible in terms of people. They are measured, assessed, selected, appraised, developed and motivated. Human resource management identifies what new know-how is needed, what different personal relationships are wanted and whether a culture change is required. Those who deliver the goods may be human resource specialists, or line managers using HRM systems, or more likely a combination of both.

At this point it is important to remember the distinction Purcell (1989) makes between different levels of strategy in an organization. He defines 'upstream first order decisions' as those to do with planning the long-term direction of the firm; 'downstream second order decisions' as those to do with consequent changes to organizational structure and operating procedures; and 'downstream third order decisions' as those to do with HRM strategic choices. If we accept his definition of HRM as a third order strategic function, then whoever it is who wills the strategic 'ends', it is HRM which has to deliver many of the significant 'means' through people. Selection issues related to both these means and ends are the focus of this chapter.

Strategic management, if it is to merit the description, involves a design for the future which has at least a degree of grandness. This implies that the managers are not blind. Indeed, they are required to see the present clearly, predict future probabilities and make choices about where they want to be. In one study (Price Waterhouse Cranfield, 1992) half the organizations surveyed claimed to manage strategically. It would seem reasonable to assume that the strategic 50% undertook some kind of 'visioning' involving scanning their internal and external environments, drawing conclusions about how they wanted to be different, where they wanted to go and how they were going to get there.

Human resource specialists may have been involved in this strategic visioning and planning process prior to implementation. Practice varies widely, depending upon organizational politics and the status of the HRM function within the organization. If people are a significant part of the environment and the plan, then human resource expert input to strategic decisions about the future would seem appropriate. This issue will be addressed later. In any event, HRM will at this point have interpretive and implementation functions.

Whether the strategy is the outcome of vision, plan or 'mission statement', whether the process is deliberate or emergent, clear or coded, the HRM role is to interpret it and translate it into 'people' terms. Even if human resource managers operate within an organization with no discernible corporate plan, as perhaps half of them do, their HRM function is best served by operating as if there is one. This is necessary if they are to operate strategically and develop human resource policies and plans related to the organization's future.

Strategic management is not solely the province of the board. As we saw in Chapters 1 and 2 there are different levels of strategy, with 'corporate' dealing with overall priorities and planning; 'business units' fitting into the corporate whole and devising their own individual goals in 'local' circumstances; and 'functional', such as human resources, listening there below with their own strategies to service the superordinate needs of the higher levels (Thompson and Strickland, 1992).

Like other functions, human resource management is subjected to diverse strategic management styles. They may be clear directives about future developments upon which selection and development strategies must be devised; those primarily responsible for the function may be consulted or share in corporate decisions which affect HRM plans; or they may be subjected to short-termism or even silence. When they listen but hear nothing from above, apart from the occasional emergency call for help, they must actively seek a strategy from top management. If this fails, they must themselves seek a pattern for the future by their own environmental scan.

HR as an upstream strategic function

If human resource specialists are represented in the primary strategic management visioning processes, their expertise could help in the formulation of plans and goals, particularly when there is a strong people and selection dimension such as a major cultural or socio-technical change. They would, of course, be in a position to influence the initiation of change themselves at this level, rather than reacting to strategies designed by others.

Such primary influence could have two kinds of outcome. The first is that the human resource scan of the external environment may reveal a different order of threats and opportunities which could affect the organization's business strategy and competitiveness. The second possible outcome is that a different range of values may come to influence strategic policy. This assumes that human resource specialists do see the world in a different way from other functions. If they do, they could, for example, present the business case for equal opportunity selection policy as effective human resourcing, and the socially responsible strategy to adopt, as suggested in Chapter 8. In this way they could urge the case for 'humane HRM' (p. 72) in ways that focus none the less on business needs. Selecting for diversity through employment of underutilized groups, as a means of defusing the (smaller cohorts of younger employees) demographic time-bomb that may eventually explode through high unemployment levels, is one of the kinds of human resource argument which should be exercising strategic management.

Another powerful illustration is provided by Malcolm Greenslade (1991), Grand Metropolitan's group employment policy director.

> It was felt that the success of any (equal opportunity and diversity) programme would not be in the statement of policy . . . but in the commitment to action that would implement the policy. . . . A proposal was submitted by the corporate HR department . . . recommending a policy and implementation programme for managing diversity. . . . This sought to provide a business case. . . . A corporate review measuring progress towards the corporate goals will take place every six months.

The business case was the US experience that the organization can profitably reflect the cultural diversity in the marketplace. For example, Hispanics represent a $160 billion market and is the fastest growing in the United States. Grand Met's subsidiary, Burger King, now has as strategic policy the recruitment of a higher proportion of Hispanics. It had already increased its African–American employee proportion from 12% to 18% in four years and its selection goal is to continue that trend. The selection strategy in the United Kingdom is similarly based on the premise that it is profitable for the organization membership to move towards matching the diversity of the market.

This is the first type of outcome of human resource management operating at a primary strategic level. It involves environment scan and contribution to business strategy and effectiveness, and in this case it led to a new recruitment strategy.

The second type of outcome could be human resources taking the strategic initiative in people issues of a moral and ethical nature, reflecting the concept of social responsibility, such as equal opportunity in all its aspects, *for its own sake*. In other words, human resource strategists could urge the cause of humane HRM, despite concerns already noted in that respect, (p. 72) and could also assume the ethical role that is implicit, for example, in the Institute of Personnel Management's professional code. This point is discussed further at the end of the chapter.

If a study by the University of Westminster (Burke, 1992) reflects reality, this second option is not likely to have many champions. Those constant members of strategic management, finance and marketing directors, were low in the ethics league. Personnel staff topped the table, although this could be the reason why they are often not invited to the strategic table in the first place!

The possibility is that if human resource specialists are not involved in setting them, strategic goals will be defined in technical and not people terms in a way which will inhibit the effective selection and harnessing of the human resources. As we saw in Chapter 1 (p. 29):

> Giles (1991) maintains that the technical side of strategy generation is overemphasized, to the neglect of the human aspects of strategy. He suggests that the wider ownership of strategy among the organizational members is the key to successful implementations.

The technical orientation of the primary strategic groups does not appear to be universal. Storey (1992), reporting on numerous cases and interviews with line managers, indicated that strategic people issues were increasingly occupying senior line management.

HR as downstream strategic function

If human resource specialist managers are excluded at the primary stages of strategy, there is still the supporting role of implementation to be carried out to facilitate the achievement of goals set by others. The relationship between the goal setters and the implementers appears to be critical for the effectiveness of planned goal achievement. If it is a close and involved relationship, as will be seen in the case study of Pension and Life Insurance, there is a good chance that the organization will move in the planned direction through its selection and development policy.

Another possibility is that the primary strategic group may wish the ends but not will the means, nor have an explicit method of harnessing the collaboration of those functional departments who would have to deliver the plan. This is wishful thinking strategic management. At best it involves planting the vision and goals like a banner on a peak, leaving those below, such as HRM functions, to scramble upwards as best they can. At worst there is no articulated strategy and the secondary groups are only aware that they have a mountain to climb. How assertive and strategic the human resource function is in its climb is then in large measure dependent upon its own choice.

Which of the strategic positions HRM occupies and how it performs will be substantially influenced by how the function is perceived by others and how it perceives itself. There are no universals here. The General Food case is a clear illustration of strategic and proactive HRM influencing business policy and translating this directly into recruitment policy. Similarly, Mueller and Purcell (1992), in their international study of the car industry, cite Ford as an illustration of personnel management not being marginalized but being part of a functionally integrated strategic management team.

However, looking at the car manufacturing industry generally in Europe, Mueller and Purcell concluded that the managers responsible for initiating change were not personnel people but operations managers and directors. The personnel role was administrative or facilitative in support of other managers' initiatives. They suggest that many studies agree with their conclusion that:

> . . . the pressure for change in *personnel* practice . . . comes from line managers and senior executives. Personnel is not at the forefront of change but can play a major role in the facilitation of change *if they wish to*.
>
> [my italics]

In a survey of line managers' perceptions of personnel management and its role (Allen, 1991), already referred to in Chapter 3, the most frequent activity wanted from the personnel function was a human resource contribution to the business strategy, particularly in relation to recruitment, compensation, motivation and performance:

> Many of the managers were clearly looking for a strategic management input allied to professional knowledge to apply the strategy. Yet those who had the clearest view of this role of the function . . . were frequently disappointed . . .

Only 5% of the respondents had experience of human resource staff as contributors to strategic management.

It would seem that although HRM professionals are rarely included in first or second order strategic management, at least in the United Kingdom, their role at these and the third order support and implementation level is as much a function of their perception of themselves and their role as it is of other managers' perception of them. If they are neither assertive nor strategic in their vision of the HRM function, their contribution to the strategic design will be minimal. If HR managers are neither creative nor proactive in their response to that design, they will fail to translate it into people terms. Selection of who to move in, up and out will then be nonstrategic. HRM will probably be guided by short-term expedient 'ad hocery' and past patterns rather than by a strategic assessment of what the organization needs in the future.

Perhaps it is time for the human resource profession to conduct a Johari window exercise, assessing how it sees itself and seeking feedback about how others see it. If such an exercise were to suggest that the profession is not generally where it wants to be in terms of strategic role and competence, the remedy will probably be in the areas of 'best practice modelling' and its profession's strategic leadership, image, entry population, training and development.

In the absence of such an exercise, Durham University Business School, a number of human resource professionals and other senior line managers are drawing their own conclusions with their coming together on a part-time

MBA which offers a specialization in strategic human resource development (Arkin, 1991). Learning about each others' functions and integrating their knowledge in a strategic context within a collaborative educational environment would appear one way to approach the issues. A broad base, wide vision, confidence in their own expertise and accepting the value of that of others are prerequisites for individual contributions to strategic management teams.

Translating strategic goals into selection requirements

To arrive at the implications for selection, the impact of the corporate strategy on the organization's socio-technical system has first to be assessed. At its simplest this may be a three-part checklist of the projected strategy's effect upon technical, organizational and people factors. At its most sophisticated, it would be a projection of the interaction between these three subsystems and an assessment of the resultant changes which have human resource implications:

- *Technical* Will the strategy involve changes in the technical systems, methods, procedures, equipment or technology that people use to do their jobs?

- *Organizational* Will the strategy involve changes in structure, roles, communication, decision-making, planning or management styles affecting people's accountability, responsibility and authority?

- *People* Will the strategy directly, or through technical and organizational aspects, involve people changes? Will it affect attitudes, relationships and motivation? Will it require differences in them in terms of these factors and other personal attributes, knowledge, experience and skills?

This concept has been developed from that first used by the Tavistock Institute and described by Biddle and Evenden (1989).

Complex interactions between the three subsystems may have effects which require strategic HRM responses. For example, the external environment scan could identify threats and opportunities which are interpreted as demanding a high rate of technical innovation and rapid response to local circumstances. This may be seen to require organizational devolution and decision-making based upon technical expertise rather than position. Human resource management may interpret that the nature and quality of the know-how needed may well be a scarce resource in the organization. In addition, a turbulent environment could demand a more organic form of organization, with frequent change and higher levels of uncertainty.

To seize the opportunities and avoid the threats, the organization may require a radical change in its culture, or in 'the way we do things around here'. Much has already been written about this complex area in Chapter 2. The organization could need its people to be different and it may need different people. Line management and human resource specialists will have to collaborate to identify these differences, as well as when and how to get them in place (Figure 9.1). It may involve new selection policies and criteria with recruits and promotees selected from new specifications and attracted from new sources. Development will have a key role, and decisions will have

CONDUCT THE PROCESS OF **strategic management**

(1) **Strategic vision**   Scan the environment
What we want to be like
What goals we want to achieve

(2) **Strategic plan**   How we are going to get there

(3) **Implementation**   Getting there

ASSESS IMPACT UPON **socio-technical system**

Technical ⟷ Organizational

People

TRANSLATE INTO **HRM system**

Job analysis   *Job description*   What are the job changes?

translated into

Person specification   Do we need different attributes from our people?

People audit   What attributes do we have in individuals?
What are our collective attributes?

TRANSLATE INTO

SELECTION   *Recruitment*   Do we need different person specification criteria in recruits?

Promotion   Do we need to promote on different criteria?

Dismissal   Who will not fit the new specification adequately even with development?

DEVELOPMENT   What are the person specification shortfalls that can be met by training and development?

Figure 9.1 *Strategic management, HRM and selection policy.*

to be made about those who will not fit the organization in the future. The projected socio-technical system will now need to be translated into an HRM system.

The translation of strategy into selection terms continues through the medium of job analysis. The initial analytical activity is the assessment of the impact that strategic changes will have on what people have to do in their jobs and how they have to do them. This job description phase will lead to the identification of the changes to the person specifications, which spell out the different attributes now needed from people (Evenden and Anderson, 1992). These key HRM tools will be dealt with briefly at this point in order to explore connections between strategy and selection and the case study illustration which follows. A more detailed discussion of job analysis and other selection methods can be found towards the end of the chapter.

Job descriptions are standard HRM tools, but they are frequently inadequate for the tasks they need to perform within organizations. One problem is that they are often too brief and superficial to produce person specifications which aid effective differentiation between candidates for selection. Another difficulty is that they are not sensitive to organizational change, because their construction is treated as an infrequent bureaucratic exercise rather than as a human resource management of change tool. For selection, the main purposes of the job need to be identified, along with the major tasks to be performed; the people conditions of the job, such as reporting line, internal and external contacts and staff management; special aspects; and the rewards and condition attached to the job.

'Tasks' need to be more than a label in the job description. There should be a sufficient description of the nature of the activity for the selectors to be able to specify clearly the qualities they are looking for in the candidates. As we shall see in the case study shortly, to describe the main task of a Pensions and Life Insurance direct salesperson as: 'Client Sales: To present product benefits to potential clients and to secure sales' gives no indication about the nature and complexity of the sales process. It could be a routine clerical operation with a limited decision-making role, or a sophisticated underwriting procedure carrying considerable financial responsibility. The person specification would be very different in the two cases, and the job description needs to have enough information for an appropriate person to be specified. The job description category 'special aspects' would not have been included a few years ago, when change was less prevalent. Now it is a useful repository of reminders and information to selectors about unusual, temporary or changing features of a job and its context.

The **person specification** is derived from the job description, and indicates the ideal person to perform the job to the level required. It underpins selection strategy by:

■ describing who you are looking for;

- indicating where you look inside and where you need to look outside, in conjunction with people audit data;
- determining your selection methods, such as interview, tests or assessment centres and how to apply them;
- assisting selection decisions through the systematic comparison of candidates.

Hall's intangible strategic resources (1992) are made tangible by the person specification categories, within which the ideal person is described. Those categories which feature in some form in many schemes are as follows:

- Physical: impact and health.
- Qualifications: educational, technical and professional.
- Work experience and achievements.
- Learning and change.
- Special skills.
- Interests: personal and work motivation.
- Personality: relating to self, others and situation.
- Personal circumstances.

The human resource managers or selectors specify what they are looking for in each category in such a way that they will be able to find evidence, compare candidates and make a decision which successfully predicts the best fit for the job. It is here, in these person specification profiles, that the people changes required by strategic decisions will emerge, perhaps in a few individual cases or possibly across the entire organization. Like the corporate strategies themselves, the HRM interpretation and resultant profiles are judgements. They are not scientific, but can be assisted by systematically applied tools derived from operationalized concepts and HRM experience.

Job analysis can help us identify the people we want in the organization. Through a people audit, it can reveal the existing collective and individual profiles. Matching the two sets of data reveals some of the main information necessary for HRM selection and development decisions. Bentley (1990) suggests that this type of integrated system not only aids selection for recruitment and promotion, but also offers improved individual and corporate results, faster reaction to change, better response to market opportunities and a sharper competitive edge.

In a small organization it would be possible to create an integrated HRM system by using a manual database fed by recruitment, training and appraisal information. The same sources could provide the bases for a computer system in larger organizations or a confidential personal file for individual managers to assist their own HRM.

The case study which follows is intended to illustrate the translation of strategic goals into selection requirements. It also identifies connections between strategic management and HRM with examples of the application of the tools in a selection context. It would lend itself to a study assignment as indicated in Part 3.

CASE STUDY: *The Pension and Life Insurance plc*

■ Stage one

☐ *Background*

The Pension and Life Insurance (PLI) company offers its products to the market through the traditional broker intermediaries. However, during the last decade, in line with its competitors, an increasing proportion of its business has been through direct sales, which offer substantially better profit margins by eliminating the brokers. Clients respond to media advertisements through telephone contact with a direct salesperson.

PLI operates strategically through visioning and planning. This process is marketing and product centred. The main focus is short term, usually reflecting back six months and projecting forward its plans for a similar period. In terms of Mintzberg's model (p. 22) this aspect of the strategic management process can be classified as nearer 'emergent' than 'deliberate'. 'Strategic learning' occurs by the divination of patterns and trends in the market, as indicated by a series of six-monthly visioning sweeps. This trend analysis and the subsequent implementation process move the strategic management closer to 'deliberate'. Financial and marketing goals are set for intermediate (three years) and longer term (five years) periods. Occasionally, 'watershed' strategic decisions are made, which have major socio-technical implications for the organization and HRM.

☐ *Strategic scan: SWOT analysis*

The strategic management team conducted a review of their internal strengths and weaknesses in the light of their assessment of the opportunities and threats in PLI's external environment:

Opportunities: It was predicted that Europe would climb out of the recession of the early 1990s and that the trend towards an increasing proportion of income being invested in long-term savings would continue. A new niche market was developing – this was medium-income groups who were more demanding and sophisticated in relation to life insurance and pensions.

Threats: The market had hardened. Margins were narrowing and competition was intensifying through the single European market. PLI had a declining market share.

Strengths: Primarily technical. PLI had a special competitive advantage through its substantial lead in computer systems. In organization terms it listened to the market through those closest to it, its salespeople. This intelligence was used strategically.

Weaknesses: Its organization was bureaucratic and centralized, so that its underwriting decision response time was slow. The strategic team discovered through its total quality feedback system that 70% of the direct sales enquirers did not eventually purchase, often because the sale could not be closed during the initial telephone contact: the salespeople had neither the role, system nor ability to do this.

☐ *Strategic plan*

PLI made a strategic watershed decision to build upon its technical strength by substantial investment in its computer systems. It would offer a wider and constantly varying range of products to respond to market conditions. It would also incorporate higher level underwriting know-how in a system which could be accessed by its direct salespeople who could analyse client needs and make sales on the spot. PLI would need a 10% increase in sales to cover the investment and expected 20%.

If this case is used as a study assignment, do not read the remainder of the case analysis yet. See Part 3 for the assignment.

■ **Stage two**

☐ *The strategic plan and the socio-technical system*

Technical: The strategy involved developments in the computer systems and the methods and procedure used in direct sales.

Organizational: The level of underwriting management previously used to make product sales decisions would no longer be needed. These responsibilities were passed down to salespeople, whose role in client relations, client need analysis, underwriting awareness and computer operation would change considerably. They would now be accountable for decisions and sales performance.

People: The motivation base of the sales role and the skill and knowledge demands would be substantially different. There would be frequent changes to product, autonomy and more responsibility. Risk and decision-making became part of the new job.

☐   *The HRM response to the strategy*

HRM specialists were not party to the strategic visioning and planning process but were central to its implementation. They were fully informed, however, and had to assess its implications in socio-technical terms and form an HRM strategy satisfactory to the board and capable of delivering the people to achieve the outcomes required.

Part of this involved 'delayering' the underwriting department, assessing the profiles of those involved and liaising with them and line management to identify redeployment opportunities. This was a selection and matching task using the human resource tools considered earlier. The major effort needed was to assess the strategy's impact upon the front-line sales jobs and its effect upon the person specification profile. The job analysis would inform the judgements that had to be made about the suitability of the present incumbents in the new roles, and training and development, as well as recruitment policy in the future.

A simple job description would not be adequate. For example: 'To discuss clients needs, sell the benefits of products, establish a relationship and facilitate sales' is accurate but would apply equally to the new and the old sales roles. The description must enable the user to highlight the significant differences that result from socio-technical change. An illustration of part of a more helpful job description is given in Table 9.1.

Table 9.1 *The effect of PLI's strategy change on job descriptions*

Job factor	Previous job	New job
Client contact	Brief telephone	Extended telephone
Information		
– given	Limited/standardized	Wide/varied
– sought	Simple/standard	Complex/varied
Product range	Narrow/basic	Wide/complex
Computer		
– support	Simple	Complex
– operation	Easy	Moderate
Decisions	Refer upwards outside narrow underwriting limits	Made within wide underwriting limits but with powerful system support
Change	Infrequent	Constant

The new job description now had to be translated into the person specification, which is the key HRM operational tool at this stage. Did PLI need new people found by new recruitment methods or the old people made different by development? Some differences between the old and new person specifications were as follows:

- *Work experience and achievements*

  PLI estimated that a higher level of conceptual and analytical skills would be required. Additionally, a higher underwriting awareness and greater knowledge of principles and practice of insurance were called for. There were a number of combinations of achievements in these two dimensions which would satisfy the selectors that the candidate had or could develop the level of competence required.

- *Learning and change*

  This was previously not specifically assessed during selection. In the light of the expectation of frequent change, the individual's capacity to learn, unlearn and respond positively to change was given significant weight.

- *Interests: personal and work motivation*

  The aim was to select not simply on the skill to work to an acceptable level but in terms of whether this *particular* job would stimulate the will to work well in a candidate. It was probable that many who found the previous job motivating might find the challenges of the new role stressful and demotivating, leading to early separation.

- *Personality: relating to self, others and situation*

  PLI felt that a number of factors would change in this dimension. The person would need to cope with different and greater pressures than in the previous role. There would, for example, be less dependence upon managerial support, higher accountability and risk. In addition to the higher 'adjustment' specification, there was now a different order of relationship development skill needed to maintain rapport with clients in a lengthy and more complex sales relationship.

HR managers and specialists in PLI compared the existing staff against the new specification using line managers' and self-reporting assessments. None were found able to move directly into the new role. They split equally into three groups. The first were those felt to have the potential to develop during the transitional six months. The second were those where there was a degree of uncertainty on key parts of the specification but it was felt appropriate to offer an extended trial and the same development opportunities as the first group. Two-thirds of this group failed to last the course. The final group were regarded as without the potential to fill the new job requirements. Those who did not fit the new role were 'audited' in a rudimentary way and most were matched with other more routine posts within PLI, but several chose to leave.

The human resource strategy had to revolve around a higher salesperson specification. This was judged to mean recruiting for an extensive development programme those with good educational attainments at 18 years and whose personal profiles also fitted the new job description. The previous recruits were assessed for modest levels of literacy and numeracy at 16 years.

The human resource team were aware of a sharp decline in the numbers of 18 year olds in the labour market owing to the higher proportion entering higher education. So it was also found appropriate to plan to recruit modestly achievement-motivated graduates, who would also add to the pool which fed into the future management structure.

A substantial number of experienced staff with appropriate profiles were drafted in from shrinking parts of PLI, including some of the dispossessed underwriting managers. It still left a large number to be attracted from competitors, which PLI expected to achieve by projecting its well-known computer leadership and 'professionalized' sales role. For the first time HRM practitioners decided to include new selection methods in their strategy. Previously the company had gathered its evidence for selection from application forms, interviews and references. It felt that these would not supply sufficient useful information to assess the now critical learning and change, motivation and personality dimensions of the new person specification.

The changed sales roles were central to PLI's achievement of its strategic goals and, in addition, the investment in training and development was substantial. The cost of selection mistakes would be high in consequence. A human resource investment was also made in an assessment centre which incorporated personality testing. It was considered that this would increase the probability of successful selection.

In the case study PLI was able to translate successfully its business strategy into the selection requirements necessary to deliver its corporate objectives. The strategic management team listened to the 'wisdom of the anthill' and incorporated it into their plans. They involved the personnel specialists and line management in the implementation process and received a positive and professional response from both groups, so that the broad design was interpreted accurately and carried out at the workface. This resulted in the development of new strategies regarding recruitment and transfer policies and methods.

In many cases organizations find it difficult to achieve this strategic congruence, collaboration and effectiveness. At this point we should focus again on the discussion on pp. 76–9 about the relationship between line managers and human resource specialists, and also on Chapter 2's analysis (p. 43) of the need for sensitivity, creativity and political skills in strategic HRM.

Achievement of strategic plans: strategies and techniques in selection

Getting the right people in the right jobs, with effective development and motivation, and providing the appropriate blend of know-how, relationships and culture to exploit the organization and technical system so that strategic goals are achieved, is the human resource manager's role in life. Missing out on any element will reduce the chances of accomplishing the mission.

Matching people to jobs is the selection function. A good hit rate is difficult to achieve even in stable organizations in static environments, when the methods may have been attuned by precedent and practice to effective targeting of people. There are many hazards even in these conditions and they are multiplied considerably when selection is undertaken during change.

Some selection methods are no better than chance and the most popular are barely better than choosing at random (Makin and Robertson, 1986). Methods are often inappropriate for the type of evidence they are trying to gather and are made worse as predictors by the fallibility and lack of competence of some who use them. Conversely, they are made better by the application of professionalism, skill and effective support systems. These aspects need reviewing as critical aspects of the human resource contribution to strategic management.

Job analysis and people auditing: Orwellian or oracular?

One major support system for strategic selection is, as we have already seen, job analysis. In essence, this should provide information about who you want to recruit, transfer or promote through describing jobs and specifying the profiles of individuals or groups needed. A second system is the people audit, which tells you the characteristics of the human resources already in membership. A people audit means that all individuals have information about them kept on record. These profiles describe them in relation to all the dimensions of a person specification and need to be altered as individuals alter, for example through experience and development (see earlier case study).

If the two systems are fully integrated, the human resources are described in a tangible way so that future patterns can be assessed against strategic needs, and individuals selected as candidates for development, transfer or promotion. The data would be obtained from recruitment, appraisal and other assessments that are made, for example, through psychological tests.

The advantages of a comprehensive and integrated computer-based system to strategic HRM are extensive (Bentley, 1990), but its development is inhibited in many organizations. Job analysis is often regarded as a bureaucratic exercise which requires time-consuming attention to maintain its accuracy. Even more investment is necessary for it to be sufficiently detailed to be sensitive to the job-related implications of strategic organizational and technical changes. These cost arguments need to be assessed against the benefits of the oracular power of such a system to inform the strategists about the future and to guide its HRM.

The fear of Orwellian 'big brother' intrusions into personal privacy could emerge when such personal information is held and accessed by faceless human resource managers contemplating the future of individuals. However, it is likely that organizations with modestly advanced selection and appraisal systems already have most of the personnel data required by such a system, probably held locally and in manual records. The issue is not where the data is located, but its openness. Data protection, equal opportunity and ethical management would suggest that all assessments and related evidence from selection procedures and appraisal should be open to inspection, discussion and appeal by the individual in any case. This not only has moral arguments about individual liberty in its favour, but also is a sound discipline, encouraging carefully made judgements based upon valid methods and sound evidence. Organizations which practise giving feedback about selection and appraisal assessments could fairly claim that their HRM policies are oracular rather than Orwellian, and are equitable rather than arbitrary.

The application of job analysis does not need to be carried out comprehensively as part of a fully integrated system for it to be the means of translating strategic plans into people and selection terms. It can be used selectively to focus upon only those parts of the organization subject to socio-technical change, as in PLI's sales and underwriting functions in the case study. Its main purpose is to spell out thoroughly and systematically the people changes required. Without it this aspect of HRM would at best be dealt with in a partial and limited fashion and at worst not dealt with at all.

Attraction of recruits

Before an organization can recruit it must attract appropriate candidates. Its approach to attraction needs to relate to organizational analysis and strategy, which informs not only the criteria for selection but also the keynote attractors. The person specification, translated from strategic changes to the socio-technical system, is the tool which guides HRM in its presentation of the job to the labour market. The aim is to achieve helpful self-selection by potential candidates, attracting only those approximately fitting the specification and deterring those who do not.

PLI in the case study, for example, would indicate the new higher level demands of the sales role, especially in the areas of self-management and

Pension and Life Insurance plc

Current role	Job Motivational Rewards	New role
Security		Independence
Good conditions		Interesting work
Support		Responsibility
Stability		Achievement

Attraction motif

Join the team	Rise to the challenge
Well established company	Leading the way in IS

Figure 9.2 Attracting staff. Reassessing the person specification to account for the impact of strategic change on roles.

responsibility. This would involve flagging the new key personality and motivational aspects of the specification. When PLI is aiming at those it hopes to attract from insurance competitors, its attracting would need to include the enhanced role and personal development opportunities, to elicit a response from those frustrated by lesser responsibilities in other companies. It would also need to highlight its market-leading characteristic of distinctive competence and its innovative information support systems.

Strategic change is translated into 'attraction' policy by emphasizing ways the organization can say:

- *We are special*
  'A key role in a unique college' – Sheffield College
  'Will the work you do today stand as a landmark for 250 years?' – Thomas Coram Foundation

or

- *We have a key personality and motivational requirement*
  'Do you have backbone?' – British Army

Among other things, the attractor review would reassess the motivational rewards of the modified roles, repackage them and target them at the new market segment as in Figure 9.2. The HRM task is in some senses a public relations exercise, informing the world in general, its current staff and labour market in particular, that the organization is now 'different'.

Strategy and hazards in selection methods

Strategy involves a broad view of the future and selection involves predicting the part that individuals could play in it. The prediction of individual performance at recruitment or promotion is made hazardous by the limitations of selection methods and those using them. For example, selection methods may be:

- *Invalid*   By their spurious nature unable to predict, such as astrology and graphology.
- *Flawed*   Open to distortion and filtering, such as references.
- *Limited*   Evidence not readily available, such as personality data from written applications.
- *Unfair*   Discriminate against a person on matters not related to job performance, such as questions to women which would not be asked to men.
- *Difficult to handle*   Acquisition of valid evidence requires considerable skill, such as the interview.
- *Difficult to interpret*   Valid interpretation requires extensive knowledge, such as personality tests.
- *Difficult to assess*   Valid assessments from methods such as assessment centres require skill and trained judgement.

The involvement of human resource professionals with specialist skills to advise and design systems and methods reduces the hazards. In most cases, line management play a significant and often decisive part in the process. Allen's survey (1991) indicated that 75% of line managers expected human resource-specialists to be advisory only, with the remainder seeing them involved in joint decision-making.

If non-HRM specialists are untrained and unsophisticated in their handling of this aspect of their human resource role, the hazards are increased and getting the right people in place to achieve strategic goals is less likely.

To assist the review of selection methods related to strategic management, it will help to have an illustration as a theme, and as 'the learning organization' is currently a much discussed strategic vision, that will be used. It is a strategy to develop an organization that is sensitive to environmental change so that it creates opportunities and deals with threats by a process of continuous learning and adaptation that ensures its survival and growth effectiveness.

A learning organization has a number of characteristics, including a learning approach to strategy, participative policy-making, environmental scanners, learning climate and self-development for all (Pedler *et al.*, 1991). However, it is the people in organizations who have to learn and behave in ways that will achieve these results (Honey, 1991; Harrison, 1992), so the person specification will need to incorporate the appropriate characteristics. A few illustrative personal behavioural dimensions are listed in Figure 9.3. The selector would be looking for those who are to the left of the scales.

In assessing the capacity of a selection strategy to help deliver a business strategy, it is essential to review the current methods in the light of the

Appropriate	**Inappropriate**
Experiments	Cautious
Admits mistakes	Rationalizes mistakes
Open	Defensive
Encourages ideas	Discourages ideas
Makes joint decisions	Dominates

Figure 9.3 *Person specification: behaviour appropriate to a learning organization.*

demands which will be placed upon them by any new requirements. Will a new range of methods be needed and what could increase their predictive value? The line managers' selection role is already significant and may well be increasing, so that there is a need for them to develop substantial skill and knowledge. The following is a brief review of selection methods and their effectiveness (see Table 9.2). (A fuller examination is made in Evenden and Anderson, 1992.) It focuses on selecting people for a learning organization.

Application information

This is one of the better ways of gathering evidence to help selection decision-making (Makin and Robertson, 1986). People rarely lie when giving factual information, perhaps because it is checkable. The selector needs to indicate the information needed or it may not be forthcoming.

In recruitment this is the major source of evidence for matching against the person specification to produce a short list. If the application guide does not seek information relevant to behaviour appropriate to a learning organization (Figure 9.3), then there will be little opportunity to have it represented in the people on your short list.

To assess the less tangible 'softer' personal attributes like openness, admitting mistakes and learning to change, you could include questions or statements like: 'How have you developed during the last five years?' or 'Describe a mistake you have made at work and its significance'.

Unless attempts are made to seek more than facts in the written application, there is unlikely to be a great deal of evidence to form even an impressionistic view of what the individual is like as a person in terms of the attributes helpful to develop the learning organization.

References

The vast majority of recruiters in the United Kingdom and United States use references (Dobson, 1989) to verify factual statements in a candidate's application, and this is a strong inducement to be truthful. However, any additional information given by a referee fails to make their predictive value

Table 9.2 *Selection methods: general predictive value*

Method	Predictive value	Improvement conditions
Application information	Moderately good	Indicate the facts wanted Encourage self-revelation
References	Very poor	Steer referees to key aspects Talk with them
Aptitude and ability tests	Very good	Professional administration and interpretation
Personality tests	Good	Professional administration and interpretation Target scales to person specification
Assessment centre	Good	Design/target to person specification Train assessors
Appraisal	Good	Assess against relevant future person specification criteria
Work sampling and testing	Very good	Ensure it relates to the job and person specification
Interview	Poor	Train selectors Use job analysis
Astrology and graphology	Nil	Seek help from post-modern magicians

little better than tossing a coin (Makin and Robertson, 1986). Typically they are not helpful, but they become more so if these guidelines are followed:

- give referees full details of the post;
- indicate the facts you want verified;
- seek opinions and illustrations about the aspects of behaviour that are important that the referee may have observed;
- talk to the referee about aspects of the candidate's behavioural style, such as openness and decision-making.

Psychological tests

Psychological, or psychometric, tests offer the selector evidence based upon the assessment and measurement of:

- aptitude – the potential to learn to do something;
- ability – being able to do something now;

- attitudes – what you think about something, and therefore how you might respond to it;

- personality – what you are like as a person, in terms of how you see yourself and relate to others and situations.

Tests for ability and aptitude can be among the best predictors of future job performance (Makin and Robertson, 1986). Personality tests, which provide information about a person's potential contribution to a 'learning organization', for example, are much more controversial. Although such tests would claim to give clues about aspects such as 'openness–defensiveness' and 'experimentation–caution', they have been challenged on professional grounds. Critics argue that their administration and interpretation are often poor, and that they are frequently asked to make predictions beyond their capacity. Sometimes they have not been validated to show they do measure what they are supposed to measure. Some of the issues were aired in a written debate (Fletcher *et al.*, 1991), which offered qualified support for the use of personality tests:

> Routine large-scale personality testing is unlikely to be useful, whereas the focused application personality tests, based on clear hypotheses about which scales are related to job performance, will have the best chance of success.

Makin and Robertson (1986) concluded that they are valuable predictive tools for recruitment and promotion. Their place in the strategic methods of selection depends upon whether they are validated, specific to a job or job family, administered and interpreted professionally and used in conjunction with other tools.

An issue highlighted by psychological tests but applicable to all methods, is whether they have an adverse impact upon equal opportunity codes and legislation, an issue which needs to be addressed by all HRM strategies. Some test scores produce a marked disparity between ethnic groups, so that one group is disproportionately preferred to another. Unless this can be justified test users will be guilty of unfair discrimination.

To avoid failing legal definitions of unfairnesss, the test or other method has to measure a skill or competency that is really needed for the job. Furthermore, selection decisions have to be based upon the *level* of skill that is required. Thorough job analysis is needed for both factors to be established and justified (Wood and Baron, 1992).

Test results may reflect test-taking behaviours as well as ability and aptitudes. Some ethnic minority groups may not be 'test wise' and could be unfairly discriminated against as a result. Many employers such as British Rail, Midland Bank and West Midlands Police have followed the advice of the Commission for Racial Equality (1993) and provide test access training to reduce the impact of cultural rather than intrinsic personal factors in selection.

Wood and Baron suggest that job analysis is a necessary tool for arriving at the right choice of test. British Rail dropped a test after job analysis revealed it was not relevant for the job. They conclude that although some tests have been used unfairly:

> . . . if care is taken . . . there is every reason to use tests with all job applicants. . . . To rely instead on interviews, which, unless they are carefully planned and conducted, are untrustworthy, could actually work against both fair selection and effective selection.
>
> (p. 37)

Assessment centres

An assessment centre is a method which uses a series of exercises and activities, usually in a group context, to produce behavioural evidence upon which individuals can be assessed for recruitment, promotion or development. If it is carefully designed to yield evidence linked to person specifications, and if behaviour is accurately assessed by trained assessors, it is a good predictive tool (Makin and Robertson, 1986). For example, the 'learning organization' behaviours (Figure 9.3) can more readily be assessed by this than by any other method apart from rigorous observation and assessment of an individual at work. Individuals can be seen behaving in relation to risk-taking, reacting to mistakes, openness, ideas and decision-making, and so on.

The basis for selection is often reviewing an individual's track record to predict future performance. However promotion, or new roles produced by strategic change, may demand attitudes or competencies that were not called forth previously. Speculative assessment can be made surer by defining these new person specification dimensions and by providing opportunity for their display during an assessment centre. The costs in terms of time, accommodation, design and training are high, but a significant proportion of the top 1000 UK companies use them (Dulewicz, 1991; Harrison, 1992).

Work sampling and testing

A work sample test uses tasks that are a significant part of the job. Individuals are asked to provide samples of their work, or to allow their work to be sampled. It provides concrete evidence of individual performance, a commodity which is rare in selection processes. Examples are British Rail's recruiting potential bridge examiners by asking them to examine bridges, and HM Customs and Excise's selecting trainers by asking them to experience, design and run training activities (Evenden and Anderson, 1992).

Makin and Robertson (1986) rate these the highest predictors of success in selection and Wood and Baron (1992) conclude that:

> Work sample tests have not been greatly used in this country (UK), but the experience to date, here and in the USA, is that candidates perceive them

as fairer, more acceptable and of a more appropriate level of difficulty than traditional ability tests.

(p. 37)

Appraisal

Effective appraisal is the pivotal HRM tool for performance management and development (Harrison, 1992; Anderson, 1993). If its assessment aspect is based upon careful observation of the individual's performance-related behaviour, it can also provide vital information which the HRM system could harness for selection for promotion or transfer.

If, as in the PLI case, new person specifications had emerged from strategic change that were not directly covered in the appraisal criteria, line managers could still provide assessment for selection based upon their knowledge of the individual at work. In the learning organization illustration (Figure 9.3) they would report their assessment against these criteria.

The selection interview

The selection interview is still the most popular selection method, perhaps because it is the cheapest, simplest to conduct and uses the managers' confidence in their infallible ability to select the right person. Makin and Robertson (1986) and many others, however, show that its real predictive value is only marginally better than chance. As with other methods, the issue is not to abandon but improve the method.

Human resource management support through preparation and job analysis, as well as training in the special skills of selection interviewing, would make it more effective (Evenden and Anderson, 1992): for example, learning how to go beyond the candidates' assertions that they are open, participative and responsive to 'learning and change', by illustration-seeking, indirect and hypothetical questioning and offering screens upon which the person's attitudes and values can be projected. Self-awareness, in terms of bias, rapport, listening and interview style, as well as knowledge about structuring the interview, assessment and decision-making, would also help the selection interview to be more effective.

Social responsibility and strategic selection goals

There are many cases where business and social responsibility strategic goals coincide. The example given of Burger King's approach to cultural diversity through targeting recruitment at ethnic minorities with high and growing aggregate incomes is an illustration (Greenslade, 1991).

Other cases have been mentioned where legal requirements or socially responsible codes of fairness have influenced the methods of selection, perhaps through the medium of the Commission for Racial Equality (Wood and Baron, 1992, 1993). Business goals could have been met at lower cost in most of these cases; British Rail, West Midlands Police and Midland Bank may have achieved the quantity and quality of resources they needed, without investing in ways of improving the opportunities for disadvantaged or minority groups to enter the organization.

Human resource management has many social responsibility issues affecting selection (see Chapter 8). The long-term unemployed are frequently treated as pariahs by recruiters. It is a group which grew dramatically during the 1980s. A positive illustration of social responsibility goals in this area is Abbey National recruiting long-term unemployed as a policy decision. The majority are women and from ethnic minorities, and initial indications are that they will meet the person specification and performance requirements in all respects.

Human resource managers could bring equal opportunity enlightenment to strategic planning and decision-making groups, and challenge stereotypes which contaminate selection processes. They could address social responsibility goals that may be good in themselves but which do not always maximize the achievement of bottom-line business goals, although in many cases this is eminently debatable (Graham, 1992). As was explained in Chapter 8, the long-term business benefits to culture, commitment and public image of social goals require assessment by strategic decision-makers even if they are unable to embrace altruism in their vision of the future.

Conclusion

This chapter has examined how selection can contribute effectively to strategic management, and its relation to other processes in HRM. It has considered selection issues which have strategic implications or which need addressing strategically and has reviewed selection methods and their practical implications for an organization.

Human resource management has to translate planned strategic changes into the three interrelated technical, organizational and people systems. This in turn has to be interpreted by job analysis in terms of the human resource requirements which need to be met by fair and effective selection methods.

If the selection strategy requires competencies and attitudes which cannot be gauged from the simple factual dimensions of education, qualifications and experience, then the methods will need to include a battery of approaches that are judged likely to help assess individuals against the more personal and less tangible aspects of the person specification.

Selection strategy will need to ensure that the person specifications are sensitive to change. It will also need to make provision for the careful selection and training of the selectors. Human resource practitioners must constantly review and validate their methods and be open to creative innovation in response to the threats and opportunities present in their own environment. Finally, they must consider whether they have a special role in relation to ethics and social responsibility as goals of organizational strategy.

10

Performance management: its role and methods in human resource strategy

Gordon Anderson and
Robin Evenden

By the end of this chapter the reader will:

1. understand the relationship between performance management and wider HRM strategy;

2. understand the relationship between performance appraisal and performance management systems, and the factors that have encouraged some organizations to transform the former into the latter;

3. appreciate the nature of performance management and what makes it effective;

4. become familiar with developments and techniques that can be used by managers in their own performance management role.

Performance management and wider human resource strategy: an overview

It is people who make effective strategic decisions, or make the sale, or make the quality suggestion, or make the change, or not; in other words, they perform. How they perform is a critical factor in organizational effectiveness.

In Chapter 1 (p. 8), it was suggested that:

> . . . strategic management is not just about finding a congruence between organizational strengths and weaknesses and environmental opportunities and threats. . . . Similarly it is not just about communicating the chief executive's vision down the line. It is also about harnessing the abilities, innovative capacity and drive of everyone in the organization. . . .

It is this 'harnessing' in relation to mission and objectives that is performance management's concern in the strategic process.

Performance management involves having in place systems and methods which translate the goals of strategic management into individual performance terms through HRM. If the selection function's contribution to strategic management involves getting the right people, then performance management and development means getting the people right. This includes appraisal of individuals as well as planning and influencing their future performance through targets and development.

Performance management also needs to be concerned with the manager's relationship with the individual in general, and with the appraisal process and motivation in particular (Evenden and Anderson, 1992). Performance-related pay is often a part of this integrated HRM system (Figure 10.1).

Page 39 in Chapter 2 refers to the difficulty of achieving:

> . . . smooth interaction between the various HRM functions relating to performance, and then integration of the entire human resource cycle with business goals.

For example, the skill and application needed to translate broad strategic plans into specific individual actions are considerable; the collaboration and communication required between decision-makers and implementers, specialists and line managers, is of a high order; and parts of the cycle may conflict, such as when the impact of performance-related pay pulls self-assessment in a direction different from the needs of self-development. As Chapter 2 suggests, these tensions cannot be eliminated, but must be recognized and managed.

Although there are problems of integration between levels, functions and systems, many of the operational aspects of performance management focus upon one individual, the manager in human resource mode. Integration should be easier at this level, provided the manager is aware of the

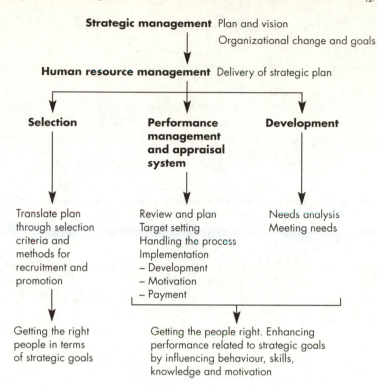

Strategic management Plan and vision

Organizational change and goals

Human resource management Delivery of strategic plan

Selection	**Performance management and appraisal system**	**Development**
Translate plan through selection criteria and methods for recruitment and promotion	Review and plan Target setting Handling the process Implementation – Development – Motivation – Payment	Needs analysis Meeting needs
Getting the right people in terms of strategic goals	Getting the people right. Enhancing performance related to strategic goals by influencing behaviour, skills, knowledge and motivation	

Figure 10.1 *Strategic management and HRM: the role of performance management*.

connections between the elements of the performance management role (see Figure 10.1).

The individual is not a passive, compliant and manipulated element of the system. Indeed, many models of HRM see the process as one of exchange between the individual and the organization, with commitment, involvement and initiative as key variables for effectiveness (Storey, 1992). Mismanagement, conversely, will result in alienation, disengagement and passivity. The crucial factors here are the HRM systems that are in place in the organization, and the commitment, involvement, initiative and skill of those operating them.

Performance appraisal: systems, objectives and tensions

Performance appraisal systems have been widely recognized as forming a central element in the management of people's performance. Long (1986) showed that in a study of 306 organizations in the United Kingdom, 82% operated some kind of formal system for appraising employee performance. In the United States similar surveys (for example, Bureau of National Affairs, 1983) also revealed high levels of use of formal performance appraisal. Although performance appraisal is subject to differing interpretations, it is usually considered to involve written assessments of employees carried out in a systematic way at regular time intervals (Anderson, 1980).

Performance appraisal schemes are usually expected to serve multiple objectives. This can benefit both individuals and organizations if useful purposes are achieved, but can lead to problems characterized by a dissipation of effort and lack of focus. A necessary condition for the effective management of performance appraisal in any organization is the clarification to all concerned of the objectives which the system is intended to achieve.

Performance appraisal objectives can be classified in a number of ways. One of the best known classifications was produced many years ago by McGregor (1960) who grouped objectives as follows:

- *Administrative* Providing an orderly way of determining promotions, transfers and salary increases.

- *Informative* Supplying data to management on the performance of subordinates and to the individual on his or her strengths and weaknesses.

- *Motivational* Creating a learning experience that motivates staff to develop themselves and improve their performance.

McGregor's groupings are useful in drawing attention not only to the variety of purposes but also to different organizational philosophies towards performance appraisal.

Cummings and Schwab (1973) adopted a similar perspective, contending that organizations typically view appraisal as having two broad purposes: an evaluative function, and a development function. Bevan and Thompson (1991, p. 39) were concerned about the 'reward-driven' aspects of evaluation, seeing increasing evidence (in their UK survey) of these reducing or even rendering impotent the developmental function.

Over the last two decades the literature on performance appraisal has reinforced the issues recognized and clearly articulated by Cummings and Schwab that well-designed systems of performance appraisal should pursue forward-looking developmental objectives, such as the setting of targets for different aspects of job performance and the identification of training needs, as well as evaluative objectives concerned primarily with the assessment of the actual performance of employees over a given time period, often six months or a year, against what are considered to be desirable standards. Over the years, one of the issues commented on in the literature of performance appraisal has been just how to achieve balance and compatibility among the various objectives of performance appraisal systems. There is evidence (see, for example, Mohrman *et al.*, 1989) to suggest that the more effective, sustainable performance appraisal schemes are those where both evaluative and developmental objectives are considered important, but where greater emphasis is placed on developmental objectives. There is also, however, evidence to indicate that, at least in the United Kingdom, appraisal schemes are being used increasingly to control, rather than to develop, performance (Harrison, 1992, pp. 320–4).

These possible conflicts between the evaluative and developmental dimensions have been much discussed in the appraisal literature (see Mohrman *et al.*, 1989) and constitute an equally relevant issue to consider in the wider context of performance management. Various conflicts can occur and are summarized in Figure 10.2.

Beer (1981) stressed that both organizations and individuals have certain goals that they attempt to achieve through performance appraisal; tensions, again, are inherent here. Writers as far back as Festinger (1954) have drawn attention to the fact that individuals want and seek feedback on their performance, to help them evaluate their own performance, learn how they are progressing, and make changes to improve their future performance. Mohrman *et al.* (1989) pointed out that everyone develops a sense of self that includes beliefs about competence and capabilities. In most people these beliefs are strongly held and well developed. Information that confirms them is easy to accept, but people often attempt to avoid receiving information that does not match their self-perceptions, frequently rejecting it. Rejection can take several forms, including discrediting the source and/or appraiser, and distorting the information so that it becomes more compatible with existing beliefs. While these problems apply mainly to negative feedback, they can also apply in situations where feedback is more favourable than expected.

In performance appraisal systems where the evaluation of performance is linked to reward decisions, especially financial rewards, individuals have an important reason for seeking favourable evaluations and are more likely to present themselves in the most favourable way possible even if it means a loss of opportunity for giving and receiving valid feedback which would subsequently assist in improving their performance.

Other conflicts, as shown by arrows in Figure 10.2 occur when organizations seek comprehensive and accurate data about the performance and development needs of individuals, but it is not always perceived by

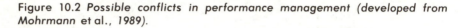

Figure 10.2 *Possible conflicts in performance management (developed from Mohrmann et al., 1989).*

individuals as being in their best interests to provide it. This kind of conflict applies less in the case of high performers, but more in the case of employees whose performance is moderate or deficient.

The linkages between performance evaluation and financial rewards, and the tensions to which they give rise, are seen as increasingly important but also problematic in modern performance management systems, and are examined in greater detail later in the chapter.

Outcomes of performance appraisal

Despite the fact that performance appraisal is a well-established practice in many organizations, it still generates a wide range of views about its usefulness. The range of views is well illustrated in the title of a recent journal article: 'Performance appraisal: effective management or deadly disease' (Carson *et al.*, 1991). At one end of the spectrum there are those who see performance appraisal as making a key contribution to HRM. For example Brent Miles, training manager of Yorkshire Television describes performance appraisal as 'the vital factor which enables Yorkshire TV to achieve a high level of competence in its management team' (Miles, 1991). Towards the other end of the spectrum are those who emphasize the problems which often frustrate performance appraisal systems in achieving their objectives.

George (1986) observed that while companies may have become much better and more enlightened in designing and implementing performance appraisal, the concept of performance appraisal is inherently very demanding, and asks a great deal of people in terms of openness and honesty. Typical appraisal problems include:

- lack of honesty in exchanging opinions and feelings;
- failure to face up to deficiencies in performance;
- failure to agree actions that genuinely help the individual.

Formalized performance appraisal is also, to some extent, self-limiting, being concerned fundamentally with periodic one-off events when managers and employees sit down together to take part in appraisal interviews, and agree the contents of a written appraisal report. The best performance appraisal practice has to some extent moved beyond that situation, and extends into other areas by emphasizing the links between formal appraisals and informal day-to-day management.

In summary, if care is given to the design and implementation stages, formalized performance appraisal can yield useful benefits both to individuals and to organizations. Problems and tensions, however, can readily emerge and prevent the objectives from being achieved. We shall return to ways of making performance appraisal an effective function, both for the organization and for the individual, later in this chapter.

From performance appraisal to performance management

Performance management builds on, rather than replaces, performance appraisal. Indeed most writers on performance management systems (for example, Fletcher and Williams, 1992) regard performance appraisal as an essential characteristic, but only one of several essential characteristics, of a good performance management system.

Connock (1991) has suggested that in the late 1980s a shift of emphasis began to take place from performance appraisal to performance management. Bevan and Thompson (1992) indicate that a performance management system can be defined as being in operation when the following conditions are met by the organization:

- it communicates a vision of its objectives to all employees;
- it sets departmental and individual performance targets which are related to wider objectives;
- it conducts a formal review of progress towards these targets;
- it uses the review process to identify training, development and reward outcomes;
- it evaluates the whole process in order to improve effectiveness.

Performance management focuses very much on the future. Connock stresses that a major contribution of performance management is to place great emphasis on:

- setting key accountability;
- agreeing future objectives in each of these key accountability areas;
- agreeing measures and standards to be attained;
- assigning timescales and priorities.

This emphasis on the future represents an evolutionary rather than a revolutionary change since, as previously discussed, it has long been recognized that well-designed systems of performance appraisal should pursue forward-looking developmental objectives such as the setting of targets for different aspects of job performance for each employee, and the identification of employees' training needs, as well as historical, evaluative objectives concerned primarily with the assessment of actual employee performance over a given time period of the previous 6 or 12 months. In this respect, again performance management builds upon and extends the best performance appraisal practice.

The emergence of the concept of performance management, however, places emphasis on using performance appraisal as a platform for establishing targets and making a range of decisions aimed at improving the performance of employees in organizations. Connock (1991) has suggested four main reasons for an increasing preoccupation with tightly focused management of human performance in organizations:

- more intense competition, associated with the globalization of markets for many goods and services, with increased deregulation and liberalization of trade resulting from political and economic change, and through the emergence of developing nations;
- greater awareness that the corporate mission and strategic objectives are more likely to be achieved through the development of carefully formulated links between strategic objectives and departmental and individual objectives;
- the increasing use of performance-related pay, a major feature of reward strategies in many modern organizations;
- greater emphasis on quality, and on Total Quality Management (TQM).

At first sight there would seem to be clear links between TQM and performance management. Both concepts, it could be argued, are concerned with quality of service delivery. Oakland (1989) sees performance management harmonizing with TQM in clarifying responsibilities, developing performance objectives and indicators, and preparing action plans. At another level, the links between TQM and performance management are less straightforward than implied by Connock. A major difference is that TQM philosophy emphasizes that the control of quality rests upon individual employees themselves, while conventional performance management approaches imply that the manager or supervisor takes responsibility for the quality of work of employees through evaluation and assessment.

Fowler (1990) raises the question whether performance management is simply management by objectives with a new title, in so far as there are some common features, with emphasis in both placed on goal-setting, linking individual and departmental goals in a coordinated way with corporate goals, and the appraisal of performance against goals as the basis for setting and agreeing new goals. Fowler, however, concludes that there are crucial differences in philosophy as well as in methods of implementation.

In performance management the starting point is a definition of the organization's mission, aims and values, giving performance management a stronger strategic and cultural focus than generally prevailed in systems of management by objectives. Performance management is thus a process that has a vital role to play in ensuring that human resource strategies support the business direction of the organization by providing a basis for evaluating and improving individual and company performance against predefined business strategies and objectives.

Fowler also draws attention to the fact that in many organizations initiatives in performance management are being undertaken by chief executives and senior managers from a range of functions. Even where changes are being led by personnel or training specialists, strong attempts are made to involve line managers as much as possible in the design stages, to give them feelings of ownership of the schemes that evolve. In keeping with recent trends in performance appraisal (for example, Anderson *et al.*, 1987), performance management systems increasingly are being applied to nonmanagerial staff. Furthermore, to develop successful schemes, organizations are recognizing to a greater extent that they must be tailor-made to harmonize with organizational values and address organizational needs.

The nature of performance management

Elements of a performance management system

To be integrated and effective in its support of business strategy, a performance management system needs at least the following four elements (this approach corresponds closely to the principles outlined by Williams (1992)).

1   The determination and setting of individual objectives which support the achievement of overall business strategies

This of course requires that business strategies have been formulated through the analysis and evaluation of a range of internal and external factors, and is a reiteration of points made on pp. 248, 249 and 255.

2   Performance appraisal

Performance appraisal is, as we have already seen (pp. 250–3) the system and process for the provision of both feedback to employees on all aspects of their performance, and the opportunity for discussion to agree actions to assist their future development. For performance appraisal to make an effective contribution to a system of performance management, a number of elements should be present:

- The appraisal of employee performance against preset objectives, which should be linked in an effective and reliable way with departmental and corporate objectives.

- Awareness of reasons for barriers to effective performance, and for performance deficiencies resulting from joint analysis and discussion of performance involving appraiser and employees.

- New objectives for employees emerging from the appraisal discussion.

- Action plans to assist performance and personal development emerging from the appraisal discussion.

- A linkage between performance appraisal and rewards that is perceived by all parties as fair, and contributing to the motivation of employees and to the creation of a performance-oriented culture, with widely held values accepting and encouraging the giving of greater rewards to those identified as high performers, and lesser rewards, or in extreme cases, no rewards or negative measures for those identified as low performers.

- A linkage between performance appraisal and the provision of on-going, informal feedback, coaching, mentoring and counselling to employees, stressing that performance appraisal does not consist of a set of periodic, isolated events, but rather forms an integral part of the management process connected to on-going activities that contribute to improved performance and the development of employees.

- A culture and climate characterized by openness and trust between appraisees and employees, so that both parties enter into candid, constructive discussions on performance issues with defensiveness and anxiety kept to a minimum.

We shall examine the elements of effective performance appraisal in more detail at a later point in this chapter.

3 Review of pay and rewards

An important element in a system of performance management is, as previously noted, the inclusion of a linkage between performance appraisal ratings and the distribution of rewards that is perceived to be fair and reasonable to all the parties involved. A company can select various options:

(a) A *direct linkage*, where a particular performance appraisal rating leads to a specific pay increase.

(b) *Discretionary merit pay increases* This approach is operated in some organizations, where decisions on merit pay are not closely tied to performance appraisal ratings. Instead, managerial discretion is used in arriving at merit pay decisions, constrained by a number of factors often including budgeting controls, market wage rates and position in salary grade. They have the advantages of:

  (i) involving appraisers and reviewers actively in the decision-making process about merit pay;

  (ii) providing flexibility in the system;

  (iii) giving employees the opportunity to improve their performance after appraisal interviews, and have this reflected in higher merit increases.

Potential difficulties include possible disparities and perceived unfairness in the way the system of merit payments is implemented through decentralized managerial discretion.

(c) *Limited managerial discretion*, an intermediate option, with performance appraisal ratings being linked to ranges of values of merit pay, has most of the advantages and few of the disadvantages of the two options identified above.

In introducing merit payments, it is easier to introduce a direct linkage scheme, and then move later to either the intermediate option or the managerial discretion approach. This strategy provides greater organizational control in the early stages of implementation, later delegating some element of discretion to managers.

CASE STUDY: *Performance management in a major UK financial institution (no contextual details are given, as the organization wishes its anonymity to be preserved)*

A major UK financial institution uses the 'direct linkage' approach, based on an eight-point set of overall performance appraisal ratings (one is low, eight is high), with the following pay increases awarded in 1991.

Appraisal ratings (0 = low, 8 = high)	Pay increase (%)
1	0
2	0
3	7.5
4	10.5
5	11.5
6	12.5
7	13.5
8	15.0

The advantages of the direct linkage method identified by this bank include:

1. *Strong management control.* The decision on the nature of the linkage can be made at a very senior level, and implemented.

2. *Avoids relativity/potential grievance problems among departments.* All those evaluated at the same performance level receive the same percentage merit increase.

3. *Adds credibility to the performance appraisal scheme.* It is seen as having important, direct financial implications.

The bank, however, has identified several problems and issues which need to be addressed:

1. *The need to avoid upward inflation of performance appraisal ratings.* This can be helped through active participation by those in the 'grandfather' or 'reviewing' role, who monitor the accuracy and fairness of appraisers' ratings and comments. Typically, they are at more senior organizational levels, often being the persons to whom appraisers report in the organization structure.

2. *The development of linkages that are seen to be fair and reasonable.* These should aid the motivation of managers, if worked out carefully on a sound basis.

3. *The need to avoid the merit pay issues overshadowing all other aspects of performance appraisal.* This implies the need for some separation in time between the appraisal interview and the merit payment decision.

Armstrong and Murlis (1988) stress that developing sound linkages between performance evaluations and reward decisions is by no means easy, and emphasize that there are no easy-to-follow general techniques; mechanisms must be devised that match the culture and core values of the organization. More detailed discussion of financial incentive and reward strategies follows in Chapter 11.

4   Organization capability review

In some organizations, the consolidation of the individual outputs from performance appraisal provide the basis for a review of the capability of the organization to undertake particular activities. Salaman (1979) has argued that a limitation of performance appraisal is an underlying assumption that variations in performance are explained in terms of differences in individual contribution. The review of organizational capability as an element of performance management remedies this problem by recognizing that factors relating to organizational design and organizational structure may explain variations in performance attributed, under traditional performance appraisal, to individual causes. The organization capability review forms part of the process of reviewing how effectively strategy is being implemented, as well as contributing to performance management.

Performance management: wider implications for HRM

The various elements of a performance management system are interdependent. Adjustments should be based on regular feedback and review, since the aim of any performance management system should be continuous performance improvement. While changes are likely to be evolutionary rather than revolutionary, performance management is likely to become increasingly important in terms of helping organizations to achieve their strategic goals. Peters (1989), for example, pointed out that the process of strategic planning, at times of rapid change, relies heavily on a bottom-up approach, starting with a clear assessment of how far 'front-line' employees are responsive, flexible and attentive to customers. While other issues are inevitably involved in formulating strategy, it is important that an organization does not lose sight of the information the performance management system can contribute to the formulation of strategic plans.

Schneir (1981) provides a model for performance management which assists in highlighting some of the wider implications for HRM. The model draws attention to ways in which the performance management system can assist organizations in developing human resource strategies to achieve corporate goals. The planning process of the performance management system links the objectives of individuals to the wider goals of the organization. Performance appraisal is central to the whole process; the outcomes clearly highlight two sets of human resource activities that impact upon the individual – **judging** and **coaching**. Judging activities contribute to other evaluative areas of HRM like compensation decisions, succession planning and discipline situations. The coaching activities relate to the identification of training and development needs, methods of improving performance and the discussion of career options.

Strategic HRM stresses the importance of integration, and the need for a coherent set of human resource policies. In the case of systems of performance management, Bevan and Thompson (1991, 1992) identify two approaches to integration:

- **Reward-driven integration**, implying particular emphasis being given to the role of performance-related pay schemes in changing organizational behaviour (the dominant mode of integration, in their belief, which is emerging in the United Kingdom).

- **Development-driven integration**, stressing the importance of ensuring that human resource development activities are appropriate to the needs of the organization, and that they are coordinated.

They remind us of the major problems inherent in performance management when they write (1991, p. 39):

> There is a strong possibility that the tension between the two integrating processes may cause both to malfunction and that the reward-driven strategy will dominate at the expense of the development-driven strategy.

Fletcher and Williams (1992) believe that four issues need to be addressed if performance management systems are to form an effective, central element of HRM.

1   Ownership and commitment

Performance management should be driven by line managers, with line managers possessing strong feelings of ownership of the system rather than the driving force behind performance management being only the CEO or the head of the human resource function. Good consultation processes in the design phase are vital, as are training programmes to ensure line managers fully understand performance management – the philosophy, the techniques, the challenges and the links with other areas of HRM.

2   Human resource specialists as facilitators

According to Fletcher and Williams, human resource specialists need to reassess their own role and contribution, with regard to performance management. They are likely to have an important facilitating and support role to ensure that policies develop in a coordinated way, while balancing the need to devolve ownership to line managers.

3 Motivation and rewards

The development of a sound rewards strategy is, as previously discussed, central to performance management systems. A major challenge is to produce systems that can be controlled yet contain sufficient flexibility to cover the different needs of different individuals in organizations. More discussions of this area follows in Chapter 11.

4 The well-being of employees

Performance management is increasingly seen as a concept which contributes to the profitability of organizations. There is a danger that this emphasis will tend to deflect attention from the needs and well-being of employees (see Harrison, 1992, pp. 317–24).

Performance management at the workface: strategies and techniques

Human resource management systems may be designed by 'personnel' specialists but they rely for their success upon implementation by line managers. It is managers who have the task of planning the future by reviewing the past with the individual in the appraisal interview, agreeing performance gaps and targets before identifying development needs. They are the monitors of individual performance and progress, the coaches and counsellors who support, guide and motivate (Figure 10.3). Strategic HRM stands or falls very largely by their own performance of their people-management role at the workface.

It has to be said that the degree of commitment and priority that managers give to their HRM role varies widely. Although, as was pointed out in Chapter 2, there is evidence to show the positive bottom-line impact of effective HRM systems and their integration with corporate strategy (Fox *et al.*, 1992), that chapter also shows that there are cultural, political and human realities in organizational functioning which can prevent this occurring. The research and consultancy experience of the writers of this chapter reinforces this. Many managers lack the will to invest sufficient time in their people role and to manage performance effectively, and changing this is costly and difficult.

This lack of commitment may be due to cultural factors, where values and norms support 'technical' orientations and short-termism rather than 'people' and the strategic view. It can also stem from organizational politics

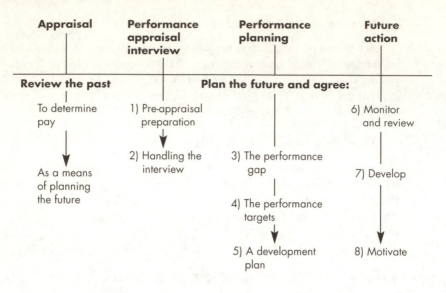

Figure 10.3 *Performance management: the manager's role.*

related to departmental and functional power and influence rivalry. It often results from the attitudes and role interpretation of individual managers, whose experience of organizational life, among other things, has led them to give their HRM role a low priority (Biddle and Evenden, 1989, Chapter 2).

Having indicated that the *will* to manage people and performance may often be lacking, and that this may be a major cause of HRM failing to connect with strategic management, the lack of performance management *skill* has the same effect. What are these skills? The remainder of this chapter will explore them. It will also consider the role the line manager needs to take in performance management to energize HRM systems and focus individuals' performance towards the achievement of job objectives which contribute to emerging strategic policy and goals. Their effectiveness is a crucial factor in the achievement of HRM strategies.

CASE STUDY: *Performance management at HM Customs and Excise*

HM Customs and Excise are investing significantly in training managers to enable them to develop the skills to operate effectively within new human resource systems of appraisal, development and payment. This is part of the HM Customs and Excise board's pursuit of strategic goals related to efficiency, effective performance management and responsiveness to change. It is operating in a situation which has required an internal assessment of strengths and weaknesses in the light of a scan of opportunities and threats in the environment external to the organization.

These external factors have been significant and varied. They include political demands upon the civil service in general, such as enhanced account-ability and resource management, market testing and the Citizen's Charter. Particular demands are the need to enhance its protective role in relation to drugs, its relationship to other agencies in this field, and the impact of customs control changes related to the EC. In addition, it is expected to main-tain and even increase its efficiency and effectiveness as revenue collector.

Performance-related pay, appraisal and development form an integrated HRM strategy aimed in part at changing leadership style and management culture. It is connected to strategic policy and mission statements, which in turn link directly to the environmental changes outlined above. The Customs and Excise appear to be conforming with several aspects of Fox *et al.*'s (1992) research model of HRM strategy's integration with corporate strategy and successful business performance.

It is an illustration of corporate strategy being translated through HRM into performance management terms, with the aim of harnessing individual abilities and focusing them on strategic goals (see Figure 10.1). The translation from strategy to workface is on three fronts:

1. *Performance management systems* Performance-related pay has been intro-duced and personal development planning and enhanced delivery are in the process of installation. A new appraisal system is being put in place, continuing progress from the closed reporting of several years ago to open, future-oriented appraisal which puts emphasis on performance assessment within an accepted and standardized competence-based framework.

2. *Expectations and attitudes* A long-term programme is being undertaken to achieve organization development and culture change, part of which involves changing expectations and attitudes about the 'people and performance management' role of managers. This is being achieved through a range of approaches. At board level a series of mission and policy statements of values and intent have been communicated to all staff, including 'next steps' and the 'people initiative'. Opinions have been fed back to the board and to each executive unit through a comprehensive and independently administered attitude survey. The results were available to all staff and reinforced the need for change. Personal and team development has been extensive and focused upon expectations and attitudes, as well as business needs. Finally, the assessment centre for senior management selection now includes people and performance management criteria.

3. *Skill training* Training is being provided to enable individuals to operate the new people and performance roles and systems effectively at the workface. There is opportunity to develop professional management skills and all staff are being trained to achieve the positive performance outcomes possible from appraisal.

HM Customs and Excise provide a case where strategic planning and policy have been informed by external demands and internal opinions. It has been translated into HRM strategy and performance management by considering the integration of selection, payment, appraisal and development. It is being transmitted to the workface by culture change initiatives, management action down the line and training and development. This illustrates an attempt to achieve congruence between people and technical and organizational change in order to meet environmental challenges.

Pre-appraisal preparation

The first stage in the line manager's performance management role (see Figure 10.3) is preparation prior to the appraisal interview. This involves both parties reflecting upon performance in relation to the job and standards which may have been set. The appraisee and appraiser will cast their minds back over the review period and identify evidence to aid assessment. Ideally, they will both arrive at some thoughts on the future in terms of performance and development. Hopefully, they will not develop fixed views at this stage in the process, but will have clear ideas that will be the basis of exchange and discussion.

It is helpful at this point to distinguish between the two terms **assessment** and **appraisal**. **Assessment** means making a judgement about or measuring a person's performance against standards. **Appraisal** is the process of reviewing and making decisions about past performance with the performer, prior to planning for the future. Both appraisal and assessment are central to performance management and are best seen as a continuous process, with a periodic 'patterns and planning' appraisal interview which demands particular prior thought and preparation.

The role of job analysis, outlined in Chapter 9 on selection, is important in the performance management process. It should be the means of defining jobs, job-specific and core competencies and their performance, as well as a vehicle for translating role changes required by strategic decisions. It will reveal the key aspects of a role and lead on to what has to be done for successful accomplishment. This involves the definition of performance standards in precise and concrete terms so that both appraiser and appraisee are clear about what is expected, perhaps in the light of role changes which result from strategic decisions. We shall return to this aspect in relation to agreeing performance gaps and targets.

Apart from clarifying the role and performance, the appraiser needs to be creative in gathering evidence to feed the appraisal and assessment process. Line managers often find their performance management role is enhanced by keeping confidential personal files of their staff to aid memory, assessment, appraisal, planning and development. It can include previous appraisal reports, reviews, agreements, plans and actions related to performance and development. It can also be a repository of evidence and illustrations regarding the individual's performance, perhaps from observation, work sampling, results analysis, achievements, failures and data gleaned from the observations of others.

Such personal files may be seen as intrusive, but need not be so if they are treated as open only to the two people involved. This information proves invaluable in preparing for the periodic appraisal interview, which can then more easily become an effective vehicle for managing the individual's performance.

Handling the performance appraisal interview

Experience and research indicate that the periodic appraisal interview can be the critical element in individual performance management. It is often handled inadequately by managers who are untrained and uncommitted. When it is prepared for by both parties, handled with some skill and sensitivity, given adequate time (1–2 hours) and seen as a two-way exchange aiming at agreement about future plans which the appraisee expects to be followed up, it is very likely to be regarded by both parties as important for development and performance (Anderson and Barnett, 1986; Harrison, 1992).

The classic definition of style choices available to appraisal interviewers is that given by Norman Maier (1976). The approach which is appraiser dominated is the judgemental 'tell and sell' style which Maier regards as likely to produce defensiveness and low commitment. This is still a problem to a degree in the more appraisee-orientated 'tell and listen' style, although appraisees may find that a listening appraiser gives them a measure of influence over their future. These two styles spring from traditional bureaucratic or command cultures. Organizations which are sophisticated enough to embrace performance management explicitly are likely to have appraisal systems which require a 'shared' approach, described by Maier as the 'problem solving' style. This means that the appraisee plays an active part in identifying difficulties, suggesting solutions, developing plans and offering self-assessment as well as being free to discuss those offered by the appraiser.

If the aim is to gain the individual's commitment and ownership of personal development and to change performance, for example to cope with a new set of specified requirements to meet strategic needs, then certain characteristics of the interview appear necessary (Evenden and Anderson, 1992).

A supportive approach which is based upon shared rather than imposed ideas is likely to be required to make performance appraisal systems effective. Praise for achievements (missing, however, from many organizations' culture) is prescribed, and negative feedback needs to be given nonjudgementally with positive future development top of the agenda. Joint problem-solving, target setting and planning rather than authoritarian or paternalistic imposition are also needed – although they may not always 'fit' the value system of appraising line managers. An informal conversational style and good active listening are frequently cited by interviewees as significant influences upon positive perception of appraisal.

Agreeing the performance gap

Managers influencing the performance of others must be clear about how well individuals are performing in relation to how well they need to perform. What constitutes performance will vary from job to job, but will be assessed in terms of:

- Priorities – Are they doing the right things?
- Quantity – Are they doing enough?
- Quality – Are they doing it well enough?
- Time – Are they doing it at the right time?

Human resource management appraisal schemes are likely to require assessment of performance against objectives and standards agreed at the last formal appraisal and modified by subsequent reviews as a result of change. They focus upon behaviour or competencies, the things that people *do* in jobs, rather than the traditional personal trait criteria which focused on what the appraiser thought people were *like*, such as industrious/lazy, or shy/sociable. The latter are more open to dispute, more subjective and perhaps less remediable, although 'personal development' may be a prerequisite of people changing what they do. The difference between actual performance and the upper limit of what could be achieved is the **performance gap** (see Figure 10.4).

In times of transition, perhaps through strategic change, the roles and required performance may alter as a result of social-technical modification. (See the PLI case study and discussion in Chapter 9.) The new performance requirements can be specified during appraisal, and new targets, objectives and development plans assessed and agreed, related to the performance gap which is the result of changes stemming from policy or technical change.

As already noted (pp. 256, 257, 259) Williams (1991) suggests that there are four elements in performance management: individual objectives supporting business strategy; appraisal; pay and other rewards; and organization capability. This is a similar proposition to that made by Biddle and Evenden (1989) regarding individual performance limits and their implications for HRM (Figure 10.4). It identifies four factors which directly influence an individual's performance and provides an analytical and diagnostic device for performance managers, as well as a focus for the appraisal discussion itself.

The upper limit shown in Figure 10.4 describes the ceiling of an individual's performance, which can be raised by improving the **technical system** of operational practices, procedures and technology. This may be a legitimate topic for appraisal. Certainly, issues may be raised at that time, but more likely it will be pursued elsewhere, in quality circles, TQM or in a separate discussion. This aspect coincides with Williams' organization capability. The limit can also be raised by enhancing the individual's current **ability**, which is the development aspect of appraisal in performance management.

The third factor indicates the lowest limit of performance which management are prepared to **tolerate**. In a static situation this would imply that the performance management system has failed in terms of motivation, appraisal, feedback or relationships. In a major change situation (see the PLI case), the new role may be beyond the ability and potential of some individual incumbents. The upper and lower limits would in this case be identical, and the issue no longer one of performance management but of redeployment or severance.

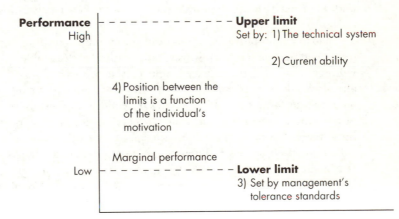

Figure 10.4 *Individual performance limits.*

The fourth factor in performance management is the individuals' will to work well, or their **motivation** to perform. The higher the motivation, the closer the individual is to the upper limit. The lower the motivation, the closer to the lower limit and the status of marginal performer.

During appraisal, the two parties need to articulate and agree the gap between actual and possible performance, establish why it exists and what needs to be done to close it. This is the essence of individual performance management. It focuses upon future targets; development planning; monitoring and reviewing; development delivery; and motivation.

Agreeing performance targets

Individual performance management requires that people know both what is expected from them and how well they are doing. This is enhanced in direct proportion to the degree of clarity and concreteness of the performance targeting.

The procedure is for the manager to agree with the individual the key parts of the job and significant changes required in new circumstances. Each key part is likely to have a broad objective for the performer to focus upon in the future. The different levels of achievement possible for each objective are the standards of performance. Target setting means specifying and, hopefully, agreeing a standard of performance to achieve in the future.

An illustration of this process could be a manager's staffing role. A key task could be to 'manage staffing in the department' and the objective here could be 'to reduce staff turnover'. Standards might be 'over 50% poor' to 'less than 5% excellent' and the individual target to 'reduce staff leaving from the current rate of 30% to 15% during the review year'. How to achieve this and what needs to be done differently would then be the subsequent focus of agreement and planning.

This is a simplistic example, and many managers find it difficult to be this clear and precise. However, application of learnable techniques and willingness to devote sufficient time to the process of target setting could always result in both manager and managed articulating in concrete terms what the performer should be trying to achieve, and establishing the means of agreeing subsequently on what has been achieved. It is not necessary for these targets to be in quantitative terms. Clear qualitative descriptions will suffice for both parties to know what is expected and what is accomplished (Evenden and Anderson, 1992, pp. 263–77). With appropriate steering and questioning, managers experience that most individuals are able to articulate and identify this for themselves, with obvious enhancement in ownership and commitment.

This aspect of performance management does, like the other parts, require effort, creativity, time and probably learning new techniques. This is, of course, no different from the behaviour demanded of managers in accounting, finance, marketing, engineering or any other function needing the application of procedures. Whereas managers accept that they are not born with inherent sets of technical functional skills, they often seem to believe they do arrive in this world complete with a performance management toolkit which needs no further development.

Agreeing the development plan

If the appraisal wishes the ends, in terms of performance change, it must also will the means of achieving it. Learning needs have to be identified and ways of meeting them established. Agreement on this and other aspects of the individual performance management process are not always easy. Rosemary Harrison (1992, pp. 317–20) suggests that defensiveness and low confidence can inhibit appraisees. A lack of skill and knowledge will restrict the appraiser, who may also be embarrassed by discussions of the performance of others.

If the manager has been supported and developed in performance management skills and applies them sensitively, agreement is likely. Creative insights are often needed to identify what will help an individual to develop in order to improve performance. Typically, plans revolve around courses, coaching, visits or temporary attachments, reference material and guided self-development.

Monitoring progress and reviewing plans

The importance of follow-up actions resulting from performance appraisal discussions, to enhance the credibility of performance appraisal and bring about improved performance on the part of those who have been appraised, has been stressed in the literature (see, for example, Locke *et al.*, 1981; Anderson, 1988).

Survey data analysed by Bevan and Thompson (1992) identifies six methods of expressing performance requirements. These are:

- *Clear and measurable accountabilities*   Setting targets linked to outcomes for which the job holder is answerable.
- *Broad responsibilities and roles*   Including descriptions of the key elements of jobs expressed as obligations.
- *Objectives/targets*   Reflecting the aims of the job and the outputs expected of a competent performer.
- *Main job activities and tasks*   Describing the main components of jobs in terms of activities and tasks.

- *Written job descriptions*   Explaining core responsibilities and lines of accountability.
- *Lists of competencies*   Statements of performance outcomes often expressed in behavioural or output terms.

Bevan and Thompson note that organizations which operate more formalized performance management systems are significantly more likely to express the performance requirements of senior managers in terms of clear and measurable accountabilities, objectives/targets, main job activities and tasks, and lists of competencies. This implies an approach which emphasizes outcomes and accountabilities rather than broader, general statements of job expectations.

Performance management stresses that feedback on performance should be provided on an on-going basis, not confined only to periodic performance appraisals. This implies the need for regular, informal communications between appraisers and appraisees, with managers developing and making use of coaching and counselling skills.

Appraisal is really a continuous process with a periodic 'high ground' interview to see patterns and trends and alter direction. It is essentially a forward-looking planning activity which requires frequent progress monitoring and review, both in terms of performance and development. This is particularly important in times of turbulence, when new strategies emerge and roles may be altering frequently and need may be translating into personal performance.

Another reason for monitoring is to ensure that development is effective, or indeed to check that plans are actually carried out. In one study reported in Evenden and Anderson (1992), only two-thirds of agreed planned development was actually carried out. There is no guarantee that it was effective in all cases, but it is likely that the credibility and effectiveness of the entire performance management system would be jeopardised in many of the one-third where promises and plans were not delivered.

Sharing development delivery

Current emphasis is upon the efficacy of the performer owning their own performance and having responsibility for self-development. The key lies in the development relationship between manager and performing individual. It stems from individual values and organizational culture and is closely linked to the concept of the learning organization discussed in the last chapter of this book.

Evenden and Anderson (1992) argue that development is a mutual responsibility requiring different activity but equal commitment from the individual on the one hand and from the organization and performance manager on the other. The manager has a choice of three types of development relationship: usurper, which is directive and requires learning dependence; abdicator, which involves opting out of development responsibility; and supporter/sharer, in which the manager has some responsibility for providing opportunity and support, for example by coaching, and the learner makes and takes them.

> Individuals are responsible for their own learning. If development takes place through a process of choice, it is because individuals choose to learn and change, not because the manager chooses that they should. . . . The organization may offer opportunity and incentive. The manager may appraise, assess and agree purpose, direction and objectives. The means of development through coaching, counselling experience and courses may be made available. This is the organization and manager's side of . . . the development relationship. Learning . . . requires effort and investment on the part of the developing person . . . and ownership. This is the individual's side of the development relationship.
>
> (Evenden and Anderson, 1992, pp. 287–8)

Paradoxically, although great weight is now being placed upon individuals' active pursuit of their own development, the role of the manager in this is, in many senses, increasing. We have examined the demands of effective assessment and appraisal if line managers are to perform their HRM role. Performance development may also be becoming a central activity and is increasingly associated with learning at the workface. This includes coaching, counselling to help individuals overcome blocks to performance and creating opportunities for job-related growth (Evenden and Anderson, 1992, Chapter 27).

Coaching is essentially a two-way process, normally involving manager and employee, concerned with analysing and finding jointly agreed solutions to work problems facing the employee, and helping the employee to develop his or her potential through a two-way dialogue designed to enhance learning that takes place on the job.

Counselling is a wider process that involves deliberation between the manager and employee on a range of issues, often concerned with giving guidance or encouraging the appraisee to talk through and think through personal problems that may be impeding performance or career development, and with career progression issues that may be causing the appraisee anxieties or concerns. Mumford (1985) has suggested that the more effective forms of development are often the less structured, on-the-job approaches associated with coaching and counselling, and that they can make an important contribution towards performance management.

The role of coach is an amalgam of four other HRM activities:

- *Appraiser*   Agrees what development is needed; performance targets and development plans
  Observes and assesses.

- *Supporter*   Creates opportunity
  Provides support, services and resources
  Counsels and helps with problems.

- *Communicator*   Gives balanced and constructive feedback
  Offers advice and suggestions
  Develops positive relationships
  Is clear and informative.

- *Motivator*   Encourages
  Gives recognition
  Challenges
  Exhorts
  Has expectations
  Understands the developer.

Influencing motivation

Performance management involves developing the skill to work well, but as we indicate in the 'performance gap' model, it also requires influence upon the will to work well, or motivation.

Most of the many models of motivation at work suggest that understanding must come before motivator skills can be applied, and that this understanding has to relate to an individual's internal processes, such as needs (Alderfer, 1979). This means that managers must focus upon individuals and anticipate differences between them. Personal profiles vary substantially, so the 'triggers' of motivation will too.

The influence of work motivation comes through structuring a situation so that individual performance will be instrumental in meeting that individual's needs, and the better they perform the more their needs will be met (Nadler and Lawler, 1977). This means identifying the motivation triggers and endeavouring to provide them for people at work.

As in all aspects of social perception, managers develop stereotypes of what motivates others at work, and evidence suggests these work against effective performance management by motivation. In the first place, they militate against necessary tailoring to individual profiles, and in the second they are usually wrong in general terms. For example, one study revealed that managers believed the top three performance motivators of staff were salary, security and personal development, in a list of 10 factors; however, the staff themselves saw interesting work, recognition and being kept in the picture as most important (Couger and Zawaki, 1980).

We have suggested that performance management through motivation requires finding situational triggers that will stimulate performance, which itself will be meeting individual needs. There are, of course, no universal motivators, but the authors' review of the evidence and their own research (Evenden and Anderson, 1992) in the public and private sectors suggest that the three key sources are the job, the manager and colleagues.

Conclusion

In this chapter we have attempted to show how the concept of performance appraisal, while still considered of central importance to HRM, is in some organizations evolving into a wider concept of performance management, the nature of which has been outlined in terms of philosophy and developments. We have concluded by reviewing strategies and techniques that can be used by managers in their performance management role at the workface, when the need is to translate broad strategic plans and goals through HRM into performance management, and the difficulties that this entails when people enter the equation.

Performance management systems and the skill of the line manager attempt to focus and influence the performance of individuals at work so that effective contributions are made to the achievement of corporate goals. The philosophy of performance management is clear, in supporting the achievement of corporate strategies, but many issues still have to be thought through fully, in terms of how performance management systems can be designed and implemented satisfactorily, and integrated within wider HRM strategy.

11

Choosing and using relevant financial reward systems

David Bright and Frank Needham

By the end of this chapter the reader will:

1. understand the role and the functions of reward systems in an HRM strategy;

2. understand the nature of the key ingredients of reward packages;

3. be able to identify the most important ingredients in reward packages for particular organizations or sectors.

Introduction

This chapter examines the nature of reward systems, their usage by business organizations and the role of reward management in an HRM approach. To this end, attention is given to the function of rewards in an enterprise, the direction of current trends in pay and other benefits, and to the application of different types of reward packages to support an organization's business strategy.

For a contract of employment to exist, as well as an offer and acceptance of terms there must be 'consideration', the exchange of tangible benefits for effort and ability. These rewards in the form of payment systems are critical, not just to the existence of the employee–employer relationship, but to the management of that resource:

> For employers, pay represents not only a cost but an important management tool for achieving all sorts of aims.
>
> (Duncan, 1989, p. 217)

There are many kinds of reward systems in existence which make use of a wide variety of ingredients but for any system to be an effective part of a strategic human resource approach it must possess the following criteria:

- it must be understood by those personnel affected by it, so that these staff can see the impact of their performance and the equity of the scheme;

- it must support the organization's corporate objectives;

- it should reward effort and development, measured both in qualitative and quantitative terms;

- it should be reasonably flexible;

- it should mesh with other parts of the HRM strategy.

If a reward scheme possesses these characteristics it will form a coherent element in overall human resource strategy; will focus clearly on improving performance; will encourage development; and will relate to both the individual's and the organization's targets.

Within a reward strategy a number of elements interlink. Armstrong and Murlis (1988) identify the following as the major elements in this linkage:

- pay levels and relativities;

- reward structures;

- performance-related pay;

- benefit packages and total remuneration;

- special reward management programmes for particular groups of staff;

- programmes for *managing* the reward systems.

Such elements demonstrate the cohesiveness and the strategic nature of a system. In Britain and many other countries, leading employers are increasingly developing reward mechanisms which they believe possess such cohesiveness and strategic importance. Before moving to a consideration of the elements and trends in these mechanisms of reward strategy, it is important to recognize the nexus between reward management and HRM strategy.

Reward management and HRM strategy

Speaking at the 1990 IPM Conference at Harrogate, David Guest suggested that the following were required conditions for the successful cultivation of HRM techniques:

- the perception of the organization that HRM is about tackling specific human resource development goals;
- a desire to invest heavily in quality;
- an ability on the part of the organization to encompass employee commitment;
- adaptability and reliability; and
- the ability of the employer to successfully integrate all of these.

Reward management relates to all of these areas. Thus the package or packages should be sufficient to attract and retain valued staff and should reward quality of performance and also quality of behaviour. At the same time, reward packages have to take cognizance of wider trends in specialized and more generalized labour markets. The chemical multinational, ICI, encapsulates all these points in its approach to salary management for their expatriate managers by taking into account the following factors (with acknowledgements to Aitken, 1990):

- Organizational requirements
  - stage of business development
  - organizational structure
  - organizational culture.
- External and social trends
  - labour market
  - personal values
  - reward packages.

- Internal considerations
  - reasons for expatriate assignments
  - expatriate profile
  - type of assignment
  - corporate policies/standards.

Thus, for an employer to achieve a successful reward management programme, which is itself a part of an effective HRM strategy, a degree of planning must inevitably take place with regard to both systems. The planner must be aware of the business goals of the organization. He or she must be cognizant of all the elements of the HRM strategy and must have given consideration to the areas of interlock between its elements, particularly recruitment, human resource development, negotiation practices and reward management. Having satisfied the above requirements, the major task remaining for the manager is to construct and implement the most suitable type of reward system to meet the needs of that specific business. This is where the wider policy targets and priorities interface with the pragmatics of reward management. Bowen (1990) offers us one example in his analysis of the restructuring of remuneration policies at the retail group, W.H. Smith. He explained that the objective of his review was to design a remuneration strategy that covered all grades of management and staff, across the whole group of companies.

> Our staff are in direct contact with the public and need to be motivated and encouraged. It was and is, therefore, essential that our strategy was fair, that it motivated and encouraged. If it was seen so to be then we would recruit and retain – for growth.
>
> (Bowen, 1990, p. 4)

The W.H. Smith review had five clear but related phases. These were:

- review of current practice;
- review of incentive schemes;
- profit-related pay;
- job evaluation;
- the clean salary (benefits as part of total package).

It can be noted, then, that for reward management to sit well as part of a wider HRM approach the person responsible for developing the rewards will have had to address a series of key issues. These include: an awareness of the organization's business objectives and the contents of any related mission statement; an understanding of the other HRM elements and their likely points of interface with the reward policy; the objectives that the reward strategy should itself possess; an understanding of how the organization currently handles its reward business; knowledge of the various reward elements available; an understanding of how implementation will have to be handled; and an appreciation of the timescale involved in implementation. Let us consider the types of reward elements and their uses.

The determination of pay schemes

Types of pay scheme

Reward systems inevitably concentrate on basic pay, but a series of additional pay-related and other benefits apply to many forms of employment. These benefits may include bonus schemes, overtime payments, merit or performance-related payments, profit bonuses and paid holiday leave.

Additional non-pay items also make up part of the reward package, and such items may include occupational pension schemes, sick pay schemes, paid holiday leave, company cars, clothing allowances and subsidized meals and accommodation.

Often, pay-related issues are categorized into those reflecting payment by time and those reflecting payment by results (Duncan, 1989). We shall deal with each of these in turn.

Payments by time

Schemes in this category are based on payment for hours worked weekly, monthly or annually, regardless of any direct measure of performance. Underperformance is dealt with outside the pay relationship as a counselling or disciplinary issue. While the rate for the job can change through a process of revision (often the product of collective bargaining), there is no other incremental or grade development built into the system. The straightforward 'rate for the job' approach is easy to apply, though is somewhat inflexible, and has been criticized as lacking the capability to reward effort and merit. A simple scheme of this nature would not be of high value in seeking to achieve the objectives set down earlier, in particular, those of rewarding effort, quality and development.

A more sophisticated variant of the simple time rate is that of a grading structure based on a scheme of systematic job evaluation. Here the payment structure is underpinned by a series of grades and scales, with similarly graded jobs being linked in the same scale. From a strategic viewpoint this more sophisticated structure has the advantages that (Armstrong and Murlis, 1988, p. 33):

- the *relative levels* of jobs in different functions can be readily assessed and recognized;

- consistent methods of grading jobs and establishing differentials between them can be maintained;

- a well-defined and comprehensible framework exists within which salary and career programmes can be planned and controlled;

- better control can be exercised over salaries for new starters, merit increments and promotion increases.

Most job evaluation schemes are based on the related techniques of points rating and factor comparisons. In the former, actual jobs are examined by a team or a panel of evaluators and the inherent tasks and responsibilities broken down in a manner resembling reverse model building. Each factor is then allocated a number of points which, in turn, make up the relevant weighting. The points are then summed and the amount of the totalled points determines the grade to which the job is allocated.

Factor comparisions are an extension of the points system but are more reliant on a series of 'benchmark' jobs. The scheme compares the actual jobs with the benchmark on a factor-by-factor basis which, in turn, produces a ranking of the benchmark jobs for each factor. The actual wage rates are dissected in an exercise to ascertain how much of each rate relates to each factor. This procedure results in a scale of pay for each of the factors which reflects the factorial contribution to the benchmark jobs. The actual jobs are then evaluated factor by factor against these scales.

The use of these types of job evaluation schemes should allow for more objectivity and systematization to be applied to the reward structure. Where employers use such schemes, they need to be sure to construct or utilize schemes which are free from any direct or indirect sex discrimination which would be unlawful under the 1970 Equal Pay Act and other antidiscriminationary pieces of legislation.

A recent survey in the *Industrial Relations Review and Report* suggests that employers had become more cognizant of this requirement over the last few years:

> Amid concern, often prompted by the unions they negotiate with, that existing pay structures and job evaluation systems open them up to equal value claims a number of major employers have revised, or are planning to revise, their old arrangements for pay determination.
>
> (Industrial Relations Review and Report, 1990a, p. 12)

Such employers from this British survey included the textile giant Courtaulds, Findus Foods and Tesco, the supermarket chain.

While movement from one grade to another comes through job change, the scales are usually regularly revised on a cost-of-living basis. A different method of monetary progression applies to a number of other jobs, often white collar, where a process of incremental moves based on length of service allows the employee to be paid more over time. Here emphasis is placed on length of service to the employer, with the reward being justified as a reward for loyalty and increased knowledge and skill over time. This type of scheme has been particularly associated with public sector employers, such as the civil service and local government, but current developments are reducing the importance of incremental programmes for many employers.

Shiftwork premiums

In the 1992 New Earnings Survey, a regular statistical analysis covering a random sample of occupations, it was noted that 24% of all male manual workers received some sort of shift premium, which represented 5.5% of the average gross weekly earnings. Such premiums are generally calculated in one of two ways, being either a fixed percentage of the basic pay rate or a flat-rate cash amount. While variations in rates abound, the former appears to be the more common type. In situations where premiums are linked as a percentage of basic pay, they reflect the wage structure, protecting differential rates and positions. Where the overtime rate is paid as a flat-rate figure, reflecting the logic of equal inconvenience, all employees receive the same cash figure for working what are considered anti-social hours.

Shift working is predominately associated with manufacturing and process systems where the technology and the process requires round-the-clock throughput. Not surprisingly, therefore, the majority of shiftworkers are employed on manual work:

> According to a recent CBI survey just over 80% of manufacturing organisations have employees working shifts in one form or another, with just under half of all manual employees in this sector actually working shifts at any one time. The incidence of manufacturing companies operating shifts for non-manual employees is markedly lower – around 5% of organisations operate shifts for 'clerical' staff and around 35% of companies operate shifts for 'white collar' employees.
>
> (Industrial Relations Review and Report, 1989b, p. 8)

Overtime payments

These payments apply in many organizations, predominantly to manual workers, where the standard working week is exceeded because of increased product demand, increasing schedules or some unforeseen event such as a machine breakdown. Overtime is generally of a 'noncontractual' nature wherein payment would only be made if the employee was required to work the excess hours, though in some workplaces staff are paid for a guaranteed number of excess hours regardless of whether they are required to work them (contractual overtime). Employees who work overtime can be paid at standard time rate though more often at a premium rate, with time plus one half time being common, with a double-time rate for Sundays and public holidays being a traditional norm. The amount of overtime work may be seasonally or cyclically related and is also related to the state of the economy: if a company is comparatively buoyant with demand for its products rising one would expect overtime to rise. Correspondingly, if the economy is in a state of comparative recession then overtime would inevitably fall across the range of industries.

In the New Earnings Survey for 1992, the UK Department of Employment noted that the average working week, for those full-time employees for whom weekly hours were reported, was 39.9 hours, of which 2.4 consisted of paid overtime. Manual employees worked on average almost 44 hours per week, non-manual employees less than 38 hours. Two-thirds of this difference was due to overtime.

Another recent survey supported the view that overtime as a working practice remained well established:

> We found that despite well publicised moves to annual hours in some companies, with a consequent loss of payment for overtime, payment for out of hours working continues to be made to non-managerial grades in most companies.
>
> (Industrial Relations Review and Report, 1990b, p. 11)

For employers seeking to manage reward systems effectively the amount of overtime needs to be closely monitored for, just as some overtime may always be necessary, a significant amount of it can throw the control of the relevant reward system out of kilter:

> The payment of overtime pay is generally held to be reasonable as long as the nature and amount of overtime working is strictly controlled. People do not work well and consistently if excessive overtime is worked and they should never be allowed to take on too much to supplement what may be, or perceived to be, an inadequate basic salary.
>
> (Armstrong and Murlis, 1988, p. 236)

Payments by output and results

As in the case of payments by time there are a number of varieties of payment by output and results. Much interest has been focused in the United Kingdom and elsewhere recently on performance-related systems linked to appraisal schemes, and certainly developments of these kinds have been seen as central to an HRM approach. We shall deal with these in some detail later in the section. Before doing so, however, brief mention should be made of the concepts of piecework and bonus payments.

In a piecework system, traditionally associated with production and assembly work, the employee is rewarded by payment for the amount of production and assembly completed. Not surprisingly, the range of income could be large, with the employees being able to exercise their own degree of control over the production process. Elements of this type of system can also be seen in commission-based selling in the financial and other service sectors. As Guest (1989) notes, however, such schemes are unlikely to support HRM approaches to the management of employees and their conditions of service:

> If workers have been selected to minimum specifications and display a strong instrumental orientation, they are unlikely to fit comfortably into the kind of environment necessary for HRM.
>
> (Guest, 1989, p. 30)

Under a range of bonus schemes extra payment is made in situations where production exceeds set targets or where work of acceptable quality is completed within a predetermined deadline. Duncan (1989) notes the distinction in the variation in the amount that earnings change dependent upon performance:

> In geared schemes the rate of change of earnings, although constant, is greater than the rate of change of performance. If the change of earnings is less than the change of performance the scheme is known as stabilized.
>
> (Duncan, 1989, p. 223)

Relating types of payment scheme to HRM strategy

There are, however, three particular limitations with mechanistic schemes of pay determination. The first, as noted by Duncan and others, is that they are prone to 'decay' as working conditions change. The second is that they take away a degree of control from management, in that the scheme develops almost an arbitrary existence. The third limitation is that such schemes, while having some benefits, lack a great deal of flexibility of application, and it is exactly this flexibility that Guest noted as being critical for the successful implementation of HRM. In addition to these specific points such schemes, and indeed most of the traditional methods of rewarding staff, possess a conceptual difficulty, in that they reflect a particularly mechanistic image of the organization wherein the workforce are treated similarly, if not identically, in matters of reward. Thus groups of staff would be employed on fairly rigid contractual terms, all receiving a similar return that would be underpinned by a shared logic which suggested that any developments, changes or increases in performance had to be driven by extra pay.

Put simply, such traditional systems of pay reflect a pluralistic image of the organization, helping to engender a 'what's in it for us?' set of attitudes. Readers of this book will already be aware of the lack of fit between the above outcomes and the objectives of HRM. As Cooke and Armstrong comment:

> HR strategies will therefore be concerned with the design and management of the culture and organisational processes of the business to ensure that the good can be made better. They will assess critical success factors and the competences required and decide how to get and keep the high-calibre people

the business needs. They will address the main issues relating to the management of performance and quality, gaining the commitment of members of the organisation and developing harmonious relationships with trade unions and employees.

(Cooke and Armstrong, 1990, p. 31)

It can be seen then that, just as the effective reward package needs to be flexible and relevant, it should also possess features which help more convergent values to be developed and retained between senior management in an organization and the workforce as a whole. This is one of the features believed by many employers to be associated with some of the more modern and qualitatively based systems of performance-related pay.

Performance-related pay

Although performance-related pay is now fairly widespread among managerial employees in the manufacturing sector of the British economy, the most far-reaching changes in this direction recently have occurred within the service sector. In the public service sector, performance-based salary structures have been introduced in the National Health Service, public authorities and parts of the civil service. These have largely been confined to more senior positions or specialists such as computer staff. However, more significant examples of the adoption of performance-related pay are found within the British financial services sector which during the 1980s was subject to significant structural and organizational change as a consequence of deregulation, mergers, technological developments and increasing competition.

Surveys in the late 1980s by ACAS and IDS revealed that increasingly companies which may initially have confined performance-related pay to senior managers have extended the numbers covered to incorporate all employees. This trend is particularly evident in the British financial sector where it is common practice to include all permanent staff in the performance-related pay scheme.

This development has been encouraged by a number of HRM-related factors, the most significant of which are as follows:

- The need to *change employee attitudes to their work performance*.
- The need to make the *most cost-effective use of salary increases* by distributing awards differentially to reward high performance.
- The need to *address recruitment and retention problems* by developing a more attractive and competitive salary structure to enable rapid progression through salary scales.

■   The development of *more sophisticated and objective appraisal* systems to assess performance according to output – both quantitative and qualitative – to overcome the defects of earlier merit rating systems which were based on a subjective assessment of an employee's input.

■   The acquiescence of the unions in *adopting a pragmatic approach* even though they may be sceptical of all the claims made for performance-related pay. This may involve negotiating on the size of the overall pot and method of distribution, while accepting wide variations in the size of individual awards.

■   The desire to adopt *flatter systems of grading and responsibility* as part of an overall strategy to achieving harmonization and flexibility in the workplace.

The logic of paying more to those who make the most effort is difficult to refute and even without the introduction of performance-related pay, the proportion of a salary award directly related to merit became greater during the 1980s as inflation rates fell. A typical UK pay settlement in the financial services sector in 1980 – with inflation at 17% – would have been 17.5% across the board, with an additional 2.5% for merit awards. By 1987 with RPI down to 4.4% a typical settlement would have been 5% across the board, and again 2.5% allocated to merit. Thus the merit element, which accounted for just 12.5% of the total award in 1980, had increased proportionately to one-third of the total by 1987.

Management in companies which adopted this type of performance-related pay were therefore able to take advantage of the relatively low levels of inflation which applied in Europe in the 1986–88 period (RPI was below 5% for two years to July 1988), in persuading employees and unions that the annual pay award and merit review should in effect be merged to make all salary progression dependent on individual performance. In those British building societies which adopted performance-related pay during that period (Abbey National, Alliance and Leicester and National and Provincial), the overall award was more generous than the unions believed would have been the outcome of a traditional across-the-board plus merit settlement. In two cases (Abbey National and National and Provincial) the change to performance-related pay was also accompanied by the introduction of profit-related bonus schemes.

The emphasis in these developments was on the organization's 'ability to pay', rewarding individual performance to engender corporate success. However, it should be remembered that even systems of performance-related pay are influenced by external factors. For example, market pressures and comparative settlements continue to be significant elements in determining the overall size of salary awards, even though the total award is then distributed differentially. Fowler (1988) argues that:

> . . . the description of these schemes as being entirely performance based
> is however misleading . . . and their operation would be prejudiced by any
> significant increase in pay or price inflation.
>
> (Fowler, 1988, p. 31)

Fowler maintains that higher inflation would lead to increases being necessary just to keep pace, outweighing the 'pure' performance element and diluting any motivational effect.

Within British building societies and banks the introduction of performance-related pay often followed job evaluation exercises which had been implemented as a consequence of structural changes made necessary by deregulation of the industry, technological developments and in some cases, mergers. In this context it is interesting to note the role and influence of consultants whose job evaluation systems had been adopted by a range of building societies, insurance companies and banks.

One attraction of outside consultants for these organizations is the access they have to a salary database, enabling them to obtain information on comparative rates of pay using points systems as the basis of comparison. A very common approach relates individual performance appraisal to the achievements of specific objectives which are, in turn, related to the principal 'accountabilities' identified in the job description. An assessment is then made of the level of performance achieved in relation to each accountability, using five defined categories, usually described as:

- marginal or initial;
- incomplete or developing;
- fully competent or fully acceptable;
- superior;
- outstanding.

An overall performance rating is then assessed which determines the size of the performance-related pay award, dependent on the individual's existing position on the salary scale, using a matrix to determine the size or range of the pay award.

Some care needs to be taken with this method to make sure that the appraisal process is as fair and objective as possible. At the same time, sufficient training must be given to appraisees and appraisers alike to ensure that the scheme is understood, manageable and evokes confidence.

While performance-related pay offers the HRM-oriented organization a number of aids to the achievement of an overall effective approach, one particular tension surrounding it needs to be noted and handled carefully. Much of the changed patterns of work and identification in businesses today revolve around teams and team working. Teams support just-in-time and quality developments, they are an important ingredient in the communication process and they offer a type of peer group management. It is important, therefore, that the cohesiveness and synergetic benefits of good team working are not dissipated by a performance-related pay scheme which is seen to set one worker against another by paying too stark a rate difference for the same type of work. Thus differential rate has to be managed equitably, be linked to some measurable indicator, such as skill level achieved, and should be robust enough to stand against any allegation of unlawful discrimination. It may be that the employer who wishes to manage the tension between differentiation and group identity has to limit the amount of money related to performance and link it to a type of team-related enhancement.

One further caveat should be noted with regard to performance-related pay. While underperformance can be dealt with in financial terms, it would be wrong for an employer to rely solely on this to bring about a change in behaviour. Underperformers also require remedial attention in the form of counselling or training to support a move to full competence. Where this is unsuccessful, the disciplinary process needs to be applied. While it is true that regular poor pay increases or no increases at all may encourage the poor performer to leave the organization, strategic management requires that the human resource manager does not rely on this possibility as an answer to the problem.

Profit-related pay

Although they are sometimes confused and frequently bracketed together, the two concepts of performance-related pay and profit-related pay must be clearly distinguished. Performance-related pay refers to a method or system of distributing pay awards by reference to individual performance appraisal, whereas profit-related pay refers to a system of determining part of a pay award, usually in the form of a lump sum bonus payment, by reference to a measure of corporate success. A wide range of companies, particularly in retailing and finance, have established profit-sharing schemes, some of them such as those at Rowntree's, Sainsbury's and the John Lewis Partnership have particularly long pedigrees.

Although the idea of employee participation in corporate performance through profit-sharing schemes is not new (their history can be traced back to the nineteenth-century work of Robert Owen), there has undoubtedly been a revival of interest in profit-related pay, cash or share-based bonus schemes and more recently employee share ownership plans.

Greenhill (1988) cites the American economist Martin Weitzman, who argues that the linking of an element of pay to corporate profit would raise employment levels by reducing the marginal cost of labour. There is little empirical evidence of this effect to date, however, even in those schemes where a significant proportion of overall remuneration is accounted for by a direct profit relationship. The evidence from the banks and from major retailers who have long-established profit-sharing schemes would suggest that such schemes become institutionalized with the annual bonus, whether in the form of cash or shares, being anticipated and taken account of by both employers and unions in determining overall remuneration levels.

A revival of interest in profit-related pay was expected to follow the British government's tax concessions for profit-related pay schemes, which were initially announced in the 1986 budget speech followed by a Green Paper, which met with a mixed response and some scepticism. When the proposals were finally revealed in the 1987 Finance Act, the maximum amount of tax relief had been doubled. Despite subsequent extensions to the amount of profit-related pay which can be paid tax free and some liberalization of the somewhat complex requirements laid down by the Inland Revenue for registration, the number of schemes registered by the end of 1988 had only reached 830, covering just 122 000 employees. Similar low figures exist in the 1990s. Thus, so far the scheme has failed to meet the expectations of the then Chancellor, Nigel Lawson, who believed that the widespread adoption of profit-related pay, encouraged by the government's tax concessions, would curb inflationary wage pressures by linking a significant slice of overall pay to corporate profitability.

Cash-based profit-sharing schemes which have not been registered for tax relief continue to be the most common form of profit-related pay. Such schemes have the advantage of relative simplicity and flexibility and, in most cases, have been set up and operated without negotiation or consultation with employee representatives. Most companies operating profit-sharing schemes therefore retain the element of discretion to withold or reduce payments, however in a few cases the terms have been negotiated with trade unions – at British Nuclear Fuels and at Vauxhall, for example.

The objective of employers in establishing profit-related pay or bonus schemes is to create a sense of participation and loyalty in the workforce and to encourage individual employees to contribute to corporate achievement by giving them a direct interest in corporate profits. This sits well with the type of attitude set required for an effective HRM approach. A few companies, such as Vauxhall and the Halifax Building Society, publicize bulletins during the year to draw their employees' attention to the achievement of the profit target, and some such as Pitney Bowes pay a quarterly bonus.

As has been noted earlier in this chapter, the trend towards performance-related pay and, to a lesser extent, profit-related pay has been closely associated with and could be described as a move towards more cost-effective reward programmes. Such a move has been assisted in the United Kingdom by relatively low inflation rates, by deregulation of some specialized markets and the whole ethos of a government which has stressed the values of individualism and self-development. In view of this background, it is perhaps not surprising that organizations within the finance sector have been at the forefront of these developments and have provided a number of models for performance-based salary structures and rewards systems which others have subsequently adapted.

Key current trends in reward systems

From the attention given thus far to the increasing importance of performance-related pay it can be noted that changes in emphasis in payment systems have been taking place in UK industry and commerce in recent years. There are a number of features associated with this trend. Some of the most important are;

- the adherence by employers to strict 'rate for the job' reward systems has been lessened;

- many reward packages possess built-in areas of variability or flexibility;

- there has been an increasing priority given to reward of effort, behaviour, development or results rather than crude output;

- the above tendencies can be linked to one of the features discussed in Chapter 6, the move to decentralized collective bargaining.

Such developments have, to an extent, reflected and been assisted by the industrial relations policies of the British government. The Conservative government have, since their election in 1979, repealed a number of initiatives or rules related to pay regulations. These include: the winding up of the Comparability Commission; the repeal of the House of Commons Fair Wages Resolution which required companies working with parts of the public sector to pay 'fair wages' to their employees; the repeal of Schedule 11 of the 1975 Employment Protection Act which allowed unions to take a complaint to the Central Arbitration Committee on the grounds that their members in a particular place of employment were not receiving wages as good as a national wage agreement or the general level of pay for the type of job in the district; and the removal of minimum wage protection for young workers in industries covered by wages councils.

The broad rationale for these changes is as Mackie (1989) notes:

> . . . 'deregulation' in order to allow the labour market to work more freely and to allow employers to concentrate on the question of goods and services rather than on external systems of wages and legal diversions
>
> (Mackie, 1989, p. 274)

This has provided for the employer a freer hand in the organization of reward systems. A further factor assisting in the development has been the preparedness of unions to sit down with employers and negotiate new reward systems in which the traditional principle of the rate for the job is given less credence and significance.

In addition to the payment element of reward, improvements in a number of other non-wage benefits need to be considered. Of greatest probable importance are holidays, working time, occupational pensions, sick pay schemes and a range of fringe benefits or 'perks', such as a company vehicle.

Three general points can be made with regard to trends here. First, the numbers of employees covered by such terms has been steadily increasing through the last decade. Second, this process of extension has been linked in a number of organizations to a process of 'harmonization', and third, the concept of a 'cafeteria package' is emerging in some companies where staff can select elements in their reward package within a range. The first two of these trends are linked, with companies extending non-wage benefits to groups of employees who traditionally were not in receipt of them.

Harmonization

ACAS (1989) defines harmonization as the 'narrowing or elimination of the differences in the basis of the treatment of manual and non-manual workers regarding pay, fringe benefits and other conditions of employment'. In a recent survey of 83 employers, the research company IRS concluded the following regarding the extension of harmonization:

> holiday and leave entitlement, redundancy pay and occupational pensions are the major areas of terms and conditions where harmonisation has been most evident, while of the peripheral terms and conditions, harmonization is most common in canteen/restaurant facilities, product discounts and allowances, car parking and loans . . . harmonisation is least advanced in pay systems, grading structures, hours of work and methods of recording attendance . . . half the companies surveyed had implemented most harmonisation in the last five years, half before that time . . . employers usually instigated harmonisation moves, but the process itself was typically the subject of negotiation with unions . . . nearly two thirds of companies expect the pace of harmonisation generally to increase in the 1990s.
>
> (Industrial Relations Review and Report, 1989a, p. 5)

Thus, it appears that harmonization is most readily found in non-wage areas. Apart from any ideological rationale three factors have been at work in influencing employers and unions to move down such a route:

1.   In areas such as pensions and retirement ages the decisions of British courts and, in particular, the European Court of Justice, have made it necessary for employers to standardize rules in order to remain within the law.

2. In some of the last years of the 1980s (though not in the 1990s) in Britain and elsewhere in Europe critical skill shortages in areas of industry and commerce have required employers to offer better packages of benefits to attract and retain key staff.

3. Organizations which seek to initiate a bond between the organization and the employee need to minimize traditional and often outmoded differences in terms of employment and related conditions.

Thus, whereas at one time, benefits such as pensions and longer holidays were enjoyed more by white-collar staff, employers today, particularly in greenfield operations, desire to demonstrate that all staff are of critical value to the company and should enjoy similar non-wage conditions.

The cafeteria approach

At the same time, however, that harmonization is increasing, greater flexibility allows employers to offer a more selective range of package ingredients to their staff should they so wish. This has led to the initiation of a **cafeteria approach** to benefits in a few organizations where certain groups of staff can select the nature and mix of their benefits from a range. The mix can be varied to suit the particular needs of individuals at certain stages of their career.

Such a practice is now quite well established in the United States (Friedman, 1990) and European companies have become more attracted to it of late. For example, the Mortgage Corporation, a finance house, allows staff to select benefits within overall parameters. The organization believes that this approach allows it to retain key staff by matching their needs at different stages of their career. The benefits include pensions, long-term disability insurance, life assurance and subsidized mortgages. In Hewitt Associates staff can select from company cars, holiday entitlements, pension and medical insurance.

Although cafeteria schemes are a comparatively new development in the United Kingdom, their logic, reflecting as it does choice and individual contract agreement, fits well within a cohesive approach to HRM. Friedman is one writer who sees their use expanding:

> Although cafeteria benefit systems are only just obtaining a foothold in the UK their popularity looks likely to increase throughout the 1990s.
>
> (Friedman, 1990)

The European dimension

Although the British government has felt unable to ratify the 'Social Charter' of the EC, its implementation elsewhere in the next few years will influence further changes in pay and benefits in European companies. The majority of member states have ratified the full Maastricht Treaty. This will require businesses in those states to adopt systems for minimum pay levels, to treat their part-time staff no less favourably in proportionate terms to their full-time workers and to improve some of the terms for female staff. While some employers might already match the criteria, many will have to change their practices.

At the same time, because of recruitment patterns and union campaigns, European employers have come under increased pressure to improve a range of benefits in the area of working time. Some examples include:

- career breaks;
- family and paternity leave;
- more flexible working time patterns;
- improved schemes for career development.

A further reflection of the changing times is the predicted increase in nationals of European states working elsewhere in the Community. Employers will need to be aware of labour markets, not just in their home country but across the Community. Human resource specialists will need to be competent in income and taxation levels, employment rights, vocational qualifications, retirement and pensions at the pan-European level if they are going to be able to assist in the provision and retention of highly skilled and motivated staff.

Reward systems and HRM

In the foregoing pages we have examined some of the key elements in the make-up of reward systems and have assessed current trends of thinking in these areas. We have looked, in particular, at how developments in performance-related payment schemes have been increasingly adopted by UK employers and by foreign-based multinationals in the last few years. We can now reiterate the importance of reward management to an overall HRM approach. The key point in this relationship is that of flexibility, with the organization being able to apply differing levels of payment in response to differing levels of application and results from their employees. As Fowler notes in an examination of performance-related pay:

> are the trends [described in this article] leading to permanent changes in UK salary practice? It seems probable that at least some of them are. Paying for how well work is done rather than for highly subjective assessments of personal qualities, seems likely to set the scene for most future performance–pay policies. In the public sector, the precedent of incremental salaries has

been broken to too great an extent to envisage any fundamental reversion.
As the principle of single status spreads, the extension of performance pay
throughout workforces will become commonplace.

(Fowler, 1988, p. 44)

However, before any employer rushes to bring in a radically new system of
pay based on performance, Fowler sets out some caveats which should be
noted. In essence these are:

■ organizations will need to consider very carefully the operation of any
scheme which does not enable the majority of employees to benefit from
it;

■ those organizations which have introduced performance pay mainly to
improve salary levels will have great difficulty in applying real performance principles;

■ as happened with MBO (Management by Objectives) some schemes are
becoming so structured that their operation runs the risk of becoming an
end in itself – sophisticated performance–pay schemes can too easily be
or become the property of personnel managers.

Within these notes of caution three points are worthy of being underlined:

1. Any new payment system, whether related to performance or not, needs
to be carefully chosen, designed and, where necessary, adapted.

2. Employers should be wary of expecting long-term changes in employees'
attitudes and behaviour from schemes which have been introduced to
solve short-term exigencies.

3. Any reward system which is not understood and owned by line managers
as well as the personnel specialist is unlikely to work efficiently over time.
If payment systems are to be effective then they, like other facets of
HRM, need to be supported by key operational staff as well as the
specialists.

    In the USA the prevailing view appears to be that HRM is too important
    to be left to personnel managers . . . HRM is now a central component of
    MBA programmes for managers who are unlikely to pursue a career as
    HRM specialists.

(Guest, 1989, p. 51)

A further important issue in the management of rewards within HRM
is for employers to recognize the reward package as a whole and to manage
it coherently rather than as a set of often unrelated elements. This, for
Armstrong and Murlis, is the notion of 'total remuneration' or 'remuneration package' management:

    Application of the 'total remuneration' or 'remuneration package' concept
    involves treating all aspects of pay and benefits policy as a whole. It gives

valuable discipline and perspective to the overall process of salary and benefits planning and creates a framework within which the different elements of remuneration can be adjusted according to the needs of the organisation and the individual. The cost to the company and the value to the individual of each element is assessed with the aim of achieving an appropriate balance between the various components of remuneration for each employee grade or category,

(Armstrong and Murlis, 1988, p. 315)

The third important issue in reward management is for employers to recognize that the elements of the system must change with time to respond to changes in labour markets, social expectations and governmentally determined rules. This means that, while reward systems should always underwrite stability, they will undoubtedly require regular amendments and revision. To accomplish this, any employer attempting to manage pay and benefits successfully within HRM must initiate and maintain a monitoring operation. To recall the discussion in Chapter 3 about the HRM roles of specialists and line managers, this is where the personnel specialist comes into his or her own, for while the HRM philosophy requires commitment from the line manager, the personnel specialist can become the consultant in all matters of HRM and for our purposes in this chapter this rests largely on providing a pay and benefits monitoring facility.

The final important issue in reward management is strongly related to the one dealt with above, and it is patience. Payment and benefit systems in most organizations have been set down or have emerged over many years. It would be foolish for management in such an organization to expect radical changes to be successfully achieved in a short time, particularly where the changes have to be negotiated through the trade unions.

In such situations it would serve companies well to agree a timescale for the introduction of changes which is realistic and allows for:

- adequate communication of the scheme elements to all affected by the changes, management and staff alike; additionally, time may well be required for negotiation with recognized trade unions;

- discussions by employees of the benefits and details of the scheme;

- the possibility of piloting the scheme in some areas of the company initially;

- possible revision of the scheme within a reasonably short time.

The adoption of such a staged process will undoubtedly make the implementation of a scheme slower to achieve but will at the same time significantly reduce the risk of a major early catastrophe.

A recent case study of a change in salary determination in Coates Viyella, a leading textile company, serves to underline the need for careful planning at all stages:

Other companies contemplating decentralisation of collective bargaining can draw a number of lessons from the initial experience of the Coates Viyella companies. These include:

- The need for careful planning
- The need to win the support of senior managers who will have to implement the change
- The need to train such managers properly for their new roles and responsibilities
- The need to keep employees informed of developments
- The need to reassure the union of its role in representing employees

(Jackson and Leopold, 1990, p. 66)

There is no doubt that the successful management of reward systems is critical to successful HRM. Principles such as flexibility, stability and the reward of skill and effort are inherent in the former as well as the latter. There is no universal rewards package for companies to adopt. On the contrary, it behoves them to meet their needs by the careful planning and implementation of elements best suited to their organization. Successful reward management is not an easy thing to achieve. It needs care and effort but as Armstrong and Murlis conclude, it possesses many benefits for the organization utilizing HRM:

> Reward management is becoming an integral part of human resource management with its stress on the strategic nature of personnel management as a means of influencing and achieving organisational objectives.
>
> (Armstrong and Murlis, 1988, p. 421)

They argue that future trends will reinforce this process of integration in that reward management can help manage organizational culture, performance and career paths.

Finally, it should not be forgotten that while effective reward management can and does support HRM in these ways, it also makes the organization more cost effective, which in these days of high levels of competition for markets is of critical importance in itself.

Thus as Brewster and Connock (1985) note:

> In the area of pay and other rewards, control over costs remains fundamental to organisational success. To improve cost effectiveness, we have stressed the emphasis on the employees' contribution to organisational objectives. Cost control can also be exercised through cash limits, the use of the kitty principle, or through self-financing productivity arrangements. For all except those few organisations whose pay is a very small percentage of total costs this is a key challenge.
>
> (Brewster and Connock, 1985, p. 102)

Conclusion

Much of this chapter has been associated with change, in particular the way businesses have changed their systems of reward to allow a more strategic approach to HRM to proceed or, for those wishing to change, the steps required to achieve it.

It has been noted throughout that many organizations have moved away from traditional time-based systems and the more mechanistic payment-by-results modes. Rewards have a critical role in HRM. They can be used to support commitment, achievement, team working and organizational performance.

We noted that any effective rewards package must be:

■   understood by those to whom it applies;

■   supportive to corporate objectives;

■   able to reward performance and development;

■   flexible; and

■   able to fit with other elements of HRM.

Businesses should be particularly careful to ensure that any changes in rewards, be they in pay forms or in nonwage areas, should be cost effective and should be right for that organization. This is particularly the case with the more individualistic trends such as performance-related pay. If a company wishes to build strong team identity and responsibility then attaching too much importance to performance pay could well prove to be counterproductive.

Early in 1993 in the UK the level of pay settlements had fallen to a typical range of 2–3%, while public sector pay was limited to 1.5% and many firms were given no increase at all. Against such a backcloth, individual performance pay is even more difficult to administer fairly and effectively. Greater interest is likely to be shown in systems which link pay increases to organizational performance. Typical features of these schemes are:

■   they are often nonconsolidated additions;

■   they can support team achievements by being linked to intracorporate unit performance;

■   they can be paid quarterly, six-monthly or annually;

■   they can qualify for exemption from income tax.

Throughout the 1990s it is likely that we will continue to see pay being linked to a 'something for something' method of thinking where increases are merited rather than being a normative expectation. Flexibility in packages will continue to be a keynote. Emphasis will lie on teams, business units and, to an extent, individuals. It is also likely that more and more erosion will take place with regard to traditional status-related benefits though a process of harmonization.

As employers and trade unions work to amend pay and benefits systems and to locate them within a tighter strategic framework, it is important that they bear in mind the three notes of caution stated earlier in the chapter:

1. Any new system has to be *carefully* chosen and/or adapted.

2. It is difficult to achieve long-term results from schemes which have been introduced to meet short-term problems.

3. Any system which is not understood and owned by *line managers* is unlikely to work effectively.

If these issues can be successfully resolved, reward systems can, with careful planning, be designed to play their part in effective HRM. If this is not achieved then a fully cohesive and strategic approach will not be possible.

12

Developing people – for whose bottom line?

Rosemary Harrison

By the end of the chapter the reader will:

1. understand how the development of people can contribute to organizational performance and growth, and the ways in which that contribution can be measured;

2. understand the relationship between developing people and wider HRM strategy, and the forces that trigger the need for human resource development in an organization;

3. understand some of the most typical attitudes related to investing in people's learning and development in organizations, and some of the major differences in attitudes towards training and development in the United Kingdom and major competitor countries;

4. understand the circumstances and ways in which an active commitment to human resource development in an organization can be achieved;

5. know how to develop the kind of strategic developmental processes that will both meet identified business needs and aid the growth of 'the learning organization'.

Some definitions

This chapter examines the kind of impact that the development of an organization's workforce can have on its short-term performance and longer term strategic growth. The examination will be in the wider context of human resource strategy and the general needs of the business.

First, some definitions. These are important, because there is such imprecision attached to terms like 'business success' and 'employee development' that it is hardly surprising that the needs of the one are so hard to relate to the outcomes of the other.

Business success refers here to the achievement of the organization's corporate mission, its business strategy, and its formal business goals, **Develop** means, literally, 'to unfold . . .; make or become fuller, more elaborate or systematic' (Oxford, 1988). **Education** and **training** both contribute to the development process, but development is more wide-ranging and more enduring than either, and there are many other factors that affect it, notably the values and behavioural norms of those who influence the individual both in and outside the workplace. **Learning** can be described as the process by which skills, knowledge and attitudes are acquired and translated into habitual forms of behaviour and performance, whether by design or through the natural passage of time.

The phrase **human resource development** (HRD) is now widely used, to the undoubted annoyance of many who prefer 'softer' phrases such as 'employee development', 'development of people' or just 'training and development' (used to distinguish between the immediate and job specific on the one hand and the longer term developmental on the other). However, it is becoming an internationally recognized way of describing the kind of process that, when used in the context of the wider phrase 'human resource management' refers to the planned learning and development of people as individuals and as groups to the benefit of the business as well as themselves:

> Developing people as part of an overall human resource strategy means the skilful provision and organization of learning experiences in the workplace in order that business goals can be achieved. It must be aligned with the organization's mission and strategic goals in order that, through enhancing the skills, knowledge, learning ability and enthusiasm of people at every level, there will be continuous organizational as well as individual growth.

Triggers to human resource development (HRD)

A business-led approach to training and development is typical of organizations like Halfords, Britain's biggest retailer of car accessories and cycles (Sparrow and Pettigrew, 1988). Halfords needed to invest heavily in training when, from 1982 onwards, the company began to pursue a series of strategic changes in its business. These related to increasing competitive edge by improving store productivity and margins, moving into superstore management, and introducing car servicing. Skilful management and development of people became an essential process to support these changes, involving a number of interrelated activities that included major training initiatives to tackle specific business needs.

Success in the initial series of business changes led to further strategic goals being set, and that expansion process generated further training needs. It was at this stage that the emphasis began to move from short-term training, related to the need for new interpersonal and technical skills, to a longer term programme of management training and continuous development. That, in turn, revealed unexpected areas of potential in many managers, who began to produce new business initiatives that had not even been under consideration at the initial stages. In this way business needs, training and development, the increasing pace of change, the generation of new business possibilities and needs and a consequent further cycle of training and development formed a continuing and interactive process which unlocked new possibilities for the business and its workforce.

The Halfords case shows that focused development of people can not only satisfy immediate business needs, but can also make possible a widening choice of business actions as the real potential of people at various levels of the organization comes to fruition. It is a good example of that process of incremental learning and its impact on strategic management to which reference was made on p. 22. It demonstrates that HRD should be managed as a dynamic process, moving in line with the continued cycle of business change. (For two more real-life case studies exemplifying the points made in this paragraph, see Harrison, 1992a and 1993/4.)

In the Halfords example a number of factors initially triggered a major investment in training and an eventual move into organization-wide developmental programmes. There is a body of research, notably that done at Warwick University in the United Kingdom, to show that training and development do tend to get a higher profile when an organization, reacting to a variety of business-related pressures and opportunities, has to take a generally more strategic approach to the management of its human resources (Pettigrew *et al.*, 1988). Triggers to such activity include:

- Business strategy
  - renewal of competitive edge
  - changes in product design
  - changes in manufacturing process
  - changes in management systems
  - offering new services
  - improving quality of existing services/products.

- External labour market shortages.

- Internal labour market needs
  - reduced numbers, leading to need for a multiskilled workforce
  - high attrition rates
  - need to attract and keep high-quality recruits.

- Internal values and systems
  - commitment to HRD at various levels, and systems and roles to support it.

- External support for training
  - various linkages with the outside world, legislative requirements, and funding opportunities.

The forces that 'trigger training' in an organization will affect the development of people in ways specific both to that organization and to its internal and external environment. Generalizations cannot be made about the form development should take, or the targets it should aim at. However, there is one underlying principle that always holds true; simply investing in people's learning and development cannot guarantee an effective contribution to the achievement of business goals. As has been noted in Chapter 2 (p. 54) and as is made clear in the full account of the Halfords story (Sparrow and Pettigrew, 1988), the development of people must operate as an integral human resource process, falling within the umbrella of a general human resource strategy that is aligned to corporate strategy.

There are a growing number of British companies who use developmental initiatives as a way of recruiting, retaining and rewarding the kind of people they need for the business. One widely publicized initiative is in the motor industry, at Ford UK.

CASE STUDY: *Ford, UK*

(See also Hodges, 1990)

In June 1989, a company-wide Employee Development and Assistance Programme (EDAP) was introduced at the Ford UK Motor Company. The scheme is a joint initiative between Ford and the unions, and is independent of the Ford company although funded by Ford money of £2.5 million. The programme is not about job-related or vocational training – the company already has a wide-ranging job training programme – but about the personal and educational development of all the company's employees. The scheme was agreed in the 1987 pay negotiations, and through it every employee is offered up to £200 per year to pay for courses that will enhance their personal development.

For Ford the scheme offered an opportunity to collaborate with the unions in a significant but nonconfrontational area. John Hougham, director – personnel at Ford, clearly believed it would enhance people's motivation and commitment to the company: 'If people are enjoying learning and this is associated with the company, the company must be the better for it'.

In the scheme's first year of operation, 30% of the 43 000 workforce, compared to an expected 5%, took the opportunity to do voluntary study in their own time, with educational courses proving much more popular than health and lifestyle courses. An independent evaluation of that first year concluded that the scheme had in that respect proved extremely successful, although there needed in future to be a greater focus on monitoring the effectiveness of the programme and on determining how best it should be developed. However, for both the unions and Ford, the overwhelming response to the scheme and the interest shown in it by other large companies give sufficient short-term justification for a programme which, relative to each individual, cost them so little.

A particular point of interest about this case study is that while there was a strong commitment to employee development at Ford, the investment made arose from negotiations with unions, and payoff for the company was a consideration only in the loosest sense of the word. The EDAP scheme can be seen more as a 'fringe benefit' to enhance motivation and commitment in the workforce than as a strategic approach to HRD.

CASE STUDY: *Rover Learning Business' REAL programme*

(By permission of Rover Learning Business, 1993)

There is a similar scheme at the Rover Group where Rover Learning Business (RLB) was set up in 1990 as

> 'a company within a company with a £35 million budget and a mission to sharpen Rover's competitive edge . . . RLB expects to make the Rover Group number one in Europe at attracting, retaining and developing people'
> (Vallely, 1992).

One of its major initiatives is the Rover Employee Assisted Learning (REAL) programme, whereby every associate (all employees are now called 'associates' at Rover) is entitled to £100 per year from the group to undertake any kind of course (usually, but not in every case, accredited). There must be some kind of agreed benefit to the company, but the term 'benefit' is interpreted in its widest sense to include a wide range of initiatives that promise to develop the individual in some significant way. The aims of this company initiative are to release individual motivation to learn, and to develop unexplored potential and skills which, even if they do not immediately relate to the workplace tasks of associates, do involve core transferable skills (even campanology could be included, given its emphasis on highly skilled, dedicated team effort), and to encourage self-directed learning.

RLB is developing a wide range of learning products, including Personal Development Files (PDFs). An associate can request their manager to provide them with a PDF which, after initial briefing from the manager and a self-assessment process by the associate, is used to record all the associate's achievements and can be related to a personal learning plan agreed between the two parties and updated at regular intervals. Many of these achievements may in time enable the individual to obtain accreditation towards a national vocational qualification. The PDF thus offers a way of manager and individual working together to link personal and work-related goals through developmental activities undertaken by the individual. It is thus an aid to self-initiated career development as well as to improved shorter term job performance.

The Rover Group is looking to a heavy investment in the development of people not only to improve immediate business performance but also to uncover and develop potential, build up a culture of continuous learning and of commitment to the company, and to increase people's levels of excitement, energy, effort and creativity in the workplace. People policies in such companies tend to be characterized by:

- an emphasis on recruiting and promoting those who demonstrate the competences, attitudes and behaviour that are needed to help achieve the organizational mission through time;

- a stress on skilled leadership and management of people at all levels;

- a high investment in HRD at every level of the business, covering job-related training and retraining, team-building and team-working, job development to enhance job satisfaction, appraisal and counselling programmes relating to developing the core competences needed in the business, and related systems of career planning and development (see Harrison, 1992b);

- an increasing attempt to provide, as far as is realistically possible given contingencies of the business, an internalized career system: that is, continuous employment for regular employees who perform satisfactorily, show a desire to learn, and are adaptable in the face of change;

- incentives and rewards related to specific targets of performance and of behaviour (as explained in Chapter 11);

- the kind of many-faceted communications policy already described at BET (Chapter 7) – one that not only stresses the need for everyone in the company to understand fully the organization's vision, mission and goals, but also provides open channels whereby employees can clarify their understanding of those goals and feedback their views and ideas to key strategic decision-makers.

Such policies represent 'development of people' in the broadest meaning of the phrase, and fit well in the context of an overall human resource strategy aimed at meeting the demands of business strategy and long-term growth by attracting, retaining and developing a high-quality, committed workforce. They are not restricted to large organizations – their elements are present, for example, in the small but highly successful British firm, HMH Sheetmetal Fabrications Ltd, described in Part 3. There, HRD has been built into the fabric of the enterprise and is an essential component of its business strategy and of its culture that brings benefits to the company as a whole and to every individual who works there.

To summarize:

- Employee-oriented learning and developmental initiatives are sometimes introduced as a component in more wide-ranging industrial relations negotiations. When used in that way they may be relatively short-lived and should be viewed mainly as a form of fringe benefit for the employee.

- In a number of organizations, however, such initiatives focus clearly on improving an organization's general capability and strategic growth. They are underpinned by strong beliefs about the value of people to the business and the need to recognize this value in ways that benefit individuals as well as the organization.

- Whether HRD is used mainly as a fringe benefit or as a function expected to produce results for the business, it should always be part of, and consistent with, wider human resource processes which, in turn, are aligned with corporate strategy.

Attitudes to training and development at organizational and national levels

Given the key part that the development of people can play in helping to achieve business goals, why is support for the function so variable from one organization to the next in the United Kingdom, and performance in it so often questionable? Why, too, do UK competitor countries invest so heavily and have a generally more focused and productive approach? Before looking

iefly at some differences between national policies and levels of investment,
us first examine some views typically encountered in organizations and
k at their likely practical consequences.

Attitudes to HRD in organizations and their practical implications

'We're doing it already' or 'We don't need it here'

These attitudes stem from a mix of ignorance and complacency, not only among key managers, but too often among the very practitioners who should be taking a systematic and collaborative approach to the diagnosis of needs, demonstrating political sensitivity in obtaining agreement on priorities, promoting appropriate learning opportunities, and evaluating results in language that management best understands (Coopers and Lybrand, 1985).

   Such attitudes breed complacency, with one of two typical outcomes: no significant investment in training and development because no one is convinced that it will 'pay', or because whatever is done is assumed to be 'OK' although, never being evaluated, is in fact out of control; or a continuation of existing training and development activities, however costly, without any real attempt to evaluate them, so that meeting key business needs will occur only accidentally.

'There's no point in training people for our competitors'

Fear of poaching is one of the major reasons in the United Kingdom why many employers do not do more than is absolutely essential to train or develop their workforce. This in turn, of course, perpetuates a vicious cycle:

> Some organizations hoard skills; some overinvest and then retain their skilled
> people by long-term internal development and reward policies and systems;
> others overinvest but are unable or unwilling to restructure in those ways
> and lose many of their skilled people to 'poachers'; the poachers do no
> investment unless poaching fails. Meanwhile few individuals have incentives
> to invest for themselves.
>
> (Harrison, 1992b, p. 60)

Development is a 'good thing'

This view has been influenced by the work of organizational psychologists like Hertzberg and McGregor in the 1950s, and arises from a belief that development is *of itself* a 'good thing', because all human beings seek to realize their potential, will respond positively to opportunities to do so, and will then become fully committed members of the organization that provides these opportunities. They will also become more flexible and creative.

In fact, unless (as with the REAL programme at Rover) this view is expressed within a clear framework of business-led development strategy, it begs many questions; it makes generalized and unproven assumptions about the nature of human needs, and is essentially prescriptive. It tends to:

> . . . focus too much on the individual manager and the organisational systems dedicated to [their] development, and too little on . . . development for the organisation as a whole.
>
> (Burgoyne, 1988)

It often breeds a fragmented approach to the development of people (Sadler and Barham, 1988), in which training and development are done on a whim, becoming a cost and a luxury, rarely if ever evaluated or related in any meaningful way to business goals.

In this connection it is interesting to look at the findings of a survey of senior managers in 254 of Britain's top companies, reported in *Personnel Management* (1991). Around one-third criticized trainers' overacademic approaches and ineffective performance, with only 29% blaming inadequate training on the unavailability of training services. This correlates with findings in a report by the Employment Institute (Mayhew, 1991), that Britain's problem was 'not just insufficient training but also . . . inefficient training; with too little being done to adequately measure the outcomes of training, so that a culture existed where 'training is not thought of as an investment'.

Development is a necessary business investment

At first sight this attitude is concerned with specific business aims, but it is in fact still too unfocused on the needs of the business. The view being expressed here is that HRD will *automatically* lead to improved business performance because HRD is part of the strategies of leading 'successful' organizations both in the United Kingdom and throughout the western world. The American literature of excellence (already discussed in Chapter 1) and, in the United Kingdom, reports like 'Competence and Competition' (Institute of Manpower Studies, 1984) have fostered this view. Critical comment has already been passed on the literature (pp. 18–20). The stance itself smacks of missionary zeal, with exhortations to 'train more' rather than to undertake the tedious but necessary process of analysing business needs and of relating people's development and strategy to those needs.

Employee development should be a strategic activity, focused on the needs of the business and helping the organization to achieve its business goals

Such an attitude will tend to lead to training and development that comes downstream of business strategy, is generated by collaborative analytical processes, and is linked to the achievement of specific targets at every level. This may be a reactive rather than a proactive approach, but it will result in development that underpins the implementation of strategy in the workplace. This would eliminate the 'major weakness' reported in the Employment Institute's survey (1991a): employers' failure to think strategically about their skill needs and how to use skilled workers.

Firm overall direction will be needed with this approach, to avoid the problem highlighted in the same survey – detailed training decisions being too often left in the hands of line managers, resulting in an inadequate integration of those decisions into the firms' general strategic decision-making.

The aim of employee development should be to achieve a learning organization, continuously positioned to innovate and to adapt effectively to change of all kinds, thus enhancing the likelihood of its enduring success

Acting on this kind of attitude, training and development will be transformed into a corporate learning process that permeates the organization and, at corporate level, influences the choice of decision-makers as well as the business strategy that results from their decisions. HRD thus becomes an intrinsic and proactive part of overall long-term business strategy, fundamentally shaping as well as reinforcing the culture of the workplace. This is the concept of the learning organization, already discussed in Chapter 9. We shall return to this theme towards the end of this chapter.

Attitudes to vocational training and development in the United Kingdom and some competitor countries

Among the attitudes we have just identified are a number that, negative though they are, do unfortunately appear to characterize many British organizations. They lead either to a minimal investment in the training and development of people or to investment that is unfocused and unevaluated.

Why are such attitudes so widespread in the United Kingdom, yet so rare in her key competitor countries? And how far, and in what ways, can they be overcome? (It should be noted that although in the following discussion the focus is on training, firms not investing in training are unlikely to invest in other forms of focused developmental activity either.)

The United Kingdom seems unique in regarding overtraining as generally wasteful and foolish:

> In the US overtraining means richness and diversity of competence which can be brought to bear on innovation and change; in Germany it reinforces the confidence born of the long-cherished aim of technical excellence; and

in Japan it is the basis of the twin aims of perfection and the ability to learn so as to assume any new work role successfully.

(Hayes *et al.*, 1984)

In the United Kingdom investment in training is a matter largely left to the employer, both in terms of deciding on that investment, and in terms of meeting the costs, The situation is very different elsewhere:

> German employers voluntarily bear the burden of most of the cost and effort involved, working closely with unions and the authorities to provide a high-quality, rigorously administered and controlled NVET [national vocational education and training] system. In Japan, the costs are shared by the education system and the employer, with only limited state-sponsored public sector provision. In France . . . the use of targets of vocational attainment and the introduction of a coherent range of academic, technical and applied vocational courses into secondary schools has achieved an exceptional improvement in levels of skill and vocational qualifications.
>
> (Harrison, 1992b, p. 92)

With regard to adult training, both in and out of employment, the record in the United Kingdom remains patchy and inadequate (see, for example, Johnson, 1984).

Reasons for national underinvestment in vocational training in the United Kingdom

Basically there are two reasons for the apathy towards training in Britain – a historic culture of *laissez-faire*, coupled with lack of incentives for organizations and individuals to invest in Vocational Education and Training (VET).

With the exception of a few brief periods of panic-driven regulation, the attitude towards VET in the United Kingdom at national level has always been one of *laissez-faire*. Individual employers who fail to invest adequately in the development of their people are thus simply mirroring at their level the attitudes and philosophy evident in the wider national context.

Such employers probably constitute a majority. A Warwick University paper (IRRU, 1990) showed that over 50% of employers surveyed had no plans, related either to recruitment or to training and development, to introduce measures to deal with demographic changes in the labour market, even though existing older workers were 'closed to new concepts', 'lacking in motivation' and 'not adaptable'. Perhaps even more worrying, given their role, a 1991 Hatfield Polytechnic Survey for the Employment Institute (1991b) reported that Chairmen of Training and Enterprise Councils – the 82 local employer-driven bodies set up in 1989 in Britain to act as the spearhead to encourage and facilitate training and development in organizations – showed in many cases no real commitment to training in their own companies. Only 8 of the 31 surveyed intended to provide increased training for their own workforces in 1991, and almost a quarter of their companies were expecting to take on fewer trainees than in 1990.

In another 1991 report, this time on an Economic and Social Research Council-funded project (University of Sheffield, 1991) on Sheffield engineering companies needing new skills because of adoption of new manufacturing technology, it was noted that training 'was not high on the agenda to overcome these shortages, with firms instead preferring short term measures such as raising pay and increasing overtime'.

For their part, many individuals and organizations see no incentives to invest. Yates (1990) commented in this connection that smaller companies, lacking financial and other resources and in a generally vulnerable position, could not be blamed for poaching, nor could larger companies for failing to 'act as charities and overtrain'.

Even if there were to be legislation enabling employers to draw up contracts offering training on condition that employees worked for a period to repay some of the cost, this could be seen as unfairly penalizing individuals with good reason to leave, and as presenting a real obstacle to free movement of labour. It would, in any case, be unlikely to present any significant disincentive to those firms determined to use poaching as a quick way of obtaining skills that they need. Individuals, for their part, have little reason to invest in vocational education and training when employers' recruitment and reward systems are rarely tied to the possession of vocational qualifications or to a record of systematic training and development.

Underlying these problems of apathy and lack of incentives are more fundamental issues, one of the most important being that successive UK governments have consistently failed to build the kind of framework for NVET that would ensure in the immediate and longer term the provision of the kind of workforce the country needs. Lack of the necessary vision, mission and strategy at government level has led to reactive and politicized approaches to education and training, whereby social and economic crises may trigger wide-ranging initiatives on a sporadic basis, but basically HRD is treated as subordinate to wider economic and political issues and consistently underresourced (see Harrison, 1992b, Chapter 3).

A decisive turnaround did seem to occur at government level in 1989, with the White Paper 'Employment for the 1990s' announcing a clearly articulated and detailed national policy, with related objectives and a strategy for NVET in the United Kingdom for at least the forthcoming decade. However, the implementation of strategy was left dependent largely on a framework of voluntary partnership of government, employers and individuals, revolving around 82 new employer-driven but underresourced local Training and Enterprise Councils (and 20 Local Enterprise Councils in Scotland).

Officially, the view was that short-term planning had at last given way to long-term vision and strategy (Training Agency, 1989, p. 19). In reality, there seemed little to sustain that optimism:

> There is every likelihood that such a national policy and framework will be insecure as long as they are held in place by little more than the shifting philosophy, politics and reactions of successive Governments, together with a reliance on voluntary, collaborative and effective effort in a decentralized structure which still contains inadequate incentives for individuals and for employers.
>
> (Harrison, 1992b, p. 69)

The 1991 Hatfield Polytechnic survey report suggested that a recession would reveal the fundamental flaws of a voluntary training strategy, with TECs unable to counter similar cutbacks in training to those seen in the last recession and facing repeated government cutbacks in their training budgets. The government was urged to take a lead by formulating a long-term training strategy when 'even the most enthusiastic companies are likely to place short-run cost considerations above investment in skills as the recession bites'. Sadly, the Hatfield predictions have so far proved valid (see, for example, Graham, 1992).

It seems clear that to make any real impact on levels of investment in training in Britain, one of two things needs to happen:

1. The structure of business ownership in the United Kingdom needs to change from one dominated by a financial sector that demands short-term returns on investment and discourages long-term strategic investment in anything that cannot show some immediate results or guarantee tangible and substantial longer term profits.

2. Given that the financial structure of business in the United Kingdom is unlikely to change, the alternative must be for government to establish a much tighter regulatory system for NVET, coupled with meaningful financial incentives and rewards for organizations and individuals.

In its 1990 report on 'Vocational training and retraining' the House of Lords Select Committee on European Communities drew attention to the fact that among EC partners the United Kingdom has far less legislative underpinning of its vocational training system and far fewer equitable methods of dealing with the funding of training than most. In a Policy Studies Institute report (1990) further legal measures were also called for by Sir John Cassells, former director-general of NEDO, who believed that without legislation 'the labour market will continue to operate as it has in the past'. Companies should, he stated, regard 18 as the normal age at which to recruit young people, and should make it clear to recruits that they expect them to have acquired relevant qualifications.

To conclude this section: it would seem logical to take the view that without change at the macro level little change in attitudes – and therefore in behaviour – can be expected at the micro level. However, such a view is not necessarily valid, because it ignores one important consideration: what research indicates about the typical triggers to training in organizations

(p. 301). The presence of a range of such triggers can point to the need for a greater focus on training and development: at that stage, provided that there is sufficient vision and commitment at the top of an organization and the necessary expertize to plan and implement developmental strategies and initiatives to support corporate goals, there is the opportunity to achieve a more coherent, long-term and adequately resourced investment in the development of people – one that can make a profound contribution to the organization's bottom line in the short and longer term.

Achieving a greater commitment to people's business-led learning and development

We have surveyed the reasons for the underinvestment in training that characterize the United Kingdom at macro and micro levels, and some of the differences that help to explain the higher levels of investment in her major competitor countries (for a fuller exposition of international differences, see Harrison, 1992b, Chapter 4; Brewster and Tyson, 1991). We then concluded that if certain conditions exist in an organization, there is still the possibility – and certainly the need – to achieve an increased level of support and resources for a powerful, business-led HRD function that will add real value to the business and to all its people.

Now let us examine at a practical level what can be done to convince key parties of the need for a higher level of investment in people's learning and development in an organization, and to produce and implement relevant strategies in the workplace.

A change in attitudes can only be created by showing that the situation in which those attitudes have developed has changed

This means the need to show, using convincing factual data, that there are now a number of pressures that call for focused learning processes to be developed in the organization.

The most compelling pressures will be those relating directly to business performance and to internal labour supply (see pp. 301–2). However, to explain the significance of those pressures there must be sound data, a convincing analysis, and logical, feasible recommendations. Proposals will need the active support of certain key people (Rover Group call them 'champions' – see Figure 12.1) who will in their turn ensure support throughout the organization.

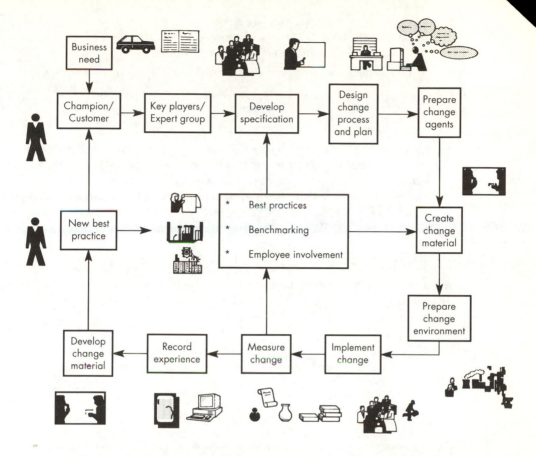

Figure 12.1 *Corporate learning at Rover Group (by permission of Rover Learning Business, 1993).*

At this stage, the ability to quote examples of other, benchmarking, companies who have a higher level of investment in developing people and whose business strategy is clearly successful will be an important tactic. So also will be obtaining external funding to support some of the proposed initiatives: this will probably give greater internal credibility to those initiatives as well as helping to offset their immediate cost to the company.

An important example of success in convincing a company of the need for higher investment can be found in Harrison (1992a) where there is a description of how in 1990/91 the new group training manager of an international construction firm with its headquarters and subsidiaries in the United Kingdom obtained the support of top management for a major investment in employee development through a variety of collaborative planning initiatives which included:

- building up strong links with key senior managers in the subsidiaries and working with them to identify key employee development needs related to the company's mission and business goals;

- involving them in formulating a strategy and plan to meet these needs;

- regularly presenting full and validated information to the company's board, and obtaining their approval for strategy and plans;

- establishing a comprehensive manpower databank;

- identifying an area in the business – sales training – where rigorous evaluation showed high costs for relatively low returns for the company, and where carefully researched and imaginative plans for a new, job-related and in-company flexible learning scheme obtained substantial funding from a local Training and Enterprise Council, thus helping the group training manager gain the financial commitment of the company to the scheme.

In trying to change attitudes to development of people at corporate level, thought should be given to how to influence decisions made about strategy as well as how to ensure that HRD plays its full part in supporting implementation of that strategy in the workplace:

> Given the valuable yet volatile nature of the human resource, [someone] has to keep people development on the business agenda as plans are being formulated. Sometimes this means posing uncomfortable questions – do we believe that we can compete effectively in Europe without making a substantial investment in language skills training? Will our salesforce have the resilience to respond to increased competition? . . . If the Board and top management believe that training expenditure is being focused on essential profit-influencing or long-term business survival tasks, their commitment is more likely. . . . Where top management develop an initial and ongoing commitment to people development, in turn is fostered a business culture which is supportive of training.
>
> (McKee, 1990)

Relate people's learning and development to corporate vision, mission and strategy

With the backing of top management for a more business-led and strategic approach to HRD, the next step is to analyse the business mission, goals and critical success factors, and to establish what is needed, in terms of people's training and development, to support them.

There will need to be a strategy for people's development across the whole organization that is related to the **business drivers** (those key processes, or critical success factors, usually between four and eight in number, that all senior management agree will be necessary and sufficient to achieve the organization's mission, and so realize its long-term vision for the kind of business it aspires to be). There will then need to be detailed plans to achieve that strategy at the level of every business unit or division, and of every team and individual.

CASE STUDY: *Rover Group, UK – The corporate learning process and its contribution to company vision, mission and strategy*

(By permission of Rover Group Limited 1993)

The Rover Group is Britain's largest motor manufacturer, formed from Austin Rover in 1986 and since 1988 a subsidiary of British Aerospace. Since the late 1980s it has achieved a striking turnaround story, becoming a highly competitive, versatile, high-quality business in a very tough world environment.

When Graham Day joined the company as CEO in 1986, at a low point in its history, he saw the need to focus on its people as well as on its products, profits and processes, if Rover was to reach and maintain world-class excellence. He spearheaded a major and continuous investment in the development of employees, and the launch of Rover Learning Business (p. 303) was one manifestation of that commitment.

Since 1988 the group has undergone major changes in its organization, systems and processes. It has formed close partnerships with its dealers, and has formed links with Honda UK. The latter has influenced many innovations including a total quality strategy, just-in-time, cell structures, flexible working practices, and the introduction of sophisticated technology into its production systems.

Rover now officially aspires to be a learning organization, that is, one which has the following characteristics:

- A *memorable and compelling vision* (Rover's vision is to be 'internationally renowned for extraordinary customer satisfaction').

- *Corporate objectives* constituting the most important subgoals of the team, necessary and sufficient to achieve its mission (at Rover there are four key business thrusts).

- *Aligned and dynamic business processes*, with corporate learning as one of the key processes. (At Rover, corporate learning is one of nine key business processes as well as being one of three primary drivers for the key business thrusts.)

- *Management-led learning* (By early 1993 25% of line managers at Rover were fully responsible for creating a learning environment and for coaching a significant number of Rover's 30 000 + employees. By the end of 1994 the percentage will have risen to 75%).

- *Learning is not only a primary business driver but also enhances the quality of on-going strategic decision-making at all levels, and ensures the supply of effective leaders for the future.* This closing of the strategic loop is arguably the most difficult and uncertain of all stages to achieve or to measure, but it has to be a defining characteristic of the learning organization.

Rover's corporate learning process permeates its business strategy, serving the needs of the eight other business processes as well as having its own vision, strategy and plans. It consists of 13 simple steps (Figure 12.1) and incorporates line management ownership, employee involvement, best practice by reference to past internal trends and external benchmarks, and regular milestones against which progress towards achieving targets can be monitored and measured.

The pace of change and the degree of business success achieved by Rover in the late 1980s and early 1990s have been remarkable. Belief in the powerful contribution of corporate learning to those achievements is clear among its top and line managers, and the motivation to learn and develop among its associates (employees) has been evidenced in two striking ways: in the detailed 75% response rate to an unprecedented survey covering every member of the group, in 1988, asking for their views and suggestions related to learning and development; and on the take up of the REAL programme (see pp. 303–4) which has outpaced the expectations of RLB. There are now learning resource centres on every Rover site, and they are in continuous use by associates; personal development files are increasingly popular, and, as already noted, about one-third of managers are now involved directly in the development and guidance of personal development plans for their associates.

Large size is not a necessary qualification for being a learning organization. Kwik-Fit, specializing in motor maintenance and repairs, is famous for its high standards of quality and customer service. It is an outstanding example of a learning organization, where the vision, values and direction of the chief executive (Tom Farmer) ensure that in every garage across the United Kingdom continuous development promotes individual and organizational growth:

> Top management must learn to understand that every action they take either produces healthy growth in the workforce or it inhibits it. They must review the systems, the organisation structure, the physical layout and the human resource policies . . . with the specific purpose of creating through them the environment in which people may thrive.
>
> (Webster, 1990, p. 47)

Webster describes five distinctive features of Kwik Fit as a learning organization. These can be shown in diagrammatic form, as in Figure 12.2.

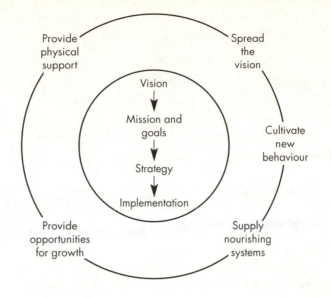

Figure 12.2 *The learning organization (based on the five Kwik-Fit learning processes).*

In such very different businesses, both of which are, however, successfully maintaining their leading competitive edge in unpredictable and tough environments, the 'learning organization' underpins the process of strategic management by continuously developing the kind of people needed by the business and by creating an environment where they are encouraged and enabled to 'think strategically' at every level, knowledgeable about external challenges and threats, and creative in their responses to them. It is this strategic ability to which, arguably, Japanese companies owe more of their business success than simply their traditional but now vulnerable human resource policies (see pp. 56–7), and it is in the learning organization that people can become a major source of competitive ability, positioned to take advantage of every opportunity, while taking a positive stance when confronted with adversity.

The case study on the Rover Group illustrates ways in which learning organizations seek to relate people's learning and development continuously to corporate vision, mission and strategy. The investment of all kinds is high, and has to be maintained over the long term; in the end, as at IBM in the early 1990s, the advantages of creating over time a culture that binds highly skilled and motivated people together in the service of the company may backfire, inhibiting the very strategic ability and creativity that, originally, it was the aim of that culture to develop. Learning organizations need to monitor not only their on-going and fairly visible outcomes, but they must also watch to see that the organization does not move into complacency and introversion – learning must pull, not push, the organization and its members.

Now let us look at how practical plans for business-led learning and development can be tackled.

Create and implement plans for employee learning and development in the organization

Plans must be drawn up which will ensure that, in relation to each of the organization's corporate objectives, appropriate activities and processes take place to help achievement of those objectives – either directly, or by supporting other organizational activities that in their turn will have a direct impact on such achievement.

Figure 12.3 shows in simple form how developmental plans can be produced and activated. The system is in widespread use in the Rover Group, ensuring that for each of the company's 'critical success factors' (of which quality strategy is one) and in relation to each of its nine key business processes, appropriate learning will take place.

Once the necessary learning initiatives have been identified, there must be, with the full involvement of managers:

■ identification of both the extent to which employees' performance and behaviour are fully supporting the achievement of business goals and are likely to continue to do so, and of those significant gaps in performance or behaviour which will best be remedied by some form of consciously planned learning;

■ agreement by managers on the ways in which that learning will be carried out and monitored, and on their own roles and responsibilities in those processes.

To facilitate business-led learning throughout the organization, and to help progress individual planned career development, a databank must be built up, recording basic information on individuals that is relevant to their continuous development – this would include noting current position, previous experience, training, education and general development, and assessed potential. This record must be kept up to date, either through the mechanism of formal appraisal reviews or in some other way.

There will, of course, need to be some form of written employee development master plan (although the aim should be to keep this as clear, simple and focused as possible). This will operate on a rolling basis, related to the budget cycle.

Objectives set for planned learning and development at every level must

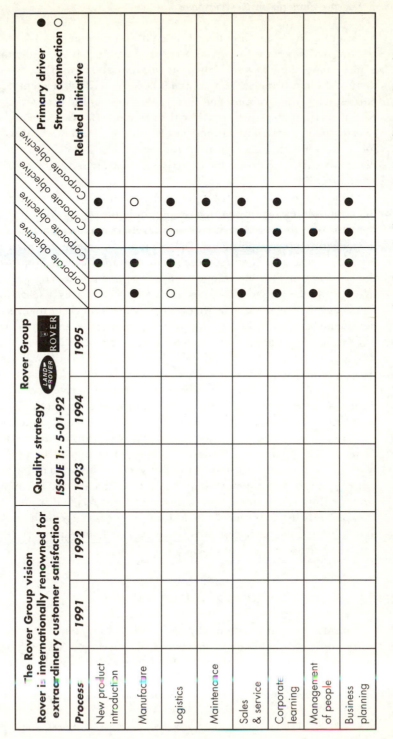

Figure 12.3 Some key business processes at Rover Group and their planning implications (by permission of Rover Group).

be realistic in order that they can gain commitment and be adequately resourced. They must be agreed between the parties if the individual learner is to be motivated by seeing them as relevant and rewarding. At this point there will often be tensions, sometimes because of disagreement between the parties as to what training and further development is needed, and why; or because certain objectives urged by the one party (for example, the manager) as essential in relation to business needs will not, if achieved, bring meaningful rewards for the other party (for example, the individual); or because of disagreement on priorities for objectives (see Harrison, 1992b, Chapter 13; Fairbairn, 1991).

One of the major contributors to the resolution of such tensions can be the appraisal discussion that focuses not only on work review and planning, but also on job-related training and development and on the individual's longer term career aspirations. The **personal development plan** is another vehicle increasingly used (sometimes in conjunction with appraisal, sometimes not) to involve the employee in assessing and agreeing with his or her manager on the personal learning needs and goals; forms of learning are then negotiated between the two that will improve job performance as well as developing the individual in line with learning goals important to them.

However, it has to be emphasized that unless there is a real learning and development culture in the workplace, processes like these will become controlling rather than developmental (as was explained in Chapter 10). Indeed, it is doubtful whether they can be otherwise except in true learning organizations – and those, and the skills and commitment to maintain them over the long term, are as yet very much in the minority in the United Kingdom.

HRD mission, strategy and plans must be realistic and feasible, given their specific organizational context. Thus, for example, there will be times when a relatively limited short-term and selective investment in training and other forms of development may be not the ideal, but the most feasible strategy. Success in modest learning events that respond to immediate and critical needs in the business should lead to a greater credibility for training, and will often enable a movement into ever-widening areas of development – as proved to be the case at Halfords (p. 301).

Measuring outcomes and evaluating results

Measuring the results of employees' consciously planned learning is notoriously difficult, and many complex models have been designed as an aid to the process. In the end, however, what is needed is a simple, easily operated approach that presents the right kind of information, at the right time, to those who need it most. With that in mind, all that is offered here is a number of basic principles. They do not amount to a model, but they may help the manager or HRD practitioner who is anxious to assess the contribution of such development to the business, and to convince others of its value. More specific guidelines on evaluation and on how to measure training and development in relation to business performance are given in Jackson (1990), in Hall (1984), and in Harrison (1992b, Chapters 11 and 17).

Evaluation of employee development strategy and activities should be related to the objectives originally set for that strategy

The process of obtaining agreement between key parties on the ways in which consciously planned learning in the organization will aid achievement of business goals will identify those outcomes that must occur if the learning is to be judged successful. If those outcomes do occur, and if the learning has taken place as originally agreed by reference to parameters such as time, cost and learners, then in most cases that will probably suffice. Of course, any weaknesses or unexpected outcomes of learning must be noted, to aid future planning – and more detailed evaluation may have to be done if circumstances dictate. However, it is important to remember that measurement and evaluation are time-consuming and therefore expensive activities: they should only be done when, and to the extent that, the key parties see them to be important, and in order to enable data to be established on trends in learning processes and their outcomes through time.

If needs have not been met, then information will have to be gathered to discover the causes. If these causes are to do with planned learning and developmental activities and processes having failed in some way, then reasons must be identified and appropriate action taken. Again, all failure in learning processes and events must be noted, as those failures will themselves form important learning data.

Measurement of itself will not achieve credibility for training and development – it is measurement of a kind already agreed between the key parties that is essential

Measurement can look at:

- Specific important activities and achievements in the organization that have been directly facilitated by individual, group or corporate learning – the aim being to identify the importance of the contribution of that learning as distinct from any other factor.
- How far major tangible improvements in areas such as waste reduction, customer hit rate and customer complaints, can be seen to be associated with employee development as distinct from other causes.
- How far learning by one individual, or from one event, or in one sector in the organization has been consciously spread across the company to

the benefit of a wider audience. This helps to measure the extent to which learning is becoming a genuinely corporate process.

Knowledge is a key business intangible (p. 29). Rover Learning Business, for example, has recognized this and is building up a computerized database, recording, on a standard form filled in by the individual concerned, learning achieved by anyone in the company as a result of a particular project, event, or incident. The records are easily accessible to any associate in the company, are available for future reference, and form part of the company's inventory of intangible assets.

Training and development should be measured against performance indicators, benchmarks and best practice, and planned milestones

> For example, a series of training programmes designed to improve marketing/buying skills should have a positive impact on key performance indicators, such as stockturn or gross margins. Similarly a training programme with the objective of enhancing staff and management awareness of shrinkage should have a beneficial impact on the level of unidentified stock loss being incured. In a non-manufacturing environment, it can be more difficult to establish measurement criteria, but absentee levels, labour turnover, percentage of internal promotions vs. external recruitment into key jobs, level of customer complaints, productivity per employee, all can be valid indicators of effective training activity.
>
> (McKee, 1990)

Cross and Mitchell (1986) looked at the introduction of advanced packaging equipment in three multinational food processing companies. They found that the main reason why one of the three outperformed the others on several indicators, including a 20% lower labour cost per unit of output, was the provision of more than 10 times the training for operators and craftsmen. Results included:

- less frequent breakdowns;
- much reduced repair time;
- plant running at full capacity for higher proportion of time, because of greater speed and quality of anticipation and responses to changes in machine status.

Having established clear indicators made the evaluation of the success of training straightforward in this case. That, of course, is only going to occur when indicators can be quantifiable, and to do with immediate outcomes, but as McKee pointed out, qualitative indicators can be agreed too, thus facilitating agreed methods of assessing outcomes.

Benchmarks and best practice are a major aid to evaluation. They can be generated internally, from past best practice; they can relate to chosen benchmark organizations, and to best practice across an industry or sector, as well as at national or international levels. A company whose mission, as at British Airways and Rover Group, relates to achieving 'world best-in-class excellence' will seek international benchmarks related to their business processes, including the learning and development of their people. Although absolute correlations between such benchmarks and the competitive position achieved by organizations can never be established with certainty (as was discussed in Chapter 1 in relation to the Peters and Waterman literature), the practices they represent are none the less a fundamental part of other leading companies' competitive strategy; this will tend to give the practices themselves credibility, stimulate those emulating them, and encourage analysis and creativity in organizational learning policies and processes.

Planned milestones enable more effective monitoring of employee development; this was well illustrated in the case of County NatWest Bank in Chapter 3.

Assessing the cost of *not* training and developing people can have considerable impact

This approach is used by commentators on national training strategies such as Prais (1990). He has for years been examining and reporting on differences in educational and training standards between Britain and Germany, France and Japan, building up a formidable databank of trends and outcomes. Asking in 1990 why British companies were not able to deliver the goods like their competitors, he spelt out the costs of lack of investment in training in compelling terms:

- *Lack of enough trained personnel* The problem concerned intermediate skilled staff responsible for executive running and administration of a wide range of activities. Prais examined matched plants in the metalworking, wood furniture, clothing and hotel industries. In each, because of lack of training at the intermediate levels, higher grade personnel – graduates – had to spend much longer on basic chores, to the detriment of business development, strategy and other more relevant tasks that they should have been performing.

- *Lack of skilled people on production lines* His research also showed that when machines broke down the people manning the line were usually unable to rectify even simple mistakes, and had to wait for skilled maintenance people to arrive – so increasing downtime.

- *Lack of people with technological education and skill* This meant that British managers tended to be less ambitious about the type of technology they used. Insead's 1990 survey of 224 large manufacturers, reported by De Meyer and Ferdows (1991), claimed that 'manufacturing must be a link in the integrated enterprise which combines vendors, the company and its customers in one system'. However, without people who possess technological education and skills, such manufacturing flexibility cannot be achieved. Insead's 1990 survey did indeed show that only one in four European companies has any kind of integrated computer-aided design (CAD) and computer-aided manufacturing (CAM) equipment.

■   *Lack of an educated workforce again hampers the company's ability to be flexible and respond to the need for change.*   Two-thirds of companies in the Insead survey said that only top and middle management understood the strategies, goals and objectives of their companies. On the other hand, the way in which Japanese supervisors and managers are continuously developed and trained in the workplace ensures that they have an inbuilt strategic ability, far superior to their average British counterparts.

Such detailed, insightful information can dramatically raise awareness of the need for more or different individual and corporate learning approaches if future productivity, innovative capacity and growth are not to be endangered.

Employee learning and development as strategic approach to organizational change

Although 'training', especially at national level, is often the most widely used term used in relation to people's planned learning in the workplace, it is as we have seen only a part of the overall continuous process whereby people can be developed to the benefit of the business as well as of themselves. Much of the emphasis in this chapter has been on the fact that an increasing number of organizations (and this includes those in the public as well as the private sector) are now moving away from a stable, routinized past, through an uncomfortable present and towards an unpredictable future. To cope with the challenges and threats they face, an increasing number are also turning to a wide range of human resource management and development techniques and approaches (Storey, 1992) to help them manage the necessary changes in organization structure, culture and systems, and develop people with new ways of behaving and performing.

In such organizations, development of people virtually absorbs all HRM processes:

■   *Recruitment and selection*   Recruitment is 'the gateway of entry into the human resource development system' (Pettigrew *et al.*, 1988). As we saw in Chapter 9, focused recruitment and selection lead to employment conditions and career development strategies appropriate to each sector of entrants, and to processes whereby performance can be monitored and appraised, potential can be assessed, and abilities be developed. An important objective will be to attract into the organization those whose attitudes, as well as competencies and potential, will fit the emergent culture. The popularity of assessment centres in the selection as well as the development process, together with a considerable level of interest in biodata (which explores the whole motivational pattern of an individual's career to date, as well as their strengths and skills (see Townley, 1989)) is to a large degree explained by a perceived need to obtain insights into the 'whole person' rather than a superficial contact with those aspects of themselves that they choose to bring to, say, a selection interview.

- *Strategies for motivating, retaining and rewarding people*   Induction programmes can be designed to introduce individuals to the culture of both the organization and their particular part of it, while job-related training helps to equip them with the specific knowledge and skills needed to perform to standard in their role and workplace. Training can also play a vital part in unfreezing existing attitudes that may clash with the organization's culture, and in beginning to develop new values and styles of behaviour; outdoor training and development courses are growing in popularity in this respect, both for groups of new recruits and for established teams (Harrison, 1992b, p. 284).

- *Appraisal and development of people*   These initial processes should be followed up by planned job experience and other forms of continuous learning and development (Wood, 1988; Harrison, 1992b). Regular reviews of performance, development planning, and appropriate incentive and reward structures – the last aiming to encourage people to work as part of wider groups and teams, and to focus on business performance rather than on individual competitive position – will help to motivate and retain a skilled and adaptable workforce. This continuous process of learning, focusing strongly on the real tasks, problems and challenges facing the organization, will help to build a learning organization where, through incremental change, redundant skills, knowledge and attitudes are continually giving way to those more appropriate to the needs of the time.

Thus a sequence of activities as indicated in Figure 12.4 aims to transform people's learning and development into a corporate, business-led activity, relying on a collaboration between key parties to generate information, agree on strategies and plans, and monitor, evaluate and act on outcomes.

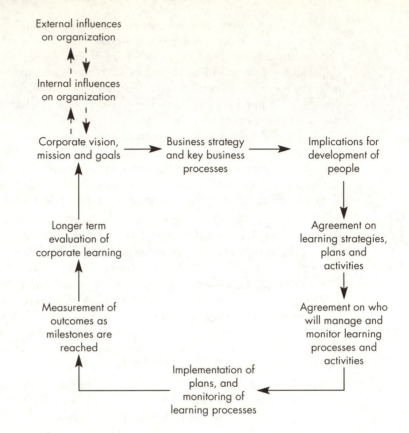

Figure 12.4 *Employee learning and development as a strategic process in the organization.*

Management development

Managers are the key decision-makers of the organization, therefore management development must be a priority for any company seeking to sustain or improve its competitive advantage:

> Management development can be defined as the planned process of ensuring through an appropriate learning environment and experiences the continuous supply and retention of effective managers at all levels to meet the requirements of an organization and enhance its strategic capability.
> (Harrison, 1992b, p. 416)

Regarded as a rationally ordered set of activities, management development is about ensuring that there are the competencies to run the business at corporate, unit and operational levels, both now and in the future, striking an appropriate balance between internal development and external recruitment; between on-the-job and external activities; between carefully structured programmes and exposure to continuing developmental ways of working and behaving.

Regarded, however, as an on-going process, management development must recognize the inherent confusion, unpredictability and political tensions involved in the work managers do. Particular insights into this hectic and fragmented role have been offered by researchers, notably Mintzberg (1973, 1989). Thus the stress in management development needs to be on developing skills of social interaction, attitudes which are conducive to constantly adapting to changing internal and external pressures and opportunities, and the ability to think and manage strategically. Such skills and capabilities do not come easily to the poorly educated, and there is much evidence to show that the British educational system is slow to produce people with the required levels of intellectual capability and achievement; France, Germany, Japan and the United States are all ahead in this respect, with even underdeveloped countries investing heavily in their education systems to produce capable leaders and workforces for the future. With the predicted rise of the knowledge worker (Drucker, 1993) and the demands that sector in particular will make on managers, the problems caused by a deficient education system will accelerate.

Thus in the management development field UK organizations have considerable cause for concern. They may well now possess some of the leanest, most efficient, low-cost workforces in Europe, but they also possess some of the most poorly educated, poorly trained and poorly developed managers. The lost opportunities that this represents in terms of ability to cope with new technologies, to manage and develop people, and to think and act strategically in order to achieve high organizational performance and competitive advantage are formidable. It is reassuring to have some signs (Storey, 1991) that attitudes are at last changing and that there is experimentation with an ever-widening range of approaches and methods in management development, even though these are only exceptionally being incorporated into any long-term, coherent strategy.

Although there is, in the United Kingdom, a significant move towards competency-based management training and educational programmes (Harrison, 1992b, Chapter 19), many argue powerfully for work-based development, since what seems to promote the most effective learning is usually experience and role models (Mumford, 1989) – and also because the tasks of managers are hard, if not impossible, to define at any but the most generalized level, so that Lead Body tables of competencies may not prove a reliable guide to skills and attitudes needed to manage in a particular situation.

Other commentators believe that the most effective strategy is to make management development a holistic function in organizations, with all actions by every employee becoming part of a total process of learning, improving and change (Wille, 1990). Such a learning environment should ensure a continuous supply of leaders and managers with the competencies, values and style that fit the organization and its mission and strategy through time.

Conclusion

For learning and development of people to become a strategic process in an organization, contributing to business goals and to corporate and individual growth, there must be a clear vision, mission and corporate objectives to which employee development can be aligned. There must also be belief, which the champions of employee development must seek to promote throughout the organization, that a significant investment in people's learning and development will pay, even though not always with easily quantifiable benefits or immediate impact. Those champions, and the managers of learners at every level, must be politically skilled, knowing how to achieve and maintain support for consciously planned learning in the organization, and they must monitor and evaluate progress and outcomes of learning and development as planned milestones are reached, making sure that evaluation information goes to those who need it, aiding future planning and strategy.

There is a catch in this, however. Setting out a stall that proclaims 'everything we do here can be measured' too often leads to the cry 'we will do nothing here unless it can be measured'. Who can precisely measure the worth of Kwik-Fit's or Rover's learning organizations? Who can quantify the contribution of a single violin in an orchestra? It is only in the United Kingdom that there is such a widespread concern with 'proving' the benefits of developing people: elsewhere, because of the fundamental values and missions related to education, training and development from governments downwards, the question is less 'should we develop?' more 'how can we improve the development of our people in order to drive the business forward and guarantee us the human potential we need for the future?'. As in so much else in strategy, so here too: values and vision are crucial determinants. In those organizations where rigid financial control is the order of the day, HRD will tend to be forced into a defensive position, continually required to quantify its worth or risk its demise.

Thus proponents of a strategic, business-led approach to organizational learning need to consider their options carefully. They are only likely to succeed where those who control key resources accept – or can be persuaded to accept – that it is less important to measure each specific outcome of training and development than to assess how well-planned learning processes and events are integrated with wider human resource and business strategies.

The ultimate aim which, however, can only be achieved in the longer term and must therefore be a conscious strategic decision is to build and sustain an environment of self-directed, continuous learning across the workforce, thereby promoting initiative and creativity as well as job-related competencies. This should provide a continuous supply of the kinds of managers needed by the business, and it will ensure that people are improving their own stock of competencies and their own learning skills all the time, thus increasing their personal chances of future job security and career mobility. There is thus a powerful contribution to the individual's as well as to the organization's bottom line.

Finally, the consciously planned continuous learning and development of people will lead to that key process of incremental organizational learning to which the first chapter of this book drew attention. Without this kind of learning organization, the process of strategic management, and with it the future direction of the business and the security of all its people, are at risk.

PART 3

Applying the Concepts: Practical Assignments and Case Studies

1 Assignments: Strategic management

2 Case study: Strategic human resource management at HMH Sheetmetal Fabrications Ltd, 1993

3 Case study: Putting TQM into practice – the role of the personnel function

4 Case study: Analysing the links between employee involvement, strategic human resource management and organizational change

5 Case study: In search of enterprise – a consultancy assignment

6 Assignment: Moving to local bargaining arrangements

7 Assignment: How well do you know your employees?

8 Assignments: Equality in the workplace

9 Assignment: Strategic aspects of selection in human resource management

10 Case study: The Fair Value case study

11 **Case study: Wharfedale Water**

12 **Case study: Thorn Lighting Ltd, UK – a learning organization**

1 Assignments

Strategic management

Susan Miller

1. Use Porter's five force framework, generic strategies and value chain to discuss the competitive position of your own organization (or one of your choice) at present and comment on potential strategic directions for the future. Evaluate the utility of these models in strategic analysis.

2. What are the critical factors which would need to be taken into account in order to implement your chosen future strategic options successfully?

3. Evaluate how far present strategy would appear to be more of a deliberate or emergent process in your chosen organization. What implications do your conclusions have for your proposals for the future strategic direction of the organization?

2 Case study

Strategic human resource management at HMH Sheetmetal Fabrications Ltd, 1993

Rosemary Harrison

(By kind permission of Albert Moss, managing director of HMH Sheetmetal Fabrications Ltd, Burnopfield, County Durham.)

The following case study offers an illustration of one firm's attempt to take a coherent, integrative approach to the direction and management of its workforce. The principles involved can be applied to any organization, although the firm in this case is in the small firm sector.

The organization

HMH Sheetmetal Fabrications is a small, owner-managed firm in the North East of England. It was started in 1972. Its present turnover is £2 million, and it is a successful growth enterprise whether defined by profitability, by widespread product recognition, by its sustained reputation for high quality, or by its stable, high-performing workforce. It employs between 50 and 60 full-time workers.

Business strategy

HMH Sheetmetal Fabrications seeks to differentiate itself from other sheet-metal companies in four ways:

- a clear market focus;
- a high-quality product;
- quality of service; and
- the continuous development of its workforce.

Its vision is to achieve world-class excellence and become a benchmark for other sheetmetal companies. Its mission is:

> We combine traditional craftsmanship with technology to delight our customers

Albert Moss, its owner, is 52, an ex-shipyard worker who left school at 15. He is the driving force of the enterprise, with the charisma, shrewdness and toughness of a businessman who is there to survive and succeed. He has a clear vision of the business, and instills this into his workforce. He believes that communication must be graphic, to the point, couched in language that his workforce can clearly understand, and be constantly making its points for the business; a typical example is his insistence that copies of the mission statement should hang on large notices all over the factory, so that no one can ever lose sight of it.

Customers are treated as partners in the undertaking, closely involved in its operations and always receiving the best possible service, with a product that is famous for its superior quality and reliability.

Albert has invested highly in sophisticated computerized manufacturing and planning systems. Key business measures are used extensively throughout the business.

Managing the workforce

Albert sees his workforce as the unique factor which can give the business its leading edge; it is they who, in the way they treat the product and the customer, can make the critical difference in moving the business forward and maintaining its success. The model of HRM he uses is simple, but it stresses the interactive wheel of functions shown on p. 40.

Let us look more closely at the HRM system that results in high performance and growth at HMH Sheetmetal.

Recruitment

Albert believes that a good workforce starts with the raw material – people recruited must be of the standard and potential upon which training, development and reward systems provided by the firm can build. He recruits only what he sees as high-calibre people – those who can quickly achieve and consistently maintain the demanding targets that the business requires and will stay with the firm to ensure that, in the longer term, it maintains its competitive advantage and has a high-performing team. To attract such people he offers above-average pay. When he brings people in from outside he does this by word of mouth and networking, in order to ensure not only that the right skills and potential are obtained, but also that whoever is recruited will bring with them attitudes and values that conform with, rather than challenge, the overall culture of the firm. The values that are particularly important relate to the need for high-quality, customer orientation, continuous development of people and product, teamwork, and commitment to the firm.

Training and development to standards and for quality

Albert saw the importance of quality in product and service long before 'quality' became fashionable in the United Kingdom. He invested early in just-in-time and total quality management, and his was the first company in his industry sector in the UK to attain BS 5750 (the universal British quality standard) approval. Albert's belief is that the investment made at the recruitment stage must be maintained by good training and development thereafter; this will ensure that essential skills related to mastering tasks specific to Sheetmetal's processes and product will be acquired quickly and to the same high standards across the workforce, and that individuals rapidly become effective performers and team members. The firm is seeking Investors in People status in recognition of the commitment to business-led human resource development.

Career development

Although Albert's firm may seem too small both in size and type of operation to offer internalized careers, none the less a system does exist. Team leader positions have been created, and promotion to those positions is normally from within. Recruits are taken from the shopfloor and trained in the skills they need, usually by external consultants who have developed a long-standing relationship with the company. Teams are carefully chosen to contain a good balance of personalities and skills. External sources of funding are used to do much of this training and other forms of development – the employer-led Training and Enterprise Councils set up in 82 regions in the United Kingdom in 1989 have some funds to disburse to programmes that relate to small and medium-sized enterprises like Albert's, provided that they promote business enterprise and growth and offer training in vital skills that are in scarce supply in a locality.

Provision for succession

There is also a succession plan for the company. Albert has identified those capable of replacing him, and is developing a number of people to secure succession into key posts in the future, including its own.

Financial incentives and rewards

Pay rates are above the norm, but work targets are clear and demanding, and people are appraised and rewarded in relation to how far they achieve them. All shopfloor workers are on performance-related pay, although the concept of team bonuses is now being examined, given the need for the firm to operate as an integrated and flexible group of people, committed to achieving a common mission. All managers are on profit-related pay.

Termination policy

The firm is high performing and must be fast reactive. While pay and rewards are high if performance and growth are sustained, there is no room for poor performance which does not respond to training, development and incentives. As is typical of life in most small firms (see Chapter 4), there are many tensions: there is little tolerance for those who do not through time fit into the culture, which has many social as well as task norms at its core. The firm is tight knit, cohesive, often frenetic in the pace of its activities. It is also characterized by an intimate knowledge of its goals and targets by all of its workforce; by its flat structure; and by the dynamic leadership which for 21 years has steered its course through the storms that face small, owner-managed businesses in a competitive and unpredictable economy.

Outcomes

Productivity, morale, efficiency and quality are high at HMH Sheetmetal Fabrications; turnover and absenteeism are, for this kind of business, exceptionally low. The company is a market leader in a field where differentiation is extremely difficult. Its success stems not only from expertise in a range of business skills, and from effective investment in new technology, but also from its workforce and the way that workforce is led and managed. Human resource strategy is, even if at a more intuitive than formal level, an essential part of general business strategy at HMH Sheetmetal, and takes the form of a well-integrated and carefully monitored range of policies and practices that both serve the short and longer term needs of the business and ensure individual motivation and growth for those who prove by Moss's standards to be capable, adaptable and committed.

Task

You are a management consultant with whom the owner, Albert Moss, is discussing his future plans for the firm. His concern is with areas such as marketing, new technology and quality. He has not indicated a concern to discuss the area of people management. On the assumption that there are no major changes envisaged for the firm in the immediate future, what would you wish to raise with him about the management and development of his workforce, and how are you going to persuade him to take that advice seriously?

3 Case study

Putting TQM into practice – the role of the personnel function

Adrian Wilkinson and Mick Marchington

(The material in this chapter is extracted from case study work carried out for the Institute of Personnel Management as part of their research report 'Quality, People Management Matters'. We are grateful to the Institute for their support and for their permission as publishers to reproduce material from the research report.)

Introduction

The practice of quality management is now becoming much more widespread throughout the United Kingdom. Recent interest has focused on the shortcomings which are associated with the 'hard', systems-type initiatives, and their failure to pay sufficient attention to the 'people' elements in the drive for continuous quality improvement (see, for example, Wilkinson *et al.*, 1992).

There is growing evidence that TQM is unlikely to achieve its objectives unless there is a greater awareness of the people factors in quality management (Wilkinson, 1993). However brilliant a strategy and the tools which are employed to put it into effect, nothing will be achieved if the people side of the equation is not properly addressed. Although writers and organizations often refer to the human factors, this is rarely treated at anything more than a superficial level – the need for more training, better communications, empowerment of staff, open management styles, and so on. There is a feeling, not just confined to those within the personnel function, that greater emphasis needs to be placed on the human aspects of quality management. It is thus interesting to note that both the American Malcolm Baldrige Award and the European equivalent – the European Quality Award – provide points for human resource issues as a specific category (see note on page 344).

This introduction sets the backcloth to the case study which follows. The case aims to shed light on some of the links between TQM and HRM and to examine in particular the contribution which personnel practitioners can make to the successful operation of a company and its TQM goals.

Four questions appear at the end of the case study. They can be used as student assignments, as topics for group work, or as self-tests for general readers.

Carcom: the TQM initiative

'Carcom' is a supplier of automotive safety components employing around 700 staff which is located on two sites in Northern Ireland. The company was originally American owned but after a joint venture with a Japanese partner in the late 1980s it was eventually bought out by the latter.

The quality initiative began in 1988–89 with a five-year plan based on the Kaizen philosophy, this concept having been picked up from the Japanese partner. This was driven by senior management in response to what they saw as increasing customer demand and operating considerations. The achievement of ISO 9001 registration in 1990 brought together processes carried out by departments which had previously been undertaken in isolation. The company is now focusing on Kaizen with the principles of improvement, customer delight, systems focus and participation. A range of quality management tools and techniques are used. A TQM steering committee is responsible for overall direction but there is also a further steering committee to oversee implementation of the Quality Improvement Teams (QITs) as well as a full time coordinator. There are teams of shopfloor operators based on natural workgroups, and these tend to focus on product problems and environmental issues (such as working conditions). In contrast, Kaizen teams focus on process improvements (for example, die change) and problem-solving workgroups are established in response to specific customer concerns (for example, warranty claims).

Senior managers stress that a long-term approach is now being taken which is in contrast to some of the programmes in the early 1980s. These former piecemeal initiatives included quality circles which had been characterized by considerable changes in personnel, with a number of champions having moved on leaving behind a flagging initiative. In contrast, the company is now taking time to get the processes right and providing a central focus through quality for change. Cultural change is the aim but it is recognized that only incremental progress can be achieved and that a supportive attitude is required from management. Thus, QIT members are given extensive training and are encouraged to tackle problems which give early success and build teamwork, rather than put pressure on teams to deliver immediately on big issues.

The impact of the TQM initiative

While it is still early days, the initiative is already felt to have had a major impact. The management structure has been reduced by one layer, shopfloor layout has been improved, and scrap rates, stock, work-in-progress and inspection times have been reduced, so too have the numbers of inspectors whose role is now seen as one of analysts. Employee response to these changes has generally been positive, and the company has spent considerable effort in relating 'quality' directly to employees' work, particularly through the use of measures which are displayed adjacent to the workstation and maintained by staff themselves. The unions were assured that there would not be job losses as a result of Kaizen, although they continue to have concerns about this and also raise the issue of payment for changes in job roles – particularly in relation to SPC. The company has adopted an open information policy to foster greater trust at the workplace, and business-related issues are given greater prominence at the joint works committee meetings. Management also believe that the quality initiative has led to a reduction in union influence, although this was not an original objective.

The strategic nature of the human resource function

The human resource function has emerged from a welfare to a more strategic role in recent years. This has been assisted by an MD who is regarded as a 'people's person' claiming that 'you can't divorce people from quality'; and by the appointment of a personnel director to the board together with a new industrial relations manager. This has broadened the role of human resources and enhanced its status. The appointment of a training manager was significant, since under the previous regime little off-the-job training was conducted. Training budgets have actually increased in volume and monetary terms despite the company's recently recorded trading losses. Recruitment and selection are becoming more sophisticated as the company wish to iden-tify teamworkers.

The links between human resources and quality were made explicitly by the MD: 'We cannot separate HR from TQM, and without HR the QIP will not work effectively'. In addition to the issues mentioned above, the function was also seen as being important in building the people aspect into the strategic quality planning process, addressing the problem of absenteeism, and supporting line management by helping to change employee attitudes/organizational culture. In addition, the function has provided appropriate training programmes for quality, in which there has been considerable investment in time and resources, it has counselled the mentors to the QIT, and ensured that managers communicate with staff by providing advice on the best means of doing this. Quality principles are also being developed in relation to the human resource function, with specific targets being set (for example, for absenteeism) as well as more general aims (for example, on training).

Note

The Malcolm Baldrige National Award for Quality Improvement provides for 150 out of 1000 points to be based on human resource utilization. Other categories are leadership, information and analysis, strategic planning, quality assurance of products and services, quality results and customer satisfaction. The European Quality Award has allocated 90 points for people management and 90 points for people satisfaction out of a total of 1000 points. The assessment model is one where customer satisfaction, people satisfaction, and impact on society are achieved through leadership drive, policy and strategy, people management, resources and processes leading, ultimately to excellence in business results.

Tasks

1. Analyse the links between TQM and HRM with reference both to this case study and more generally.

2. What does the case study demonstrate about the contribution a personnel/HRM function can make to the development of TQM in an organization?

3. How might the principles of TQM be applied to a personnel/HRM function?

4. What general implications does TQM have for industrial relations?

4 Case study

Analysing the links between employee involvement, strategic human resource management and organizational change

Peter Ackers,
Mick Marchington
and Adrian Wilkinson

(The case which forms the basis of the case study is part of a larger project funded by the Employment Department. 'NTC' is a pseudonym. We are grateful to the Employment Department for their financial assistance. The views expressed here are entirely those of the authors and do not necessarily represent those of the funding organization.)

The background

National Transport Corporation (NTC) is a large, complex transport business undergoing a process of commercialization. Over the past decade, it has attempted to transform a bureaucratic, centralized culture into a more entrepreneurial one. This has been accompanied by intensified cost pressures. NTC has a wide range of transport-related activities, but the research concentrated on two workgroups: a northern vehicle maintenance plant employing about 200, and at some distance from the customer; and a southern group of conductors in constant daily contact with passengers.

NTC is highly unionized, with a complex, centralized, union-centred history of national negotiation and joint consultation structure. At national level, this entails centralized bargaining and consultation, which establishes

347

detailed wages and conditions. At local level, works committees combine bargaining and consultation. In both areas, the unions had a strong say in decisions about work organization. For the conductors, this accompanied good relations with local management, while at the maintenance plant relations were more conflictual.

Apart from collective bargaining and joint consultation, NTC has a major, longstanding, central suggestion scheme, whereby employees from all parts of the business submit suggestions through a formal procedure. This is well resourced, and while local managers are not directly involved, they sponsor good ideas from staff, sometimes linked to local quality schemes. Otherwise, Employee Involvement (EI) is a more recent development, interwoven with cultural change and commercialization. It is directed at individual employees, which marks some departure from a tradition of channelling communications almost exclusively through union representatives. So far, this takes three interrelated, but potentially conflicting forms.

1 The TQM scheme

There is a TQM scheme, with board level sponsorship, which aims to improve customer service and safety by increasing the motivation and commitment of the staff who must deliver this. This has a five-year span, during which it will cascade down through the whole organization. At the apex, it involves a management development programme geared to the new high-performance enterprise culture. At the shopfloor base, the emphasis shifts to customer care. The national programme is at mid-term, having just reached line management, who are now undergoing a series of off-site training sessions on both of the above elements. For the conductors, the TQM programme is still in the future. However, in maintenance, management has taken a more vertical slice, including shopfloor workers. But this became embroiled with industrial relations problems linked to organizational restructuring and rationalization, and is now 'blacked' by shop stewards. The unions fear bypassing, linked to a wider unease about the uncertain future of centralized national bargaining.

2 Team briefing

A limited form of team briefing, in which the briefs are written by the chief executive, stops at clerical and supervisory level, short of the shopfloor. At local level, there is great uncertainty about the future in such a large and complex organization. This often extends to line management, and when the maintenance manager briefed his manual employees in shifts, he was embarrassed by national news affecting them, which had leaked out in the press. He has since discontinued briefing, and there is no shopfloor briefing by the conductors' line managers. However, NTC has a monthly national newspaper and a plethora of other specialist papers, which carry the briefings and other news. These do not seem widely read, but developments are also well covered in the national press.

3 Organizational restructuring

An on-going organizational restructuring programme is replacing geographical and functional hierarchies with a new business focus. This has a quality motif, but its objectives are much wider. It has a contradictory impact on wider EI developments. It complements them by encouraging local initiative, often linked to survival, which involves employees in problem-solving. This was originally true of the maintenance site, where management focused EI issues, including TQM, on obtaining BS 5750. Organizational change, however, can swamp other EI moves. By subdividing NTC, it may undermine TQM, questioning its company-wide sweep, and causing anxiety among its line management subjects. Uncertainty among manual staff about their job prospects, and the priority of cost-cutting, may both threaten employee morale in the short term.

The new EI at NTC is hard to evaluate. The key schemes have scarcely reached the main manual workforce, and are linked to a wider state of flux and uncertainty in the whole organization. There are apparent contradictions between them, and some evidence that short-term commercial considerations take priority over human resource objectives. As yet, the well-established union-centred collective bargaining and joint consultation structures, at national and local level, are still perceived as the main conduit of employee influence on and information about management decision-making.

Task

What insight does this case study offer into real-life tensions involved in trying to make EI play a more central role in strategic HRM?

5 Assignment

In search of enterprise – a consultancy assignment

John Ritchie

In search of enterprise?

The human resource division of a developing management consultancy, recently diversified into smaller and entrepreneurial business consulting, faces several challenges. In particular, it has been consulted by a major regional development forum about possible strategies for 'mobilizing human resources so as to arrest and reverse local economic and industrial decline'. The forum – a novel partnership between party political, governmental, industrial, trade union, and educational and training interests – has only recently come together with the object of facilitating change through persuasion and 'investment in people'. In working together for the first time themselves, forum members differed considerably over how they saw its problems and priorities. A general feeling that 'something needs to be done' about smaller businesses thus emerged from their early discussions, but nothing clearer than that. They therefore approached this consultancy division hoping that any 'professional' strategic advice received would not only focus their thinking but help members work together better too. 'This is our first major task', said their chairperson, 'so we need to look particularly professional and competent in everything we do, otherwise our partnership might easily come apart'. The incoming consultants therefore first asked individual members jointly to agree one common brief they could work to. This came back as:

> To research, advise and consult on the types of people, kind of businesses, range of problems, and nature of advice and support necessary for encouraging new small businesses and creating more employment right across the forum's region, and help produce appropriate strategies which partners can agree upon.

Important differences of outlook and opinion persisted throughout these early consultations, however. From tapes and notes of relevant meetings the following key statements were isolated:

CHAIRPERSON: All manner of people start their own businesses these days. There should be huge potential here. In fact more should have been done before. The more the better as far as I'm concerned. We can't rely on the big firms any more. And because they've got such widespread appeal our helping small businesses should boost our own image too. If I had my way we wouldn't look very much further.

DEPUTY CHAIRPERSON: Well, I've known the chairperson for some years now, and he's always been liable to get carried away with bright-sounding new ideas you know. I'm a bit more reserved about these firms myself. A few others have dabbled with these firms, but it seems to me only certain types succeed, while others fall away, and one thing we can't be seen to be associated with are more failures, not at this stage anyway. The types who succeed presumably already have business backgrounds, capital resources, plenty of personality and energy, that sort of thing. I couldn't put the finger on it myself, but I hope you consultants can give us the spec, so to speak.

MAJOR COMPANY REPRESENTATIVE: It's true we used to think of small businesspeople as a sort of oddball type but things are beginning to change. Even we are beginning to change in that respect, looking at who we buy from, that sort of thing. Nothing dramatic, I grant you, but it's a start. I've heard all this 'human resources' talk in our company, however, and I'm none too happy with it. We believe it's more important to channel resources towards those businesses and sectors which will stay and grow here rather than throw money at anyone who happens to come along. True, the people are important, but you need to be selective about what firms and sectors need developing first, which is where you consultants come in.

TRADE UNION REPRESENTATIVE: I'll not waste words. It's jobs I'm interested in. Pure and simple. Heaven knows how many we lost before and are losing now. Not least among men. There are lads out there who think they'll be lucky ever to work again. And you can't rely on some of the companies their wives have found jobs in – here one day, gone the next some of them, and there's not much the women can do about it. It's that which makes me think twice about some of these so-called entrepreneur types, you know. Sure, I'll go along with everyone else, and see what smaller firms can offer, but I doubt whether they're the all-purpose solution some here think they are. Some of these entrepreneurs are just get-rich-quick types, ducking and diving, laying people off as quick as they set them on, looking to the main chance, not really to be relied upon. They're not all like that, of course, but responsible bodies like ours should exercise care, that's all I'm saying.

PROFESSIONS REPRESENTATIVE: Some of us have been dealing with people like these for years so I reckon we know the inside story better than most. In fact, many accountants and solicitors, for example, are basically just small business people themselves, there to provide a service at a reasonable price. Naturally we're well placed to help, and do some hand-holding, but only provided we're properly paid, given the amount of time this usually takes up.

EDUCATION AND TRAINING REPRESENTATIVE: Now we've been reorganized we're keener to get involved than ever. Our own management strategy recognizes this, and we'll tailor everything to what local people need, subject to agreed national standards, provided money for staff is forthcoming, because we like to think we're becoming more businesslike too. If we're 'investing in people' then education and training should be right to the front of everything the forum does. We might make a start just offering small business courses free – or at worst cheap – right across the board, and seeing what follows. It's all about people, you know, but we'll need a picture of who is likely to come forward before we can plan ahead.

SMALL BUSINESS REPRESENTATIVE: I'm glad you came to speak to me because – believe it or not – we're usually the last to be consulted about the things that really affect us, despite what the politicians say. In case you're wondering, I think I should warn you that while we carry the flag for small businesses around here, things are not all they seem. Our people are under a lot of pressure, just struggling along, making do amid cutbacks, downturns and the rest. We all look for the silver lining, but the public encouragement is wearing a bit thin just now. There are more of us now, but the competition can be intense, verging upon cutting each other's throats. Courses and training are all very well, but unless you can sustain businesses themselves you've nothing to show, and I often wish there was more practical help there than anywhere else. There is an awful lot that needs to be done, and reasonably quickly too, but it's always difficult bringing people together, and finding out what they really need, because they all have very individual needs. Some are pretty doubtful about consultants too, as you might realize, so you might have credibility problems too, unless something really practical gets going.

The consultants' dilemma

On reconvening later, the consultants first found themselves mirroring the forum's own internal differences until they questioned their respective purposes. Their original brief made small business development the 'presenting' problem, but what did forum members imagine such businesses generally were, and how much/what sort of additional employment were they expecting? Even when it came to the people concerned, they needed to be much more particular and specific – and how much of a 'people problem' was there anyway? Even if they could discover more about smaller businesses, how exactly would they research it, and would it not be better if they helped them work together better first, even if that meant confronting individual differences?

In short, there were so many questions to be answered, and pathways they could follow, that their leader asked them to define and debate clearly all the key issues beforehand, focusing on what the forum had asked for/really needed, what was actually known about smaller businesses, what else they could research, how they would go about it, how they would deal with each individual forum member's likely response, what their range of strategic choices might actually be, and how/with what expectations they would go about implementing such choices.

Task

Assume you are shadowing this entire consulting assignment on behalf of the new consultancy division's corporate headquarters. How precisely would you expect the new consulting team to respond to each issue posed by their leader at the end of the case? What other issues might this assignment raise for the new division's own professional development? How could such development best be facilitated?

6 Assignment

Moving to local bargaining arrangements

David Bright

Background

The Chemical Industries Association (CIA) has a membership of some 200 companies many of which operate nationally, accounting for about half the chemical industry's employment. The CIA is involved in three national agreements. Association members who automatically apply terms and conditions agreed nationally, such as Albright and Wilson and RTZ, are known as 'conforming members', while those who do not, such as ICI, are commonly referred to as 'nonconforming members'.

The agreements are closely adhered to with regard to working hours, holiday entitlement, overtime premiums and holiday pay, while the terms on basis pay, shift pay and call-out payments tend to be regarded as the minimum. For example, the agreement tends to 'impose rigid standards' for hours, with most companies operating a 38-hour week, and very few having moved to 37.5 hours – generally as part of harmonization programmes.

Actual pay rates in member companies tend to be well above the national minimum rate, with many companies enhancing the industry minimum by incorporating regular bonus or allowance payments into the basic rate. In recent years, the JICs have attempted to bring total earnings into line and make national rates more relevant by consolidating an element of these superstructure payments (which include all payments other than those agreed by the JIC) into the national minimum.

Task

You are human resource manager for one of the above companies. The company wants to move away from centralized negotiations to develop its own in-house policy for cost-effective industrial relations within an HRM programme. You have been asked by the managing director to prepare a brief on what the industrial relations policy should comprise. Set down the key points you would wish to include in such a policy. Be prepared to discuss the importance of each of these with the managing director.

7 Assignment

How well do you know your employees?

Stephen Pain

How well do you know your employees? You have recently arrived as human resources director at a company which manufactures specialist components for the motor vehicle industry. It is a highly competitive business where product and service quality are the keys to success. The company has a turnover of £5 million and employs 100 people on two sites, one with 60 employees near the centre of Birmingham, the other with 40 employees in Milton Keynes.

You have noticed a rise in customer complaints and a rise in staff turnover at both sites among what had, hitherto, been a very stable workforce. You aim to find out the causes of the problems and decide to review the company's recruitment, training and remuneration policies. You realize that research and communication will play an important part and that it will be vital to undertake the exercise with the full support of the trade unions.

Outline the steps you might take, the obstacles you might encounter and the subsequent action you might take.

8 Assignments

Equality in the workplace
Monica Shaw

Assignment 1: Equality in the workplace: policy and practice

A Equal opportunity policies and human resource outcomes

Pages 192–9 of Chapter 8

Students should refer to the case studies of the BBC and British Telecom, and collect further case study material in order to:

- draw out and discuss the practical links between equal opportunity policy; and practice and strategic HRM;

- establish what types of organization have been most actively relating equal opportunity policies to human resource outcomes;

- identify factors which impede or promote the development of equal opportunity practice in the workplace.

B Demographic change and human resource planning

Pages 200–2 of Chapter 8

The task on page 360 is intended to promote reflection and discussion about the ways in which organizations are currently responding to the implications of demographic change and what they should be doing about it. It is assumed that students can refer to an organization in which they are employed. If not, students should explore the issues in relation to the literature.

<u>TASK</u>   **Equality in the workplace**
Consider these questions in relation to your own (or a selected)
organization:

■   What steps, if any, are being taken to allow for the changing
shape and nature of the labour force?

■   Who in the organization is most aware of demographic
change?

■   In what way has concern about demographic change fuelled
debates about equality of opportunity in the organization?

■   What would be the most appropriate human resource strategy
for the organization in the light of demographic change?

Assignment 2: Equality in organizations: working for change

Agenda setting for implementing equal opportunity policies

Readers are required to develop a plan for implementing equal opportunity
policies related to specific human resource outcomes in a selected organization
(that is, the organization in which they are employed or one which will give
them access).

9 Assignments

Strategic aspects of selection in human resource management

Robin Evenden

Assignment 1: PLI case study

The case is described in Chapter 9. Stage one should be read prior to undertaking this assignment and Stage two will help its subsequent evaluation.
Using the information in Stage one of the case, describe how you would translate PLI's strategic plan into a human resource selection strategy.

Assignment 2: Strategic change and HRM selection strategy

Either describe how an organization known to you translated strategic change into selection strategy and assess its effectiveness, *or* show how an organization known to you could effectively translate strategic change into selection strategy.

Assignment 3: Selection strategy and issues

Describe the selection strategy and methods of an organization known to you. What major issues should it be concerned with and how should it address them?

10 Case study

The Fair Value case study

Robin Evenden

The case study tasks focus upon the need to translate broad strategic plans and goals through HRM into performance management, and the difficulties that this entails when people enter the equation. Performance management systems and the skills of the line manager attempt to focus and influence the performance of individuals at the workface so that effective contributions are made to the achievement of corporate goals.

TASK 1. *Individual assignment*: Interpret the situation at Walltown, suggesting how performance management could help the achievement of Fair Value's strategic plan. With reference either to Duncan or Smith, suggest how their performance could be influenced. Illustrate with examples from your creative interpretation of the people and situation.

TASK 2. *Group assignment*:
   (a) Select small groups to represent Marsh, Morgan, Duncan, Peters, Arnold and Smith. After study, each group should offer the others its perception of the performance situation at Walltown from their individual's perspective, exploring differences in perceptions and their causes. Consider the implications of people's subjectivity for human resource management strategy and performance management systems.
   (b) Prepare and role play performance appraisals. The group should agree who will appraise whom, perhaps using the same small groups/characters as in part (a) of this task.
   The 'appraiser' groups' role players should discuss their aims and methods with their respective small groups. Similarly the 'appraisees' should discuss their 'self-assessment' and approach to the appraisal with their respective small groups. It is more effective

to run the role plays as spontaneous rather than scripted activities.

The appraiser is the 'performance manager'. His or her task is to prepare, assess, handle the appraisal, motivate the appraisee and agree a performance and development plan with objectives and targets for the key task areas. If time is limited, treat the interview as a cameo lasting about 15 to 20 minutes, focusing perhaps upon one key task area in some depth.

Each interview should be observed by the full group and discussed in terms of handling and outcomes to illustrate the techniques considered in the chapter.

Case study: Fair Value supermarket

Fair Value is a countrywide food retailing organization which has a strategy of growth by acquisition. Against intense competition it aimed to gain an additional 5% share of the market in the next three years. To support this, Fair Value had launched a major campaign to project its image of quality food and super-efficient friendly service. The theme was: 'We are pleased you trust us to please you', and it was proving successful.

Fifteen months ago they acquired Cousins, which owned four small stores in the Midlands. This case focuses upon the Walltown store which was developed and opened as a modern supermarket six months ago.

Cousins, Walltown, at the time of the takeover

Cousins had survived by niche marketing, providing 'traditional fare by traditional service'. The Walltown store had two departments: provisions, which was personal service, and groceries, which was self-service. Customers valued the friendly atmosphere and helpful service, although the layout was unsystematic and the display was unimaginative.

The manager was Charles Morgan, who had spent all 35 years of his working life with Cousins. After eight years of running provisions he was appointed manager twelve years ago. He was well content with his career, feeling he had progressed without the advantage of educational or training opportunities. The customer goodwill was largely due to his efforts. He was liked and respected by all staff, with whom he had frequent contact on the shopfloor.

His provisions manager was John Peters. Aged 42, he had long service at Cousins. His department was almost a store within a store. He was frequently consulted by Morgan on store policy and found job discussion with him easy. Their good relations extended to social contact out of the workplace.

Mary Williams was staff manager. She was highly motivated and was regarded as very helpful by the staff. Groceries was managed by Arthur Jones, who was recruited from a large supermarket to convert the department to self-service four years ago. He hoped for career development and training in management, but had received little encouragement.

Morale was high and staff turnover was low at 10%. Communication was informal and largely spoken. The managerial staff had frequent friendly conversations with each other and the sales staff. There was a weekly management team meeting.

Fair Value: the new Walltown supermarket

Nine months after the acquisition, the new store opened on the much developed old site. 'Fruit and vegetables' and 'wines and spirits' were added to the existing departments. The store was modernized, rationalized and run on an efficient self-service basis. Both the sales and preparation/processing areas trebled in size and the staff doubled. All the old staff were retained and everybody received some training in the new operations. Decor was attractive and staff facilities were much improved.

Morgan remained as manager, responsible directly to the divisional operations director, Stanley Marsh. His job became largely administrative. Communication became mostly paper or electronic rather than spoken.

A new post of deputy manager was created. This was occupied by James Duncan, previously a provisions manager at another Fair Value store. Aged 30, he had a diploma in management studies and was considered by top management to have considerable potential and to be knowledgeable in supermarket methods. Duncan was directly responsible for the departmental managers; operational efficiency; staffing and training. He took over the warehousing from Peters and was responsible for the preparation and processing areas. Most of his time he walked the job and kept his relationships on a formal basis and discouraged the use of first names. He gave appearance and hygiene a high priority and took every opportunity to impress this upon everybody. He ensured that jobs were precisely defined and rotation of jobs was discouraged.

The position after six months' trading

Business had exceeded expectations. Performance-related pay, linked to sales turnover, meant that earnings were significantly higher than previously. However, Morgan had reservations. The cooperation and friendly relations had disappeared and the weekly team meeting was strained and full of 'trivial bickering' in Morgan's view. Staff turnover had grown dramatically to 30% and half the Cousins' employees had left. In addition, customer complaints related to service, packaging and quality had increased sharply and had been noted by Marsh. Morgan felt if these trends continued it would have a sharp effect upon commercial performance.

A particular problem was relations between Duncan, the Deputy, and Peters. Duncan informed Morgan that Peters' department was frequently understocked; packs were often not sealed; sell-by dates were often exceeded; and too often items were wrongly labelled, weighed or priced. He said he had drawn these matters to Peters' attention, but it had made no difference. Peters had told Morgan that he and his staff resented Duncan's unhelpful interference and negative attitude. He felt the deputy went out of his way to be critical.

Some critical incidents and perceptions in provisions

Chris Arnold is responsible for the day-to-day running of the provisions department, and deputizes for the provisions manager Peters in his absence, which is frequent because they work different shifts and rest days.

In Fair Value, provisions includes all dairy produce, such as eggs, bacon, cold meats, milk produce, chill and freeze cabinets. The department has two sections:

Stockers – three people, usually two working at any one time, who stock the display cabinets and check for shortages and correct packaging, sell-by dates and so on.

Packers – five people, usually three working at any one time, who take deliveries from the warehouse; respond to stockers' requests when goods are short in cabinets to give fresh supplies; process and package the provisions; and ensure that their part of the processing area is hygienic and tidy. For example, they operate a machine-assisted process line for bacon, which involves slicing, packing, weighing and labelling. This requires some skill, dexterity and concentration.

Chris Arnold is the provisions senior assistant, experienced in provisions, and trained in the processing and hygiene aspects of the role at head office and on the job at Fair Value store in the large town 12 miles from Walltown. This is the first supervisory position for Arnold, who replaced the previous senior assistant who left six months after the takeover. Fran Smith is a provisions packer who was previously employed for four years by Cousins and worked on the old methods of personal counter service with Peters, and they remain on friendly terms.

Chris Arnold's perceptions

Arnold joined the Walltown store as provisions senior assistant two months before it began its modernized service. At that time Arnold thought that Smith was keen, often arriving early for work, cooperating with the refurbishing and was friendly with everybody, getting on well with colleagues and customers alike.

Smith applied to join the new wines and spirits department, thinking it would be interesting work, with customer contact and a higher grade post, but was not given the job. The new staff appointed all had wines and spirits experience. After this, Smith became much more distant towards Arnold, although remaining on good terms with others by continuing to organize social activities, raffles for charity and so on.

The stockers complained about slowness in meeting their requirements for restocking cabinets. These were most frequent during Smith's shifts. Duncan had timed the average response time at 30 minutes. Arnold had noted that Smith often took twice that. Also, an average shift, for example, produced 500 bacon packs. When Smith was on shift this average was 440. Duncan undertook periodic quality checks on merchandise on display. This involved checking for wrong price or weight, wrong labelling, faulty packaging and goods past the sell-by date. One fault per 500 items was the norm; Smith averaged 5 per 500.

Arnold noticed that Smith's workstation had become increasingly untidy, and on a few occasions the food processing equipment was not cleaned at the end of the shift. This had been brought to Smith's attention by Arnold, but the problem was usually minimized or excuses found – often owing to lack of time because of last-minute requests from stockers, or discussions with Peters about the social committee where Smith was secretary.

The Fair Value health and safety officer had recently had a word with Duncan about standards in provisions. Duncan told Peters to raise safety and hygiene standards. Peters was rather short with Arnold about it. Arnold felt Smith was the main culprit, and furthermore, was having a bad effect on the other packers. Duncan caught Smith smoking in the processing area and issued a strong reprimand on the spot, much to Peters' anger, because he felt he and Arnold should have dealt with the issue.

Fran Smith's perceptions

Fran Smith had enjoyed the last four years at Cousins. When the takeover was announced Smith felt that it might not be a bad thing, because there could be more chance of promotion in a bigger firm. Smith was a very social person and had been secretary of the Cousins' social committee, continuing this after the takeover. It was time-consuming, but Smith felt that the staff appreciated it and it added interest to the daily chores.

The new wines and spirits department seemed very attractive. It had prestige in Fair Value, and the work conditions were good, with a lot of independence. It also offered employment at higher grades. Peters told Smith that there would be a good chance of getting the job. Smith applied but received a letter from head office saying that the posts were filled. This was disappointing, and Peters intimated that unless you were a favourite with Duncan you would not get anywhere in Fair Value.

Peters had trained the staff in the new methods, but Smith was not attentive, feeling that Peters was not very good at it himself. Smith thought Arnold was not bad at the job but did not seem to appreciate the social side of things. Arnold was a bit over-critical too, so Smith tried to keep out of the senior assistant's way as much as possible.

Arnold had suggested that Smith was not as fast as other staff, but Smith made excuses about the equipment, a bad wrist and the time demands of the charity work Fair Value was supporting. The supervisor had complained about Smith's quality and tidiness recently, but Smith ignored this and put it down to Peters' complaining and Arnold's needing somebody to blame. Smith was aware that the others seemed more comfortable with the new equipment and were able to use it better, but did not want to draw attention to it, hoping to get the hang of it soon.

Smith also had a domestic problem which was distracting and rather worrying. A phone call at work last week had been very stressful and Smith needed a cigarette to relieve the pressure. Of course, it was typical of the current run of luck that Duncan had appeared and given a strong reprimand. In addition, Smith had finished with a verbal warning from Peters, with Arnold there too looking rather smug and self-righteous. Smith did not mention the problem, knowing that it was wrong to smoke in the work area.

Smith had not revealed the problem or job concerns to anybody, feeling that the supervisor was not very helpful or sympathetic and that Peters was preoccupied with his own difficulties. The only reason for staying seemed the social side of the job.

11 Case study

Wharfedale Water

David Bright

While this case study is related to trends in employment relations generally and to changes in the structure of the UK water industry particularly, the company referred to does not exist and the events described are not associated with any one particular business.

The study describes three phases of development of employment relations in Wharfedale Water plc. Three tasks have been set, one following each phase. First, some general information about the company.

Until 1989 most of the British water industry was in public ownership. The major issues of industrial relations, such as pay bargaining and the setting of other key employment terms, were carried out centrally through three national negotiating bodies. For the 10 employers' side, representation was handled initially through the National Water Council and, from 1983, the Water Authorities Association. The major union players in the companies were TGWU, GMB, NUPE and CSEU for the craft and manual staff and NALGO, NUPE and MATSA for the white-collar staff.

In 1989, following the government's privatization of the water industry in the late 1980s, the process of national bargaining was abolished, leaving each of the 10 regional companies free not only to negotiate the main terms at the domestic level but also, and perhaps more fundamentally, to determine the culture of their own employment relations.

Phase 1 1989 – The new culture

Following privatization Wharfedale moved quickly to appoint some new non-executive directors with significant commercial experience, and a new chief executive from outside the industry. The new board adopted two watchwords from the start – 'profit' and 'quality'. To achieve these targets the board used the services of leading management consultants, who advised the company to reorganize its structure on enterprise lines. This was acted upon, and within the group umbrella there are six businesses, by far the largest being the water services enterprise, Wharfewater. This part of the group is the biggest employer, having 1100 staff, compared to the next largest at 200. It is the business responsible for the supply of water and the processing of sewage and water recreation in the region. It is the most significant contributor to group profits.

While the managing director of Wharfewater is a long-standing water industry employee, the newly appointed director of human resources has no previous experience in the industry or in any other public utilities. His main career stages have been spent in the retail sector and in engineering. In 1989, 82% of the employees of Wharfewater were union members, with 9 unions being recognized.

On taking up his position, the HR director was determined to make significant changes in what he considered to be old-fashioned and irrelevant industrial relations practices. He was keen that the management of all aspects of human resources should relate to the group's mission statement and contribute to the overall corporate objectives. He saw as a central plank in this approach the method of employee representation. To that end he considered that a more 'round table' system of representation would be a better vehicle than traditional collective bargaining for managing contractual and consultative issues between management and the workforce. He took this model to Wharfewater's board and the plan received enthusiastic backing. He announced to his HR team that he wished a 'Wharfewater Council' to be in place by mid-1990 and set up a working party to advise him on the practicalities of constitution and membership.

Task 1: Union recognition

You are the chair of the above working party. The constitution of the council has been agreed in draft form and you now have to give your attention to the membership of it. There are nine unions represented in the company, as well as a separate managers' association. This latter body has 145 members and three of the unions have 650 members between them. The HR director and the board are very keen to have a system in place which allows them to deal with industrial relation issues in ways best suited to Wharfewater and which allows them to communicate directly with their staff.

Given these considerations what type of representative system should the new council have? Give particular thought to the following:

- Should all the existing unions have seats?
- Should only the three largest unions have seats?
- Should no unions have a seat?
- Should the managers' association have a seat?
- How should the company be represented?

Give reasons for your recommendations. Identify and analyse the main difficulties associated with achieving each of the options considered.

Phase 2 The new system is established

In 1990 Wharfewater set up a company council with four feeder district councils which were based upon geographical districts within the company's operational area. The company council was chaired by the managing director with the other three company representatives being the HR director, the operational director and the director of finance. The seniority of these positions was seen as a reflection of the importance the company attached to the new system of employment relations. Of the other seats there were four elected employee representatives, one from each district, an employee vice-chair, elected from all of the employees, and two observers, one from the unions and one from the managers' association.

The constitution was agreed. It was based on a shared belief that the council has been established to promote 'effective employment relations based on trust, understanding and tolerance of the views of all stakeholders'.

The company embarked on a major training programme for its elected representatives, and all members of the company council participated in a series of team-building events throughout the year. In order to give the council time to become established, the main employment relations event of the year, the pay review, was handled by the group's management with all employees receiving an increase of RPI plus 2%, a figure which accorded well with typical settlement levels for the year. At the same time, the group gave all employees a number of shares in the business as the first part of a venture to encourage employers to invest in Wharfedale financially as well as through their work efforts. Group management stated that from 1991 all pay and major conditions would be settled at the enterprise level through the councils.

1991

Meetings of the council were held every two months with a special one in June being set aside for pay and benefits matters. As June 1991 approached, the HR director began to plan for the discussions. He was anxious to avoid what he considered the ritual dance of traditional negotiations and repeatedly told the council members this. While he was reasonably pleased with the progress made, he was aware that a considerable amount of suspicion existed among many employees about the new system. The view that 'the whole thing is a management con trick' was articulated more than once. He was aware that quite a few workers, particularly in the craft and industrial ranks, would prefer to see a return to the practices of pre-privatization.

Task 2: Negiotiation

It is now May 1991 and the HR director wants advice on two fronts:

1. How should the process of negotiation be handled: should he allow the reps to submit a claim or should he make an offer first? If he moves his position how far should he move?
2. Should he just concern himself with basic pay or should he be more ambitious and try to introduce performance or profit-related systems?

Examine each of these issues and give your advice, both on concepts and implementation, to the HR director.

Phase 3 Developing rewards

In the event, the pay negotiations passed without anything radical happening. The reps gave an advance indication of the sort of issues on which they were hoping to see improvement and the level of settlement for which they were looking. No written claim was submitted. Management made an offer and following discussions improved it slightly; at the same time management indicated that it would make no further improvement.

This second offer was accepted by the elected members as being reasonable, but no great enthusiasm was evident in their acceptance. The offer was then balloted by all the workforce and was accepted, though only 58% voted in favour of it.

By 1992, management was keen to move with more radical developments in employment relations and felt that the area of pay and benefits warranted attention. It was slightly disappointed that little change had been made in the previous year but felt that with each year that passed the workforce would identify less with history and with the 'water industry' and more with Wharfewater.

One view was that the company should proceed with speed to a system of performance-related pay. The supporters of this approach believed that staff responded better if pay was linked to a performance culture. Additionally, a number of other water businesses had introduced such schemes without any apparent problems.

The opponents of performance-related pay cited three arguments against such a development:

- performance-related pay was losing currency in many firms that already had it;

- performance-related pay was divisive and undercut attempts to increase the bonding between the employee and Wharfewater;

- it would be difficult to implement performance-related pay in times when the level of settlements was low, as was the case that year.

These opponents tended to be more supportive of schemes of pay which were linked not to individual performance but to business performance, that is, linked to Wharfewater or Wharfedale's profits.

Task 3: Payment systems

Critically examine the arguments for implementing either a performance-related or a profit-related pay scheme in the company. The HR director believes that only one major development can be handled in the year so that if you see advantage in both you should prioritize them. In considering profit-related pay, consider the benefits and problems associated with linking pay to Wharfewater and Wharfedale's profits.

12 Case study

Thorn Lighting Ltd, UK – a learning organization

Rosemary Harrison

(By kind permission of Thorn Lighting Ltd)

Thorn Lighting is one of the world's largest lighting fittings manufacturers and an acknowledged leader in lighting technology. It has established operations in 22 countries and manufacturing activities in 8.

The manufacturing site at Spennymoor, Co. Durham, is one of three in the United Kingdom. It employs 1100 people, and since 1988 has been transformed from a traditional batch-production system into one of the most modern factories in Europe for the design and manufacture of lighting fittings and control gear with the latest flexible manufacturing technology, CAD/CAM systems, cellular production, and just-in-time production practices. Production changeover time, which used to take hours or days, has been cut to minutes, and lead times and backlogs have been cut dramatically and, in some cases, eliminated. A new technology centre provides the latest facilities for computerized design and analysis.

Quality is regarded as a profit centre, and consequently a total quality system has been developed. Inspection and basic maintenance are carried out by operators as an integral part of the production process.

Spennymoor is the spearhead in Thorn Lighting's drive to achieve its mission: 'to be a world class supplier of lighting solutions'. Central to its new outlook is its commitment to developing its people. Since 1988 it has been working to create and sustain a multiskilled, high-quality workforce, committed to its business goals and to their own continuous development. It invests heavily in HRD through processes aimed at attracting those with the competencies and values that have been defined as essential to the company's high performance and growth, and at sustaining the culture by induction and job-related training based on attitude development as well as skills acquisition. There is a cell group structure where everybody is trained in all the different tasks involved and encouraged to exchange tasks regularly. Team work and team building courses are conducted regularly at an outdoor development centre.

At the Spennymoor site, future supervisors are identified through annual internal assessment centres which identify either longer term or immediate potential in those who apply (the centres are open to anyone in the company and are strongly supported by the workforce). Those with longer term supervisory potential move into a two-year development programme at the completion of which they can apply for promotion. Those ready now for promotion move, on appointment to their new position, into a higher level development programme, involving 32 days of modular training and development across 2 years. The modules cover areas such as team leader skills, action-centred leadership, advanced management techniques, continuous improvement, problem-solving and so on. All new supervisors are moved to monthly staff status, and thereafter their earnings growth is linked to successful modular completion (80%), and to proven competence in new skills (20%).

All middle managers are encouraged (and almost none fail to do so) to go through a development workshop out of which will come discussion on strengths and weaknesses and an individualized training plan. There is a similar format for established supervisors who, like the managers, fully support the process. The process is repeated every three years for each manager and supervisor.

On the shopfloor there are continuous improvement teams, a shopfloor training centre including facilities for distance learning, and the knowledge that there will be no restriction on education and training for anyone (provided it promises benefits for the company as well as the individual): the only conditions are that people must take the initiative and ask for development, and that, once started, they maintain success in it.

Priority throughout the site is given to targets that derive from business needs; on regular, voluntary assessment from which training needs are identified and development plans ensue; on training and education at the initiative of the individual, for the mutual benefit of themselves and the company; and on high day rates and an internalized career system. There are no financial incentive or reward schemes (except those tied to the modular training programme): the aim is to develop people whose motivation relates to the success of the company and to work to encourage and help them together to improve its performance continually (see Figure CS12.1).

Thorn's *Manufacturing Policy Manual*, the outcome of a 1988 workshop of managers across the country, and a small human resources team, is reviewed

WHAT IS A WORLD CLASS MANUFACTURER?

The few companies in the world that can call themselves World Class Manufacturers are those which provide the customer with a total service in terms of product, design, quality, speed of delivery, low cost, reliability, and which are the first choice every time when it comes to that product range.

In order to eliminate all the factors which can destroy world class performance we need to revolutionise the way we do things at present and this booklet explains what we must do.

Make no mistake we have no choice in the matter, we must change now if we are to avoid being swallowed up by our competitors particularly as the single European Community becomes a reality from 1992 onwards. Every single person in the Thorn Lighting Systems Team has a contribution to make to this change.

– WHY DO WE NEED TO BE ONE?

Any team member who either does not understand what we must do or why we must do it or perhaps in a very small minority of cases simply does not care, is letting all the other team members in our business down.

For this weakness in our organisation we will be exploited by our competitors so that they can steal our business and our customers and in consequence our jobs.

So let's play to win the game outright, there's no place for the team that comes second in the Lighting Systems market.

If there are any points outlined in this handbook on which you'd like clarification please speak to your team leader.

Good luck.

**PETER ALMOND
DIVISIONAL HUMAN RESOURCE
MANAGER, MANUFACTURING
AND TECHNOLOGY**

Figure CS12.1 *Being a world class manufacturer; and importance of people at Thorn (by permission of Thorn Lighting Ltd, UK).*

and updated by a similar group every year. It spells out Thorn Lighting Manufacturing Division's mission, its manufacturing policy and the benefits of that policy (pride, challenge, security and resources for growth) as well as the implications of these for the factories, and a range of policies – including human resource policies (see Figure CS12.2) – which together drive the business. In each policy, the focus is on one major problem that must be overcome in order to achieve the 'world class excellence' mission; on the aim of the policy concerned; and on the policy itself, expressed in a number of specific statements against which success can ultimately be measured.

Performance indicators and benchmarks are used as business measures, relating mainly to level of inventory, customer hit rate, cost of quality, added value, labour variance, value analysis and health of the business (as measured by an internal questionnaire that examines sharing the vision, integrating the effort, sustaining a healthy community and making intelligent decisions). Measurements against all these criteria are taken every year, and

EMPLOYMENT POLICY
-ongoing commitment, from you and us

Quite simply, we're looking to build ourselves into a fully committed equally determined and motivated workforce, so that we are guaranteed to reach our goal of being number one in the world.

In order to do that, we will continue to build a genuine working partnership - with all our employees.

- an on-going commitment to recruit high quality people

That means:

- recruiting and maintaining high-quality people and rewarding them accordingly;

- applying just-in-time and short cycle manufacturing principles, where appropriate, in our factories;

- improving communications and understanding both ways whenever possible;

- offering terms and conditions that reward excellent performance and skills

- maintaining a positive relationship with the trade unions;

- ensuring that each person employed understands that he or she is working in a supplier to customer environment where our daily input <u>will</u> have an impact on the next person down the line. (In other words, the person who supplied you with his work for you to work on, is your supplier and the person whom you supply with your work, is your customer. This principle is true whether you are a manager, an engineer, a manufacturing employee or a salesman. <u>No-one must let the next in line down</u>.

- giving people responsibility for product lines and the ability to determine how to achieve the required targets.

- providing the necessary training at all levels to enable a full understanding and ultimately, the achievement of

WORLD CLASS EXCELLENCE.

Figure CS12.2 *Employment policy at Thorn (by permission of Thorn Lighting Ltd, UK).*

are compared to previous norms in the company, to external norms in comparable businesses (Cranfield Business School holds manufacturing norms which offer competitive benchmarks) and to general UK norms.

In 1992 the site won a National Training Award in recognition of major initiatives in training. More important, the company itself has improved steadily between 1988 and 1993, achieving profits even during the recession; recruiting people, not downsizing; absorbing inflation costs and, by every measure used, improving efficiency throughout the site.

In all of this, it is the goals of the business that determine the direction of HRD. Every year an HRD budget is drawn up. It is based on the training and development needed to generate the percentage profit, turnover and return on capital needed for the business to reach its targeted level of success. No one in Thorn Lighting UK doubts that the improvement achieved over the past few years has been in a major way influenced by the people policies at Spennymoor. The mission of HRD there is absolute flexibility, positioning the organization to adapt to whatever comes along and take advantage of it, turning threats into challenges, and rising to these challenges in ways that produce increased benefit to the company and its workforce.

To give employees greater ownership of the business, and to breed strategically capable managers, Thorn at Spennymoor has gone for a decentralized strategy, with its site split into six separate factories, each a business unit with a high degree of autonomy. Operations focus on internal and external customer service (the three UK manufacturing sites serve each other as well as the outside world). Currently at Spennymoor there is only a small core human resources team whose manager operates across the three UK sites. HRD is the critical function in the human resources wheel (see page 40), and there is a focus on the development of a learning organization and the integration of development into on-going functions of the business.

This kind of approach, which has broken completely from the formalized, imposed, bureaucratized systems of old to a holistic, business-led but highly developmental process, enhancing individual as well as organizational growth, typifies the concept of a learning organization. Abilities unfold as potential is revealed and nurtured. The vision, mission and strategy of the business lie at the centre of all activity, with strategy subjected to incremental changes as the workforce becomes an increasingly active part of the feedback loop referred to in Chapter 1.

Such an approach is evident in a growing number of organizations, large or small, which are in a highly competitive market, aim to be world leaders in their field, operate complex technology and seek to attract, train, retain and develop a skilled, flexible and committed workforce (see, for example, Harrison, 1992, Chapters 11 and 21). The major principles are of a strategic and integrative approach to HRD aligned to the needs of the business. They are found in many Japanese parent and subsidiary companies (Wickens, 1988; Sawers, 1986). Often, as at Thorn and at Rover Group UK (a company which officially aspires to be a learning organization and shares all the essential features of the HRD mission and strategy pursued at Thorn), the Japanese influence has been very strong and has led to new ways of working, new production processes and new manufacturing systems and philosophies.

Task

The aim of this task is to carry out some primary research to discover more about trends and strategies related to HRD in organizations.

Take an organization of your choice, in the private or the public sector, where it is apparent that there is a considerable investment in development of people, particularly in ways similar to those described in the Thorn case study.

Find out as much as you can, preferably by visiting the organization and talking with some senior and middle managers, HRD practitioners and one or two of the operational personnel, about the following:

1. What have been the main triggers to an increased commitment to HRD in the organization, and how far are these triggers similar to those already identified in research? (cf. Pettigrew *et al.*, 1988)

2. What are the stages whereby HRD becomes aligned with business strategy in the organization, and how are its outcomes assessed?

3. What specific policies and systems have been established relating to recruitment and selection, skills training, appraisal, and financial and nonfinancial rewards, and how far are these consistent with the mission and strategy for HRD?

4. Can the organization be called a 'learning organization'? If not, what more would need to be achieved to enable it to reach and maintain that status?

Appendix A

Industrial disputes

The rate of strike activity in the United Kingdom is not high, either in absolute terms or when compared internationally with other industrialized nations. Because of the low level of action in the 1990s it has not been discussed as a separate issue in the text. However, the reader might find it helpful to read the brief analysis set out here.

Figure A.1 sets out the recent picture for the United Kingdom. It can be seen from the table that the statistics for industrial disputes, while low, have slightly different trends. The incidence of stoppages shows a clear downward trend over the years, particularly of late, while the other two series of data oscillate more. This trend difference can largely be explained by an analysis of the types of stoppage. One traditional distinction is between official and unofficial strikes. The former type is sanctioned (being either authorized or endorsed) by the union's rule-making body or bodies. In the latter situation the action tends to be more spontaneous, often being what Hyman has referred to as a 'perishable dispute' (Hyman, 1989). These unofficial strikes used to be considered a peculiarly British issue when compared with other countries, giving rise in the 1960s to a belief in some quarters that the British economy was generally strike prone and suffered particularly from a type of industrial anarchy in terms of unofficial and unconstitutional action.

Since the late 1970s the official dispute has featured more prominently than in previous eras. With disputes such as these there is a likelihood that the figure for days lost will be of a higher magnitude as the disputes tend to be of a more protracted nature and involve more workers than do unofficial stoppages. It should also be noted that the statistics on stoppages include 'lockouts' (where management decide to close a plant to press their point in a dispute) though these are not particularly numerous in any year.

Currently, Britain is in the middle order of a 'disputes league table'

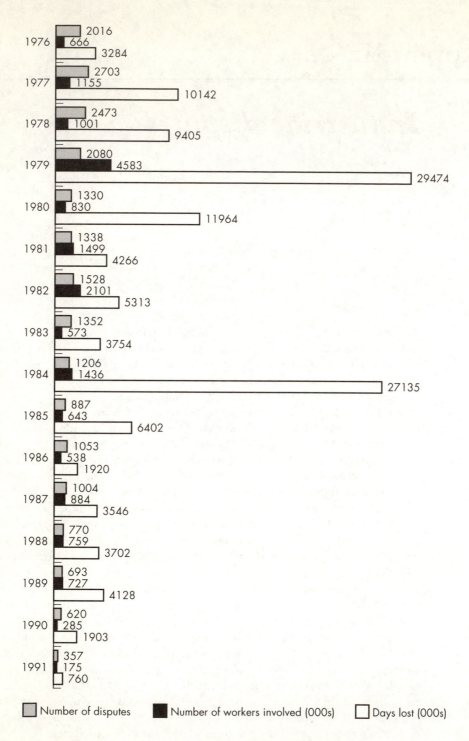

Figure A.1 *Industrial disputes in the United Kingdom (1976-91).*

according to data published by the OECD in 1989. Between 1978 and 1988 the United Kingdom was somewhat above mid-table with Spain, Italy, Greece, Canada and Ireland losing most days per employee. Countries with a low dispute return were Austria, Japan, Holland and what was West Germany.

Reference

Hyman R. (1972). *Strikes*. London: Fontana.

References and useful reading

Preface

Blyton P. and Turnbull P. (1992). *Reassessing Human Resource Management*.
London: Sage

Guest D.E. (1989). Personnel management and HRM: can you tell the
difference? *Personnel Management*, **21**(1) 48–51

Guest D.E. (1990). Human resource management and the American dream.
Journal of Management Studies, **27** (4 July), 337–97

Legge K. (1989). Human resource management: a critical analysis. In *New
Perspectives on Human Resource Management* (Storey J., ed.), pp. 19–40. London:
Routledge

Mackay L. and Torrington D. (1986). *The Changing Nature of Personnel Management*.
London: Institute of Personnel Management

Salaman G., ed. (1992). *Human Resource Strategies*. London: Sage

Sisson K., ed. (1989a). *Personnel Management in Britain*. Oxford: Blackwell

Sisson K. (1989b). Personnel management in transition? In *Personnel Management
in Britain* (Sisson K., ed.), pp. 22–52. Oxford: Blackwell

Storey J., ed. (1989). *New Perspectives on Human Resource Management*. London:
Routledge

Storey J. (1992). *Developments in the Management of Human Resources*. Oxford:
Blackwell

Storey J. and Sisson K. (1989). Limits to transformation: human resource
management in the British context. *Industrial Relations Journal*, **20**, 60–5

Towers B., ed. (1992). *A Handbook of Human Resource Management*. Oxford:
Blackwell

Chapter 1

Braybrooke D. and Lindblom C. (1963). *A Strategy of Decision*. New York: Free Press

Chakravarthy B.S. and Doz Y. (1992). Strategy process research: focusing on corporate self-renewal. *Strategic Management Journal*, **13**, 5–14

Child J. (1972). Organizational structure, environment and performance: the role of strategic choice. *Sociology*, **6**(1), 1–22

Clarke C. and Brennan K. (1988). Allied forces. *Management Today*, November, 128–31

Dror R. (1964). Muddling through – science or inertia? *Public Administration Review*, **24**, 153–7

Fine C.H. (1983). *Quality control and learning in productive systems*. Doctoral dissertation, Stanford University, Graduate School of Business

Giles W.D. (1991). Making strategy work. *Long Range Planning*, **24**(5), 75–91

Goold M. and Campbell A. (1991). *Strategies and Styles: The Role of the Centre in Managing Diversified Corporations*. Oxford: Blackwell

Guest D.E. (1992). Right enough to be dangerously wrong: an analysis of the *In Search of Exellence* phenomenon. In *Human Resource Strategies* (Salaman G., ed.), pp. 5–19. London: Sage

Hall R. (1992). The strategic analysis of intangible resources. *Strategic Management Journal*, **13**, 135–44

Hamel G. and Prahalad C.K. (1989). Strategic intent. *Harvard Business Review*, May–June, 63–76

Hendry C. and Pettigrew A. (1992). Patterns of strategic change in the development of human resource management. *British Journal of Management*, **3**(3), 137–56

Hill C.W.L (1988). Differentiation versus low cost or differentiation and low cost: a contingency framework. *Academy of Management Review*, **13**(3), 401–12

Johnson G. and Scholes K. (1989). *Exploring Corporate Strategy*. Hemel Hempstead: Prentice-Hall

Lindblom C. (1959). The science of muddling through. *Public Administration Review*, **19**, 79–99

Lindblom C. (1969). The science of 'muddling through'. In *Readings on Modern Organizations* (Etzioni A., ed.). Englewood Cliffs, NJ: Prentice-Hall

Miller S. (1990). *Successfully implementing strategic decisions*. PhD Thesis, University of Bradford, England

Mintzberg H. (1987). Crafting strategy. *Harvard Business Review*, July–August, 66–75

Mintzberg H. (1990a). The design school: reconsidering the basic premises of strategic management. *Strategic Management Journal*, **11**, 171–95

Mintzberg H. (1990b). Strategy formation: schools of thought. In *Perspectives on Strategic Management* (Fredrickson J.W., ed.), pp. 105–235. New York: Harper Business

Mintzberg H. (1991). Learning 1, Planning 0. Reply to Igor Ansoff. *Strategic Management Journal*, **12**, 463–6

Mintzberg H. and Waters J.A. (1985). Of strategies, deliberate and emergent. *Strategic Management Journal*, **6**, 257–72

Moore J.I. (1992). *Writers on Strategy and Strategic Management*. London: Penguin

Murray A.I. (1988). A contingency view of Porter's 'generic strategies'. *Academy of Management Review*, **13**(3), 390–400

Nelson R. (1992). Recent writings on competitiveness: boxing the compass. *California Management Review*, Winter, 127–37

Peters T. (1989). *Thriving on Chaos*. London: Macmillan

Peters T. and Waterman Jr R.H. (1982). *In Search of Excellence*. New York: Harper & Row

Pettigrew A. (1973). *The Politics of Organizational Decision-making*. London: Tavistock

Pettigrew A. (1990). Is corporate culture manageable? In *Managing Organizations* (Wilson D.C. and Rosenfeld R.H., eds.), pp. 266–72. London: McGraw-Hill

Phillips L.W., Chang D.R. and Buzzell R.D. (1983). Product quality, cost position and business performances: a test of some key hypotheses. *Journal of Marketing*, **47**(2), 26–43

Porter M.E. (1980). *Competitive Strategy*. New York: Free Press

Porter M.E. (1985). *Competitive Advantage*. New York: Free Press

Porter M.E. (1990). The competitive advantage of nations. *Harvard Business Review*, March–April, 73–93

Prahalad C.K. and Hamel G. (1990). The core competence of the corporation. *Harvard Business Review*, May–June, 79–91

Purcell, J. (1992). The impact of corporate strategy on human resource management. In *Human Resource Strategies* (Salaman G., ed.), pp. 59–81. London: Sage

Quinn J.B. (1978). Strategic change: logical incrementalism. *Sloan Management Review*, Fall, 7–21

Quinn J.B. (1980). *Strategies for Change: Logical Incrementalism*. Homewood, Illinois: Irwin

Ring P.S. and Van de Ven (1992). Structuring cooperative relationships between organizations. *Strategic Management Journal*, **13**, 483–98

Simon H.A. (1957). *Administrative Behaviour*. New York: Free Press

Stalk G., Evans P. and Shulman L.E. (1992). Competing on capabilities: the new rules of corporate strategy. *Harvard Business Review*, March–April, 57–69

Storey J. (1992). *Developments in the Management of Human Resources*. Oxford: Blackwell

Thompson Jr A.A. and Strickland A.J., III (1992). *Strategic Management: Concepts and Cases*. Boston, MA: Irwin

Wilson D.C. (1992). *A Strategy of Change*. London: Routledge

Wilson D.C. and Rosenfeld R.H. (1990). *Managing Organizations*. Maidenhead: McGraw-Hill

Chapter 2

Ackroyd S., Burrell G., Hughes M. and Whitaker A. (1988). The Japanisation of British industry? *Industrial Relations Journal*, **19**(1), 11–23

Ahlstrand B. and Purcell J. (1988). Employee relations strategy in the multi-divisional company. *Personnel Review*, **17**(3), 3–11

Allen K.R. (1991). Personnel management on the line: how middle managers view the function. *Personnel Management*, **23**(6), 40–3

Armstrong M. (1987). Human resource management: a case of the emperor's new clothes? *Personnel Management*, **19**(8), 30–5

Bell D. (1989). Why manpower planning is back in vogue. *Personnel Management*, **21**(7), 40–3

Blackhurst C. (1993). Branson to demand 'millions' from BA. *The Independent on Sunday (Business Section)*, 24 January, p. 1

Blyton P. and Turnbull P., eds. (1992). *Reassessing Human Resource Management*. London: Sage

Brewster C. and Tyson S. (1991). *International Comparisons in Human Resource Management*. London: Pitman

Briggs P. (1991). Organisational commitment: the key to Japanese success? In *International Comparisons in Human Resource Management* (Brewster C. and Tyson S., eds.), pp. 33–43. London: Pitman

British Institute of Management and Aston University (1989). *The Responsive Organization*. London: BIM

Dore R. (1987). *Taking Japan Seriously: A Confucian Perspective on Leading Economic Issues*. London: Athlone Press

Faith N. (1992). Brought low by arrogance. *Independent on Sunday*, 26 January, p. 11

Fombrun C., Tichy N.M. and Devanna M.A. (1984). *Strategic Human Resource Management*. Chichester: Wiley

Fowler A. (1987). When chief executives discover HRM. *Personnel Management*, **19**(1), 3

Fox S., Tanton M. and McLeay S. (1992). *Human Resource Management, Corporate Strategy and Financial Performance. Executive summary of research project undertaken for HM Government's Economic and Social Research Council's 'Competitiveness and Regeneration of British Industry' Initiative*. Lancaster University and University of Wales

Gleave S. and Oliver N. (1990). Human resource management in Japanese manufacturing companies in the UK: 5 case studies. *Journal of General Management*, **16**(1), Autumn, 54–68

Gluck F.W. (1985). In *Handbook of Strategic Planning* (Gardner J.R., Rachlin R. and Allen Sweeny H.W., eds.). New York: Wiley

Gouldner A. (1965). *Wildcat Strike*. New York: Harper

Gribben R. (1991). Rover plans 30 pc cut in drive to match Japanese. *Daily Telegraph*, 6 November

Guest D.E. (1989a). Personnel and HRM: can you tell the difference? *Personnel Management*, **21**(1), 48–51

Guest D.E. (1989b). Human resource management: its implications for industrial relations and trade unions. In *New Perspectives on Human Resource Management* (Storey J., ed.), pp. 41–55. London: Routledge

Guest D.E. (1990). Human resource management and the American dream. *Journal of Management Studies*, **27** (4 July), 337–97

Guest D.E. (1992). Right enough to be dangerously wrong: an analysis of the *In Search of Excellence* phenomenon. In *Human Resource Strategies* (Salaman G. *et al.*, eds.), Ch. 1. London: Sage

Harrison R. (1992). *Employee Development*. London: Institute of Personnel Management

Hendry C., Pettigrew A.M. and Sparrow P. (1988). Changing patterns of human resource management. *Personnel Management*, **20**(11), 37–41

Herriot P. and Fletcher C. (1990), Candidate-friendly selection for the 1990s. *Personnel Management*, **22**(2), 33–5

Institute of Personnel Management (1980). *Official Definition of 'Personnel Management'*. London: IPM

Kanter R.M. (1983). *The Change Masters*. London: Allen and Unwin

Koike K. (1988). *Understanding Industrial Relations in Modern Japan*. London: Macmillan

Leadbetter C. (1993a). Tough middle age for lifetime jobs. *Financial Times*, 13 January

Leadbetter C. (1993b). Manufacturers' profits 'spurred by cheap finance'. *Financial Times*, 1 February

Legge K. (1977). Contingency theory and the personnel function. *Personnel Management*, **9**(8), 22–5

Legge K. (1989). Human resource management: a critical analysis. In *New Perspectives on Human Resource Management* (Storey J., ed.), pp. 19–40. London: Routledge

Mackay L. and Torrington D. (1986). *The Changing Nature of Personnel Management*. London: Institute of Personnel Management

Maguire K. (1991). Rover offers jobs for life in effort to counter Japanese. *Daily Telegraph*, 18 September

Malloch H. (1990). Strategic management and the decision to subcontract. In *Flexibility in the 1990s* (Blyton P. and Morris J., eds.), Ch. 10. Berlin: Walter de Gruyter

Malloch H. (1992). Human resource strategy in Hutton Borough Council. In *Case Studies in Personnel: Tutors' Manual* (Winstanley D. and Woodall J., eds.), pp. 133–5. London: Institute of Personnel Management

Marlow S. and Patton D. (1992). Employment relations, human resource management strategies and the smaller firm. In *Proc. United Kingdom Enterprise Management Research Ass. 15th National Small Firms Policy and Research Conf. Small Firms in a changing market place – local, national and European issues*, 25–6 November. Southampton: UKEMRA

McKinley A. and Starkey K. (1992). Competitive strategies and organizational change. In *Human Resource Strategies* (Salaman G. *et al.*, eds.), Ch. 8. London: Sage

Meek V.L. (1992). Organizational culture: origins and weaknesses. In *Human Resource Strategies* (Salaman G. *et al.*, eds.), Ch. 12. London: Sage

Miller P. (1987). Strategic industrial relations and human resource management – distinction, definition and recognition. *Journal of Management Studies*, **24**, 347–61

Mumford J. and Buley T. (1988). Rewarding behavioural skills as part of performance. *Personnel Management*, **20**(12), 33–7

Personnel Management (1989). Focus shifts to line managers in BA human resource shake-up. *Personnel Management*, **21**(3), 5

Peters T. and Waterman R. (1982). *In Search of Excellence*. New York: Harper & Row

PM Plus (1993). Chief concern of HR directors is communications. *PM Plus*, **4**(1), 7

Purcell J. (1989). The impact of corporate strategy on human resource management. In *New Perspectives on Human Resource Management* (Storey J., ed.), pp. 67–91. London: Routledge

Salaman G., Cameron S., Hamblin H., Iles P., Mabey C. and Thompson K. (1992). *Human Resource Strategies*. London: Sage

Sawers D. (1986). The experience of German and Japanese subsidiaries in Britain. *Journal of General Management*, **12**(1), Autumn, 5–21

Schein E.H. (1992). Coming to a new awareness of organizational culture. In *Human Resource Strategies* (Salaman G. *et al.*, eds.), Ch. 14. London: Sage

Silverman D. (1970). *The Theory of Organisations: A Sociological Framework*. London: Heinemann

Sparrow P. and Pettigrew A.M. (1988). Contrasting HRM responses in the changing world of computing. *Personnel Management*, **20**(2), 40–5

Storey J., ed. (1989). *New Perspectives on Human Resource Management*. London: Routledge

Storey J. (1992). *Developments in the Management of Human Resources*. Oxford: Blackwell

Thomas M. (1985). In search of culture: holy grail or gravy train. *Personnel Management*, **17**(9), 24–7

Towers B. (1992). *A Handbook of Human Resource Management*. Oxford: Blackwell

Chapter 3

Allen K.R. (1991). Personnel management on the line: how middle managers view the function. *Personnel Managemet*. **23**(6), 40–3

Arkin A. (1991). Still looking for a strategic role. *Personnel Management Plus*, **2**(6), 18–19

Armstrong M. (1989a). *Personnel and the Bottom Line*. London: Institute of Personnel Management

Armstrong M. (1989b). Personnel directors' view from the bridge. *Personnel Management*, **21**(10), 53–5

Armstrong M. (1989c). The personnel manager as entrepreneur. *Proc. Institute of Personnel Management National Conference*, Harrogate, UK. October 1989

Brewster C. and Smith C. (1990). Corporate strategy: a no-go area for personnel? *Personnel Management*, **22**(7), 36–40

Brewster C. and Tyson S. (1991). *International Comparisons in Human Resource Management*. London: Pitman

Burns T. and Stalker G.N. (1966). *The Management of Innovation*. London: Tavistock

Coulson-Thomas C. (1991). What the personnel director can bring to the boardroom table. *Personnel Management*, **23**(10), 36–9

Guest D. (1991). Personnel management: the end of orthodoxy? *British Journal of Industrial Relations*, **29**(2 June), 149–75

Institute of Personnel Management (1980). *Official Definition of 'Personnel Management'*. London: IPM

Keenan T. (1991). Graduate recruitment à la française. *Personnel Management*, **23**(12), 34–7

Keenoy T. (1990). HRM: a case of the wolf in sheep's clothing? *Personnel Review*, **19**(2), 3–9

Korn Ferry International and Columbia University Graduate School of Business (1989). Reinventing the CEO. *21st Century Report: A Journal on Critical Issues affecting Senior Executives and the Board of Directors*, **1**(1), 61–6. London: KFI

Legge K. (1977). Contingency theory and the personnel function. *Personnel Management*, **9**(8), 22–5

Legge K. (1988). Personnel management in recession and recovery. *Personnel Review*, **17**(2), 1–72

Legge K. (1989). Human resource management: a critical analysis. In *New Perspectives on Human Resource Management* (Storey J., ed.), pp. 19–40. London: Routledge

Mackay L. and Torrington D. (1986). *The Changing Nature of Personnel Management*. London: Institute of Personnel Management

Miller P. (1987). Strategic industrial relations and human resource management – distinction, definition and recognition. *Journal of Management Studies*, **24**, 347–61

Neale R. and Mindel R. (1992). Rigging up multicultural teamworking. *Personnel Management*, **24**(1), 36–9

Personnel Management (1989). US human resource managers told to throw away the rule book. *Personnel Management*, **21**(9), 11

Prokopenko J. (1992). *Human Resources Management in Economies in Transition: The East European Case*. Geneva: International Labour Office (Entrepreneurship and Management Development Branch)

Reitsperger W.D. (1986). Japanese management – coping with British industrial relations. *Journal of Management Studies*, **23** (1 January), 72–87

Riley K. and Sloman M. (1991). Milestones for the personnel department. *Personnel Management*, **23**(8), 34–7

Scullion H. (1992). Attracting management globetrotters. *Personnel Management*, **24**(1), 28–32

Sisson K., ed. (1989). *Personnel Management in Britain*. Oxford: Blackwell

Storey J., ed. (1989). *New Perspectives on Human Resource Management*. London: Routledge

Storey J. (1992). *Developments in the Management of Human Resources*. Oxford: Blackwell

Storey J. and Fenwick N. (1990). The changing face of employment management in local government. *Journal of General Management*, **16**(1), Autumn, 14–30

Storey J. and Sisson K. (1989). Limits to transformation: human resource management in the British context. *Industrial Relations Journal*, **20**, 60–5

Thurley K. (1981). Personnel management in the UK – a case for urgent treatment? *Personnel Management*, **13**(8), 24–9

Tyson S. and Fell A. (1986). *Evaluating the Personnel Function*. London: Hutchinson

Williams R. (1989). Chairman's Summary. In *Proc. The Economist Conference: 1992 and beyond: Practical Approaches to the Human Resource and Management Development Issues*. Brussels, Belgium, 2–3 March 1989

Chapter 4

Ackers P. and Black J. (1991). Paternalist capitalism: an organisation culture in transition. In *Work and the Enterprise Culture* (Cross M. and Payne G., eds.), pp. 30–56. Falmer: BSA

Ackers P., Marchington M., Wilkinson A. and Goodman J. (1992). The use of cycles? Explaining employee involvement in the 1990s. *Industrial Relations Journal*, **23**, 268–83

Brewster C., Gill C. and Richbell S. (1983). Industrial relations policy: a framework for analysis. In *Industrial Relations and Management Strategy* (Thurley K. and Wood S., eds.), pp. 62–72. Cambridge University Press

Buchanan D. (1986). Management objectives in technical change. In *Managing the Labour Process* (Knights D. and Wilmott H., eds.). Aldershot: Gower

Buchanan D. and Besant J. (1985). Failure, uncertainty and control: the role of operators in a computer integrated production system. *Journal of Management Studies*, **22**(3), 292–308

Cressey P., Eldridge J. and MacInnes J. (1985). *Just Managing: Authority and Democracy in Industry*. Milton Keynes: Open University Press

Dawson S. (1992). *Analyzing Organisations*, 2nd edn. London: Macmillan

Fox A. (1974). *Beyond Contract: Work, Power and Trust Relations*. London: Faber

Gearey J. (1992). Autonomous work groups and worker participation. In *Fourth International Workshop on Employee Involvement*, Brussels, 23–4 March

Guest D. and Dewe P. (1991). Company or trade union: which wins workers' allegiance? – a study of commitment in the UK electronics industry. *British Journal of Industrial Relations*, **29**, 75–96

Kelly J. and Kelly C. (1991). Them and us: a social psychological analysis of the new industrial relations. *British Journal of Industrial Relations*, **29**, 25–48

Marchington M. and Parker P. (1988). Japanization: a lack of chemical reaction. *Industrial Relations Journal*, **9**(4), 272–85

Marchington M. and Parker P. (1990). *Changing Patterns of Employee Relations*. Hemel Hempstead: Wheatsheaf

Marchington M., Goodman J., Wilkinson A. and Ackers P. (1992). *New Developments in Employee Involvement*. Employment Department Research Paper Series no. 2. London: HMSO

Metcalf D. (1989). Water notes dry up: the impact of the Donovan Reform proposals and Thatcherism at work on labour productivity in British manufacturing industry. *British Journal of Industrial Relations*, **27**(1), 1–31

Oakland J. (1989). *Total Quality Management*. London: Heinemann

Pettigrew A. (1985). *The Awakening Giant: Continuity and Change in ICI*. Oxford: Blackwell

Pettigrew A. and Whipp R. (1991). *Managing Change for Competitive Success*. Oxford: Blackwell

Ramsay H. (1977) Cycles of control: worker participation in sociological and historical perspective. *Sociology*, **2**, 481–506

Roberts I. and Wilkinson A. (1991). Participation and purpose – boilermakers to bankers. *Critical Perspectives on Accounting*, **2**(4), 385–413

Schonberger R. (1990), *Building a Chain of Customers*. New York: Free Press

Smith C., Child J. and Rowlinson M. (1991). *Reshaping Work: The Cadbury Experience*. Cambridge University Press

Storey J. (1992). *Developments in the Management of Human Resources*. Oxford: Blackwell

Wilkinson A., Marchington M., Goodman J. and Ackers P. (1992). Total quality management and employee involvement. *Human Resource Management Journal*, **2**(4), 1–20

Useful reading

Boxall P. (1992). Strategic human resource management: beginnings of a new theoretical sophistication? *Human Resource Management Journal*, **2**(3), 60–79

Guest D. (1987). Human resource management and industrial relations. *Journal of Management Studies*, **24**(5), 503–21

Hendry C. and Pettigrew A. (1992). Patterns of strategic change in the development of human resource management. *British Journal of Management*, **3**, 137–56

Hendry C., Pettigrew A. and Sparrow P. (1988). Changing patterns of human resource management. *Personnel Management*, **20**(11), 37–41

McKinlay A. and Starkey K. (1992). Competitive strategies and organisational change. In *Human Resource Strategies* (Salaman G., ed.), pp. 107–23. London: Sage

Miller P. (1987). Strategic industrial relations and human resource management – distinction, definition and recognition. *Journal of Management Studies*, **24**(4), 347–61

Purcell J. (1989). The impact of corporate strategy on human resource management. In *New Perspectives on Human Resource Management* (Storey J., ed.), pp. 59–81. London: Routledge

Schuler R.S. and Jackson S.E. (1989). Determinants of human resource management priorities and implications for industrial relations. *Journal of Management*, **15**(1), 89–99

Snape E., Redman T. and Wilkinson A. (1993). Human resource management in building societies: making the transformation? *Human Resource Management Journal*, **3**(3), 43–60

Storey J. and Sisson K. (1990). Limits to transformation: human resource management in the British context. *Industrial Relations Journal*, **21**(1), 60–5

Chapter 5

Anheier H. and Seibel W., eds. (1990). *The Third Sector*. Berlin: De Gruyter

Arkin A. (1991). Personnel policies in professional practices. *Personnel Management*, **23**(5), 32–8

Armstrong M. (1989). *Personnel and the Bottom Line*. London: Institute of Personnel Management

Arthur M. and Hendry F. (1990). HRM and the emergent strategy of small to medium sized business. *International Journal of Human Resource Management*, **1**(3), 233–50

Ball M. (1988). *Rebuilding Construction*. London: Routledge

Belussi F. (1989). Benetton. In *Technology Strategy and the Firm* (Dodgson M., ed.), pp. 116–33. Harlow: Longman

Boswell J. (1973). *The Rise and Decline of Small Firms*. London: Allen & Unwin

Bosworth D. (1989). Barriers to growth: the labour market. In *Barriers to Growth in Small Firms* (Barber J. *et al.*, eds.), pp. 58–80. London: Routledge

Brown C., Hamilton J. and Medoff J. (1990). *Employers: Large and Small*. Harvard University Press

Butler R. and Wilson D. (1990). *Managing Voluntary and Non-profit Organizations*. London: Routledge

Chalmers N. (1989). *Industrial Relations in Japan*. London: Routledge

Christensen R. (1953). *Management Succession in Small and Growing Enterprises*. Harvard University Press

Collins O. and Moore D. (1964). *The Enterprising Man*. Michigan University

Collins O. and Moore D. (1970). *The Organization Makers*. New York: Meredith

Commission of the European Communities (1988). *Labour Law and Industrial Relations in Small and Medium Sized Enterprises in the EEC Countries*. Luxembourg: Office for Official Publications

Curran J. (1987). Employment and employment relations in the small enterprise: a review. *London Business School Small Business Bibliography*, pp. 13–25

Curran J. and Blackburn R., eds. (1991). *Paths of Enterprise: The Future of the Small Business*. London: Routledge

Curran J. and Stanworth J. (1989). Education and training for enterprise. *International Small Business Journal*, **7**(2), 11–22

Curtis D. (1983). *Strategic Planning for Smaller Businesses*. MA: Lexington Books

Dailey R. and Reuschling T. (1979). Human resource management in the family owned company. *Journal of General Management*, **5**, 49–57

Department of Employment (1989). *Small Firms in Britain*. London: HMSO

De Vries M. (1980). *Organizational Paradoxes*. London: Tavistock

De Vries M. (1985). The dark side of entrepreneurship. *Harvard Business Review*, **23**(6), 160–7

De Vries M. and Miller D. (1984). *The Neurotic Organization*. San Francisco: Jossey Bass

De Vries M. and Miller D. (1987). *Unstable at the Top*. New York: NAL Books

Dyer W. (1986). *Cultural Change in Family Firms*. San Francisco: Jossey Bass

Flamholtz E. (1990). *Growing Pains*. San Francisco: Jossey Bass

Gibb A. (1990). Towards ensuring the design of effective training programmes for small and medium enterprises in Europe. In *Consulting in Innovation* (Allesch J., ed.), pp. 75–90. Amsterdam: Elsevier

Gill J. (1985). *Factors affecting the Survival and Growth of the Smaller Company*. Aldershot: Gower

Goss D. (1991). *Small Business and Society*. London: Routledge

Gray H. (1987). Management consultancy and training for professional business partnerships. *Journal of European Industrial Training*, **11**(1), 17–22

Hakim C. (1989). Identifying fast growth small firms. *Employment Gazette*, January, 29–41

Handy C. (1988). *Understanding Voluntary Organizations*. Harmondsworth: Penguin

Harrigan K. (1988). *Managing Maturing Businesses*. MA: Lexington Books

Harvey-Jones, J. (1990). *Troubleshooter*. London: BBC Books

Hendry C. (1991). Corporate strategy and training. In *Training and Competitiveness* (Stevens J. and Mackay R., eds.), pp. 79–110. London: NEDO

HMSO (1971) *Committee of Inquiry on Small Firms*. Bolton Report, Cmnd 4811. London: HMSO

Katz R., ed. (1988). *Managing Professionals in Innovative Organizations*. MA: Ballinger

Kelly A. (1991). The enterprise culture and the welfare state. In *Deciphering the Enterprise Culture* (Burrows R., ed.), pp. 126–51. London: Routledge

Kirby D. (1990). Management education and small business development. *Journal of Small Business Management*, **28**(4), 78–87

Landry R., Morley D., Southwood R. and Wright P. (1985). *What a Way to Run a Railroad*. London: Comedia

LAURA (1990). *Community Business*. London: HMSO

Leach P. (1991). *The Stoy Hayward Guide to the Family Business*. London: Kogan Page

Levinson H. (1971). Conflicts that plague family businesses. *Harvard Business Review*, **9**(2), 90–8

Levinson H. (1983). Consulting with family businesses. *Organizational Dynamics*, Summer, 71–80

Miller D. (1990). *The Icarus Paradox*. New York: Harper

Miller D. and Rice A. (1967). *Systems of Organization*. London: Tavistock

Mintzberg H. (1989). *Mintzberg on Management*. New York: Harper

Mintzberg H. (1990a). Strategy formation: schools of thought. In *Perspectives on Strategic Management* (Frederickson J., ed.), pp. 105–237. New York: Harper

Mintzberg H. (1990b). The design school. *Strategic Management Journal*, **11**, 171–95

Morgan G. (1989). *Creative Organization Theory*. London: Sage

Rainnie A. (1989). *Industrial Relations in Small Firms*. London: Routledge

Redding G. (1986). Developing managers without 'management development': the overseas Chinese solution. *Management Education and Development*, **17**(3), 271–81

Redding G. (1990). *The Spirit of Chinese Capitalism*. Berlin: De Gruyter

Ritchie J. (1986a). Predictable casualties: the sacrificial role of the older small firm. In *Small Firms Growth and Development* (Lewis J. *et al.*, eds.), pp. 147–64. Aldershot: Gower

Ritchie J. (1986b). New social entrepreneur and community business development. In *Proc. Annual Small Business Policy and Research Conference*. Scottish Enterprise Foundation

Ritchie J. (1991). Enterprise Cultures: a frame analysis. In R. Burrows, ed., Deciphering the Enterprise Culture. London: Routledge, pp. 17–34

Ritchie J. and Gibb A. (1982). Understanding the process of starting small businesses. *European Small Business Journal*, **1**(1), 1–20

Scase R. and Goffee R. (1987) *The Real World of the Small Business Owner*, 2nd edn. London: Croom Helm

Scott M. and Ritchie J. (1984). Rethinking entrepreneurial failure. In *Success and Failure in Small Businesses* (Lewis J. *et al.*, eds.), pp. 29–56. Aldershot: Gower

Scott M., Roberts I., Sawbridge D. and Holroyd G. (1989). *Management and Industrial Relations in Small Firms*. Department of Employment Research Paper no. 70. London: HMSO

Smith C. (1990). Using consultants to manage change. *Employment Gazette*, January, 29–41

Stanworth J. and Curran J. (1973). *Management Motivation and the Smaller Business*. London: Gower

Storey D. (1987). *The Performance of Small Firms*. London: Croom Helm

Storey D. and Johnson S. (1987). *Job Generation and Labour Market Change*. London: Macmillan

Storey D. and Johnson S. (1990). A review of small business employment databases in the United Kingdom. *Small Business Economics*, 2, 279–99

Trist E., Higgin G., Murray H. and Pollock H. (1963). *Organizational Choice*. London: Tavistock

Whitley R. (1991). The social construction of business systems in East Asia. *Organization Studies*, **12**(1), 1–28

Chapter 6

ACAS (1988). *Developments in Payment Systems*. Occasional Paper 45

ACAS (1989). *Annual Report 1989*

Armstrong M. (1987). Human resource management: a case of the emperor's new clothes? *Personnel Management*, **19**(8), 30–5

Atkinson J. (1984). Manpower strategies for flexible organisations. *Personnel Management*, **16**(8), 28–31

Bean R. (1989). *Comparative Industrial Relations*. London: Routledge

Blain A.N. and Gennard J. (1970). Industrial relations theory – a critical review. *British Journal of Industrial Relations*, **VIII**(2), 389–407

Blyton P. and Turnbull P., eds. (1992). *Reassessing Human Resource Management (Part III)*. London: Sage

Brewster C. (1989). Managing industrial relations. In *A Handbook Of Industrial Relations Practice* (Towers B., ed.), pp. 81–94. London: Kogan Page

Brown W. (1981). *The Changing Contours of British Industrial Relations*. Oxford: Blackwell

Brown W. (1989). Managing remuneration. In *Personnel Management in Britain* (Sisson K., ed.), pp. 249–70. Oxford: Blackwell

Claydon T. (1989). Union de-recognition in Britain in the 1980s. *British Journal of Industrial Relations*, **XXVII**(2), 214–24

Donovan, Lord (1968). *Report of the Royal Commission on Trade Unions and Employers' Associations*. London: HMSO

Dunlop J. (1958). *Industrial Relations Systems*. New York: Holt

Flanders A., ed. (1969). *Collective Bargaining*. Harmondsworth: Penguin

Fox A. (1969). Management's frames of reference. In *Collective Bargaining* (Flanders A., ed.), pp. 390–409. Harmondsworth: Penguin

Fox A. (1973). Industrial relations: a social critique of pluralist ideology. In *Man and Organisation* (Child J., ed.), pp. 185–234. London: Allen and Unwin

Guest D. (1987). Human resource management and industrial relations. *Journal of Management Studies*, **24**(September), 503–22

Industrial Relations Review and Report (1989a) 434. *Merit Pay – The Growth Industry*. (Pay and Benefits Bulletin 226.) 21.2.89, p. 2. London: Industrial Relations Services

Industrial Relations Review and Report (1989b) 437. *Flexibility Moves at Colgate and Castrol*, 4.4.89, p. 15. London: Industrial Relations Services

Industrial Relations Review and Report (1989c) 499. *BT(UK)'s Employee Communications Drive*, 10.10.89, pp. 11–14. London: Industrial Relations Services.

Industrial Relations Review and Report (1989d) 450. *Suggestion Schemes: Exploiting Employees' Ideas*. 24.10.89, pp. 6–8. London: Industrial Relations Service.

Kochan T.A., Katz H.C. and McKersie R.B. (1986). *The Transformation of American Industrial Relations*. New York: Basic Books

Marchington M. (1989). Joint consultation in practice. In *Personnel Management in Britain* (Sisson K., ed.), pp. 378–99. Oxford: Blackwell

Margerison C.J. (1969). What do we mean by industrial relations? A behavioural science approach. *British Journal of Industrial Relations*, **VII**(2), 273–86

Palmer G. (1987). *British Industrial Relations*. London: Allen and Unwin

Poole M. (1986). *Industrial Relations*. London: Routledge and Kegan Paul

Purcell J. and Sisson K. (1983). Strategies and practice in the management of industrial relations. In *Industrial Relations in Britain* (Bain G.S., ed.), pp. 95–120. Oxford: Blackwell

Rainnie A. (1989). *Industrial Relations in Small Firms; Small isn't Beautiful*. London: Routledge

Rogaly J. (1977). *Grunwick*. Harmondsworth: Penguin

Sisson K. (1989). Personnel management in perspective. In *Personnel Management in Britain* (Sisson K., ed.), pp. 3–21. Oxford: Blackwell

Walton R. and McKersie R.B. (1965). *A Behavioral Theory of Labor Negotiation*. New York: McGraw-Hill

Webb S. and Webb B. (1920). *History of Trade Unionism*. London: Longman

Wickens P. (1987). *The Road to Nissan: Flexibility, Quality, Teamwork*. London: Macmillan

Useful reading

ACAS (1991) *Annual Report 1991*

Beaumont P. (1990). *Change in Industrial Relations*. London: Routledge

Guest D. (1991). Personnel management: the end of orthodoxy. *British Journal of Industrial Relations*, **29** (2 June), 149–75

Storey J. and Sisson K. (1990). Limits to transformation: human resource management in the British context. *Industrial Relations Journal*, **21**(1), 60–5

In addition, readers will find very useful sources of material in the series of journals published by Incomes Data Services and Industrial Relations Services.

Chapter 7

Arnott M. (1987). Effective employee communication. In *Effective Corporate Relations* (Hart N.A., ed.), Ch. 5. London: McGraw-Hill

Buchanan D.A. (1982). High performance: new boundaries of acceptability in worker control. In *Job Control and Worker Health* (Sauter S.L., Hurrell Jr J.J. and Cooper C., eds.), pp. 255–73. Chichester: Wiley

Burns T. and Stalker G.M. (1961). *The Management of Innovation*. London: Tavistock

Clegg S.R. (1990). *Modern Organisations*. London: Sage

Drucker P.F. (1988). The coming of the new organization. *Harvard Business Review*, Jan–Feb, 45–53

Drucker P.F. (1989). *The New Realities*. Oxford: Heinemann

Harrison R. (1992). *Employee Development*. London: Institute of Personnel Management

Majaro S. (1988). *The Creative Gap: Managing Ideas for Profit*. London: Longman

Miller P. (1989). Strategic HRM: what it is and what it isn't. *Personnel Management*, **21**(2), 46–51

Purcell J. (1989). The impact of corporate strategy on human resource management. In *New Perspectives on Human Resource Management* (Storey J., ed.), pp. 67–91. London: Routledge

Thomson K.M. (1990). *The Employee Revolution*. London: Pitman
Toffler A. (1985). *The Adaptive Corporation*. London: McGraw-Hill

Useful reading

ACAS/LBS (1986). *Participation and Communication: A Survey of Company Reports*. London: Advisory, Conciliation and Arbitration Service in association with London Business School

Beckhard R. (1989). A model for the executive management of transformational change. In *The 1989 Annual: Developing Human Resources* (Pfeiffer J.W., ed.), pp. 225–64. San Diego, CA: University Associates

Beckhard R. and Harris R. (1977). *Organisational Transitions: Managing Complex Change*. Reading, MA: Addison-Wesley

Beer M., Eisenstat R. and Spector B. (1990). *The Critical Path to Corporate Renewal*. Boston: Harvard Business School Press

Bernstein D. (1984). *Company Image and Reality*. New York: Holt, Rinehart and Winston

Drucker P.F. (1993). *Post-capitalist Society*. London: Butterworth Heinemann

Francis D. (1987). *Unblocking Organizational Communication*. Aldershot: Gower

Goold M. and Campbell A. (1986). *Strategies and Styles: The Role of the Centre in Managing Diversified Corporations*. Oxford: Blackwell

Chapter 8

Atkinson J. (1984). Manpower strategies for flexible organisations. *Personnel Management*, **16**(8), 28–31

Atkinson J. (1989). Four stages of adjustment to the demographic downturn. *Personnel Management*, **21**(8), 20–35

Bargaining Report (1990). Equal pay claims on the move. *Bargaining Report*, June, 12–15

Barnes C. (1992). Disability: an equality issue which can no longer be ignored. *Equal Opportunities Review*, (46), 52

Beechy V. (1989). Woman's employment in France and Britain: some problems of comparison. *Work, Employment and Society*, **3**(3), 369–738

Beechy V. and Perkins T. (1987). *A Matter of Women's Hours: Part-time Work and the Labour Market*. Cambridge: Polity Press

Berry-Lound D. (1990). Towards the family-friendly firm? *Employment Gazette*, February, 85–91

Bridgeford J. and Stirling J. (1993). *Employee Relations in Europe*. London: Blackwell

Cockburn C. (1991). *In the Way of Women: Men's Resistance to Sex Equality in Organisations*. London: Macmillan

Cockman, Bacon and Woodrow (1990). Report on an equal opportunities policy and practice survey. *Equal Opportunities International*, **9**(2), 19–23

Commission of the European Communities (1989). *Employment in Europe*. COM (89) 399 Final. Luxembourg: Office for Publications of the European Communities

Commission of the European Communities (1990). *Employment in Europe*. COM (90) 290 Final. Luxembourg: Office for Publications of the European Communities

Commission for Racial Equality (1989). *The Race Relations Code of Practice: Are Employers Complying?* London: CRE

Confederation of British Industry (1988). *Workforce 2000. An Agenda for Action*. London: CBI

Employment Gazette (1990). Industrial tribunal statistics. *Employment Gazette*, April, 213–18

Employment Gazette (1991a). Ethnic origins and the labour market. *Employment Gazette*, February, 59–72

Employment Gazette (1991b). Characteristics of the unemployed. *Employment Gazette*, May, 267–302

Employment Gazette (1992). Women and the labour market: results from the 1991 labour force survey. *Employment Gazette*, September, 435–44

Equal Opportunities Commission (1992). *EOC Statistical Review*. Manchester: EOC

Equal Opportunities Review (1989). Age discrimination: over the hill at 45? *EOR* (25), 10–15

Equal Opportunities Review (1992). Opportunity 2000. *EOR*, (41), 20–26

Floyd F. (1991). Overcoming barriers to employment. In *Disability and Social Policy* (Dalley G., ed.), Ch. 11. London: Public Policy Studies Institute

Foster J. (1989). Sex discrimination – the enemy of effective resourcing. In *Proc. Institute of Personnel. Management Annual Conference*, Harrogate

Gibbon P. (1989). EO in Sheffield: policies and outcomes. *Equal Opportunities International*, **8**(6), 10–15

Hammond V. (1992). Opportunity 2000: a culture change approach to equal opportunity. *Women in Management Review*, **7**(7), 3–10

Hansard Society (1990). *The Report of the Hansard Society Commission on Women at the Top*. London: A.L. Publishing Services

Hutton J. (1984). How the SDA has failed. *Legal Action*, April, 10–11

Jelnick M. and Adler N. (1988). Women: world-class managers for global competition. *The Academy of Management Executive*, **II**(1) 11–19

Labour Research (1988). How far has company equality gone? *Labour Research*, December, 11–13

Labour Research (1989). Racial equality at work – top firms fail the test. *Labour Research*, November, 13–16

Labour Research (1992). Industrial tribunal trends. *Labour Research*, February, 23

Lewis S. (1989). Maximising the potential of your under-utilized resource: a separate strategy for women? In *Proc. Institute of Personnel Management Annual Conference*, Harrogate

Liff S. (1989). Assessing EO policies. *Personnel Review*, **18**(1), 27–34

Littlewoods Organisation plc (1986). *Equal Opportunities Code of Practice*. Liverpool: Littlewoods plc Equal Opportunities Department

LMQR (1991). The labour force to 2001. *LMQR*, August, 3

LMQR (1992). Ethnic minorities in the youth labour market. *LMQR*, August, 12–15

Mahon T. (1989). When line managers welcome equal opportunities. *Personnel Management*, **21**(10), 76–9

Morris L. (1991). Women's poor work. In *Poor Work: Disadvantage and the Division of Labour* (Brown P. and Scase R., eds.), Ch. 5. Milton Keynes: Open University Press

National Economic Development Office (1989). *Defusing the Demographic Time Bomb*. London: NEDO and Training Agency

Oliver M. (1991). Disability and participation in the labour market. In *Poor Work: Disadvantage and the Division of Labour* (Brown P. and Scase R., eds.), Ch. 9. Milton Keynes: Open University Press

Paddison L. (1989). Equal opportunities makes good business sense. In *Proc. Institute of Personnel Management Annual Conference*, Harrogate

Parson D. (1990). Winning workers: rising to the demographic challenge. *Employment Gazette*, February, 63–9

Pillinger J. (1989). Women and '1992': everything to go for. *International Labour Reports*, July–October (34/35), 35–38

Powell G. (1989). Retainer and re-entry schemes. In *Proc. Institute of Personnel Management Conference*, Harrogate

Rubenstein M. (1986). Do we need an age discrimination in employment act? *Equal Opportunities Review*, Jan/Feb (5), 36

Rubery J. (1992). *The Economics of Equal Value*. Manchester: Equal Opportunities Commission

Straw J. (1990) *Equal Opportunities*. London: Institute of Personnel Management

Webb J. and Liff S. (1988). Play the white man: the social construction of fairness and competition in EO policies. *Sociological Review*, **36**(3) 532–51

Useful reading

Birkett K. and Workman D., eds. (1988). *Getting on with Disabilities: An Employer's Guide*. London: Institute of Personnel Management

Bramham J. (1989). *Human Resource Planning*. London: Institute of Personnel Management

Collinson D.L., Knights D. and Collinson M. (1990). *Managing to Discriminate*. London: Routledge

Crompton C. and Sanderson K. (1990). *Gendered Jobs and Social Change*. London: Unwin Hyman

Dowling P.J. and Schuller S. (1990). *International Dimensions of Human Resource Planning*. Kent: P&W

Equal Opportunities Commission (1988). *From Policy to Practice: an Equal Opportunities Strategy for the 1990s*. London: EOC

Equal Opportunities Commission (1990). *Women and Men in Britain*. London: EOC

Gregory J. (1987). *Sex, Race and the Law*. London: Sage

Hearn J., Sheppard D.L., Tancred-Sheriff P. and Burrell G. (1990). *The Sexuality of Organisations*. London: Sage

McRae S. (1991). *Maternity Rights in Britain: The Experience of Women and Employers*. London: Policy Studies Institute

With thanks to John Stirling, Doug Miller and Michelle Pavey for their assistance in providing useful references for this chapter.

Chapter 9

Allen K.R. (1991). Personnel management on the line. *Personnel Management*, **23**(6), 40–3

Anderson G. (1993). *Managing Performance Appraisal Systems*. Oxford: Blackwell

Arkin A. (1991). Specialising in strategic human resource development. *Personnel Management*, **23**(12), 7–8

Bentley T.B. (1990). Corporate strategy: performance management systems. *Training and Development*, **8**(4), 24–6

Biddle D. and Evenden R. (1989). *Human Aspects of Management*. London: Institute of Personnel Management

Blyton P. and Turnbull P., eds. (1992). *Reassessing Human Resource Management*. London: Sage

Burke T. (1992). *University of Westminster Survey*. Cooperative Bank

Dobson P. (1989) References. In *Assessment and Selection in Organisations* (Heriot P., ed.). Chichester: Wiley

Dulewicz V. (1991) Improving assessment centres. *Personnel Management*, **23**(6), 50–5

Evenden R. and Anderson G. (1992) *Management Skills: Making the Most of People*. Wokingham: Addison-Wesley

Fletcher C., Blinkhorn S. and Johnson C. (1991). Personality tests: the great debate. *Personnel Management*, **23**(9), 38–42

Giles W.D. (1991). Making strategy work. *Long Range Planning*, **24**(5), 75–91

Graham P. (1992). *Integrative Management: Creating Unity From Diversity*. Oxford: Blackwell

Greenslade M. (1991). Managing diversity: lessons from the United States. *Personnel Management*, **23**(12), 28–32

Hall R. (1992) The strategic analysis of intangible resources. *Strategic Management Journal*, **13**, 135–144

Harrison R. (1992). *Employee Development*. London: Institute of Personnel Management

Honey P. (1991). The learning organisation simplified. *Training and Development*, **9**(7), 30–3

Makin P. and Robertson I. (1986). Selecting the best selection techniques. *Personnel Management*, **17**(11), 38–41

Mueller F. and Purcell J. (1992). The drive for higher productivity. *Personnel Management*, **24**(5), 28–33

Pedler M., Burgyne J. and Bydell T. (1991). *The Learning Company: A Strategy for Sustainable Development*. London: McGraw-Hill

Price Waterhouse Cranfield (1992). International strategic human resource management survey reference in: New priorities for Dutch HRM. *Personnel Management*, **24**(12), 42–6

Purcell J. (1989). The impact of corporate strategy on human resource management. In *New Perspectives on Human Resource Management* (Storey J., ed.), pp. 67–91. London: Routledge

Storey J. (1992). *Developments in the Management of Human Resources*. Oxford: Blackwell

Thompson A.A. and Strickland A.J. III (1992). *Strategic Management: Concepts and Cases*. Boston, MA: Irwin

Wood R. and Baron H. (1992). Psychological testing free from prejudice. *Personnel Management*, **24**(12), 34–7

Wood R. and Baron H. (1993). *Striving for Fair Selection*. London: Commission for Racial Equality

Chapter 10

Alderfer C.P. (1979). *Existence, Relatedness and Growth*. New York: Free Press

Anderson G.C. (1980). *Performance Appraisal in Theory and Practice*. Strathclyde Business School Working Paper no. 8002, University of Strathclyde, Glasgow

Anderson G.C. (1988). Staff appraisal. *Training and Development*, **3**

Anderson G.C. and Barnett J.G. (1986). Nurse appraisal in practice. *The Health Service Journal*, **96** (5023), October

Anderson G.C., Young E. and Hulme D. (1987). Appraisal without form-filling. *Personnel Management*, **19**(2), 44–7

Armstrong M. and Murlis H. (1988). *Reward Management*. London: Institute of Personnel Management

Beer M. (1981). Performance appraisal: dilemmas and possibilities. *Organisational Dynamics*, **9**(1), 24–36

Bevan S. and Thompson M. (1991). Performance management at the crossroads. *Personnel Management*, **23**(11), 36–9

Bevan S. and Thompson M. (1992) *An Overview of Policy and Practice in Performance Management in the UK*. London: Institute of Personnel Management

Biddle D. and Evenden R. (1989). *Human Aspects of Management*. London: Institute of Personnel Management

Bureau of National Affairs (1983). *Performance Appraisal Programs*. Personnel Policies Forum Survey 135. Washington DC: BNA

Carson K.P, *et al.* (1991). Performance appraisal: effective management of deadly disease. *Group and Organisation Studies*, **16**(2)

Connock S. (1991). *HR Vision: Managing a Quality Workforce*. London: Institute of Personnel Management

Couger J.D. and Zawaki R.A. (1980). *Motivating and Managing Computer Personnel.* Chichester: Wiley

Cummings L.L. and Schwab D.P. (1973). *Performance in Organisations: Determinants and Appraisals.* Glenview, Illinois: Scott, Foresman

Evenden R. and Anderson G.C. (1992). *Management Skills: Making the Most of People.* Wokingham: Addison-Wesley

Festinger L. (1954). A theory of social comparison approaches. In *Human Relations*

Fletcher C. and Williams R. (1992). *Organisational Experience in Performance Management in the UK.* London: Institute of Personnel Management

Fowler A. (1990). Performance Management: the MBO of the '90s. *Personnel Management*, **22**(7), 47–51

Fox S., Tanton M. and McLeay S. (1992). *Human Resource Management, Corporate Strategy and Financial Performance. Executive summary of research project undertaken for HM Government's Economic and Social Research Council's 'Competitiveness and Regeneration of British Industry' Initiative.* Lancaster University and the University of Wales

George J. (1986). Appraisal in the public sector: dispensing with the big stick. *Personnel Management*, **18**(5), 32–5

Harrison R. (1992). *Employee Development.* London: Institute of Personnel Management

Locke E.A. *et al.* (1981). Goal setting and task performance. *Psychological Bulletin*, 90

Long P. (1986) *Performance Appraisal Revisited.* London: Institute of Personnel Management

Maier N.R.F. (1976) *The Appraisal Interview.* New York: University Associates

McGregor D. (1960). *The Human Side of Enterprise.* New York: McGraw-Hill

Miles B. (1991). Management appraisal at Yorkshire Television. *Executive Development*, **4**(3)

Mohrman A.M. Resnick-West S.M. and Lawler E.E. (1989). *Designing Performance Appraisal Systems.* San Francisco: Jossey Bass

Mumford A. (1985). What's new in management development. *Personnel Management*, **17**(5), 30–2

Nadler D.A. and Lawler E.E., III (1977). Motivation: a diagnostic approach. In *Perspectives and Behaviour in Organisations* (Hackman J.R. *et al.*, eds.). New York: McGraw-Hill

Oakland J.S. (1989). *Total Quality Management.* Oxford: Heinemann

Peters T. (1989) *Thriving on Chaos.* London: Macmillan

Salaman G. (1979). Management development and organisation theory. *Journal of European Industrial Training*, **2**(7)

Schneir C.E. (1989). Implementing Performance Management and Recognition and Rewards Systems at the Strategic Level: a line management driven effort. *Human Resource Planning*, **12**(3), 205–20

Storey J. (1992). *Developments in the Management of Human Resources.* Oxford: Blackwell

Williams S. (1992). Strategy and objectives. In *The Handbook of Performance Management* (Neale F., ed.), pp. 7–24. London: Institute of Personnel Management

Useful reading

Anderson G.C. (1993) *Managing Performance Appraisal Systems*. Oxford: Blackwell
Towers B., ed. (1992). *Handbook of Human Resource Management*. Oxford: Blackwell

Chapter 11

ACAS (1989). *Labour Flexibility in Britain*. Occasional Paper no. 71
Aitken J. (1990). Establishing flexible and effective renumeration strategies in an international context. In *Proc. Institute of Personnel Management Conference*, Harrogate, October, 1990
Armstrong M. and Murlis H. (1988). *Reward Management*. London: Kogan Page
Bowen H. (1990). Structuring remuneration policies to support the priorities of the business. In *Proc. Institute of Personnel Management Conference*, Harrogate, October, 1990
Brewster C. and Connock S. (1985). *Industrial Relations; Cost Effective Strategies*. London: Hutchinson
Cooke R. and Armstrong M. (1990). The search for strategic HRM. *Personnel Management*, **22**(12), 30–3
Duncan C. (1989). Pay and payment systems. In *Handbook of Industrial Relations Practice* (Towers B., ed.). London: Kogan Page
Fowler A. (1988). New directions in performance pay. *Personnel Management*, **20**(11), 30–4
Friedman B. (1990). Flexible benefits menus for employees. *Building Society Gazette*, August, p. 25
Greenhill R. (1988). Giving staff their just rewards. *Building Society Gazette*, April, p. 18
Guest D. (1989). Personnel and HRM – can you tell the difference? *Personnel Management*, **21**(1), 48–51
Industrial Relations Review and Report (1989a) 445. *Harmonisation: a Single Status Surge?* 8.8.89, p. 5. London: Industrial Relations Services
Industrial Relations Review and Report (1989b) 452. *Shiftwork: Premia for Some, Annual Salary for Others*, 21.11.89, p. 8. London: Industrial Relations Services
Industrial Relations Review and Report (1990a) 455. *Job Evaluation and Equal Value: Recent Developments*, 10.1.90, pp. 11–13. London: Industrial Relations Services
Industrial Relations Review and Report (1990b) 468. *After Hours: a Survey of Overtime Working*, 17.7.90, p. 11. London: Industrial Relations Services
Jackson M. and Leopold J. (1990). Casting off from national negotiations. *Personnel Management*, **22**(4), 66
Mackie K. (1989) Changes in the law since 1979; an overview. In *Handbook of Industrial Relations Practice* (Towers B., ed.), pp. 267–99. London: Kogan Page
Weitzman M. (1988). The share economy. Quoted in 'Giving staff their just rewards' (Greenhill R.). *Building Societies Gazette*, April 1988, p. 18

Chapter 12

Brewster C. and Tyson S., eds. (1991). *International Comparisons in Human Resource Management*. London: Pitman

Burgoyne J. (1988). Management development for the individual *and* the organisation. *Personnel Management*, **20**(6), 40–4

Coopers and Lybrand Associates (1985). *A challenge to complacency: changing attitudes to training*. A Report to the Manpower Services Commission and National Economic Development Office. Sheffield: MSC

Cross M. and Mitchell P. (1986). *Packaging Efficiency. The Training Contribution*. UK: Technical Change Centre

De Meyer A. and Ferdows K. (1991). *Removing the Barriers in Manufacturing – a report on the 1990 manufacturing survey*. Fontainebleau: Insead

Drucker P.F. (1993). *Post-capitalist Society*. Oxford: Butterworth Heinemann; New York: Harper Collins

Economic and Social Research Council (1991). *Skills Shortages in Sheffield Engineering Companies*. London: ESRC

Employment Institute (1991a). *Training – the Problem for Employers*. London: Employment Policy Institute

Employment Institute (1991b). *Economic Report No. 9*. Hatfield Polytechnic Survey. London: Employment Policy Institute

Fairbairn J. (1991). Plugging the gap in training needs analysis. *Personnel Management*. **23**(2), 43–5

Graham A. (1992). YT funding and the TECs, a tragedy in the making. *Personnel Management*, **24**(2), 4

Hall D.T. (1984). Human resource development and organizational effectiveness. In *Strategic Human Resource Management* (Fombrun D., Tichy N.M. and Devanna M.A., eds.), Ch. 11. New York: Wiley

Harrison R. (1992a). Employee development at Barratt. In *Case Studies in Personnel* (Woodall D. and Winstanley D., eds.), pp. 103–15. London: Institute of Personnel Management

Harrison R. (1992b) *Employee Development*. London: Institute of Personnel Management

Harrison, R. (1993/4). *Developing Human Resources for Productivity*. Geneva: International Labour Office

Hatfield Polytechnic (1991). *Economic Report No. 9*. Survey for Employment Institute. London: Employment Policy Institute

Hayes C., Anderson A. and Fonda N. (1984). International competition and the role of competence. *Personnel Management*, **16**(9), 36–8

Hodges C. (1990). Ford's development scheme bears fruit. *Personnel Management*, **22**(10), 19

House of Lords Select Committee on European Communities (1990). *Vocational training and retraining*. Report (October)

Industrial Relations Research Unit (1990). The impact of age upon employment. *Warwick Papers in Industrial Relations*, No. 33. Coventry: Warwick University, IRRU

Institute of Manpower Studies (1984). *Competence and competition, training and education in the Republic of Germany, the United States and Japan.* London: National Economic Development Office

Jackson T. (1990). *Evaluation: Relating Training to Business Performance.* London: Kogan Page

Johnson R. (1984). Adult training in Europe. *Personnel Management,* **16**(8), 24–7

Mayhew K. (1991). *Training – the problem for employers.* Report for the Employment Institute (May). London: Employment Policy Institute

McKee L. (1990). Ensuring increased profitability in the 1990s by recognising training and development as an investment, not an expense. In *Proc. Institute for International Research Conference,* London, 1 May

Mintzberg H. (1973). *The Nature of Managerial Work.* New York: Harper & Row

Mintzberg H. (1989). *Mintzberg on Management.* New York: Harper

Mumford A. (1989). *Management Development: Strategies for Action.* London: Institute of Personnel Management

Oxford (1988). *The Concise Oxford Dictionary of Current English,* 7th edn. Oxford: Oxford University Press

Personnel Management (1991). Failure of training due largely to management indifference. *Personnel Management,* **23**(5), 4

Pettigrew A.M., Swallow P. and Hendry C. (1988). The forces that trigger training. *Personnel Management,* **20**(12), 28–32

Policy Studies Institute (1990). *Britain's Real Skill Shortage.* Report. London: PSI

Prais S.J. and NIESR research team (1990). Productivity, education and training: Britain and other countries compared. *National Institute Economic Review.* London: National Institute of Economic and Social Research

Sadler P. and Barham K. (1988). From Franks to the future: 25 years of management training prescriptions. *Personnel Management,* **20**(5), 48–51

Sparrow P. and Pettigrew A. (1988). How Halfords put its HRM into top gear. *Personnel Management,* **20**(6), 30–4

Storey J. (1991). Do the Japanese make better managers? *Personnel Management,* **23**(8), 24–8

Storey J. (1992). *Developments in the Management of Human Resources.* Oxford: Blackwell

Townley B. (1989). Selection and appraisal: reconstituting 'social relations'? In *New Perspectives on Human Resource Management* (Storey J., ed.), pp. 92–108. London: Routledge

Training Agency (1989). *Training and Enterprise Councils: a Prospectus for the 1990s.* Sheffield: Department of Employment

University of Sheffield (1991). *Skills Shortages in Sheffield Engineering Companies.* Survey for Economic and Social Research Council. London: ESRC

Vallely I. (1992). How Rover drives its learning message home. *Works Management,* August

Webster B. (1990). Beyond the mechanics of HRD. *Personnel Management,* **22**(3), 44–7

White Paper (1989). *Employment for the 1990s.* London: HMSO

Wille E. (1990). Should management development just be for managers? *Personnel Management,* **22**(8), 34–7

Wood S., ed. (1988). *Continuous Development: the Path to Improved Performance.* London: Institute of Personnel Management

Yates I.R. (1990). Gaining competitive advantage through human resources leadership. In *Proc. Conference Board, European Human Resources Conference,* London, 28–9 November

3 Case study

References and useful reading

Fowler A., Sheard M. and Wibberly M. (1992). Two routes to quality. *Personnel Management,* **24**(11), 30–4

Giles E. and Williams R. (1991). Can the personnel department survive quality management? *Personnel Management,* **23**(4), 28–33

Guest D. (1992). Human resource management in the United Kingdom. In *A Handbook of Human Resource Management* (Towers B., ed.), pp. 3–26. Oxford: Blackwell

Hill S. (1991). Why quality circles failed but total quality might succeed. *British Journal of Industrial Relations,* **29**(4), 541–68

Marchington M., Wilkinson A. and Dale B. (1993a). Quality management and the human resource dimension: the case study report. In *Quality, People Management Matters,* pp. 25–64. London: Institute of Personnel Management.

Marchington M., Wilkinson A. and Dale B. (1993b). Who really is taking the lead on quality? *Personnel Management,* **25**(4), 30–3

Oakland J. (1989). *Total Quality Management.* London: Heinemann

Schuler R. (1989). Strategic human resource management and industrial relations. *Human Relations,* **42**(2), 157–84

Schuler R. and Harris D. (1992). *Managing Quality: The Primer for Middle Managers.* Reading, MA: Addison-Wesley

Wilkinson A. (1992). The other side of quality: 'soft' issues and the human resource dimension. *Total Quality Management,* **3**(3), 323–29

Wilkinson A. (1993). Managing human resources for quality. In *Managing Quality,* 2nd edn (Dale B., ed.), Ch. 13. Hemel Hempstead: Prentice-Hall

Wilkinson A., Allen P. and Snape E. (1991). TQM and the management of labour. *Employee Relations,* **13**(1), 24–31

Wilkinson A., Marchington M., Ackers P. and Goodman J. (1992). Total quality management and employee involvement. *Human Resource Management Journal,* **2**(4), 1–20

4 Case study

Reference and useful reading

Ackers P., Marchington M., Wilkinson A. and Goodman J. (1992). The long and winding road: tracking employee involvement at Brown's Woven Carpets. *Employee Relations*, **14**(3), 56–70

Dawson S. (1992). *Analysing Organisations*, 2nd edn. London: Macmillan.

Fox A. (1966). *Industrial Sociology & Industrial Relations*. Research Paper 3, Royal Commission on Trade Unions and Employers Associations

Marchington M. (1992). *Managing the Team: A Guide to Successful Employee Involvement*. Oxford: Blackwell

Marchington M., Goodman J., Wilkinson A. and Ackers P. (1992). *New Developments in Employee Involvement*. Employment Department Research Paper 2

Peters T. and Waterman Jr R.H. (1982). *In Search of Excellence*. New York: Harper & Row

Smith C., Child J. and Rowlinson M. (1990). *Reshaping Work: The Cadbury Experience*. Cambridge University Press

12 Case study

References and useful reading

Harrison R. (1992). *Employee Development*, Chs. 11 and 21. London: Institute of Personnel Management

Jones A. and Hendry C. (1992). *The Learning Organisation: a Review of Literature and Practice*. London: HRD Partnership

Pedler M., Burgyne J. and Bydell T. (1991). *The Learning Company: A Strategy for Sustainable Development*. Maidenhead: McGraw-Hill

Pettigrew A.M., Swallow P. and Hendry C. (1988). The forces that trigger training. *Personnel Management*, **20**(12), 22–32

Sawers D. (1986). The experience of German and Japanese subsidiaries in Britain. *Journal of General Management*, **12**(1), 5–21

Senge P.R. (1990). *The Fifth Discipline: The Art and Practice of the Learning Organisation*. New York: Doubleday

Vallely I. (1992). How Rover drives its learning message home. *Works Management*, August

Wickens P. (1987). *The Road to Nissan: Flexibility, Quality, Teamwork*. London: Macmillan

Index

A

ability   240, 241, **267**
accountabilities   254, 269, 270, 286
achievments   321
acquisition   64, 80
action plans   256, 262
age discrimination   208–10
agenda (strategic human resource
    management (HRM))   31–3
application information   239, 240
appraisal   240, 262, **264**, 325
   appraiser   272
   interview   265–6
   schemes   282, 285
   see also performance appraisal
approach, minimalist   **121**
aptitude   240, 241
architect   **74**
assessment
   appraisal   **264**
   centres   240, 242
   cost   323–4
attitudes   63, 241, 263
   changes in   312–14
   employees   185–6, 284
   to human resource development (HRD)
      in organizations   306–8
   to training and development   305–121
awareness   254

B

bargaining
   local flexibility   159, 355–6
   local in UK TV companies (case study)
      142
   localized   155
   power   143
barriers   256
   high exit   11
BBC policy statement (case study)   193–4
benchmarks   280, 322–3
benefits *see* fringe benefits
Benetton (case study)   131
board-level function   68–9, 263
   as business-led function   70–2
   corporate function, proactive   69–70
   formalized strategy at corporate level
      72–3
Bolton committee   119
bonuses   169
   bonus schemes   283, 288
   profit   **157**
Boston Consulting Group (BCG) matrix
   17
brownfield operation   142, 144
BT plc (case study)   158–9, 196–7
budgeting   **5**
business
   drivers   **314**

business (continued)
environment   77
managers   68, 75
processes   319
strategy   9, 301
success   **300**
units   24, 25, 63, 222
Business Enterprise Training option
schemes   115

C

cafeteria approach   290, **291**
capacity,   extra 11
Carcom   342–3
career
cross-career movements   78
development   337–8
opportunities   168
change, resistance to   214–15
childcare   198, 217
clerk of works   73
closed shops   139
coaching   **259–60**, 271, 272
commission   282–3
Commission for Racial Equality   198–9,
207, 241, 244
commitment and performance
management   260
communication
policy   305
strategy initiatives   173–4
systems   157–9, 170
communicator   272
community businesses   **115**
community-voluntary firms   **130**, **132**, 133
competences   270
core   **28**
competition   26–7, 254
capabilities-based   29
size of   11
concepts and issues   1–160
application   331–79
corporate mission   45–8
culture, organizational   48–51
definition   36–40
goals and contributions to 'the business'
52–5
integrated and strategic human resource
management (HRM) processes   56–63
strategic approach, development of   40–5
structure, organizational   51–2
themes   37
wheel of human resource management
functions   40
considerations, internal   278

consistency   56
constitutionalism   159
consultancy   351–4
contracts manager   **74**
contradictions   39
control   **5**
cycles   89
cooperation   26–7
cooperatives   **115**, **132**
corporate level   72–3
cost
assessment   323–4
focus   **13**
leadership, overall   **13**
levels, fixed   11
counselling   271
craft groupings   140
crafting   117, 119
culture   227, 263
adversarial   86
corporate   63
managerial   50
organizational   48–51, 62, 186–8
paternalist   86
unifying   50
Wharfedale Water (case study)   369–70
customer survey   179

D

decentralization   62, 64, 76, 154–5
deficiencies   256
definition (strategic management)
historical development   4–6
multidisciplinary nature   6–7
strategy levels   8–10
demand   117
demographic change   359
and employer responses   200–2
design   117
develop (definition)   **300**
development   249, 253
business-led   312–24
delivery   270–2
employees   305, 307–8, 318–20, 326
international   308–12
management   326–8
national   305–12
organizational level   305–12
plan   269
personal   **320**
see also learning and development
Diana Company (case study)   129–30
differentiation   11, **13**
disability   200
discrimination   208–10

Disabled Person Acts (Employment) 1944
    and 1958   204
discretion, limited managerial   257
discrimination
    age   208–10
    direct and indirect   205–6
    disability   208–10
    race   203
    reverse   206
disease, local   96
disputes, industrial   381–3
downstream
    second/third order decisions   33, 221
    strategic functions   9, 61

E

education   123, 191, **300**
    vocational   58
Employee Development and Assistance
    Programme (EDAP)   302–3
Employee Involvement (EI)   88, 89, 90,
    95
employees   88, 89, 90, 302–3
    attitudes and performance   185–6, 284
    commitment   53, 61
    development   307–8, 318–21, 324–5,
      326
    education   56, 324
    employer/employee familiarity   357
    involvement   347–9
    learning   318–20, 324–5, 326
    management   336–9
    performance   256
    rationalization   61
    recruitment   53
    relations   91, 140
    retention   325
    skilled   88
    survey   179–81, 182–4
    view   103–4
    well-being   261
    see also labour market; personnel
employers
    good   **166**, 170
    responses and demographic change
      200–2
employment   289
    continuous   304
    patterns among women   210–12
    practices   56, 57–8
    relations   97–101, **139**, 369
    small and entrepreneurial firms
      119–23
    strategies in small coal mine (case study)
      124

    see also industrial and employment
      relations; jobs
Employment Protection Act   1975 289
empowerment   89
engineering firm, overexpanding (case
    study)   128–9
enterprise, in search of   351–4
equal opportunities *see* equality
Equal Opportunities Commission   207
Equal Pay Act 1970   204
Equal Pay (Amendment) Regulation 1983
    204
Equal Treatment Act   207
equality and opportunity   204, 207, 359–60
    enlightenment   244
    individual   202–3
    legal context
      British equality legislation   204–5
      discrimination, direct and indirect
        205–6
      European legislation   203
      individual equality, principle of202–3
      the law   207–8
    legislation   204–7
    in organizations   360
    policies   359
    strong versions   190, 192, 195, 199
    in the workplace   189–218
      case study: BBC policy statement
        193–4
      case study: British
        Telecommunications plc   196–7
      case study: Wellcome Foundation
        216–17
      change, working for   213–15
      demographic change and employer
        response   200–2
      labour market, inequalities in
        208–13
      legal context   202–8
      policies and practices   192–9
      and strategic human resource
        management (HRM)   190–2
      strategy formulation   215–18
    see also Commission for Racial Equality
      espousing   147
ethnic minorities   198–9, 200, 201, 207,
    243, 244
    discrimination   208–10
    see also race; Race Relations Act
Europe
    European Commission directives   81,
      204, 205
    European Court of Justice   200
    European dimension   291–2
    legislation and equality principle   203,
      205, 210–11
expectations   263

F

fair value (case study)   363–8
family firms   **115**, 119, 127, **129**, 130
    profiles   128
fear factor   89, 96
feedback   256
finance
    financial control style   24
    financial institution and performance
        management (case study)   257–8
    see also reward systems, financial
Finance Act   1987 288
firms
    entrepreneurial   **114**, 127–30
    flexible   151
    founder   **114**, 118, 119, 123–7
        profiles   124
    franchise   **115**, **130–3**
    front-line   123–7
    infrastructure   16
    large and international   85–109
    micro-firms   **114**, 117, **123–7**, 133
    professional   **130–3**
        partnership   **115**, 131–2
    second order   127–30
    small and entrepreneurial   111–35
        differentiation   112–15
        human resource strategies   123–33
        markets comparison   115–23
        strategy crafting modes   118
        typology   114
    third order   130–3
fit, problems of   58–9, 93
five force framework   10–13
flexibility   151, **153**, 285
focus   **13**
Ford, UK (case study)   302–3
fragmentation   177
framework, paternalistic/traditional   149
Freightco   93
fringe benefits   169, 290, 303, 305
function
    business-led   70–2
    corporate proactive   69–70
    flexibility   53
    third order   38–9

G

gap *see* performance gap
General Electric Business Screen   17
goals   226–34
    see also vision and goals, organizational
grievance problems   258

H

hard times approach   96
harmonization   285, 290–1
hazards in selection methods   237–9
hierarchy   129
HM Customs and Excise and performance
        management (case study)   262–4
HMH Sheetmetal Fabrication Ltd (1933)
        (case study)   42, 51, 335–9
HMH Sheetmetal Fabrication Ltd (1933)
    business strategy   336
    the organization   335
    workforce, management of   336–9
human resource development (HRD)
        299–329
    attitudes   305–12
        in organizations   306–8
        to vocational training and
            development   308
    business-led learning and development
        312–24
        attitudes, change in   312–14
        case study: Rover Group, UK   315–16
        and corporate vision, mission and
            strategy   314–18
        outcomes, measuring of and results
            evaluation   320–4
        plans, creation and implementation of
            318–20
    definitions   300
    employee learning and development
        324–6
    issue   18–20, 27–30
    outcomes   359
    planning   359
    specialists as facilitators   260–1
    strategy   77–8
    triggers   300–5
        case study: Ford, UK   302–3
        case study: Rover Learning Business'
            REAL programme   303–4
human resource management (HRM)
    development   326–8
    hard   59–61
    international   79–82
    soft   59–61, 190
    strategy, long-term   61
human resource wheel   177

I

Ichem   93, 94
improvements   321
incentives   169, 304
    financial   258, 338

industrial and employment relations
137–60
cost-effective 144–50
case study: objectives of Council 149
management objectives 144–5
management style 145–50
nature 138–44
case study: local bargaining in UK TV
companies 142
industrial relations and management
function 140–4
industrial and employment relations
strategic human resource management
(HRM) 139–40
strategies 150–9
case study: BT's approach to
communications 158–9
communication systems 157–9
recruitment patterns 150–2
rewards and working systems 152–7
inequalities *see* labour market inequalities
influence 38
organizational 86
integration 56
and corporate strategy 54
development-driven **260**
reward-driven **260**
strategic 53
interests 233
competing 214–15
international firms *see* firms, large and
international
internationalization 64
interview (selection) 240, 243, 262
investment bank (case study) 76–8
issues *see* concepts and issues

J

jobs
activities **15**, 269, 270
analysis **221**, 229, 235–6
descriptions 221, 228, 232, 270
evaluation schemes 280
factors 168
generators 112
property rights 170
Joint Consultative Committees (JCC's) 88
judging **259–60**
'jumping out of boxes' 187

L

labour aristocracy 96
labour market

external 302
inequalities 208–13
employment patterns among women
210–12
unemployment patterns 208–10
women as flexible labour force
212–13
internal 302
learning **300**, 314–18, 321
and change 233
corporate 314
and development 306–7, 314–18,
321–3, 325, 337
business-led 312–24
employees 318–20, 324–5, 326
employee-oriented 305
management-led 315
organization 238–9, 308, 317, 375–9
processes 317
lifeboat authoritarianism 96
lifeboat democracy 89, 96, 106
linkages **16**, 257, 258

M

management 76–9, 108, 179, 233, 261,
263
business 68, 75
communication tasks 177–85
contract 74
control 258
development 326–8
function and industrial relations conduct
140–4
hard 101
line 75–6, 80, 225, 243, 260
local 172
middle 101, 107, 108
objectives 144–5
professional 127
regional 179
role 186–8, 262
skilled 76–9, 304
soft 101
strategic 333, 335–9
styles 91–2, 145–50, 147
support 17
survey 174–7
unitary 62, 146
see also performance management
markets 91, 112
growth rate 11
small and entrepreneurial firms 115–23
employment relationships 119–23
strategy making 117–19
see also labour market

merger   64, 80, 286
merit pay issues   258
meritocracy of human resource
          management   54
micro-firms   **114**, 117, **123**–7, 133
     profiles   124
milestones, planned   322–3
mission, corporate   45, 46–8, 92, 108, 173,
          222, 314–18
motivation   **268**, 325
     influence   272–3
     motivator   272
     and performance appraisal   250
     and performance management   261
Multichem (case study)   52, 87–108
     crisis and adjustment   95–7
     and human resource management
          (HRM)   92–4
     learning points   105–8
     as learning vehicle   87–90
     organizational politics   106–7
     Scotchem site   94–5
     transformation/evolution   107–9
     Way Ahead programme   97–101
          impact   101–5

N

national human resource management
          (HRM)   79–82
National Vocational Education and
          Training System   310–11
nature (of strategic management)
          1–33
     analytical view   10–18
     definition   4–10
     human issue   18–20
     human resource management (HRM)
          contribution   30–3
     processual view   21–3
     strategic success   25–30
     styles   23–5
needs, organizational and individual   117,
          164–77
     case study: corporate strategy at BET
          173–7
     case study: employer characteristics at
          BET   167–70
     decentralized organization   171–7
     employer concept   166–70
     ownership concept   165–6
negotiation (Wharfedale Water case study)
          372

O

objectives   253, 256, 269, 270, 321
     corporate   315
     of Council (case study)   149
     future   254
     individual   252, 256
     organizational   252
     of performance appraisal   250–3
     see also targets
openness   256
Opportunity 2000   210
opportunity *see* equality and opportunity
oracular policies *see* job analysis and people
          auditing
organization   231
     capability review   259
     change   324–5, 347–9
     culture   39, 185–6
     development   263
     inertia   43
     level for training and development
          305–12
     requirements   277
     restructuring   349
     small   112
     structure   185–6
     see also firms
Orwellian *see* job analysis and people
          auditing
overtime payments   281–2
ownership   **165**
     and performance management   260
     problem   213–14

P

payment
     by output   282–3
     by results   282–3
     by time   279–81
     fair   168
     increases   257, 284
     merit pay issues   258
     overtime   281–2
     performance-related   263, 284–7
     profit-related   287–9
     review   256
     schemes
          by output and results   282–3
          by time   279–81
          overtime   281–2
          shiftwork premiums   281
          Wharfedale Water case study   373
people   231, 261, 263

performance
  appraisal   243, 253–5, 256, 258
    administrative   250
    informative   250
    outcomes   252–3
    to performance management   253–5
  employees   185–6
  gap   **266**, 267–8
    model   272
  indicators   322–3
  limits, individual   267
  management   247–73
    appraisal   250–3
    appraisal interview   265–6
    case study: HM Customs and Excise
      262–4
    conflicts   252
    development delivery   270–2
    development plan   269
    employees, well-being of   261
    gap   266–8
    and human resource management
      (HRM)   259–61
    human resource specialists as facilitators
      260–1
    and human resource strategy   248–9
    manager's role   262
    motivation   261, 272–3
    nature   255–9
    ownership and commitment   260
    pre-appraisal preparation   264–5
    progress monitoring and plans
      reviewing   269–70
    system   255–9, 263
    case study: financial institution   257–8
    targets   268–9
performance-related pay   **156**, 254,
  284–7
person specification   **221**, **228–9**, 239
personality   233, 240, 241
personnel
  attraction   237
  department   76
  function   341–5
  skilled   323
  specialists   73–5
  technological education (lack of)   323–4
piecework system   282
planning
  action   256
  corporate   **6**, 222
  long-range   **5**, 262
  reviewing   269–70
pluralism   86, 87, 146, 171, 283
policies
  business   50
  espoused   90, 107
  human resource   170

  operational   90, 107
and practices in the workplace
  formal   192–5
  gaps   197–9
  integrated strategies   196–7
  ritualistic responses   195–6
politics, organizational   105, 106–7
practice, best   322–3
practices *see* policies and practices
pre-appraisal preparation   264–5
pre-existing operation *see* brownfield
  operation
premiums, shiftwork   281
priorities   266
problems, managerial   4
processes   253, 315, 319
  deliberate   222
  emergent   222
  managerial   4
  political   47
  social   47
processual view (strategic management)
  21–3
procurement   16
professionals and managers, skills of   76–9
  case study: investment bank   76–8
profit bonuses, growth in   **157**
progress monitoring and performance
  management   253, 269–70
The Pension and Life Insurance plc (case
  study)   230–4

Q

'The Quality Challenge'   93
quality   64, 254, 266, 337
  see also Total Quality Management
  (TQM)
quantity   266

R

race discrimination   203
Race Relations Act 1976   204, 205
realism, new   97, 143
recruitment and selection   219–45, 284,
  304, 324–5, 337
  attraction   236–7
  downstream strategic function   224–6
  patterns   150–2
  requirements and strategic goals
    226–34
    case study: The Pension and Life
      Insurance plc   230–4

recruitment and selection (continued)
    social responsibility and selection goals
      243–4
    and strategic human resource
      management (HRM)   220–6
    strategies and techniques   235–43
      application information   239
      appraisal   243
      assessment centres   242
      hazards in selection methods   237–9
      interview   243
      job analysis and people auditing
        235–6
      psychological tests   240–2
      references   239–40
      work sampling and testing   242–3
    upstream strategic function   222–4
    youth   201
references   239–40
relationships *see* roles, relationships and
    skills
remuneration   293–4
resourcefulness   **27–8**
responsibilities   269
    social   243–4
restructuring   64
reward systems   152–7, 253, 256, 304,
    325, 338
    financial   275–97
      current trends   289–92
      and human resource management
        (HRM)   277–9, 292–5
      pay schemes   279–84
      performance-related pay   284–7
      profit-related pay   287–9
      management   277–9
      and performance management   261
      review   256
      strategies   258
      Wharfedale Water case study   372–3
rigidity, organizational   63
roles, relationships and skills   67–83,
    269
    human resource management (HRM) as
      board-level function   68–73
    line managers   75–6
    national and international human
      resource management (HRM)
      79–82
    personnel specialists   73–5
    professionals and managers   76–9
Rover Employee Assisted Learning (REAL)
    303–4, 307, 316, 322, 328
Rover Group UK   314, 317, 319, 328
    and corporate learning process (case
      study)   315–16
Rover Learning Business (RCB)   303–4,
    315–16

S

salary *see* payment
Scotchem   88, 91, 93, 94–5, 96, 97, 106,
    107–8
selection   **220**, 249, 324–5, 361–2
    methods   240
    see also recruitment and selection
selling, commission-based   282–3
sex discrimination   208, 214
Sex Discrimination Act   1975 204, 205,
    206
share ownership, growth in   **157**
shiftwork premiums   281
skills   201
    Digital Equipment UK (case study)
      43–4
    training   264
    women   191
    see also roles, relationships and skills
small firms *see* firms, small and
    entrepreneurial
staff *see* employees; management;
    personnel
standards   254, 337
strategic *see* strategies/strategic
Strategic Business Unit (SBU) level   24,
    25, 63
strategies/strategic
    business   **300**
    consistent   61
    content   31
    control style   24
    corporate   9, 38, 173, 222, 314–18
      and integration   54
      and planning   58
    crafting   118, **119**
    deliberate   **22**
    emergent   **22**
    fit   27
    function
    downstream   224–6
    upstream   222–4
    functional   9, 222
    generic   13–15, 27
    implementation   18
    intent   **28**
    levels   8–10
    local   222
    management   5, 6, 23–5, 333
    milestone   78
    and performance management   261–73
    planning   24, 231
    process   18, 31
    scan   230–1
    selection goals   243–4
    in selection methods   237–9

small and entrepreneurial firms
    case study: Benetton   131
    case study: Diana Company   129–30
    case study: employment strategies for
    small coal mine   124
    case study: overexpanding
    engineering firm   128–9
    case study: Survival Aids Ltd.   125–6
    case study: Traidcraft   133
    micro/founder firms   123–7
    second order entrepreneurial and
    family firms   127–30
    third order franchise, professional and
    community-voluntary firms   130–3
    strategy-making   117–19
        businesslike   118
    success   25–30
        competition to cooperation   26–7
        human issue   27–30
    tough love   59, 60, 61
    vision   28
structure
    flexibility   53
    organization   51–2, 185–6
style, paternalistic and authoritarian   147
succession, provision for   338
supervisors   101, 181
supporter   272
Survival Aids Ltd. (case study)   125–6
SWOT analysis   8, 230–1
systems
    business   50
    dynamic, entrepreneurial   187
    establishment   371–2
    of performance appraisal   250–3
    socio-technical   231
    stable, mechanistic   187
    systemization   54
    technical   **267**
    working   152–7

T

targets   253, 269, 270
    see also performance targets
tasks   269, 270
team briefing   348–9
technology   16, 64, 91, 126, 231, 261, 286
TEC's   115, 311
tensions   39, 170
    of performance appraisal   250–3
    tight-loose   61–3, 171, 172, 178
termination policy   338
tests, psychological   240–2
Thorn Lighting Ltd (UK) (case study)
    375–9

time, payments by   279–81
timescales   254, 266
tolerate (definition)   **267**
Total Quality Management (TQM)   88,
    93, 254–5, 341–5
    Carcom   342–3
    impact   343
    scheme   348
    strategic nature of human resource
        function   343–4
tough love strategy   59, 60, 61
Traidcraft (case study)   134
training   123, 191, 253, **300**, 321–3, 337
    awareness   217
    good   168
    lack   120
    national level   305–12
    organizational level   305–12
    schemes   115
    support   302
    value   121
    vocational   308–12
    see also education and training
Training Agency   115
trends, external and social   277
trust   256

U

underinvestment   309–12
underperformance   287
unemployment patterns   208–10
unions   95, 107, 108
    industrial-based   141
    performance-related pay   285
    recognition   370–1
    single-union agreements   141
    super-unions   141
    views   102–3
upstream
    first order decisions   221
    functions   9, 33, 222–4

V

values
    corporate   91–2
    internal   302
    value chain   **15**–18
view, analytical
    five force framework   10–13
    generic strategies   13–15
    value chain   15–18

vision and goals
  corporate   173, 222, 314–18
organizational   163–88, 226
  communication   164
  management and communciation tasks
    177–85
  management, role of   186–8
  organizational and individual needs
    164–77
  structure and culture impact on
    employee attitudes/performance
    185–6
Vocational Education and Training (VET)
  309
voluntary firms *see* community-voluntary
  firms

W

wages *see* payment
waves concept   **89**, 90, 105, 106
Way Ahead programme   97–108
  beginnings   97–8
  employee view   103–4
  future developments   104–5
  middle management and supervisors
    101
  mission statement and cascades   98–9
  origins   97

steering group   98
testbeds   99–101
union view   102–3
Wellcome Foundation planning for change
  (case study)   215–17
Wharfedale Water (case study)   369–73
  culture, new   369–70
  negotiation   372
  rewards   372–3
  system establishment, new   371–2
  union recognition   370–1
women   198, 200, 201, 202, 214, 215, 244
  and employment patterns   210–12
  as flexible labour force   212–13
  skills   191
work
  experience and achievments   233
  part-time   217
  sampling   240, 242–3
  testing   242–3
workers/workforce *see* employees;
  personnel
workplace
  changes   215–18
  equality   359–60
    competing interests and resistance to
    change   214–15
    problem of 'ownership'   213–14
  and performance management   261–73
  strategies   161–329